T0073196

Mathematics, Physics & Chemistry
with the
Wolfram Language

Other Titles by the Author

Advanced Physical Chemistry: A Survey of Modern Theoretical Principles

Foundations of Quantum Dynamics

Introduction to Quantum Mechanics (two editions)

Guide to Essential Math: For Students in Physics, Chemistry, and Engineering (two editions)

Twenty-First Century Quantum Mechanics: Hilbert Space to Quantum Computers

Mathematical Physics in Theoretical Chemistry

Mathematics, Physics & Chemistry with the Wolfram Language

S M Blinder

University of Michigan,
USA & Wolfram Research, USA

 **World Scientific**

NEW JERSEY · LONDON · SINGAPORE · BEIJING · SHANGHAI · HONG KONG · TAIPEI · CHENNAI · TOKYO

Published by

World Scientific Publishing Co. Pte. Ltd.

5 Toh Tuck Link, Singapore 596224

USA office: 27 Warren Street, Suite 401-402, Hackensack, NJ 07601

UK office: 57 Shelton Street, Covent Garden, London WC2H 9HE

Library of Congress Cataloging-in-Publication Data
Names: Blinder, S. M., 1932–   author.
Title: Mathematics, physics & chemistry with the Wolfram language /
    S.M. Blinder, University of Michigan, USA & Wolfram Research, USA.
Description: New Jersey : World Scientific, [2022] | Includes index.
Identifiers: LCCN 2021038309 | ISBN 9789811247187 (hardcover) |
    ISBN 9789811247194 (ebook) | ISBN 9789811247200 (ebook other)
Subjects: LCSH: Mathematics--Data processing. | Wolfram language
    (Computer program language) | Mathematica (Computer file) | Quantum theory.
Classification: LCC QA76.95 .B55 2022 | DDC 510.285/5133--dc23/eng/20211027
LC record available at https://lccn.loc.gov/2021038309

British Library Cataloguing-in-Publication Data
A catalogue record for this book is available from the British Library.

Individual Wolfram Demonstrations (https://demonstrations.wolfram.com/) as referenced and displayed herein are copyrighted by S M Blinder; Wolfram Research, Inc. holds the compilation copyright in the database.

For any available supplementary material, please visit
https://www.worldscientific.com/worldscibooks/10.1142/12548#t=suppl

Desk Editor: Shaun Tan Yi Jie

Typeset by Stallion Press
Email: enquiries@stallionpress.com

Preface

I began my second career as a telecommuting computer scientist for Wolfram Research in 2007. Since 2002, I have been Emeritus Professor of Chemistry and Physics at the University of Michigan. Most of my work has been devoted to the highly acclaimed Wolfram Demonstrations Project. Stephen Wolfram conceived of the Project as a way to bring computational exploration to the widest possible audience. It is an open-code resource that uses dynamic computation to illuminate concepts in science, technology, mathematics, art, finance and a remarkable range of other fields. The stated goal is to encourage people of all ages and backgrounds to embrace computational thinking as a way to better analyze and understand the world around them. I have written over 350 demonstrations myself, mostly on topics in mathematical physics and theoretical chemistry, which were my academic career specialties. I have also served as Expert Reviewer for nearly 5000 Demonstration submissions.

Chapter 1 is a short lesson covering the essential features of the Wolfram Language (WL), which is an extension of the programming language used in the Mathematica software system. In Chapter 2, WL is used to develop several topics in applied mathematics. These are subsequently applied to the Demonstrations on physics and chemistry in Chapters 3–7. There is an emphasis on quantum mechanics and theoretical chemistry, in line with my own long-time interests. Electromagnetism and several other topics in physics are also covered.

Some 180 Demonstrations are presented in Chapters 2–7. The accompanying text can serve as a mini-lesson on the underlying scientific or mathematical principles. For compactness, the Mathematica codes for the Demonstrations are relegated to Supplementary Materials, which may be downloaded as Mathematica files (see **Instructions for Accessing Online Supplementary Material**, p. 414). The level of coding can be described as functional, appropriate to a scientist or science student who is not a computer expert. We try to "get the job done" with a fairly rudimentary set of WL commands. A more sophisticated computer programmer might enjoy revising some of the codes. All of the programming in this book is based on Mathematica version 12.

My appreciation to World Scientific, and in particular my editor Shaun Tan Yi Jie, for their competence, efficiency and responsiveness during the production of this book.

Finally, I would like to thank my colleagues in the Wolfram Demonstrations Project: Andre Kuzniarek, Ed Pegg, George Beck, Daniel Lichtblau, Glenn Scholebo, Cindie Strater and Joyce Tracewell, without whom none of this work would have been possible.

S.M. Blinder, Ann Arbor, July 2021

About the Author

**Dr. S. M. Blinder** is Professor Emeritus of Chemistry and Physics at the University of Michigan, USA. He obtained a PhD in chemical physics from Harvard University under the direction of W. E. Moffitt and J. H. Van Vleck (Nobel Laureate in Physics, 1977). He has nearly 200 research publications and 8 books in several areas of theoretical chemistry and mathematical physics. He was the first to derive the exact Coulomb (hydrogen atom) propagator in Feynman's path-integral formulation of quantum mechanics. He has taught a multitude of courses in chemistry, physics, mathematics and philosophy, mostly on the subject of quantum theory. In earlier incarnations, he was a Junior Master in chess and an accomplished cellist. He is currently a telecommuting senior scientist with Wolfram Research, and lives with his wife, Frances Bryant, in Ann Arbor.

Contents

Chapter 1

Introduction to the Wolfram Language

For a more complete account of programming in Mathematica, refer to Stephen Wolfram: *An Elementary Introduction to the Wolfram Language, Second Edition*, available online at https://www.wolfram.com/language/elementary-introduction/2nd-ed/index.html. More details on specific topics are available directly from a Mathematica notebook, by selecting "Help" from the menu, and subsequently "Wolfram Documentation". We will introduce additional elements of Mathematica functionality as needed. The format for these should be fairly evident from the context.

1.1. Basic Operations in Mathematica

We present a brief summary of the basic functional operations, used in applications to mathematics, physics and chemistry. Further operations will be introduced as needed.

The basic arithmetic operations can be carried out using the usual symbols: $+, -, =, /, (\,)$. Multiplication is represented by $*$ (as in $2 * 3$) or by a space between factors $(2\ 3)$. Raising to a power uses $\wedge$ (as in $2\wedge 3 = 8$). Algebraic symbols such as a, b, c, x, etc., can be used, as well as numbers. Here is an example:

$In[\circ]:=$ `(-b + (b^2 - 4 a c) ^ (1 / 2) ) / (2 a)`

$Out[\circ]=$ $\dfrac{-b + \sqrt{b^2 - 4\,a\,c}}{2\,a}$

The square root can be written using Sqrt[]:

In[•]:= **Sqrt[b^2 - 4 a c]**

Out[•]= $\sqrt{b^2 - 4 a c}$

The mathematical constants π, e and *i* are represented by the symbols Pi, E and I. For example:

In[•]:= **E^(I Pi)**

Out[•]= -1

To show the unevaluated formula write:

In[•]:= **HoldForm[E^(I Pi)]**

Out[•]= $e^{i\pi}$

Here is a normalized Gaussian function

In[•]:= **1 / (Sqrt[2 Pi] σ) E^(-x^2 / (2 σ^2))**

Out[•]= $\dfrac{e^{-\frac{x^2}{2\sigma^2}}}{\sqrt{2\pi}\,\sigma}$

Greek letters, as well as the symbols π, e and *i*, square root signs, exponents and many other mathematical operations can be input directly using the Basic Math Assistant palette in a Mathematica notebook. For example, we could have written for the Gaussian

In[•]:= $\dfrac{1}{\sqrt{2\pi}\,\sigma} e^{-x^2/(2\sigma^2)}$

Out[•]= $\dfrac{e^{-\frac{x^2}{2\sigma^2}}}{\sqrt{2\pi}\,\sigma}$

We can define the Gaussian function as follows:

In[•]:= **f[x_] :=** $\dfrac{1}{\sqrt{2\pi}\,\sigma} e^{-x^2/(2\sigma^2)}$

The notation indicates that evaluation of the expression for a function of x is delayed. The current value is given by

In[ ]:= **f[x]**

Out[ ]= $\dfrac{e^{-\frac{x^2}{2\sigma^2}}}{\sqrt{2\pi}\,\sigma}$

Note that square brackets in Mathematica are used only to specify functional dependence (recall Sqrt[x]). Grouping of terms uses only curved brackets ( ). When you type something and it shows up in red, this means that the expression is incomplete or incorrect. The red goes away when a valid input is completed. For example:

f[x

f[x]

Mathematica can do analytic differentiation and integration. The first derivative of $f(x)$ is found from

In[ ]:= **D[f[x], x]**

Out[ ]= $-\dfrac{e^{-\frac{x^2}{2\sigma^2}}\,x}{\sqrt{2\pi}\,\sigma^3}$

Alternatively we can write

In[ ]:= **f'[x]**

Out[ ]= $-\dfrac{e^{-\frac{x^2}{2\sigma^2}}\,x}{\sqrt{2\pi}\,\sigma^3}$

or

In[ ]:= **∂ₓ f[x]**

Out[ ]= $-\dfrac{e^{-\frac{x^2}{2\sigma^2}}\,x}{\sqrt{2\pi}\,\sigma^3}$

For the second derivative:

In[ ]:= `D[f[x], {x, 2}]`

Out[ ]=
$$\frac{\dfrac{e^{-\frac{x^2}{2\sigma^2}}x^2}{\sigma^4} - \dfrac{e^{-\frac{x^2}{2\sigma^2}}}{\sigma^2}}{\sqrt{2\pi}\,\sigma}$$

This messy expression can be simplified using

In[ ]:= `Simplify[%]`

Out[ ]=
$$\frac{e^{-\frac{x^2}{2\sigma^2}}\left(x^2 - \sigma^2\right)}{\sqrt{2\pi}\,\sigma^5}$$

where % represents the last output. Alternatively, for the second derivative,

In[ ]:= `Simplify[f''[x]]`

Out[ ]=
$$\frac{e^{-\frac{x^2}{2\sigma^2}}\left(x^2 - \sigma^2\right)}{\sqrt{2\pi}\,\sigma^5}$$

or

In[ ]:= `Simplify[∂x,x f[x]]`

Out[ ]=
$$\frac{e^{-\frac{x^2}{2\sigma^2}}\left(x^2 - \sigma^2\right)}{\sqrt{2\pi}\,\sigma^5}$$

Mathematica can do both indefinite and definite integrals. As an example, consider integrals of a simple Gaussian function e^{-x^2}. For the indefinite integral:

In[ ]:= $\displaystyle\int e^{-x^2}\,dx$

Out[ ]= $\dfrac{1}{2}\sqrt{\pi}\;\text{Erf}[x]$

in terms of the error function erf(x). The famous definite integral (Laplace, 1812) is evaluated exactly:

In[•]:= $\displaystyle\int_{-\infty}^{\infty} e^{-x^2}\, dx$

Out[•]= $\sqrt{\pi}$

Here is an approximation, obtained by numerical integration:

In[•]:= **NIntegrate$\left[e^{-x^2}, \{x, -100, 100\}\right]$**

Out[•]= **1.77245**

in close agreement with the exact result, since

In[•]:= **N$\left[\sqrt{\pi}\,\right]$**

Out[•]= **1.77245**

where N[] gives the numerical value of an expression to 6 significant figures. A larger number of significant figures can be obtained using, for example,

In[•]:= **N$\left[\sqrt{\pi}, 12\right]$**

Out[•]= **1.77245385091**

Returning to the normalized Gaussian $f(x)$ defined above, the normalization can be checked using

In[•]:= $\displaystyle\int_{-\infty}^{\infty} f[x]\, dx$

Out[•]= $\dfrac{1}{\sqrt{\dfrac{1}{\sigma^2}}\,\sigma}$ if $\mathrm{Re}\left[\sigma^2\right] > 0$

This can be cleaned up using

In[•]:= **PowerExpand[%]**

Out[•]= $\boxed{1 \ \text{if} \ \text{Re}\left[\sigma^2\right] > 0}$

To convert an expression in Mathematica notation to traditional mathematical notation use

In[•]:= **TraditionalForm[Sin[x]]**

Out[•]//TraditionalForm=
$$\sin(x)$$

In[•]:= **TraditionalForm[HoldForm[E^(I Pi)]]**

Out[•]//TraditionalForm=
$$e^{i\pi}$$

A common source of errors is the use of a common symbol, such as x or f, without recalling that it was previously defined. If you are doing some Mathematica operations involving variables, say x and y, or functions, say $f(x)$, it might be necessary to clear their earlier usage with commands such as:

In[•]:= **Clear[x, y]**

In[•]:= **Clear[f]**

1.2. Manipulate

Much of the active participation by the reader will involve the **Manipulate** command. The Wolfram language enables you to set up a user interface in which you can continually manipulate one or more variables. A simple example showing a plot of a Gaussian function, in which you can control both the average a and the standard deviation σ:

$\textit{In[•]:=}$ `Manipulate` $\Big[$ `Plot` $\Big[\dfrac{1}{\sqrt{2 \pi} \; \sigma}$ `Exp` $\Big[- \dfrac{(x - a)^2}{2 \sigma^2} \Big]$, `{x, -10, 10}, PlotRange → All,`

`GridLines → Automatic` $\Big]$, `{a, -5, 5}, {σ, .5, 2}, ControlPlacement → Top` $\Big]$

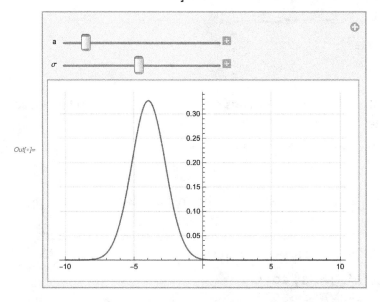

$\textit{Out[•]=}$

The two variables are selected using Sliders. Other control types that can be used with Manipulate include:

```
Animator, Checkbox, CheckboxBar, ColorSetter,
ColorSlider, FormControl, InputField, IntervalSlider,
Manipulator, PopupMenu, RadioButton or RadioButtonBar,
Setter or SetterBar, Slider, Slider2D, TogglerBar,
Trigger, and VerticalSlider.
```

Here is an example of manipulation of an algebraic formula:

In[ ]:= `Manipulate[Expand[(1 + x)^n], {{n, 2, "n"}, Range[0, 5], Setter}]`

Out[ ]=

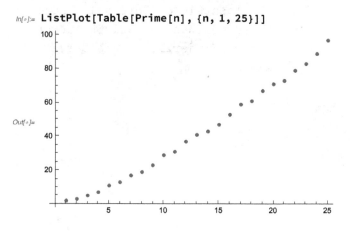

1.3. Lists

Lists provide a way to collect things together in the Wolfram Language. For example:

In[ ]:= `primes = {2, 3, 5, 7 , 11, 13}`

Out[ ]= `{2, 3, 5, 7, 11, 13}`

On their own, lists don't do anything; they're just a way to store things.

The command Table produces a list according to some specifications. For example, a table of the first 10 squares:

In[ ]:= `Table[n^2, {n, 1, 10}]`

Out[ ]= `{1, 4, 9, 16, 25, 36, 49, 64, 81, 100}`

A list plot shows a series points in the set $\{f(n), n\}$. For example the first 25 primes which are ≤ 100:

In[ ]:= `ListPlot[Table[Prime[n], {n, 1, 25}]]`

Out[ ]=

with the plot points labeled:

In[•]:= `ListPlot[Table[Labeled[n, Prime[n]], {n, 1, 25}]]`

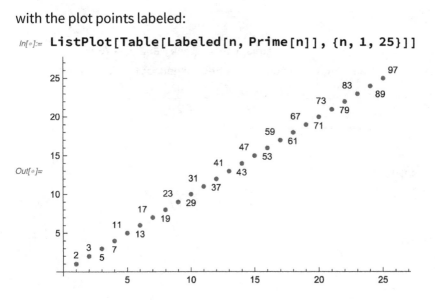

Out[•]=

Selecting a member of a list: suppose we want the 4th entry in the above list of primes

In[•]:= `primes = {2, 3, 5, 7, 11, 13}; p4 = primes[[4]]`

Out[•]= `7`

1.4. Functions and Plots

Here is a plot of the simple Gaussian function

In[•]:= `Plot[e^{-x^2}, {x, -4, 4}]`

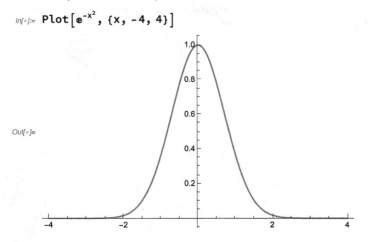

Out[•]=

Adding some options:

In[•]:= `Plot[e`$^{-x^2}$`, {x, -4, 4}, PlotStyle → Black, Frame → True,`
`    GridLines → Automatic, PlotLabel → "gaussian function"]`

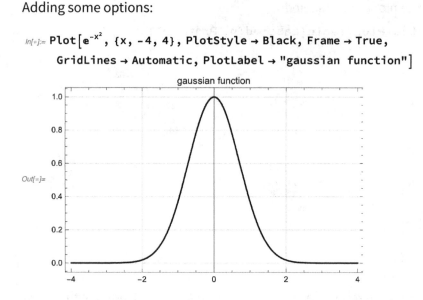

Mathematica has an immense number of built-in functions. To cite a just few examples: Sin[x], Cos[x], Tan[x], Exp[x], Sinh[x], Cosh[x], ArcSin[x], Log[x], Erf[x], Gamma[x], BesselJ[n,x], LegendreP[n,x], LegendreP[n,m,x].

The parameters in a function can be manipulated; for example, the sine function with variable frequency and amplitude:

In[•]:= `Manipulate[Plot[A Sin[ω t], {t, -10, 10}, PlotRange → {-4, 4}, GridLines → Automatic],`
`    {ω, .5, 2}, {A, 1, 4}, ControlPlacement → Top]`

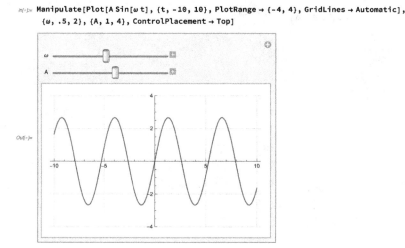

Mathematica can find series expansions for functions:

In[ ]:= **Series[Sin[θ], {θ, 0, 10}]**

Out[ ]= $\theta - \dfrac{\theta^3}{6} + \dfrac{\theta^5}{120} - \dfrac{\theta^7}{5040} + \dfrac{\theta^9}{362\,880} + O[\theta]^{11}$

In[ ]:= **Series[Cos[θ], {θ, 0, 10}]**

Out[ ]= $1 - \dfrac{\theta^2}{2} + \dfrac{\theta^4}{24} - \dfrac{\theta^6}{720} + \dfrac{\theta^8}{40\,320} - \dfrac{\theta^{10}}{3\,628\,800} + O[\theta]^{11}$

In[ ]:= **Series[$e^{i\,\theta}$, {θ, 0, 10}]**

Out[ ]= $1 + i\,\theta - \dfrac{\theta^2}{2} - \dfrac{i\,\theta^3}{6} + \dfrac{\theta^4}{24} + \dfrac{i\,\theta^5}{120} - \dfrac{\theta^6}{720} - \dfrac{i\,\theta^7}{5040} + \dfrac{\theta^8}{40\,320} + \dfrac{i\,\theta^9}{362\,880} - \dfrac{\theta^{10}}{3\,628\,800} + O[\theta]^{11}$

To verify Euler's theorem:

In[ ]:= **Series[Cos[θ] + i Sin[θ], {θ, 0, 10}]**

Out[ ]= $1 + i\,\theta - \dfrac{\theta^2}{2} - \dfrac{i\,\theta^3}{6} + \dfrac{\theta^4}{24} + \dfrac{i\,\theta^5}{120} - \dfrac{\theta^6}{720} - \dfrac{i\,\theta^7}{5040} + \dfrac{\theta^8}{40\,320} + \dfrac{i\,\theta^9}{362\,880} - \dfrac{\theta^{10}}{3\,628\,800} + O[\theta]^{11}$

Mathematica can compute the complex roots of a polynomial. Expressed numerically,

In[ ]:= **NRoots$\left[z^5 + z^4 + z^3 + z^2 + z + 1 == 0, z\right]$**

Out[ ]= $z == -1.$ || $z == -0.5 - 0.866025\,i$ ||
$z == -0.5 + 0.866025\,i$ || $z == 0.5 - 0.866025\,i$ || $z == 0.5 + 0.866025\,i$

The polynomial can be plotted in the complex plane:

In[ ]:= `ComplexPlot[z⁵ + z⁴ + z³ + z² + z + 1, {z, -1 - i, 1 + i}, ImageSize → {250, 250}]`

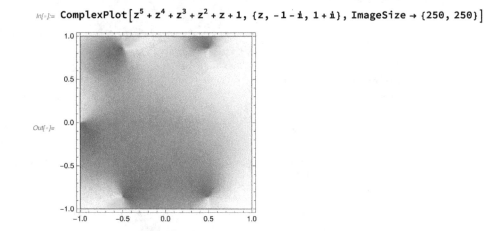

The zeros appear as white dots. The colors represent $\arg(z)$, varying as it goes from $-\pi$ to π in a counter-clockwise sense.

1.5. Other Types of Plots

Here is a bar chart showing the average monthly high temperature, January to December, in Ann Arbor, Michigan (in °F):

In[ ]:= `BarChart[{31, 35, 46, 60, 71, 80, 83, 81, 74, 61, 48, 35},`
     `ChartStyle → Blue, LabelingFunction → Above, Epilog →`
       `Text[Style["J  F  M  A  M  J  J  A  S  O  N  D", White, 22.4], {6.55, 10}]]`

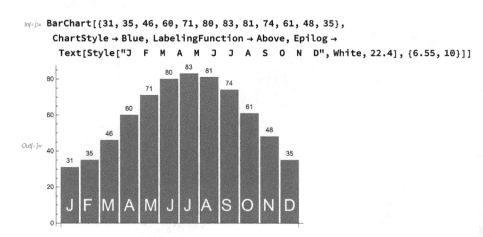

Pie charts are often visually useful:

```
In[ ]:= PieChart3D[{68.3, 26.8, 4.9},
        ChartLabels → {"dark energy 68.3%", "dark matter 26.8%", "ordinary matter 4.9%"},
        ChartStyle → {Green, Lighter[Blue], Red},
        PlotLabel → Style["Mass-Energy in the Universe", 20]]
```

Out[ ]=

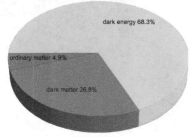

A polar plot generates a curve of the radius *r* as a function of the angle θ. Conic sections (the circle, ellipse, parabola and hyperbola) can all be represented by an equation in polar coordinates:

$$r = \frac{p}{1 - e\cos\theta},$$

where *p* is the semilatus rectum and *e* the eccentricity of the curve. For the circle, ellipse, parabola and hyperbola, the eccentricity has the values $e = 0, 0 < e < 1, e = 1$ and $e > 1$, respectively.

In[ ]:= `PolarPlot[{1 / (1 - .5 Cos[θ])}, {θ, 0, 2 π},`
`    PolarGridLines → {Automatic, {.5, 1, 1.5, 2, 2.5}},`
`    PlotStyle → Red, Frame → True, ImageSize → Medium]`

Out[ ]=

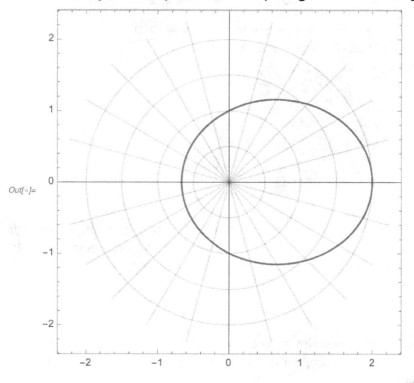

```
In[•]:= PolarPlot[{1 / (1 - Cos[θ])}, {θ, 0, 2 π}, PlotRange → 3,
         PolarGridLines → {Automatic, {.5, 1, 1.5, 2, 2.5}},
         PlotStyle → Red, Frame → True, ImageSize → Medium]
```

Out[•]=

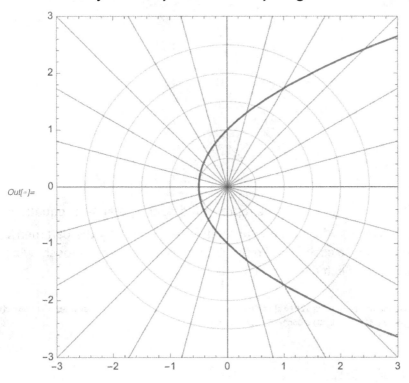

In[•]:= `PolarPlot[{1 / (1 - 1.5 Cos[θ])}, {θ, 0, 2 π},`
`        PolarGridLines → {Automatic, {.5, 1, 1.5, 2, 2.5}},`
`        PlotStyle → Red, Frame → True, ImageSize → Medium]`

Out[•]=
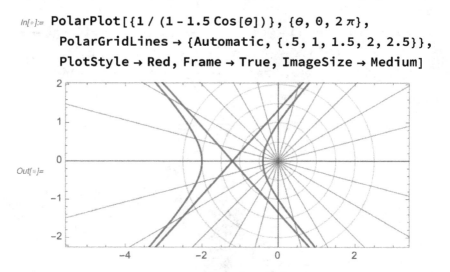

An ellipse $\frac{x^2}{a^2} + \frac{y^2}{b^2} = 1$ can be represented by the parametric equations $x = a\cos\theta$, $y = a\sin\theta$, a hyperbola $\frac{x^2}{a^2} - \frac{y^2}{b^2} = 1$ by the parametric equations $x = a\cosh\theta$, $y = a\sinh\theta$. Here is a parametric plot showing an ellipse for elected values of a and b:

In[•]:= `Manipulate[ParametricPlot[{a Cos[θ], b Sin[θ]}, {θ, 0, 2 π}, GridLines → Automatic],`
`        {a, 2, 3}, {b, 1, 2}, ControlPlacement → Top]`

Out[•]=
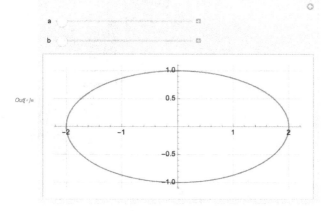

And for a hyperbola:

In[ ]:= `Manipulate[ParametricPlot[{{a Cosh[t], b Sinh[t]}, {-a Cosh[t], b Sinh[t]}},`
`    {t, -2, 2}, GridLines → Automatic], {a, 1, 2}, {b, 1, 2}, ControlPlacement → Top]`

Out[ ]=

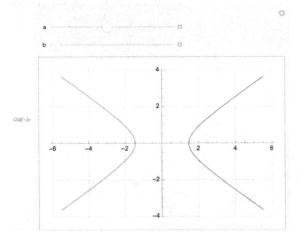

A contour plot of a function shows a series of curves $f(x, y) = c$ for varying c. For example a radial gaussian function e^{-ar^2}:

$$f(x, y) = e^{-a(x^2 + y^2)}$$

In[ ]:= `Manipulate[ContourPlot[e^{-a (x²+y²)}, {x, -1.5, 1.5}, {y, -1.5, 1.5}],`
`    {{a, 1, Style["a", Italic]}, .5, 2, Appearance → "Labeled"}, ControlPlacement → Top]`

Out[ ]=

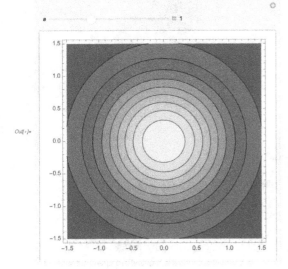

1.6. 2D Graphics

We illustrate the graphics capabilities of Wolfram Language with a visual proof of Pythagoras' theorem, $a^2 + b^2 = c^2$, which requires no verbal description. You can learn some of the graphics commands by close study of this example.

```
In[•]:= Graphics[{Blue, Polygon[{{0, 0}, {4, 0}, {4, 4}, {0, 4}}]],
        Red, Polygon[{{0, 4}, {-3, 4}, {-3, 7}, {0, 7}}],
        Purple, Polygon[{{0, 7}, {3, 11}, {7, 8}, {4, 4}}],
        Text[Style["a", Italic, White, 24], {2, 3.5}],
        Text[Style["b", Italic, White, 24], {-.5, 5.5}],
        Text[Style["c", Italic, White, 24], {2.2, 6}]
       }, ImageSize → {250, 250}]
```

Out[•]=

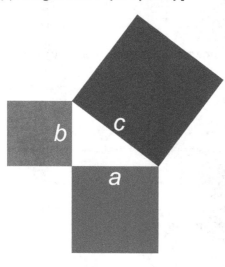

```
In[*]:= Graphics[
    {Purple, EdgeForm[{Thick, Black}], Polygon[{{-8, 4}, {-4, 7}, {-1, 3}, {-5, 0}}]],
    Red, Polygon[{{1, 7}, {4, 7}, {4, 4}, {1, 4}}]],
    Blue, Polygon[{{4, 4}, {8, 4}, {8, 0}, {4, 0}}]],
    Thick, Black, Line[{{-8, 0}, {-8, 7}, {-1, 7}, {-1, 0}, {-8, 0}}]],
    Line[{{8, 0}, {8, 7}, {1, 7}, {1, 0}, {8, 0}}]], Line[{{1, 0}, {4, 4}, {8, 7}}]]
    }, ImageSize → {300, 200}]
```

Out[*]=

Here is a sampling of the some of the more common colors used in graphics:

```
In[*]:= {White, Red, Orange, Yellow, Green, Blue, Purple, Brown, Gray, Black}
```

Out[*]= { ▢ , ■ , ■ , ▢ , ■ , ■ , ■ , ■ , ■ , ■ }

See "guide/Colors" under "Help" to explore the many variations and color schemes available in Mathematica.

1.7. 3D Graphics

On the next page is a 3D graphic showing intersections of a cone and a plane to form conic sections:

```
In[ ]:= Graphics3D[{Cyan, Opacity[1], Cone[{{0, 0, 2}, {0, 0, 0}}, 1],
      Cone[{{0, 0, -2}, {0, 0, 0}}, 1], Magenta, Opacity[.8],
      InfinitePlane[{{0, 0, 1}, {1, 0, 1.75}, {-1, -1, 0}}], Cyan, Opacity[1],
      Cone[{{5, 0, 2}, {5, 0, 0}}, 1], Cone[{{5, 0, -2}, {5, 0, 0}}, 1], Magenta,
      Opacity[.8], InfinitePlane[{{5.5, 0, 0}, {5.5, 0, 2}, {5.5, -1, -2}}]
      }, Boxed → False]
```

Out[ ]=

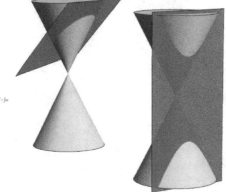

with an ellipse on the left and a hyperbola on the right. Note that you can manually rotate this figure using your trackpad (or mouse) to change the angle of viewing.

1.8. Wolfram Alpha

A central feature of the Wolfram Language is that it has an immense amount of real-world data built in. You can access the Wolfram Knowledgebase by typing the = key at the beginning of a line and asking a question in plain English.

In[ ]:=

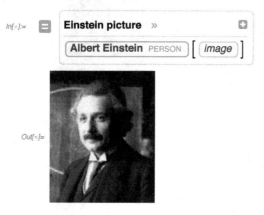

Out[ ]=

In[⚬]:= **Stonehenge picture** »

Stonehenge BUILDING [*image*]

Out[⚬]=

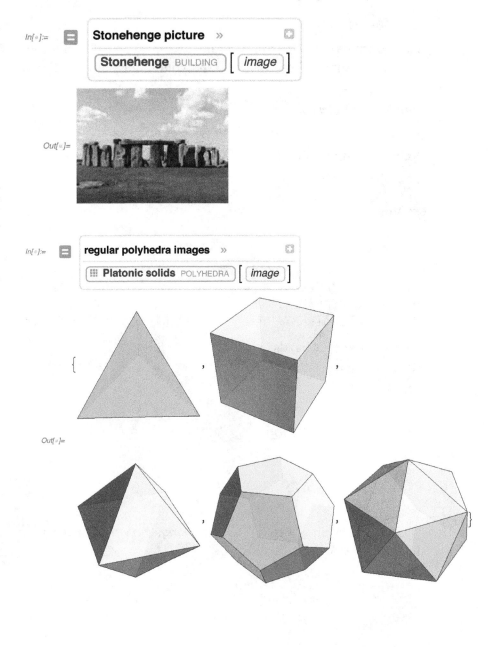

In[⚬]:= **regular polyhedra images** »

▦ Platonic solids POLYHEDRA [*image*]

Out[⚬]=

1.9. Random Numbers

Original algorithms developed at Wolfram Research can efficiently generate random numbers, both discrete and continuous, of exceptional quality. Examples:

In[•]:= **RandomReal[{0, 1}]**

Out[•]= 0.468079

In[•]:= **RandomInteger[{1, 100}]**

Out[•]= 28

Representing a series of coin tosses:

In[•]:= **RandomChoice[{H, T}, 100]**

Out[•]= {T, H, H, H, H, T, H, T, H, H, H, T, H, H, T, T, T, T, H, T, H, T, H, H, H, T, T, T, T, H, H, H, H, H, T, T, H, H, T, T, H, T, T, H, H, T, T, T, T, H, H, T, H, H, T, H, H, H, H, T, H, H, H, T, H, T, T, T, T, H, T, T, T, T, H, H, T, T, T, H, T, T, T, T, H, T, H, H, T, H, T, T, T, T, H, T, T, H, H, T, T}

To count the number of heads:

In[•]:= **Count[%, H]**

Out[•]= 48

1.10. Binomial Distributions

Binomial coefficients are defined by

$$\binom{n}{k} = \frac{n!}{k!(n-k)!}.$$

They can be visually displayed by *Pascal's triangle*, in which the nth row contains the $n+1$ possible values of k.

```
In[ ]:= Manipulate[
    Column[Table[Row[Table[Binomial[i, j], {j, 0, i}], Spacer[10 - i]], {i, 0, n}],
      Center], {{n, 5, Style["n", Italic]}, 0, 10, 1, Appearance → "Labeled"},
    ControlPlacement → Top, Alignment → Center]
```

n ──────────○────────── ⊞ 5

```
Out[ ]=
                    1
                  1   1
                1   2   1
              1   3   3   1
            1   4   6   4   1
          1   5  10  10   5   1
```

Note that each entry is equal to the sum of the two entries diagonally above, for example $10 = 4 + 6$.

Consider the expansions:

```
In[ ]:= TraditionalForm[Column[Table[
    Row[{Superscript[HoldForm["(1+x)"], n], " = ", Expand[(1 + x)^n]}], {n, 0, 5}]]]
```
Out[ ]//TraditionalForm=

$(1+x)^0 = 1$

$(1+x)^1 = x + 1$

$(1+x)^2 = x^2 + 2x + 1$

$(1+x)^3 = x^3 + 3x^2 + 3x + 1$

$(1+x)^4 = x^4 + 4x^3 + 6x^2 + 4x + 1$

$(1+x)^5 = x^5 + 5x^4 + 10x^3 + 10x^2 + 5x + 1$

Evidently:

$$(1+x)^n = \sum_{k=0}^{n} \binom{n}{k} x^k.$$

For a more general binomial expansion:

$$(x+y)^n = \sum_{k=0}^{n} \binom{n}{k} y^k x^{n-k}.$$

```
In[•]:= TraditionalForm[Column[Table[
        Row[{Superscript[HoldForm["(x+y)"], n], " = ", Expand[(x+y)^n]}], {n, 0, 5}]]]
```

Out[•]//TraditionalForm=

$(x+y)^0 = 1$

$(x+y)^1 = x+y$

$(x+y)^2 = x^2 + 2xy + y^2$

$(x+y)^3 = x^3 + 3x^2 y + 3xy^2 + y^3$

$(x+y)^4 = x^4 + 4x^3 y + 6x^2 y^2 + 4xy^3 + y^4$

$(x+y)^5 = x^5 + 5x^4 y + 10x^3 y^2 + 10x^2 y^3 + 5xy^4 + y^5$

Isaac Newton discovered this result in 1666. Remarkably, the binomial formula is also valid for negative, fractional, and even complex values of *n*, which was proved by Niels Henrik Abel in 1826. (It is joked that Newton didn't prove the binomial theorem for non-integer *n* because he wasn't Abel.) The expansions then become infinite with the binomial coefficients given by

$$\binom{\alpha}{k} = \frac{\alpha(\alpha - 1) \cdots (\alpha - k + 1)}{k!}.$$

Some examples

```
In[•]:= Series[(1 + x)^-1, {x, 0, 5}]
```

Out[•]= $1 - x + x^2 - x^3 + x^4 - x^5 + O[x]^6$

```
In[•]:= Series[(1 - x)^-1, {x, 0, 5}]
```

Out[•]= $1 + x + x^2 + x^3 + x^4 + x^5 + O[x]^6$

```
In[•]:= Series[ 1/√(1 - x), {x, 0, 5}]
```

Out[•]= $1 + \frac{x}{2} + \frac{3x^2}{8} + \frac{5x^3}{16} + \frac{35x^4}{128} + \frac{63x^5}{256} + O[x]^6$

For repeated sets of 100 coin tosses, the idealized result, which is approached in the limit $n \to \infty$, is a binomial distribution

$$f(n, k) = \frac{1}{2^n} \binom{n}{k}.$$

```
In[ ]:= Manipulate[
    Show[BarChart[Table[100 * 2^-100 Binomial[100, x], {x, 1, 100}], BarSpacing → Large,
      LabelingFunction → (Placed[Style[#2[[2]], 6], Top] &), PlotRange → {{35, 65}, All},
      PlotLabel → "binomial distribution"], Plot[ 100/(5 √(2 π)) e^-(x-50)^2/50, {x, 35, 65},
      PlotStyle → {Opacity[s], Black}, PlotRange → All, Axes → False]],
    {{s, 0, "show normal distribution"}, {0, 1}, Checkbox}, ControlPlacement → Top]
```

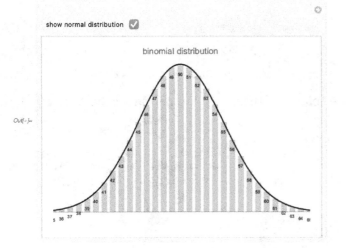

1.11. Matrices

To represent, say, a 3×3 matrix, with the 9 elements $M_{11}, M_{12}, \ldots, M_{33}$, in Mathematica, we write

```
In[ ]:= Mx = {{M[1, 1], M[1, 2], M[1, 3]},
      {M[2, 1], M[2, 2], M[2, 3]}, {M[3, 1], M[3, 2], M[3, 3]}}
Out[ ]= {{M[1, 1], M[1, 2], M[1, 3]}, {M[2, 1], M[2, 2], M[2, 3]}, {M[3, 1], M[3, 2], M[3, 3]}}
```

For better visualization

```
In[ ]:= % // MatrixForm
Out[ ]//MatrixForm=
```

$$\begin{pmatrix} M[1, 1] & M[1, 2] & M[1, 3] \\ M[2, 1] & M[2, 2] & M[2, 3] \\ M[3, 1] & M[3, 2] & M[3, 3] \end{pmatrix}$$

The determinant of this matrix is given by

In[ ]:= **Det[Mx]**

Out[ ]= −M[1, 3] × M[2, 2] × M[3, 1] + M[1, 2] × M[2, 3] × M[3, 1] + M[1, 3] × M[2, 1] × M[3, 2] −
M[1, 1] × M[2, 3] × M[3, 2] − M[1, 2] × M[2, 1] × M[3, 3] + M[1, 1] × M[2, 2] × M[3, 3]

The triple vector product $(\mathbf{a} \times \mathbf{b}) \cdot \mathbf{c} = \mathbf{a} \cdot (\mathbf{b} \times \mathbf{c})$, where $\mathbf{a} = (x1, y1, z1)$, $\mathbf{b} = (x2, y2, z2)$, $\mathbf{c} = (x3, y3, z3)$, can be represented by the determinant

$$\begin{vmatrix} x1 & y1 & z1 \\ x2 & y2 & z2 \\ x3 & y3 & z3 \end{vmatrix}.$$

This is equal to the volume of the parallelopiped shown below:

In[ ]:= **Graphics3D[{Opacity[0.35], Blue,**
Parallelepiped[{0, 0, 0}, {{1, 0, 0}, {1, 1, 0}, {0, 1, 1}}], Opacity[1], Thick,
Black, Arrowheads[.06], Arrow[{{0, 0, 0}, {1, 0, 0}}], Arrow[{{0, 0, 0}, {1, 1, 0}}],
Arrow[{{0, 0, 0}, {0, 1, 1}}]}, Boxed → False, ImageSize → 250]

Out[ ]=

In a transformation of coordinates, say from Cartesian (x, y, z) to spherical polar (r, θ, ϕ), the volume element for integration makes use of the *Jacobian determinant*:

$$J = \begin{vmatrix} \dfrac{\partial x}{\partial r} & \dfrac{\partial x}{\partial \theta} & \dfrac{\partial x}{\partial \phi} \\ \dfrac{\partial y}{\partial r} & \dfrac{\partial y}{\partial \theta} & \dfrac{\partial y}{\partial \phi} \\ \dfrac{\partial z}{\partial r} & \dfrac{\partial z}{\partial \theta} & \dfrac{\partial z}{\partial \phi} \end{vmatrix}.$$

From the transformation equations $x = r\sin\theta\cos\phi$, $y = r\sin\theta\sin\phi$, $z = \cos\theta$, we proceed as follows:

In[•]:= `x := r Sin[θ] Cos[φ]; y := r Sin[θ] Sin[φ]; z := r Cos[θ];`

In[•]:= `Simplify[Det[{{∂ᵣx, ∂θx, ∂φx}, {∂ᵣy, ∂θy, ∂φy}, {∂ᵣz, ∂θz, ∂φz}}]]`

Out[•]= `r² Sin[θ]`

which shows that the Cartesian volume element $d^3\mathbf{r} = dx\,dy\,dz$ transforms to the polar

$$d^3\mathbf{r} = r^2\sin\theta\,dr\,d\theta\,d\phi.$$

Important in several applications are the three 2×2 Pauli spin matrices:

In[•]:= `Table[PauliMatrix[i] // MatrixForm, {i, 1, 3}]`

Out[•]= $\left\{ \begin{pmatrix} 0 & 1 \\ 1 & 0 \end{pmatrix}, \begin{pmatrix} 0 & -i \\ i & 0 \end{pmatrix}, \begin{pmatrix} 1 & 0 \\ 0 & -1 \end{pmatrix} \right\}$

These are conventionally designated either $\sigma_1, \sigma_2, \sigma_3$ or $\sigma_x, \sigma_y, \sigma_z$, respectively. Evaluate the matrix products:

In[•]:= `PauliMatrix[1].PauliMatrix[2] // MatrixForm`

Out[•]//MatrixForm= $\begin{pmatrix} i & 0 \\ 0 & -i \end{pmatrix}$

such that $\sigma_x\sigma_y = i\sigma_z$. This holds for the cyclic permutations $\sigma_y\sigma_z = i\sigma_x$ and $\sigma_z\sigma_x = i\sigma_y$. Note that the Pauli matrices do not commute:

In[•]:= `PauliMatrix[2].PauliMatrix[1] // MatrixForm`

Out[•]//MatrixForm= $\begin{pmatrix} -i & 0 \\ 0 & i \end{pmatrix}$

so that $\sigma_y\sigma_x = -i\sigma_z$. The commutator of two matrices is defined by $[A, B] = AB - BA$. Thus

$$[\sigma_x, \sigma_y] = 2i\sigma_z, \text{ et cyc.}$$

The eigenvalues and eigenvectors of a matrix can be found using

In[•]:= `Eigensystem[PauliMatrix[1]]`

Out[•]= `{{-1, 1}, {{-1, 1}, {1, 1}}}`

showing that σ_x has the eigenvectors $\begin{pmatrix} -1 \\ 1 \end{pmatrix}$ and $\begin{pmatrix} 1 \\ 1 \end{pmatrix}$ with eigenvalues -1 and 1, respectively.

In[•]:= `Eigensystem[PauliMatrix[3]]`

Out[•]= `{{-1, 1}, {{0, 1}, {1, 0}}}`

The more canonical eigensystem is that of σ_z, with the eigenvectors $\begin{pmatrix} 0 \\ 1 \end{pmatrix}$ and $\begin{pmatrix} 1 \\ 0 \end{pmatrix}$.

1.12. Demonstrations

Many of the applications of Wolfram Language to mathematics, chemistry and physics will make use of excerpts from Wolfram Demonstrations. These are interactive visualizations of concepts in a wide range of topics: science, technology, mathematics, art, finance and much more. Every Demonstration published in the Wolfram Demonstrations Project has its own webpage that gives an overview of the Demonstration. The authoring notebook for a Demonstration provides sections that you fill in to create these parts of the webpage. To begin a new Demonstration select:

File ▶ New ▶ Repository Item ▶ Demonstrations Project Notebook

Here's what the page looks like:

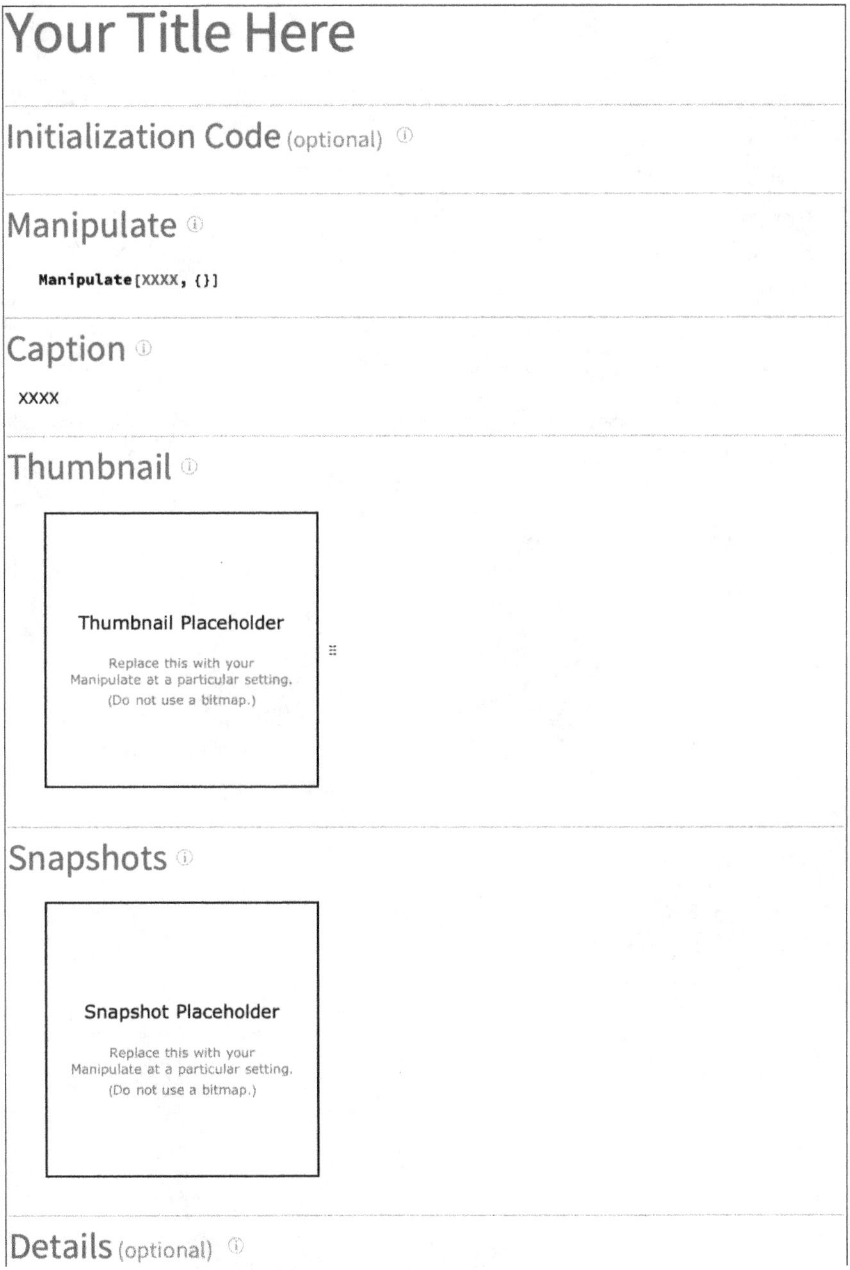
Your Title Here
Initialization Code (optional)
Manipulate
Manipulate[XXXX, {}]
Caption
XXXX
Thumbnail
Thumbnail Placeholder
Replace this with your Manipulate at a particular setting.
(Do not use a bitmap.)
Snapshots
Snapshot Placeholder
Replace this with your Manipulate at a particular setting.
(Do not use a bitmap.)
Details (optional)

Control Suggestions (optional) ⓘ

- [ ] Resize Images
- [ ] Rotate and Zoom in 3D
- [ ] Drag Locators
- [ ] Create and Delete Locators
- [ ] Slider Zoom
- [ ] Gamepad Controls
- [ ] Automatic Animation
- [ ] Bookmark Animation

Search Terms (optional) ⓘ

Related Links (optional) ⓘ

Authoring Information ⓘ

Contributed by: XXXX

Chapter 2

Mathematics: Some Applications of the Wolfram Language to Applied Mathematics

In this Chapter, we consider a selection of mathematical topics which will be of use in our later applications to physics and chemistry.

2.1. Complex Variables

2.1.1. *Visible and Invisible Intersections in the Cartesian Plane*

The circle $x^2 + y^2 = 1$ and the straight line $y = x + b$ are plotted on the Cartesian plane. Their two intersections (x_1, y_1) and (x_2, y_2), shown as black points, represent solutions of the simultaneous equations.

But suppose the value of b is such that the two curves do *not* intersect? There are still two perfectly good algebraic solutions of the simultaneous equations: $x = \frac{1}{2}(-b \mp \sqrt{2 - b^2}), y = \frac{1}{2}(b \mp \sqrt{2 - b^2})$, but these now involve *complex* numbers. You can imagine that the two intersections are now *invisible* in two-dimensional space.

A deeper understanding of functional analysis, even involving real functions of real variables, can be attained if the functions and variables are extended into the complex plane. A functional relationship $w = f(z)$ can be represented by a mapping of the z-plane, with $z = x + iy$, into the w-plane, with $w = u + iv$.

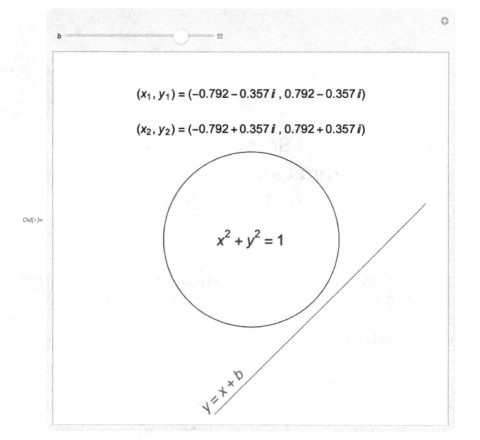

Demonstration 2.1: Visible and Invisible Intersections in the Cartesian Plane (https://demonstrations.wolfram.com/VisibleAndInvisibleIntersectionsInTheCartesianPlane/)

A very simple complex plot of $z = x + iy$, with blue and red lines showing the real and imaginary parts, respectively: $x = \text{Re}(z), y = \text{Im}(z)$.

```
ComplexContourPlot[{Re[z], Im[z]}, {z, 2},
    ContourStyle → {Blue, Red}, PlotLabel → Style["z", 20, Italic]]
```

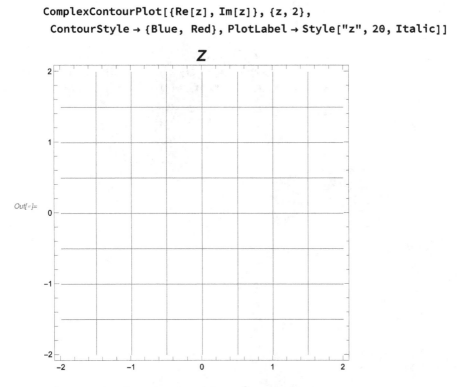

A simple complex function is $w(z) = z^2$, such that

$$w(x, y) = (x + iy)^2 = x^2 - y^2 + i2xy = u(x, y) + iv(x, y),$$

and therefore

$$\text{Re}(z^2) = u(x, y) = x^2 - y^2, \quad \text{Im}(z^2) = v(x, y) = 2xy.$$

This can be represented as a complex contour plot:

```
ComplexContourPlot[{Re[z²], Im[z²]}, {z, 2},
    ContourStyle → {Blue, Red}, PlotLabel → Style[Row[{TraditionalForm[w[z]],
        " = ", Style["u", Italic], " + ", Style["i v", Italic]}], 20]]
```

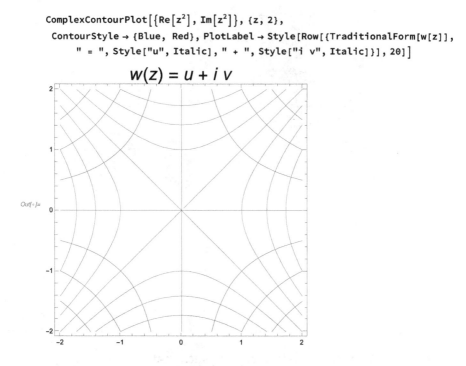

A function $w(z) = w(x, y)$ which depends on z alone, and not on the complex conjugate z^*, if certain other conditions are obeyed, is called an *analytic function*. For an analytic function, derivatives can be calculated using the usual rules for real functions. For example, $w'(z) = \frac{d}{dz}z^2 = 2z$.

A complex variable can alternatively be expressed in polar form $z = \rho e^{i\theta}$, where ρ is called the *modulus* and θ the *phase* or *argument*. Clearly, $\rho = |z|$. The function w above has the polar form $w(\rho, \theta) = \rho^2 e^{2i\theta}$.

The integral of a complex function $\int_C f(z)dz$ has the form of a line integral over a specified path or contour C between two points z_1 and z_2 in the complex plane. In the most general case, the value of the integral depends on the path C. But for an analytic function in a simple-connected region, the contour integral is independent of path, being determined entirely by the endpoints.

Cauchy's theorem is a central result in the theory of complex variables. It states that the line integral of an analytic function around an arbitrary closed path in a simple-connected region vanishes:

$$\oint f(z)\,dz = 0.$$

The path of integration is understood to be traversed in the *counter-clockwise* sense. The most important applications involve functions with singular points, applying the result known as *Cauchy's integral theorem*:

$$f(z_0) = \frac{1}{2\pi i} \oint \frac{f(z)}{z - z_0}\,dz.$$

More generally, for a function $f(z)$ with simple poles at $z_1, z_2, \ldots z_n$ within the contour of integration we have, by the *residue theorem*

$$\oint f(z)\,dz = 2\pi i \sum_n R(z_n)$$

where the $R(z_n)$ are the residues of the function $f(z)$ within the contour. If the singular points of $f(z)$ are only simple poles, the residues are simply the coefficients of $\frac{1}{z-z_n}$ in a Laurent expansion of the function.

As a simple example, the function $f(z) = \frac{1}{z-z_0}$ is analytic in the entire z plane, except for a simple pole at $z = z_0$. The function is to be integrated counter-clockwise over a unit circle, shown in red, which you can move in the complex plane. If the singular point z_0 falls outside the contour of integration, the function is analytic everywhere on and inside the contour and the integral equals zero by Cauchy's theorem: $\oint f(z)\,dz = 0$. When the singularity lies within the contour, the residue theorem applies and the integral equals 1. In the intermediate case, when the simple pole lies *on* the contour, it can be considered to be half inside, half outside. The Cauchy principal value for this segment of the integral is implied, so that the complete integral equals $\frac{1}{2}$.

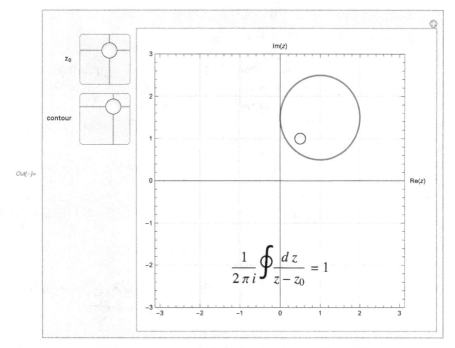

Demonstration 2.2: Contour Integral around a Simple Pole (https://demonstrations. wolfram.com/ContourIntegralAroundASimplePole/)

2.1.2. *Contour Integrals*

Contour integrals provide some very general methods for evaluating definite integrals, for example by applying *Jordan's lemma*. This can be stated as follows: let $f(z)$ be an analytic function in the upper half of the complex plane such that $|f(z)| \rightarrow 0$ on any semicircle of radius R in the upper half-plane, centered at the origin. Then, for $k > 0$, the contour integral $\int_R f(z)e^{ikz}dz \rightarrow 0$ as $R \rightarrow 0$. This can be directly applied to the evaluation of infinite integrals of the form $\int_{-\infty}^{\infty} f(x)e^{ikx}dx$ in terms of the residues of $f(z)$ at the points z_n in the upper half-plane. Specifically, $2\pi i \sum_n \text{Res}(f(z_n))e^{ikz_n}$. If z_n is a pole of order N, the residue is given by $\frac{1}{N-1} \lim_{z \to z_n} \frac{d^{N-1}}{dz^{N-1}}[(z - z_n)f(z)]$. The method is also applicable for $k = 0$, with the simpler integrals $\int_{-\infty}^{\infty} f(x)dx$, provided that $f(z)$ fulfills the requisite limiting behavior. In the following Demonstration, you are challenged to apply Jordan's lemma in 10 problems of increasing difficulty. Solutions are shown by clicking the checkbox.

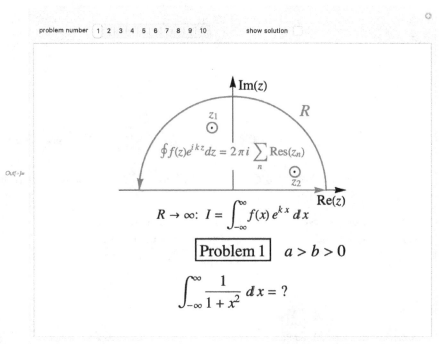

problem number 1 2 3 4 5 6 7 8 9 10   show solution

$Out[\cdot]=$

$$\oint f(z)e^{ikz}dz = 2\pi i \sum_n \text{Res}(z_n)$$

$$R \to \infty: \quad I = \int_{-\infty}^{\infty} f(x)\, e^{kx}\, dx$$

$$\boxed{\text{Problem 1}} \quad a > b > 0$$

$$\int_{-\infty}^{\infty} \frac{1}{1+x^2}\, dx = ?$$

Demonstration 2.3: Jordan's Lemma Applied to the Evaluation of Some Infinite Integrals (https://demonstrations.wolfram.com/JordansLemmaAppliedToTheEvaluationOfSomeInfiniteIntegrals/)

2.2. The Gamma Function

The factorial of an integer n is defined as the product of integers $n, n-1$, $n-2$, down to 1:

$$n! = n(n-1)(n-2)\cdots 1$$

Thus, $1! = 1, 2! = 2, 3! = 6, 4! = 24, 5! = 120, 6! = 720$, etc. The relation $(n-1)! = n!/n$ for $n = 1$ implies that $0! = 1$. The gamma function for an integer argument can be defined by $\Gamma(n) = (n-1)!$. In Wolfram Language:

In[•]:= `Table[Gamma[n], {n, 1, 7}]`

Out[•]= `{1, 1, 2, 6, 24, 120, 720}`

which agrees with our values of 0! to 6!. Next consider the definite integral

In[•]:= `Clear[n]`

In[•]:= $\int_0^\infty x^{n-1}\,e^{-x}\,dx$

Out[•]= `Gamma[n]` if `Re[n] > 0`

This can be considered as a definition of $\Gamma(n)$, valid even when n is not an integer. Here is a plot:

```
Plot[Gamma[v], {v, 0, 6}, GridLines → Automatic,
   PlotLabel → Gamma[v], Epilog → {Red, PointSize[.02], Point[{1, 1}],
     Point[{2, 1}], Point[{3, 2}], Point[{4, 6}], Point[{5, 20}]]}]
```

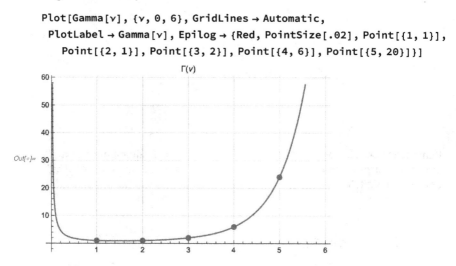

The integer values are shown as red dots. The gamma function appears to represent a smooth interpolation between the integer values of the factorial. Interesting results occur for half-integer values of the argument. For example:

In[•]:= `Gamma`$\left[\dfrac{1}{2}\right]$

Out[•]= $\sqrt{\pi}$

which is clear from the integral definition

In[ ]:= $\displaystyle\int_0^\infty x^{-1/2}\, e^{-x}\, dx$

Out[ ]= $\sqrt{\pi}$

The function $\Gamma(z)$ can actually be defined throughout the complex plane. Consider first, along the real axis

In[ ]:= `Plot[Gamma[x], {x, -5, 5}, GridLines → Automatic, PlotLabel → Gamma[x]]`

Out[ ]=

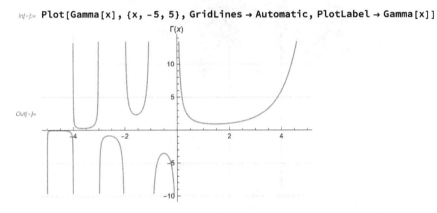

There are evidently singularities at $x = 0, -1, -2, \ldots$, as is, in fact, obvious from the definition as an definite integral. Here is a plot in the complex plane:

In[ ]:= `ComplexPlot[Gamma[z], {z, -6 - 4 i, 6 + 4 i}]`

Out[ ]=

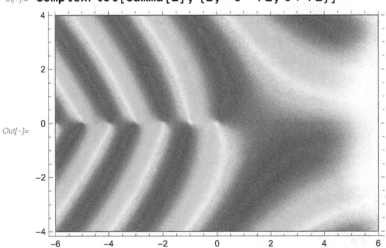

The singularities show up as white dots. Here is a 3D complex plot:

In[ ]:= `ComplexPlot3D[Gamma[z], {z, -6 - 4 i, 6 + 4 i}, ViewPoint → {-2, -2, 2}]`

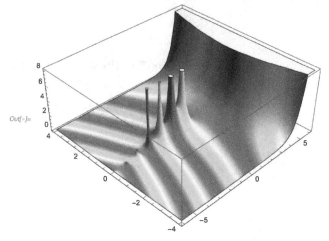

Out[ ]=

The beta function is a combination of gamma functions:

$$B(a, b) = \frac{\Gamma(a)\Gamma(b)}{\Gamma(a + b)} = \int_0^1 t^{a-1}(1 - t)^{b-1}dt.$$

The incomplete gamma function is defined by

$$\Gamma(a, x) = \int_x^\infty t^{a-1}e^{-t}dt.$$

The asymptotic approximation to the gamma function as $n \to \infty$ leads to *Stirling's approximation* for $n!$:

In[ ]:= `TraditionalForm[Asymptotic[Gamma[n + 1], n → ∞]]`

Out[ ]//TraditionalForm=

$$\sqrt{2\pi}\, e^{-n}\, n^{n+\frac{1}{2}}$$

which we can write

$$n! \sim \sqrt{2\pi n}\left(\frac{n}{e}\right)^n.$$

Compare, for $n = 10$

In[ ]:= `N[10!]`

Out[ ]= 3.6288×10^6

and

$\textit{In[•]:=} \quad \sqrt{2 \pi 10} \left(\dfrac{10}{e}\right)^{10} \text{ // N}$

$\textit{Out[•]=} \quad 3.5987 \times 10^6$

and we see an error of approximately 1%.

2.2.1. *Digamma Function*

The logarithmic derivative of the gamma function, given by

$$\psi(z) = \frac{d}{dz}\log \Gamma(z) = \frac{\Gamma'(z)}{\Gamma(z)},$$

is known as the *digamma function*. Mathematica defines the function as **PolyGamma[z]**. The gamma function obeys the equation $\Gamma(z + 1) = z\Gamma(z)$ and therefore

$$\Gamma'(z + 1) = z\Gamma'(z) + \Gamma(z).$$

Dividing by $\Gamma(z + 1)$, or equivalently $z\Gamma(z)$, then gives

$$\psi(z + 1) = \psi\{z\} + \frac{1}{z}.$$

2.2.2. *Harmonic Numbers*

For $z = k$, an integer, we can derive

$$\sum_{k=1}^{n} \frac{1}{k} = \sum_{k=1}^{n} [\psi(k + 1) - \psi(k)] = \psi(n + 1) - \psi(1).$$

The sum of reciprocals is known as the nth *harmonic number*

$$H_n = \sum_{k=1}^{k} \frac{1}{k} = 1 + \frac{1}{2} + \frac{1}{3} + \cdots + \frac{1}{n}$$

so that we can write

$$\psi(n) = H_{n-1} + \psi(1).$$

The harmonic series, the above sum as $n \to \infty$, is divergent. However,

In[ ]:= `Limit[HarmonicNumber[n] - Log[n], n → ∞]`

Out[ ]= `EulerGamma`

In[ ]:= `N[%]`

Out[ ]= `0.577216`

This is Euler's constant γ, also known as the Euler–Mascheroni constant:

$$\gamma = 0.577216\ldots$$

where

$$\gamma = \lim_{n\to\infty} \left(1 + \frac{1}{2} + \frac{1}{3} + \cdots + \frac{1}{n} - \log n\right).$$

The digamma function $\psi(1)$ can be determined from

In[ ]:= `Limit[PolyGamma[n] - HarmonicNumber[n - 1], n → ∞]`

Out[ ]= `-EulerGamma`

Thus, more explicitly,

$$\psi(n) = H_{n-1} - \gamma.$$

Here is a plot of the digamma function for real arguments:

In[ ]:= `Plot[PolyGamma[x], {x, -4, 4}, Frame → True,`
`    GridLines → Automatic, PlotLabel → TraditionalForm[ψ[x]]]`

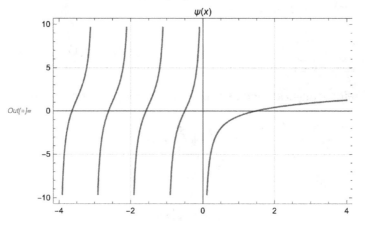

with the expected singularities at $x = 0, -1, -2, \ldots$.

2.3. The Error Function

Recall the famous definite integral

$$\int_{-\infty}^{\infty} e^{-t^2}\,dt = \sqrt{\pi} \quad \text{or} \quad \int_{0}^{\infty} e^{-t^2}\,dt = \frac{\sqrt{\pi}}{2}.$$

The error function can be defined by the definite integral

$$\text{erf}(x) = \frac{2}{\sqrt{x}} \int_{0}^{x} e^{-t^2}\,dt$$

which reduces to 1 for $x = \infty$. Following is a plot:

In[ ]:= `Plot[Erf[x], {x, -4, 4}, Frame → True,`
    `GridLines → Automatic, PlotLabel → TraditionalForm[Erf[x]]]`

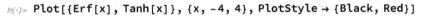

Remarkably, the function is very closely approximated by tanh x:

In[ ]:= `Plot[{Erf[x], Tanh[x]}, {x, -4, 4}, PlotStyle → {Black, Red}]`

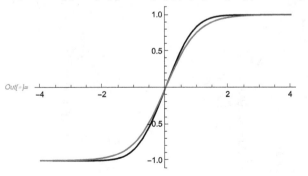

The error function occurs in computations of slices of the normal distribution function or bell curve

$$f(x) = \frac{1}{\sqrt{2\pi}\sigma}e^{-\frac{(x-\mu)^2}{2\sigma^2}}$$

with an average μ and standard deviation σ. The *standard normal distribution*, with $\mu = 0$ and $\sigma = 1$, can be written

$$f(x) = \frac{1}{\sqrt{2\pi}}e^{-x^2/2}.$$

For example, what is the fraction that is contained within ± 1 σ of the average $(x = 0)$? This is represented by the integral

In[•]:= $\displaystyle\int_{-1}^{1} \frac{1}{\sqrt{2\,\pi}}\, e^{-x^2/2}\, dx$

Out[•]= $\mathrm{Erf}\left[\dfrac{1}{\sqrt{2}}\right]$

In[•]:= $\mathbf{N[\%]}$

Out[•]=   0.682689

showing that 68.3% of the statistical sample lies between these limits. This is represented on the following graphic

```
In[•]:= Show[Graphics[{EdgeForm[{Thin, White}],
         GrayLevel[0.8], Rectangle[{-3, 0}, {-2, .45}], GrayLevel[.6],
         Rectangle[{-2, 0}, {-1, .45}], GrayLevel[.4], Rectangle[{-1, 0}, {0, .45}
         ], GrayLevel[0.4], Rectangle[{0, 0}, {1, .45}], GrayLevel[.6],
         Rectangle[{1, 0}, {2, .45}], GrayLevel[.8], Rectangle[{2, 0}, {3, .45}]}],
       Plot[ 1/√(2 π)  e^(-x²/2), {x, -4, 4}, PlotRange → {0, .45},
         PlotStyle → Black, Filling → Top, FillingStyle →
         White], Graphics[{Text[Style["13.6%", 12, White], {-1.5, .05}],
         Text[Style["34.1%", 12, White], {-.5, .05}],
         Text[Style["34.1%", 12, White], {.5, .05}], Text[Style["13.6%", 12, White],
         {1.5, .05}], Text[Style["2.1%    0.1%", 12, Black], {3, .05}],
         Text[Style["0.1%    2.1%", 12, Black], {-3, .05}]}], AspectRatio → .6]
```

Out[•]=

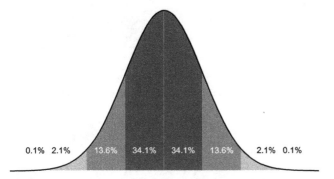

This shows that 68.3% of the data falls within one standard deviation of the mean, 95.4% falls within 2σ of the mean and 99.7% falls within 3σ of the mean.

The *complementary error function* erfc x is defined by

$$\operatorname{erfc}(x) = 1 - \operatorname{erf}(x) = \frac{2}{\sqrt{\pi}} \int_{x}^{\infty} e^{-t^2} \, dt$$

In[ ]:= `Plot[Erfc[x], {x, -4, 4}, Frame → True,`
        `GridLines → Automatic, PlotLabel → TraditionalForm[Erfc[x]]]`

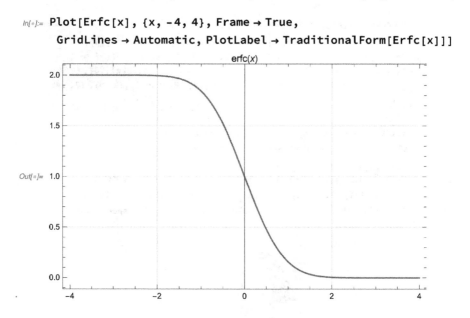

Referring to the bell curve above, the fraction *greater* than 2σ amounts to

In[ ]:=
$$\int_{2}^{\infty} \frac{1}{\sqrt{2\,\pi}}\, e^{-x^2/2}\, dx$$

Out[ ]=
$$\frac{\mathrm{Erfc}\left[\sqrt{2}\right]}{2}$$

In[ ]:= `N[%]`

Out[ ]= `0.0227501`

corresponding to 2.3% or the 98th percentile. The fraction greater than 3σ equals

In[ ]:= $N\left[\frac{1}{2}\,\mathrm{Erfc}\left[\frac{3}{\sqrt{2}}\right]\right]$

Out[ ]= `0.0013499`

in the 99.9th percentile.

Some applications in quantum theory involve erfc(z) in the complex plane:

In[ ]:= `ComplexPlot[Erfc[z], {z, -4 - 4 i, 4 + 4 i}]`

Out[ ]=

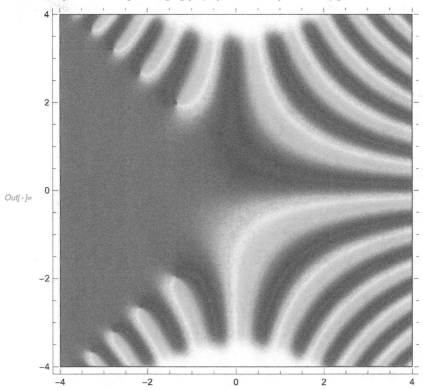

2.4. Exponential Integral

For real values of x, the exponential integral Ei(x) is defined by

$$\text{Ei}(x) = \int_{-\infty}^{x} \frac{e^t}{t} dt = -\int_{-x}^{\infty} \frac{e^{-t}}{t} dt.$$

The integral is to be understood as the Cauchy principal value for the singularity at zero. In Mathematica the exponential integral is written ExpIntegralEi[x].

In[•]:= `Plot[ExpIntegralEi[x], {x, -1, 2},`
`    GridLines → Automatic, PlotLabel → ExpIntegralEi[x]]`

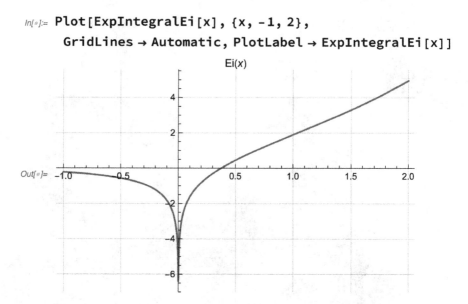

A series expansion about $x = 0$:

In[•]:= `Series[ExpIntegralEi[x], {x, 0, 4}, Assumptions → x > 0]`

Out[•]= $(\text{EulerGamma} + \text{Log}[x]) + x + \dfrac{x^2}{4} + \dfrac{x^3}{18} + \dfrac{x^4}{96} + O[x]^5$

The log term produces the singularity at $x = 0$. An asymptotic expansion is found from

In[•]:= `Normal[Series[ExpIntegralEi[x], {x, ∞, 5}]]`

Out[•]= $e^x \left(\dfrac{24}{x^5} + \dfrac{6}{x^4} + \dfrac{2}{x^3} + \dfrac{1}{x^2} + \dfrac{1}{x} \right)$

The leading form is evidently $\text{Ei}(x) \sim \dfrac{e^x}{x}$. For $x = \log z$, the integral definition of the exponential integral can be transformed as follows:

$$\text{Ei}(x) = \int_{-\infty}^{x} \frac{e^t}{t}\, dt = \int_{0}^{z} \frac{e^{\log u}}{\log u}\, d\log u = \int_{0}^{z} \frac{1}{\log u}\, du.$$

This leads to the definition of the logarithmic integral:

$$\text{li}(z) = \int_{0}^{z} \frac{du}{\log u},$$

written LogIntegral[z].

In[•]:= `FullSimplify[ExpIntegralEi[Log[z]]]`

Out[•]= `LogIntegral[z]`

2.5. The Dirac Delta Function

2.5.1. *Representations of the Delta Function*

The "delta function" was invented by P. A. M. Dirac around 1930 in order to compactly express the completeness relation in quantum mechanics. (Essentially equivalent definitions appear in earlier works of Fourier, Kirchhoff, and Heaviside.) The delta function is the limit of a function that grows infinitely large in an infinitesimally small region, while its integral remains normalized to 1. The delta function is too singular to be considered a function in the usual sense. Mathematicians have, however, accepted it as a linear functional, a "generalized function", or "distribution".

The delta function has computational significance only when it appears under an integral sign. Its defining relation can, in fact, be written $\int_{-\infty}^{\infty} f(x)\delta(x)dx = f(0)$ or, more generally, $\int_{-\infty}^{\infty} f(x)\delta(x-a)dx = f(a)$. There are a number of representations of the delta function based on limits of a family of functions as some parameter approaches infinity (or zero). In this Demonstration, five of these representations are illustrated. You can select the parameter n to take values from 1 to 10, on its way toward infinity. The most rudimentary representation is a rectangular pulse: $f_n(x) = n$ for $-\frac{1}{2n} \le x \le \frac{1}{2n}$. Then $\delta(x) = \lim_{n\to\infty} f_n(x)$ as the rectangle becomes higher and narrower.

The most commonly cited representation is based on the normalized Gaussian distribution (bell-shaped curve): $\delta(x) = \lim_{n\to\infty} \frac{n}{\sqrt{2\pi}}e^{-n^2x^2/2}$. The limit $n \to \infty$ is equivalent to $\sigma \to 0$, where σ is the standard deviation.

Closely analogous is the Lorentzian representation: $\delta(x) = \lim_{n\to\infty} \frac{n/\pi}{1+n^2x^2}$. The Lorentzian function is proportional to the derivative of the arctangent, shown as an inset. In the limit as $n \to \infty$, the arctangent approaches a step function (Heaviside function). Thus the delta function represents the derivative of a step function.

In quantum mechanics, one frequently encounters the representation $\delta(x) = \lim_{n \to \infty} \frac{\sin(nx)}{\pi x}$. The rapidly oscillating normalized sinc function gives an effective contribution of zero when $x \neq 0$.

The Fourier series for the delta function contains unit contributions from all frequencies. A delta function is approached as the number of terms in the following expansion increases: $\delta(x) = \lim_{n \to \infty} \sum_{k=-n}^{n} e^{ikx}$.

This representation applies only in a neighborhood of the origin. More correctly, this Fourier series represents a Dirac comb function or Shah function $\sqcup\!\sqcup (x - 2n\pi) = \sum_{n=-\infty}^{\infty} \delta(x - 2n\pi)$ (after the Russian letter $\sqcup\!\sqcup$).

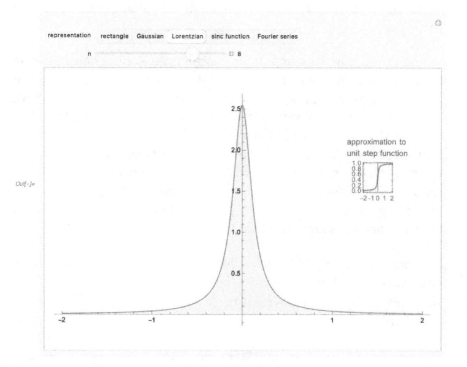

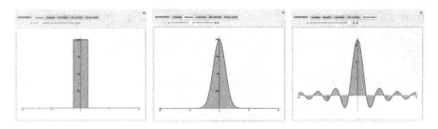

Demonstration 2.4: Representations of the Dirac Delta Function (https://demonstra tions.wolfram.com/RepresentationsOfTheDiracDeltafunction/)

2.5.2. *Delta Function as Limit of Some Special Functions*

The above Demonstration gives some representations for the Dirac delta function as the limit of elementary functions. This Demonstration illustrates several additional limiting relations involving special functions and the delta function:

Bessel: $\delta(x) = \lim_{n\to\infty} nJ_n(n(x+1))$, $(n \neq \text{integer})$.

Airy: $\delta(x) = \lim_{n\to\infty} n\,\text{Ai}(nx)$.

Hermite: The mth derivative of the delta function is given by $\delta^{(m)}(x) = \lim_{n\to\infty} \frac{(-1)^m}{\sqrt{\pi}} \frac{e^{-n^2x^2}}{n^{m-1}} H_m(nx)$. Shown is $\delta'(x)$ with $m = 1$.

Dirichlet kernel: $\text{Ш}(x) = \lim_{n\to\infty} \frac{1}{2\pi} \frac{\sin((n+\frac{1}{2})x)}{\sin(\frac{x}{2})}$, where the Dirac comb or Shah function is defined by $\text{Ш}(x) = \sum_{n=-\infty}^{\infty} \delta(x - 2n\pi)$. This is a periodic extension of the delta function.

Fejér kernel: $\text{Ш}(x) = \lim_{n\to\infty} \frac{1}{2\pi n} \left(\frac{\sin(\frac{nx}{2})}{\sin(\frac{x}{2})}\right)^2$, with the same periodicity as the Dirichlet kernel.

Sigmoid: The derivative of the sigmoid function $\delta(x) = \lim_{n\to\infty} \frac{d}{dx}\left(\frac{1}{1-e^{-nx}}\right)$.

Closure: An orthonormal set of functions $\{\phi_n(x)\}$ obeys the closure relation $\lim_{n\to\infty} \sum_{k=0}^{n} \phi_k^*(x)\phi_k(x') = \delta(x - x')$. This is shown for orthonormalized Hermite functions $\phi_n(x) = (2^n n! \sqrt{\pi})^{-1/2} e^{-x^2/2} H_n(x)$ with $x' = 1$.

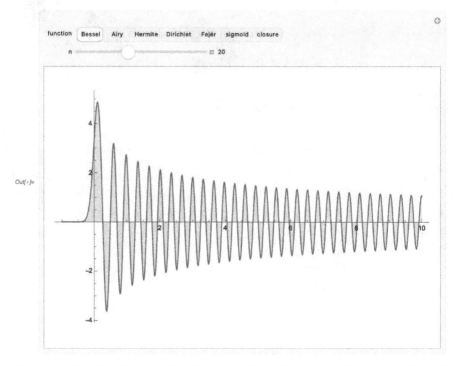

Demonstration 2.5: The Delta Function as the Limit of Some Special Functions (https://demonstrations.wolfram.com/TheDeltafunctionAsTheLimitOfSomeSpecialFunctions/)

2.6. Spherical Trigonometry

A gnomonic projection is obtained by projecting points on the surface of a sphere from the sphere's center to a plane tangent to the sphere. In this Demonstration, the tangent point is taken as the North Pole, so that loci of constant θ are circles, while those of constant ϕ are radial spokes. This projection can be used to project slightly less than one hemisphere at a time onto a finite plane. The transformation equations are $\xi = \tan\theta \cos\phi$, $\eta = \tan\theta \sin\phi$. A gnomonic projection is neither conformal nor area-preserving, but has the distinctive feature that great circle arcs are mapped into straight lines. This suggests that it might be instructive to apply the gnomonic projection to spherical trigonometry.

Spherical triangles with sides a, b, c and angles α, β, γ, all expressed in degrees, are shown on a hemisphere and on a gnomonic projection. You can drag the vertices. The triangles conform to spherical analogs of the law of cosines, $\cos a = \cos b \cos c + \sin b \sin c \cos \alpha$ and also $\cos \alpha = -\cos \beta \cos \gamma + \sin \beta \sin \gamma \cos a$, with two other cyclic permutations for each. The spherical law of sines has the form $\sin \alpha / \sin a = \sin \beta / \sin b = \sin \gamma / \sin c$. The sum of the angles of a spherical triangle is greater than $180°$, and it is useful to define the spherical excess $E = \alpha + \beta + \gamma - 180°$. The area enclosed by a triangle on the unit sphere, as well as the subtended solid angle, is equal to E, expressed in steradians.

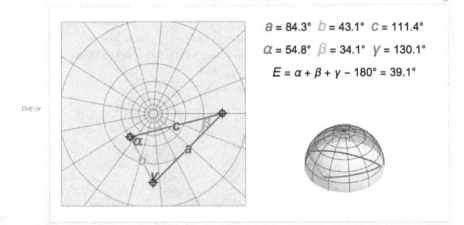

Out[ ]=

$a = 84.3°$ $b = 43.1°$ $C = 111.4°$

$\alpha = 54.8°$ $\beta = 34.1°$ $\gamma = 130.1°$

$E = \alpha + \beta + \gamma - 180° = 39.1°$

Demonstration 2.6: Spherical Trigonometry on a Gnomonic Projection (https://demonstrations.wolfram.com/SphericalTrigonometryOnAGnomonicProjection/)

2.7. First-Order Differential Equations

In radioactive decay the number of nuclei decaying per second is simply proportional to the number of nuclei, with a negative constant of proportionality since the number is decreasing. This implies a first-order differential equation $\frac{dn}{dt} = -nk$, where $n(t)$ is the number of nuclei at time t and k is the decay constant. Let n_0 be the initial number of nuclei at time $t = 0$. It is most convenient to write $\frac{dn}{dt}$ as $n'[t]$.

Mathematica can then solve the differential equation as follows:

In[•]:= `Clear[n, k]`

In[•]:= `DSolve[{n'[t] == -n[t] k, n[0] == n0}, n[t], t]`

Out[•]= $\left\{\left\{n[t] \rightarrow e^{-kt} n0\right\}\right\}$

We would write this as

$$n(t) = n_0 e^{-kt}.$$

Here is a simple plot, where you can vary the decay constant:

In[•]:= `Manipulate[Plot[e^{-kt}, {t, 0, 5}, PlotRange -> {0, 1},`
`    PlotTheme -> "Scientific", GridLines -> Automatic, FrameLabel ->`
`        {Style["t", Italic], Row[{TraditionalForm[n[t]], "/", Style["n", Italic]_0}]}],`
`    {{k, 1, Style["k", Italic]}, .5, 3, Appearance -> "Labeled"}, ControlPlacement -> Top]`

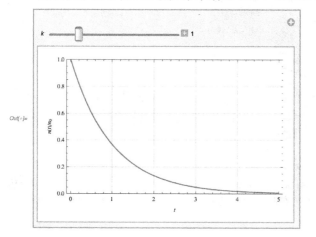

Often the rate of a radioactive decay is described by its *half life* $t_{1/2}$, the time it takes for half of the nuclei to decay. From the integrated rate law, the half life can be found from

$$\frac{n}{n_0} = \frac{1}{2} = e^{-kt_{1/2}}.$$

Taking logarithms, we find $-\ln 2 = -kt_{1/2}$, so that

$$t_{1/2} = k/\ln 2 \approx 1.44k.$$

Note that in mathematical literature the natural logarithm is written as "Log". Thus:

In[∘]:= $\mathbf{N}\left[\dfrac{1}{\mathbf{Log[2]}}\right]$

Out[∘]= `1.4427`

An exponential power law with a *positive k* can represent the growth of a bacterial colony, assuming unlimited nutrition and the absence of predators:

In[∘]:= `Manipulate[Plot[e^kt, {t, 0, 5}, PlotRange → All,`
`        PlotTheme → "Scientific", GridLines → Automatic, FrameLabel →`
`        {Style["t", Italic], Row[{TraditionalForm[n[t]], "/", Style["n", Italic]₀}]}],`
`    {{k, 1, Style["k", Italic]}, .5, 3, Appearance → "Labeled"}, ControlPlacement → Top]`

Out[∘]=

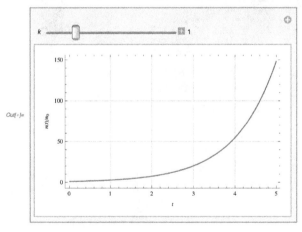

Population growth subject to limiting factors, for example overcrowding, limited food supply, predators, etc., can be modeled using the *logistic equation* or Verhulst model:

$$\frac{dP}{dt} = rP\left(1 - \frac{P}{K}\right).$$

Here r is the intrinsic rate of population growth, while K is the so-called carrying capacity, the maximum sustainable population. Taking $P(0) = 1$, we compute:

```
In[*]:= DSolve[{P'[t] == r P[t] (1 - P[t] / K), P[0] == 1}, P[t], t]
```

$$Out[*]= \left\{\left\{P[t] \to \frac{e^{r t} K}{-1 + e^{r t} + K}\right\}\right\}$$

The result can be plotted, with the parameters manipulated:

```
In[*]:= Manipulate[Plot[ (e^(r t) K)/(-1 + e^(r t) + K), {t, 0, 10}, PlotTheme → "Scientific",
        GridLines → Automatic, FrameLabel → {Style["t", Italic], Style["P", Italic]}],
       {{r, .5, Style["r", Italic]}, 0, 1, Appearance → "Labeled"},
       {{K, 1.5, Style["K", Italic]}, .5, 4, Appearance → "Labeled"},
       ControlPlacement → Top]
```

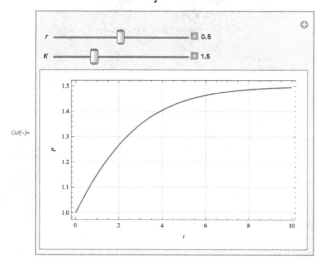

2.8. Second-Order Differential Equations

Next, we consider some second-order differential equations with constant coefficients. An idealized representation of Hooke's law is provided by a mass m attached to a massless spring with force constant k, something like this:

```
In[ ]:= Manipulate[ParametricPlot3D[{x ϕ, .5 Cos[ϕ], .5 Sin[ϕ]}, {ϕ, 0, 16 π}, Boxed → False,
         Axes → False, PlotStyle → Red, PlotRange → {{0, 12}, {-1, 1}, {-1, 1}},
         ImageSize → {300, 150}, ViewPoint → {1, -2, 0},
         Epilog → {Disk[{19.4 x - 1.64, .5}, .2], Arrow[{{0, -.25}, {3, -.25}}],
           Line[{{1.27, 0}, {1.27, -.5}}], Text[Style[TraditionalForm["x-x₀"], 20, Italic],
           {1.75, -.5}], Text[Style["m", 20, Italic, Black], {19.4 x - 1.64, 1}],
           Text[Style["k", 20, Italic, Red], {5.5 x - 1.25, 1}]}}],
        {x, .1, .2}, ControlPlacement → Top]
```

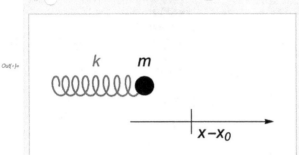

The force law is given by $f = -k(x - x_0)$, where x_0 is the equilibrium extension of the spring. The spring resists both expansion and compression from its equilibrium state, which is consistent with the minus sign. By Newton's second law, the force on the mass m is related to its acceleration by

$$f = ma = m\frac{d^2x}{dt^2},$$

leading to the second-order differential equation

$$m\frac{d^2x}{dt^2} + k(x - x_0) = 0.$$

Using Mathematica:

```
In[ ]:= DSolve[m x''[t] + k (x[t] - x0) == 0, x[t], t]
```

$$Out[ ]= \left\{\left\{x[t] \to x0 + c_1 \cos\left[\frac{\sqrt{k}\ t}{\sqrt{m}}\right] + c_2 \sin\left[\frac{\sqrt{k}\ t}{\sqrt{m}}\right]\right\}\right\}$$

If we set $x_0 = 0$ and assume the initial conditions $x(0) = 1$ and $x'(0) = 0$, we can use

In[•]:= `DSolve[{m x''[t] + k x[t] == 0, x[0] == 1, x'[0] == 0}, x[t], t]`

Out[•]= $\left\{\left\{x[t] \to Cos\left[\dfrac{\sqrt{k}\ t}{\sqrt{m}}\right]\right\}\right\}$

The motion of the mass is evidently sinusoidal with an angular frequency $\omega = \sqrt{\frac{k}{m}}$. This is known as a *harmonic oscillator*.

In[•]:= `Manipulate[ParametricPlot3D[{.06 × (2 + Cos[ω t]) φ, .5 Cos[φ], .5 Sin[φ]},`
`    {φ, 0, 16 π}, Boxed → False, Axes → False, PlotStyle → Red,`
`    PlotRange → {{0, 12}, {-1, 1}, {-1, 1}}, ImageSize → {300, 150},`
`    ViewPoint → {1, -2, 0}, Epilog → Disk[{1.2 × (2 + Cos[ω t] - 1.4), .5}, .2]],`
`    {{ω, 2, "ω"}, 1, 4, Appearance → "Labeled"},`
`    {{t, 0, "animate"}, 0, ∞, Trigger}, ControlPlacement → Top]`

Out[•]=

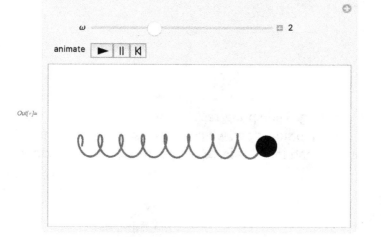

The oscillator might be subject to damping, which adds a term proportional to the instantaneous velocity $x'(t)$. The equation of the oscillator can now be written

$$mx''(t) + \eta x'(t) + kx(t) = 0.$$

With the definitions $\gamma = \frac{\eta}{2m}$, the damping constant, and $\omega_0 = \sqrt{\frac{k}{m}}$, the natural frequency of the undamped oscillator, we can write

$$x''(t) + 2\gamma x'(t) + \omega_0^2 x(t) = 0.$$

Again with the initial conditions $x(0) = 1$ and $x'(0) = 0$, we compute:

In[⬦]:= `DSolve[{x''[t] + 2 γ x'[t] + ω0² x[t] == 0, x[0] == 1, x'[0] == 0}, x[t], t]`

Out[⬦]= $\left\{\left\{x[t] \to \dfrac{1}{2\sqrt{\gamma^2 - \omega0^2}}\right.\right.$
$\left.\left(-e^{t\left(-\gamma-\sqrt{\gamma^2-\omega0^2}\right)} \gamma + e^{t\left(-\gamma+\sqrt{\gamma^2-\omega0^2}\right)} \gamma + e^{t\left(-\gamma-\sqrt{\gamma^2-\omega0^2}\right)} \sqrt{\gamma^2-\omega0^2} + e^{t\left(-\gamma+\sqrt{\gamma^2-\omega0^2}\right)} \sqrt{\gamma^2-\omega0^2}\right)\right\}\right\}$

We can simplify this by defining the frequency $\omega = \sqrt{\omega^2 - \gamma^2}$, so that $\sqrt{\gamma^2 - \omega_0^2} = i\omega$. Now

In[⬦]:= $\textbf{FullSimplify}\left[\textbf{\% /. } \sqrt{\gamma^2 - \omega0^2} \to i\,\omega\right]$

Out[⬦]= $\left\{\left\{x[t] \to \dfrac{i\,e^{-t\gamma}\,(\omega\,\text{Cos}[t\,\omega] + \gamma\,\text{Sin}[t\,\omega])}{\sqrt{(\gamma - \omega0)\,(\gamma + \omega0)}}\right\}\right\}$

which we can simplify further to $x(t) = e^{-\gamma t}(\cos \omega t + \frac{\gamma}{\omega} \sin \omega t)$. Following are some plots:

In[⬦]:= $\textbf{Manipulate}\left[\textbf{Plot}\left[e^{-\gamma t} \left(\textbf{Cos}\left[\sqrt{\omega0^2 - \gamma^2}\ t\right] + \gamma \big/ \sqrt{\omega0^2 - \gamma^2}\ \textbf{Sin}\left[\sqrt{\omega0^2 - \gamma^2}\ t\right]\right),\right.\right.$

$\{t, 0, 20\}, \textbf{PlotTheme} \to \textbf{"Scientific"}, \textbf{GridLines} \to \textbf{Automatic}\Big],$

$\{\{\omega0, 1, \textbf{"}\omega_0\textbf{"}\}, .5, 2, \textbf{Appearance} \to \textbf{"Labeled"}\},$

$\left.\{\{\gamma, .25, \textbf{"}\gamma\textbf{"}\}, 0, 2, \textbf{Appearance} \to \textbf{"Labeled"}\}, \textbf{ControlPlacement} \to \textbf{Top}\right]$

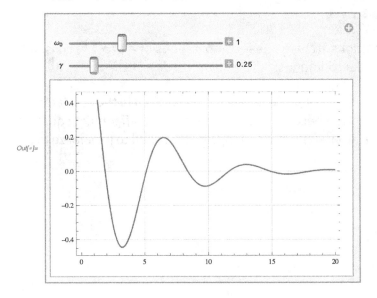

For $\gamma = 0$, the motion is undamped harmonic oscillation. For $\gamma < \omega_0$, we have *underdamping*, with the sinusoidal oscillation damped by the factor $e^{-\gamma t}$. The case $\gamma = \omega_0$ represents *critical damping*, with $x(t) = e^{-\gamma t}$, a pure exponential decay. When $\gamma > \omega_0$, *overdamping* occurs, where the oscillation decays to zero, but more slowly.

An alternative approach to the problem admits complex-valued solutions. The physically significant results are then the real and imaginary parts of these functions. For example, consider again

$$x''(t) + 2\gamma x'(t) + \omega_0^2 x(t) = 0.$$

Assume a solution of the form $x(t) = e^{i\Omega t}$, where Ω is complex. Now:

In[•]:= `x[t_] := ` $e^{i \Omega t}$

In[•]:= `Simplify[x''[t] + 2 `γ` x'[t] + w0`^{2}` x[t]]`

Out[•]= $e^{i t \Omega} \left(2 i \gamma \Omega - \Omega^2 + \text{w0}^2\right)$

Thus the solution is reduced to an algebraic problem:

In[•]:= `Solve[% == 0, `Ω`]`

Out[•]= $\left\{\left\{\Omega \to i \gamma - \sqrt{-\gamma^2 + \text{w0}^2}\right\}, \left\{\Omega \to i \gamma + \sqrt{-\gamma^2 + \text{w0}^2}\right\}\right\}$

Thus the solutions $x(t)$ are linear combinations of $e^{-\gamma t} e^{\pm i\omega t}$, chosen to satisfy the initial conditions.

When a sinusoidally varying external force is applied to the oscillator, the equation of motion becomes an inhomogeneous differential equation: $x''(t) + 2\gamma x'(t) + \omega_0^2 x(t) = f \cos \omega t$. Again, it is useful to generalize to the complex domain and rewrite as $x''(t) + 2\gamma x'(t) + \omega_0^2 x(t) = f e^{i\omega t}$. Now

In[•]:= `DSolve[x''[t] + 2 γ x'[t] + ωθ² x[t] == f e^{i ω t}, x[t], t]`

Out[•]= $\left\{\left\{x[t] \rightarrow -\left(\left(f\left(e^{t\left(\gamma+i\,\omega-\sqrt{\gamma^2-\omega\theta^2}\right)+t\left(-\gamma+\sqrt{\gamma^2-\omega\theta^2}\right)}\gamma - \right.\right.\right.\right.$

$e^{t\left(-\gamma-\sqrt{\gamma^2-\omega\theta^2}\right)+t\left(\gamma+i\,\omega+\sqrt{\gamma^2-\omega\theta^2}\right)}\gamma + i\,e^{t\left(\gamma+i\,\omega-\sqrt{\gamma^2-\omega\theta^2}\right)+t\left(-\gamma+\sqrt{\gamma^2-\omega\theta^2}\right)}\omega - $

$i\,e^{t\left(-\gamma-\sqrt{\gamma^2-\omega\theta^2}\right)+t\left(\gamma+i\,\omega+\sqrt{\gamma^2-\omega\theta^2}\right)}\omega + e^{t\left(\gamma+i\,\omega-\sqrt{\gamma^2-\omega\theta^2}\right)+t\left(-\gamma+\sqrt{\gamma^2-\omega\theta^2}\right)}\sqrt{\gamma^2-\omega\theta^2} + $

$e^{t\left(-\gamma-\sqrt{\gamma^2-\omega\theta^2}\right)+t\left(\gamma+i\,\omega+\sqrt{\gamma^2-\omega\theta^2}\right)}\sqrt{\gamma^2-\omega\theta^2}\right)\Big/$

$\left(2\sqrt{\gamma^2-\omega\theta^2}\left(-\gamma-i\,\omega+\sqrt{\gamma^2-\omega\theta^2}\right)\left(\gamma+i\,\omega+\sqrt{\gamma^2-\omega\theta^2}\right)\right)\right) + $

$e^{t\left(-\gamma-\sqrt{\gamma^2-\omega\theta^2}\right)}c_1 + e^{t\left(-\gamma+\sqrt{\gamma^2-\omega\theta^2}\right)}c_2\Big\}\Big\}$

In[•]:= `Simplify[%]`

Out[•]= $\left\{\left\{x[t] \rightarrow \frac{1}{2\,i\,\gamma\,\omega - \omega^2 + \omega\theta^2}e^{-t\left(\gamma+\sqrt{\gamma^2-\omega\theta^2}\right)}\right.\right.$

$\left.\left.\left(e^{t\left(\gamma+i\,\omega+\sqrt{\gamma^2-\omega\theta^2}\right)}f + \left(2\,i\,\gamma\,\omega - \omega^2 + \omega\theta^2\right)c_1 + e^{2\,t\sqrt{\gamma^2-\omega\theta^2}}\left(2\,i\,\gamma\,\omega - \omega^2 + \omega\theta^2\right)c_2\right)\right\}\right\}$

The terms proportional to the two constants of integration c_1 and c_2 represent *transients*, dependent on the initial conditions $x(0)$ and $x'(0)$. The remaining part is the *steady state* solution, which establishes itself after the external force operates for a sufficient time. Setting the two constants equal to zero and simplifying the remaining expression, we find:

In[•]:= `% /. {c₁ → 0, c₂ → 0}`

Out[•]= $\left\{\left\{x[t] \rightarrow \frac{e^{-t\left(\gamma+\sqrt{\gamma^2-\omega\theta^2}\right)+t\left(\gamma+i\,\omega+\sqrt{\gamma^2-\omega\theta^2}\right)}f}{2\,i\,\gamma\,\omega - \omega^2 + \omega\theta^2}\right\}\right\}$

In[•]:= `Simplify[%]`

Out[•]= $\left\{\left\{x[t] \rightarrow \frac{e^{i\,t\,\omega}f}{2\,i\,\gamma\,\omega - \omega^2 + \omega\theta^2}\right\}\right\}$

Thus the steady state solution is proportional to the forcing function with a modified complex amplitude. When the forcing frequency ω approaches the natural frequency of the oscillator ω_0, the amplitude of $x(t)$ increases to a maximum. This is the phenomenon of *resonance*. If the damping constant γ were hypothetically reduced to zero, the amplitude would become infinite. Following is a plot of the complete solution, including the transients, with the initial conditions $x(0) = 1$, $x'(0) = 0$. You can play with the parameters to see how the steady state is established and explore the onset of resonance when $\omega \approx \omega_0$.

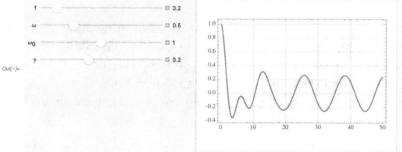

2.9. Partial Differential Equations

Many physical phenomena are described by partial differential equations (PDEs), involving two or more independent variables. They are obviously much more difficult to solve than ordinary differential equations (ODEs). Some applications, including weather prediction, econometric models, fluid dynamics, and nuclear engineering, might involve simultaneous PDEs with large numbers of variables. Such problems are best tackled by powerful supercomputers. We will be content to consider a few representative second-order PDEs for which analytic solutions are possible.

Scalar and vector fields which depend on more than one independent variable, which we write in notation such as $\Psi(x, y)$, $\Psi(x, t)$, $\Psi(\mathbf{r})$, $\Psi(\mathbf{r}, t)$, etc., are very often obtained as solutions to PDEs. Some classic equations of mathematical physics which we will consider are the wave equation, the heat equation, Laplace's equation, Poisson's equation, and the Schrödinger equation for some exactly solvable quantum-mechanical problems.

Wave equation:

$$\nabla^2\Psi - \frac{1}{c^2}\frac{\partial^2\Psi}{\partial t^2} = 0;$$

Heat or diffusion equation:

$$\frac{\partial\Psi}{\partial t} = \kappa\nabla^2\Psi;$$

Laplace's equation:

$$\nabla^2\Psi = 0;$$

Poisson's equation:

$$\nabla^2\Psi = -4\pi\rho(\mathbf{r}).$$

The Laplacian or ∇^2 operator in three common coordinate systems, Cartesian, cylindrical and spherical:

In[•]:= `Laplacian[f[x, y, z], {x, y, z}]`

Out[•]= $f^{(0,0,2)}[x, y, z] + f^{(0,2,0)}[x, y, z] + f^{(2,0,0)}[x, y, z]$

In[•]:= `Simplify[Laplacian[f[r, θ, z], {r, θ, z}, "Cylindrical"]]`

Out[•]= $f^{(0,0,2)}[r, θ, z] + \dfrac{f^{(0,2,0)}[r, θ, z]}{r^2} + \dfrac{f^{(1,0,0)}[r, θ, z]}{r} + f^{(2,0,0)}[r, θ, z]$

In[•]:= `Simplify[Laplacian[f[r, θ, φ], {r, θ, φ}, "Spherical"]]`

Out[•]= $\dfrac{1}{r^2}\Big(\text{Csc}[θ]^2\, f^{(0,0,2)}[r, θ, φ] + \text{Cot}[θ]\, f^{(0,1,0)}[r, θ, φ] +$

$f^{(0,2,0)}[r, θ, φ] + 2\,r\, f^{(1,0,0)}[r, θ, φ] + r^2\, f^{(2,0,0)}[r, θ, φ]\Big)$

In operator notation:

$$\nabla^2 = \frac{\partial^2}{\partial x^2} + \frac{\partial^2}{\partial y^2} + \frac{\partial^2}{\partial z^2},$$

$$\nabla^2 = \frac{1}{r}\frac{\partial}{\partial r}r\frac{\partial}{\partial r} + \frac{1}{r^2}\frac{\partial}{\partial \theta^2} + \frac{\partial^2}{\partial z^2},$$

$$\nabla^2 = \frac{1}{r^2}\frac{\partial}{\partial r}r^2\frac{\partial}{\partial r} + \frac{1}{r^2\sin\theta}\frac{\partial}{\partial \theta}\sin\theta\frac{\partial}{\partial \theta} + \frac{1}{r^2\sin^2\theta}\frac{\partial^2}{\partial \phi^2},$$

respectively.

For the case of monochromatic time dependence, solutions of the wave equation can be separated in the form

$$\Psi(r,t) = \psi(r)T(t).$$

Substituting into the wave equation:

$$T(t)\nabla^2\psi(r) - \psi(r)\frac{T''(t)}{c^2} = 0,$$

where it has been noted that ∇^2 acts only on $\psi(r)$ while $\frac{d}{dt}$ acts only on $T(t)$. Dividing by $\Psi(r,t)$, we obtain:

$$\frac{\nabla^2\psi(r)}{\psi(r)} - \frac{1}{c^2}\frac{T''(t)}{T(t)} = 0.$$

This equation implies that a function of r is equal to a function of t. This is possible only if the function is equal to a constant. Denoting the constant as k^2, the equation reduces to two independent differential equations:

$$\nabla^2\psi(r) + k^2\psi(r) = 0 \quad \text{and} \quad T''(t) + \omega^2 T(t) = 0,$$

where $\omega = kc$. The first is known as *Helmholtz's equation* while the second is easily solved:

In[•]:= $\mathrm{DSolve}\big[\mathrm{T''[t]} + \omega^2\, \mathrm{T[t]} == 0,\ \mathrm{T[t]},\ t\big]$

Out[•]= $\{\{\mathrm{T[t]} \to c_1\, \mathrm{Cos}[t\,\omega] + c_2\, \mathrm{Sin}[t\,\omega]\}\}$

Alternative solutions are the complex exponentials $e^{\pm i\omega t}$.

Let us consider the Helmholtz equation in two dimensions

$$\frac{\partial^2 \psi}{\partial x^2} + \frac{\partial^2 \psi}{\partial y^2} + k^2 \psi(x,y) = 0,$$

subject to the boundary conditions on a rectangle: $\psi = 0$ for $x = 0$, $x = a$ and for $y = 0$, $y = b$. The Helmholtz equation is separable with $\psi(x,y) = X(x)Y(y)$ to give two ODEs:

$$X''(x) + \alpha^2 X(x) = 0 \text{ with } X(0) = X(a) = 0 \text{ and}$$

$$Y''(y) + \beta^2 Y(y) = 0 \text{ with } Y(0) = Y(b) = 0,$$

where $\alpha^2 + \beta^2 = k^2$.

In[•]:= $\mathrm{DSolve}\big[\{\mathrm{X''[x]} + \alpha^2\, \mathrm{X[x]} == 0,\ \mathrm{X[0]} == 0,\ \mathrm{X[a]} == 0\},\ \mathrm{X[x]},\ x\big]$

Out[•]= $\left\{\left\{\mathrm{X[x]} \to \begin{array}{ll} c_1\, \mathrm{Sin}\left[x\,\sqrt{\alpha^2}\right] & n \in \mathbb{Z}\ \&\&\ n \geq 1\ \&\&\ \alpha^2 == \dfrac{n^2\,\pi^2}{a^2}\ \&\&\ a > 0 \\ 0 & \text{True} \end{array}\right\}\right\}$

Thus $X(x) = \text{const}\,\sin\frac{n\pi x}{a}$, and analogously $Y(y) = \text{const}\,\sin\frac{m\pi y}{b}$, with $n, m = 1, 2, 3, \ldots$ and $k^2 = \pi^2\left(\frac{n^2}{a^2} + \frac{m^2}{b^2}\right)$. This is, in fact, an eigenvalue problem to determine the allowed values of k consistent with the boundary conditions on an $a \times b$ rectangle. The eigenfunctions $\psi_{n,m}(x,y)$ can be represented by 3-dimensional plots in the following:

```
In[•]:= Manipulate[
        Plot3D[Sin[n π x / a] Sin[m π y / b], {x, 0, a}, {y, 0, b}, BoxRatios → {a, b, 1}],
        Row[{Control[{{a, 2, Style["a", Italic]}, 1, 3, Appearance → "Labeled"}], Spacer[10],
          Control[{{b, 1.5, Style["b", Italic]}, 1, 3, Appearance → "Labeled"}]}],
        Row[{Control[{{n, 2, Style["n", Italic]}, {1, 2, 3, 4}, Setter}], Spacer[10],
          Control[{{m, 3, Style["m", Italic]}, {1, 2, 3, 4}, Setter}]}], Alignment → Center]
```

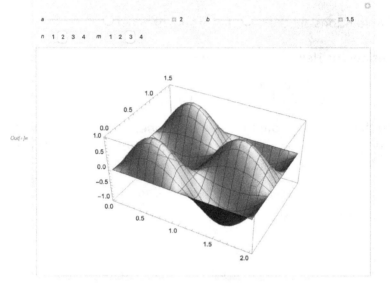

With the appropriate choice of parameters, this represents the solutions of the quantum-mechanical problem of a particle in a rectangular plate (or "two-dimensional box").

For future reference, we consider separable solutions of the Helmholtz equation in plane polar coordinates and in spherical coordinates.

In polar coordinates, the Helmholtz equation $(\nabla^2 + k^2)F(r, \theta) = 0$ is given explicitly by

$$\frac{1}{r}\frac{\partial}{\partial r}r\frac{\partial F}{\partial r} + \frac{1}{r^2}\frac{\partial^2 F}{\partial \theta^2} + k^2 F(r, \theta) = 0.$$

Assuming a separable solution $F(r, \theta) = R(r)\Theta(\theta)$, this reduces to

$$\frac{\frac{1}{r}\frac{d}{dr}r\frac{\partial R}{\partial r}}{R(r)} + \frac{\frac{1}{r^2}\frac{d^2\Theta}{d\theta^2}}{\Theta(\theta)} + k^2 = 0.$$

Multiplying by r^2 isolates the θ-dependent term. We set it equal to a negative constant:

$$\frac{\frac{d^2\Theta}{d\theta^2}}{\Theta(\theta)} = -m^2.$$

This is easily solved:

In[•]:= $\mathtt{DSolve\left[\Theta''[\theta] + m^2\ \Theta[\theta] == 0, \Theta[\theta], \theta\right]}$

Out[•]= $\mathtt{\{\{\Theta[\theta] \to c_1\ Cos[m\ \theta] + c_2\ Sin[m\ \theta]\}\}}$

where m must be an integer in order that $\Theta(\theta)$ be single valued. For compactness, we take

$$\Theta(\theta) = e^{im\theta}, \quad m = 0, \quad \pm 1, \quad \pm 2, \ldots$$

The r-equation thus reduces to

$$\frac{1}{r}\frac{d}{dr}r\frac{dR}{dr} + \left(k^2 - \frac{m^2}{r^2}\right)R(r) = 0.$$

In[•]:= $\mathtt{DSolve\left[\frac{1}{r}\,\partial_r\,(r\ R'[r]) + \left[k^2 - \frac{m^2}{r^2}\right]R[r] == 0, R[r], r\right]}$

Out[•]= $\mathtt{\{\{R[r] \to BesselJ[m, k\ r]\ c_1 + BesselY[m, k\ r]\ c_2\}\}}$

which are the Bessel functions $J_m(kr)$ and $Y_m(kr)$.

In spherical coordinates, the Helmholtz equation $(\nabla^2 + k^2)F(r, \theta, \phi) = 0$ is given by

$$\frac{1}{r^2}\frac{\partial}{\partial r}r^2\frac{\partial F}{\partial r} + \frac{1}{r^2\sin\theta}\frac{\partial}{\partial\theta}\sin\theta\frac{\partial F}{\partial\theta}$$

$$+ \frac{1}{r^2\sin^2\theta}\frac{\partial^2 F}{\partial\phi^2} + k^2 F(r, \theta, \phi) = 0.$$

We seek separable solutions of the form $F(r, \theta, \phi) = R(r)\Theta(\theta)\Phi(\phi)$. Applying the techniques introduced above, we obtain:

$$\frac{\frac{1}{r^2}\frac{d}{dr}r^2\frac{dR}{dr}}{R(r)} + \frac{\frac{1}{r^2\sin\theta}\frac{d}{d\theta}\sin\theta\frac{d\Theta}{d\theta}}{\Theta(\theta)} + \frac{\frac{1}{r^2\sin^2\theta}\frac{d^2\Phi}{d\phi^2}}{\Phi(\phi)} + k^2 = 0.$$

Multiplying by $r^2 \sin^2\theta$ isolates the ϕ-dependent term. We set it equal to a negative constant:

$$\frac{\frac{d^2\Phi}{d\phi^2}}{\Phi(\phi)} = -m^2.$$

As before, this leads to

$$\Phi(\phi) = e^{im\phi}, \quad m = 0, \pm1, \pm2, \ldots$$

The θ-dependence can analogously be isolated. We will deal with this more fully in the section on Legendre Polynomials. We will see that this introduces a separation constant $-\lambda = -l(l+1)$, so that the r-equation reduces to

$$\frac{1}{r^2}\frac{d}{dr}r^2\frac{dR}{dr} - \frac{l(1+1)}{r^2}R(r) + k^2R(r) = 0.$$

In[ ]:= **DSolve$[r^{-2} \partial_r (r^2 R'[r]) - l (l + 1) r^{-2} R[r] + k^2 R[r] == 0, R[r], r]$**

Out[ ]= $\{\{R[r] \to c_1 \text{ SphericalBesselJ}[l, k r] + c_2 \text{ SphericalBesselY}[l, k r]\}\}$

The solutions are the spherical Bessel functions $j_l(kr)$ and $y_l(kr)$.

Mathematica can directly solve a small number of partial differential equations. Following are a few examples.

In[ ]:= **DSolve$[\partial_{x,y} f[x, y] == 0, f[x, y], \{x, y\}]$**

Out[ ]= $\{\{f[x, y] \to c_1[x] + c_2[y]\}\}$

showing that, if the mixed second derivative of $f(x, y)$ equals 0, then f can be equal to the sum of arbitrary functions of x and y alone. Here is Laplace's equation in two dimensions, with unspecified boundary conditions:

$In[\bullet]:=$ `DSolve` $\left[\partial_{x,x}\, f[x,\, y]\, +\, \partial_{y,y}\, f[x,\, y]\, ==\, 0,\, f[x,\, y],\, \{x,\, y\}\right]$

$Out[\bullet]=$ `{{f[x, y]` $\to\, c_1\, [i\, x\, +\, y]\, +\, c_2\, [-i\, x\, +\, y]\}\}$

This is, of course, one of a immense number of possible solutions. But it can be surmised from this result that an analytic function of a complex variable $f(z) = f(x+iy)$ is a solution of Laplace's equation. A related result with the one-dimensional wave equation:

$In[\bullet]:=$ `DSolve` $\left[\partial_{x,x}\, f[x,\, t]\, -\, \dfrac{1}{c^2}\, \partial_{t,t}\, f[x,\, t]\, ==\, 0,\, f[x,\, t],\, \{x,\, t\}\right]$

$Out[\bullet]=$ $\left\{\left\{f[x,\, t]\, \to\, c_1\left[t\, -\, \dfrac{x}{\sqrt{c^2}}\right]\, +\, c_2\left[t\, +\, \dfrac{x}{\sqrt{c^2}}\right]\right\}\right\}$

showing possible solutions of the form $f(x - ct)$ and $g(x + ct)$.

2.10. Bessel Functions

A number of second-order differential equations with non-constant coefficients have solutions which belong to the category of *special functions*. These are particular mathematical functions that have become established and standardized by consensus by virtue of their usefulness in mathematical analysis, physics or other applications. Some of the better-known special functions are named after mathematicians, for example Bessel, Legendre, Hermite, Laguerre, Chebyshev, Jacobi, Bernoulli, and Mathieu.

Consider the differential equation $x^2 y''(x) + x y'(x) + (x^2 - n^2)y(x) = 0$, where n is an integer $0, 1, 2, \ldots$. Mathematica can solve what is known as Bessel's differential equation:

$In[\bullet]:=$ `DSolve` $\left[x^2\, y''[x]\, +\, x\, y'[x]\, +\, \left(x^2\, -\, n^2\right)\, y[x]\, ==\, 0,\, y[x],\, x\right]$

$Out[\bullet]=$ `{{y[x]` $\to\,$ `BesselJ[n, x]` $c_1\, +\,$ `BesselY[n, x]` $c_2\}\}$

The first solution is known as a Bessel function (of the first kind), designated $J_n(x)$. Here are some plots:

```
In[•]:= Manipulate[Plot[BesselJ[n, x], {x, 0, 20}, GridLines → Automatic,
         PlotLabel → BesselJ[n, x]], {{n, {0}, Style["n", Italic]}, {0, 1, 2}, CheckboxBar}]
```

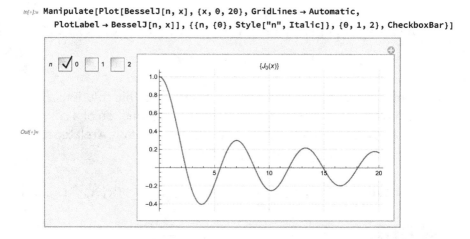

We can construct series expansions for $J_0(x)$, $J_1(x)$, $J_2(x)$, $J_n(x)$:

```
In[•]:= Series[BesselJ[0, x], {x, 0, 10}]
```

$$\text{Out[•]= } 1 - \frac{x^2}{4} + \frac{x^4}{64} - \frac{x^6}{2304} + \frac{x^8}{147\,456} - \frac{x^{10}}{14\,745\,600} + O[x]^{11}$$

```
In[•]:= Series[BesselJ[1, x], {x, 0, 10}]
```

$$\text{Out[•]= } \frac{x}{2} - \frac{x^3}{16} + \frac{x^5}{384} - \frac{x^7}{18\,432} + \frac{x^9}{1\,474\,560} + O[x]^{11}$$

```
In[•]:= Series[BesselJ[2, x], {x, 0, 10}]
```

$$\text{Out[•]= } \frac{x^2}{8} - \frac{x^4}{96} + \frac{x^6}{3072} - \frac{x^8}{184\,320} + \frac{x^{10}}{17\,694\,720} + O[x]^{11}$$

```
In[•]:= FullSimplify[Series[BesselJ[n, x], {x, 0, 10}]]
```

$$\text{Out[•]= } x^n \left(\frac{2^{-n}}{\text{Gamma}[1+n]} - \frac{2^{-2-n}\,x^2}{\text{Gamma}[2+n]} + \frac{2^{-5-n}\,x^4}{\text{Gamma}[3+n]} - \right.$$
$$\left. \frac{2^{-7-n}\,x^6}{3\,\text{Gamma}[4+n]} + \frac{2^{-11-n}\,x^8}{3\,\text{Gamma}[5+n]} - \frac{2^{-13-n}\,x^{10}}{15\,\text{Gamma}[6+n]} + O[x]^{11} \right)$$

Fixing this up a bit, noting that $\Gamma(n+1) = n!$, etc., we can write:

$$J_n(x) = \left(\frac{x}{2}\right)^n \left[\frac{1}{n!} - \frac{1}{(n+1)!}\left(\frac{x}{2}\right)^2 + \frac{1}{2(n+2)!}\left(\frac{x}{2}\right)^4\right.$$

$$- \frac{1}{6(n+3)!}\left(\frac{x}{2}\right)^6 + \frac{1}{24(n+4)!}\left(\frac{x}{2}\right)^8$$

$$\left. - \frac{1}{120(n+5)!}\left(\frac{x}{2}\right)^2 + \cdots\right].$$

The pattern becomes clear and we can surmise the general form:

$$J_n(x) = \left(\frac{x}{2}\right)^n \sum_{k=0}^{\infty} \frac{(-1)^k}{k!(n+k)!}\left(\frac{x}{2}\right)^{2k}.$$

The second solution of Bessel's equation is known as a *Bessel function of the second kind* or a *Neumann function*. It is designated $Y_n(x)$ or $N_n(x)$:

```
In[ ]:= Manipulate[Plot[BesselY[n, x], {x, 0, 20}, GridLines → Automatic,
          PlotLabel → BesselY[n, x]], {{n, {0}, Style["n", Italic]}, {0, 1, 2}, CheckboxBar}]
```

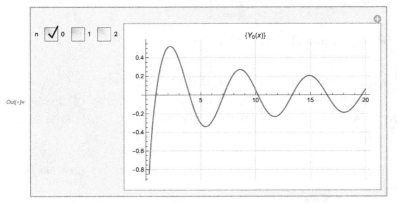

As the plots imply, $Y_n(x)$ is singular at $x = 0$. For example,

```
In[ ]:= BesselY[0, 0]
```

Out[ ]= $-\infty$

```
In[ ]:= BesselY[1, 0]
```

Out[ ]= ComplexInfinity

Bessel functions occur in problems involving the Helmholtz equation in cylindrical coordinates or, in two dimensions, plane polar coordinates. Suppose we seek a solution of the two-dimensional Helmholtz equation $\nabla^2 f(r, \theta) + k^2 f(r, \theta) = 0$ on a disk of radius r_0. Expressing the Laplacian in polar coordinates:

$$\frac{\partial^2 f}{\partial r^2} + \frac{1}{r}\frac{\partial f}{\partial r} + \frac{1}{r^2}\frac{\partial^2 f}{\partial \theta^2} + k^2 f = 0.$$

The solution of this partial differential equation is separable in the form $f(r, \theta) = R(r)e^{im\theta}$, where $m = 0, \pm 1, \pm 2, \ldots$ This leads to the ordinary differential equation for $R(r)$:

$$R''[r] + 1\frac{1}{r}R'[r] + \left(k^2 - \frac{m^2}{r^2}\right)R(r) = 0$$

In[●]:= `DSolve`$\left[\texttt{R''[r]} + \frac{1}{r}\texttt{R'[r]} + \left[\texttt{k}^2 - \frac{\texttt{m}^2}{\texttt{r}^2}\right]\texttt{R[r]} == 0, \texttt{R[r]}, \texttt{r}\right]$

Out[●]= `{{R[r]` → `BesselJ[m, k r]` c_1 + `BesselY[m, k r]` c_2`}}`

Only the first term is finite at $r = 0$. The condition that $R(r_0) = 0$ is fulfilled when $J_m(kr_0) = 0$. This involves the zeros of the Bessel function J_m. A tabulation of the first three zeros ($n = 1, 2, 3$) of the Bessel functions J_0, J_1, J_2:

In[●]:= `Table[N[BesselJZero[m, n]], {n, 1, 3}, {m, 0, 2}] // MatrixForm`

Out[●]//MatrixForm=

$$\begin{pmatrix} 2.404825557695773\text{`} & 3.831705970207512\text{`} & 5.135622301840683\text{`} \\ 5.5200781102863115\text{`} & 7.015586669815622\text{`} & 8.417244140399832\text{`} \\ 8.653727912911013\text{`} & 10.173468135062722\text{`} & 11.619841172149059\text{`} \end{pmatrix}$$

The entries in the table represent values of $k_{mn}r_0$, where k_{mn} are the eigenvalues of the Helmholtz equation for a disk. For convenience, we set $r_0 = 1$. We can now construct a contour plot of the real part of the solution

$$f(r, \theta) = J_m(k_{m,n}r)e^{im\theta}.$$

In Cartesian coordinates we use $r = \sqrt{x^2 + y^2}$ and $\theta = \arctan\frac{y}{x}$. The positive regions of the function are shaded blue, the negative regions white.

```
In[*]:= Manipulate[ k = {{2.40483, 5.52008, 8.65373},
          {3.83171, 7.01559, 10.1735}, {5.13562, 8.41720, 11.6198}};
       f[m_, n_, x_, y_] := Cos[m ArcTan[y / x]]
          BesselJ[m, k[[m + 1, n]] √(x² + y²)] Boole[1 ≥ x² + y²];
       Show[RegionPlot[f[m, n, x, y] > 0, {x, -1, 1}, {y, -1, 1}, PlotStyle → LightBlue,
          Frame → False, PlotLabel → TraditionalForm[f_{m,n}[r, θ]], ImageSize → {300, 300}],
          ContourPlot[f[m, n, x, y], {x, -1, 1}, {y, -1, 1}, Contours → 5, ContourShading →
             None, ImageSize → {300, 300}], Graphics[{Thick, Blue, Circle[{0, 0}, 1]}]],
       {{m, 2, "m"}, Range[0, 2], Setter},
       {{n, 1, "n"}, Range[1, 3], Setter}]
```

Out[*]=

The eigenfunctions for $m = 0, 1, 2$ (rows) and $n = 1, 2, 3$ (columns) are shown here:

2.11. Spherical Bessel Functions

Remarkably, Bessel functions of odd-half integer value reduce to elementary functions:

In[ ]:= `Column[Table[Row[{TraditionalForm[J_{n/2}[x]], "=", BesselJ[n / 2, x]}], {n, 1, 5, 2}]]`

Out[ ]=
$$J_{\frac{1}{2}}(x) = \frac{\sqrt{\frac{2}{\pi}} \, \text{Sin}[x]}{\sqrt{x}}$$

$$J_{\frac{3}{2}}(x) = \frac{\sqrt{\frac{2}{\pi}} \left(-\text{Cos}[x] + \frac{\text{Sin}[x]}{x} \right)}{\sqrt{x}}$$

$$J_{\frac{5}{2}}(x) = \frac{\sqrt{\frac{2}{\pi}} \left(-\frac{3 \, \text{Cos}[x]}{x} - \text{Sin}[x] + \frac{3 \, \text{Sin}[x]}{x^2} \right)}{\sqrt{x}}$$

In[*]:= `Column[Table[Row[{TraditionalForm[Y_{n/2}[x]], "=", BesselY[n / 2, x]}], {n, 1, 5, 2}]]`

Out[*]= $Y_{\frac{1}{2}}(x) = -\dfrac{\sqrt{\frac{2}{\pi}} \, \text{Cos}[x]}{\sqrt{x}}$

$Y_{\frac{3}{2}}(x) = \dfrac{\sqrt{\frac{2}{\pi}} \left(-\frac{\text{Cos}[x]}{x} - \text{Sin}[x] \right)}{\sqrt{x}}$

$Y_{\frac{5}{2}}(x) = \dfrac{\sqrt{\frac{2}{\pi}} \left(\text{Cos}[x] - \frac{3 \, \text{Cos}[x]}{x^2} - \frac{3 \, \text{Sin}[x]}{x} \right)}{\sqrt{x}}$

Spherical Bessel functions are defined by

$$j_n(x) = \sqrt{\frac{\pi}{2x}} J_{n+\frac{1}{2}}(x) \quad \text{and} \quad y_n(x) = \sqrt{\frac{\pi}{2x}} Y_{n+\frac{1}{2}}(x).$$

Following are some plots:

In[*]:= `Manipulate[Plot[SphericalBesselJ[n, x], {x, 0, 20},`
`    GridLines → Automatic, PlotLabel → SphericalBesselJ[n, x]],`
`    {{n, {0}, Style["n", Italic]}, {0, 1, 2}, CheckboxBar}]`

Out[*]=

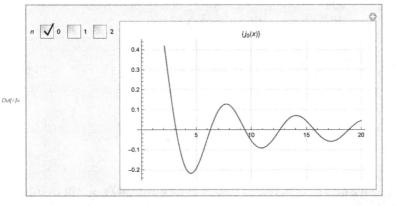

In[*]:= `Manipulate[Plot[SphericalBesselY[n, x], {x, 0, 20},`
`    GridLines → Automatic, PlotLabel → SphericalBesselY[n, x]],`
`    {{n, {0}, Style["n", Italic]}, {0, 1, 2}, CheckboxBar}]`

Out[*]=

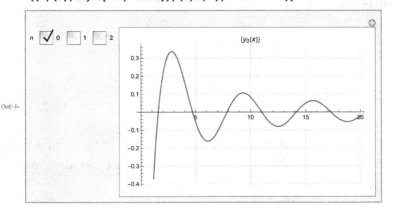

Spherical Bessel functions occur as solutions of the Helmholtz equation in spherical coordinates

$$(\nabla^2 + k^2)F(r, \theta, \phi) = 0,$$

as shown above.

2.12. Legendre Polynomials

The separated form of the Helmholtz equation in spherical coordinates led to the θ-equation

$$\frac{1}{\sin\theta}\frac{d}{d\theta}\sin\theta\frac{d\Theta}{d\theta} + \left(\lambda - \frac{m^2}{\sin^2\theta}\right)\Theta(\theta) = \odot.$$

In[•]:= `DSolve[` $\frac{1}{\text{Sin[}\theta\text{]}}$ `∂_θ (Sin[θ] θ'[θ]) +` $\left(\lambda - \frac{m^2}{\text{Sin[}\theta\text{]}^2}\right)$ `θ[θ] == 0, θ[θ], θ]`

Out[•]= $\left\{\left\{\Theta[\theta] \rightarrow c_1 \text{ LegendreP}\left[\frac{1}{2} \times \left(-1 + \sqrt{1 + 4\lambda}\right), m, \text{Cos}[\theta]\right] + \right.\right.$

$\left.\left. c_2 \text{ LegendreQ}\left[\frac{1}{2} \times \left(-1 + \sqrt{1 + 4\lambda}\right), m, \text{Cos}[\theta]\right]\right\}\right\}$

These are associated Legendre functions. Let us develop them in stepwise fashion. First consider the case $m = 0$, with the independent variable changed to $x = \cos\theta$, with $\Theta(\theta) = P(x)$. The differential equation reduces to

$$(1 - x^2)P''(x) - 2xP'(x) + P(x) = 0.$$

In[•]:= `DSolve[(1 - x²) P''[x] - 2 x P'[x] + λ P(x) == 0, P[x], x]`

Out[•]= $\left\{\left\{P[x] \rightarrow c_1 \text{ LegendreP}\left[\frac{1}{2} \times \left(-1 + \sqrt{1 + 4\lambda}\right), x\right] + c_2 \text{ LegendreQ}\left[\frac{1}{2} \times \left(-1 + \sqrt{1 + 4\lambda}\right), x\right]\right\}\right\}$

The first solutions reduce to polynomials when the index is an integer, say $l = 0, 2, 3, \ldots$. Then $\lambda = l(l+1)$. The first few Legendre polynomials are then given by:

```
In[•]:= Column[Table[Row[{P_l[x], "=", LegendreP[l, x]}], {l, 0, 4}]] // TraditionalForm
```

Out[•]//TraditionalForm=

$P_0(x)=1$

$P_1(x)=x$

$P_2(x)=\frac{1}{2}\left(3x^2-1\right)$

$P_3(x)=\frac{1}{2}\left(5x^3-3x\right)$

$P_4(x)=\frac{1}{8}\left(35x^4-30x^2+3\right)$

Since x was originally cos θ, its range is given by $-1 \le x \le 1$. Following is a plot:

```
In[•]:= Manipulate[Plot[LegendreP[l, x], {x, -1, 1},
          GridLines → Automatic, Frame → True, PlotLabel → TraditionalForm[P_l[x]]],
          {{l, 2, Style["l", Italic]}, {0, 1, 2, 3, 4}, Setter}]
```

Out[•]=

The Legendre polynomials as defined satisfy the boundary conditions $P_l(1) = 1, P_l(-1) = (-1)^l$. They appear to be mutually orthogonal in the interval $\{-1, 1\}$. Let's see if Mathematica can prove this:

```
In[•]:= 
```
$$\int_{-1}^{1} \text{LegendreP[l1, x] LegendreP[l2, x]} \, dx$$

```
Out[•]= 
```
$$\int_{-1}^{1} \text{LegendreP[l1, x] LegendreP[l2, x]} \, dx$$

Evidently not. Let's instead approach this "experimentally".

In[•]:= **Table$\left[\int_{-1}^{1}$ LegendreP[l1, x] LegendreP[l2, x] dx, {l1, 0, 5}, {l2, 0, 5}$\right]$**

Out[•]= $\left\{\{2, 0, 0, 0, 0, 0\}, \left\{0, \frac{2}{3}, 0, 0, 0, 0\right\}, \left\{0, 0, \frac{2}{5}, 0, 0, 0\right\},\right.$

$\left.\left\{0, 0, 0, \frac{2}{7}, 0, 0\right\}, \left\{0, 0, 0, 0, \frac{2}{9}, 0\right\}, \left\{0, 0, 0, 0, 0, \frac{2}{11}\right\}\right\}$

Looks like the orthogonality is verified (although not with the rigor a mathematician would like!). How about the diagonal integrals? Compute

In[•]:= **Table$\left[\frac{2}{2\,l+1}, \{l, 0, 5\}\right]$**

Out[•]= $\left\{2, \frac{2}{3}, \frac{2}{5}, \frac{2}{7}, \frac{2}{9}, \frac{2}{11}\right\}$

Thus we arrive the integral relations

$$\int_{-1}^{1} P_l(x)P_{l'}(x)dx = \frac{2}{2l+1}\delta_{l,l'}.$$

The Legendre functions of the second kind $Q_n(x)$ are designated LegendreQ[n,x] in Mathematica. Here are the first three:

In[•]:= **Table[FullSimplify[LegendreQ[n, x]], {n, 0, 2}]**

Out[•]= $\left\{\text{ArcTanh}[x], -1 + x\,\text{ArcTanh}[x], \frac{1}{4} \times \left(-6\,x + \left(-2 + 6\,x^2\right)\,\text{ArcTanh}[x]\right)\right\}$

An alternative form is given in most references. Consider the following steps:

$y = \text{arctanh}\,x$
$x = \tanh y = \frac{\sinh y}{\cosh y} = \frac{e^y - e^{-y}}{e^y + e^{-y}} = \frac{1 - e^{-2y}}{1 + e^{-2y}}$

In[•]:= **Solve$\left[x == \frac{1 - e^{-2\,y}}{1 + e^{-2\,y}}, y\right]$**

Out[•]= $\left\{\left\{y \to \frac{1}{2} \times \left(2\,i\,\pi\,c_1 + \text{Log}\left[\frac{-1 - x}{-1 + x}\right]\right) \text{ if } c_1 \in \mathbb{Z}\right\}\right\}$

With $\mathbb{C}_1 = 0$, we find an alternative form for arctanh

$$\operatorname{arctanh} x = \frac{1}{2}\log\left(\frac{1+x}{1-x}\right).$$

We can therefore write

$$Q_0(x) = \frac{1}{2}\log\left(\frac{1+x}{1-x}\right), Q_1(x) = \frac{x}{2}\log\left(\frac{1+x}{1-x}\right) - 1, Q_2(x)$$

$$= \left(\frac{3x^2-1}{4}\right)\log\left(\frac{1+x}{1-x}\right) - \frac{3}{2}x.$$

Plots of Legendre functions of the second kind:

```
In[*]:= Manipulate[Plot[LegendreQ[n, x], {x, -1, 1},
        GridLines → Automatic, Frame → True, PlotLabel → TraditionalForm[Qₙ[x]]],
        {{n, 2, Style["n", Italic]}, {0, 1, 2, 3}, Setter}]
```

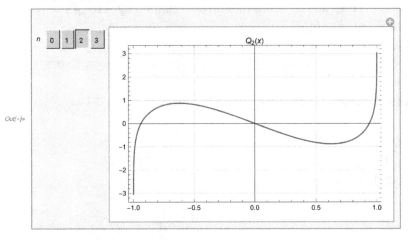

These functions are singular at $x = \pm 1$ and are therefore not usually suitable for physical applications. We next consider the associated Legendre polynomials:

```
In[*]:= Column[Table[Row[{Subsuperscript[P, l, m], "(x)=", LegendreP[l, m, x]}],
        {l, 0, 2}, {m, 0, l}]] // TraditionalForm
```

Out[*]//TraditionalForm=

$$\left\{P_0^0(x)=1\right\}$$

$$\left\{P_1^0(x)=x, P_1^1(x)=-\sqrt{1-x^2}\right\}$$

$$\left\{P_2^0(x)=\tfrac{1}{2}\left(3x^2-1\right), P_2^1(x)=-3x\sqrt{1-x^2}, P_2^2(x)=-3\left(x^2-1\right)\right\}$$

For a given value of *l*, the possible values of *m* are $0, \pm1, \pm2, \ldots, \pm l$.

Reverting to the original variable cos θ:

```
In[ ]:= Column[Table[Row[{Subsuperscript[P, l, m],
           "(cos θ) =", PowerExpand[Simplify[LegendreP[l, m, Cos[θ]]]]}],
          {l, 0, 2}, {m, 0, l}]] // TraditionalForm
```

Out[ ]//TraditionalForm=

$\{P_0^0(\cos\theta)=1\}$

$\{P_1^0(\cos\theta)=\cos(\theta),\ P_1^1(\cos\theta)=-\sin(\theta)\}$

$\{P_2^0(\cos\theta)=\tfrac{1}{4}(3\cos(2\theta)+1),\ P_2^1(\cos\theta)=-3\cos(\theta)\sin(\theta),\ P_2^2(\cos\theta)=3\sin^2(\theta)\}$

2.13. Spherical Harmonics

A *harmonic function* is defined as a solution to Laplace's equation $\nabla^2\Phi = 0$, subject to certain specified boundary conditions. The relevant equation in spherical coordinates can be obtained by setting $k = 0$ in the Helmholtz equation:

$$\frac{1}{r^2}\frac{\partial}{\partial r}r^2\frac{\partial\Phi}{\partial r} + \frac{1}{r^2\sin\theta}\frac{\partial}{\partial\theta}\sin\theta\frac{\partial\Phi}{\partial\theta} + \frac{1}{r^2\sin^2\theta}\frac{\partial^2\Phi}{\partial\phi^2} = 0.$$

We now write the separable solution in the form $\Phi(r,\theta,\phi) = R(r)Y(\theta,\phi)$

$$\Phi(r,\theta,\phi) = R(r)Y(\theta,\phi)$$

where $Y(\theta,\phi)$ is called a *spherical harmonic*. This reduces to the two separated equations

$$\frac{\partial}{\partial r}r^2\frac{\partial R}{\partial r} - \lambda R(r) = 0$$

and

$$\frac{1}{\sin\theta}\frac{\partial}{\partial\theta}\sin\theta\frac{\partial Y}{\partial\theta} + \frac{1}{\sin^2\theta}\frac{\partial^2 Y}{\partial\phi^2} + \lambda Y(\theta,\phi) = 0.$$

The *r*-equation, with $\lambda = l(l+1)$:

```
In[ ]:= DSolve[r^2 R''[r] + 2 r R'[r] - l (l + 1) R[r] == 0, R[r], r]
```

$$Out[ ]= \left\{\left\{R[r] \to r^{\frac{1}{2}\,i\,\sqrt{l}\,\sqrt{1+l}\left(\frac{i}{\sqrt{l}\,\sqrt{1+l}}-\sqrt{-4-\frac{1}{l(1+l)}}\right)}c_1 + r^{\frac{1}{2}\,i\,\sqrt{l}\,\sqrt{1+l}\left(\frac{i}{\sqrt{l}\,\sqrt{1+l}}+\sqrt{-4-\frac{1}{l(1+l)}}\right)}c_2\right\}\right\}$$

Further simplification by hand reduces this to

$$R(r) = c_1 r^{-l-1} + c_2 r^l.$$

The equation for the spherical harmonics has already been considered, and the results can be summarized as

$$Y_l^m(\theta, \phi) = \text{const}\, P_l^m(\cos\theta)\, e^{im\phi}.$$

Spherical harmonics arise in many applications of mathematical physics, including atomic orbitals, particle scattering and antenna radiation patterns. The normalized spherical harmonics, such that

$$\int_0^{2\pi} \int_0^{\pi} Y_l^m(\theta, \phi)^* Y_{l'}^{m'}(\theta, \phi) \sin\theta\, d\theta\, d\phi = \delta_{l,l'}\delta_{m,m'}$$

are given by

$$Y_l^m(\theta, \phi) = \sqrt{\frac{2l+1}{4\pi}\frac{(l-m)!}{(l+m)!}}\, P_l^m(\cos\theta) e^{im\phi}.$$

In quantum mechanics, for $m < 0$, an additional factor $(-1)^m$, known as the Condon-Shortley phase, is appended. Mathematica evidently uses this convention. The first few spherical harmonics:

```
In[*]:= Column[Table[
          Row[{Style[With[{l = l, m = m}, HoldForm[SphericalHarmonicY[l, m, θ, ϕ]]]], " = ",
            SphericalHarmonicY[l, m, θ, ϕ]}], {l, 0, 2}, {m, -l, l}]] // TraditionalForm
```

Out[*]//TraditionalForm=

$\left\{ Y_0^0(\theta, \phi) = \frac{1}{2\sqrt{\pi}} \right\}$

$\left\{ Y_1^{-1}(\theta, \phi) = \frac{1}{2} e^{-i\phi} \sqrt{\frac{3}{2\pi}} \sin(\theta),\ Y_1^0(\theta, \phi) = \frac{1}{2} \sqrt{\frac{3}{\pi}} \cos(\theta),\ Y_1^1(\theta, \phi) = -\frac{1}{2} e^{i\phi} \sqrt{\frac{3}{2\pi}} \sin(\theta) \right\}$

$\left\{ Y_2^{-2}(\theta, \phi) = \frac{1}{4} e^{-2i\phi} \sqrt{\frac{15}{2\pi}} \sin^2(\theta),\ Y_2^{-1}(\theta, \phi) = \frac{1}{2} e^{-i\phi} \sqrt{\frac{15}{2\pi}} \cos(\theta)\sin(\theta), \right.$

$\left. Y_2^0(\theta, \phi) = \frac{1}{4} \sqrt{\frac{5}{\pi}} (3\cos^2(\theta) - 1),\ Y_2^1(\theta, \phi) = -\frac{1}{2} e^{i\phi} \sqrt{\frac{15}{2\pi}} \cos(\theta)\sin(\theta),\ Y_2^2(\theta, \phi) = \frac{1}{4} e^{2i\phi} \sqrt{\frac{15}{2\pi}} \sin^2(\theta) \right\}$

Checking the orthonormality, for $m = 0$:

```
In[*]:= Table[
          ∫₀²π ∫₀π SphericalHarmonicY[l1, 0, θ, ϕ] SphericalHarmonicY[l2, 0, θ, ϕ] Sin[θ] dθ dϕ,
          {l1, 0, 2}, {l2, 0, 2}]
```

Out[*]= {{1, 0, 0}, {0, 1, 0}, {0, 0, 1}}

For $m = \pm 1$:

In[·]:= `Table`$\left[\int_0^{2\pi}\int_0^{\pi}\right.$`Conjugate[SphericalHarmonicY[l1, 1, θ, ϕ]]`

      `SphericalHarmonicY[l2, 1, θ, ϕ] Sin[θ] dθ dϕ, {l1, 1, 2}, {l2, 1, 2}`$\Big]$

Out[·]= `{{1, 0}, {0, 1}}`

Following are 3D plots of the complex spherical harmonics; the argument, in the range 0 to 2π, is indicated by the coloring, from red to magenta:

In[·]:= `Manipulate[SphericalPlot3D[`
        `Abs[SphericalHarmonicY[l, m, θ, ϕ]], {θ, 0, π}, {ϕ, -π, π}, ColorFunction →`
          `Function[{x, y, z, θ, ϕ, r}, Hue[Arg[SphericalHarmonicY[l, m, θ, ϕ]] / (2 π)]],`
        `ColorFunctionScaling → False, PerformanceGoal → "Quality",`
        `Axes → False, SphericalRegion → True, Mesh → False, Boxed → False,`
        `PlotLabel → Style[With[{l = l, m = m}, TraditionalForm[`
          `HoldForm[SphericalHarmonicY[l, m, "θ", "ϕ"]]], 16]], PlotRange → All],`
      `Row[{Control[{{l, 2, Style["l", Italic]}, Range[0, 4], Setter}], Spacer[30],`
        `Control[{{m, 1, Style["m", Italic]}, Range[-l, l], Setter}]}],`
      `TrackedSymbols :> {l, m}, ContentSize → {300, 300}, Alignment → Center]`

Out[·]=

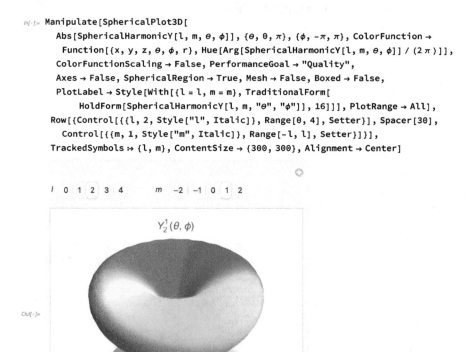

Here is a composite image of the spherical harmonics; rows: $l = 0$ to 3, columns: $m = -l$ to l:

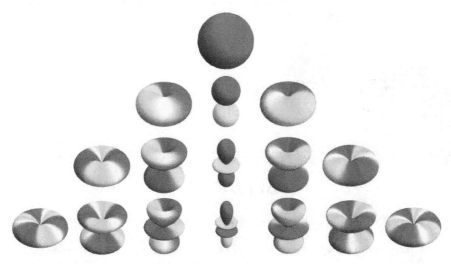

2.14. Special Functions using Leibniz's Product Rule

The nth derivative of a product of two functions can be derived stepwise:

```
In[ ]:= Clear[f, g]

In[ ]:= Column[Table[
          Row[{Style[d^n/dx^n, Italic], Style["["], f[x] × g[x], "]" = ", D[f[x] × g[x], {x, n}]}],
          {n, 1, 4}]] // TraditionalForm
```

Out[ ]//TraditionalForm=

$$\frac{d}{dx}[f(x)\,g(x)] = g(x)\,f'(x) + f(x)\,g'(x)$$

$$\frac{d^2}{dx^2}[f(x)\,g(x)] = 2\,f'(x)\,g'(x) + g(x)\,f''(x) + f(x)\,g''(x)$$

$$\frac{d^3}{dx^3}[f(x)\,g(x)] = 3\,f''(x)\,g'(x) + 3\,f'(x)\,g''(x) + f^{(3)}(x)\,g(x) + f(x)\,g^{(3)}(x)$$

$$\frac{d^4}{dx^4}[f(x)\,g(x)] = 4\,f^{(3)}(x)\,g'(x) + 4\,g^{(3)}(x)\,f'(x) + 6\,f''(x)\,g''(x) + f^{(4)}(x)\,g(x) + f(x)\,g^{(4)}(x)$$

The general formula is known as *Leibniz's product rule*:

$$\frac{d^n}{dx^n}[f(x)g(x)] = \sum_{k=0}^{n} \binom{n}{k} f^{(n-k)}(x) = f^{(n)}(x)g(x)\,g(x) + nf^{(n-1)}(x)g'(x)$$

$$+ \frac{n(n-1)}{2} f^{(n-2)}(x)g''(x) + \cdots$$

2.14.1. *Hermite Polynomials*

We will now use the product rule to construct Hermite polynomials. We begin with the function

$$u(x) = e^{-x^2}$$

In[•]:= $\mathbf{D}\left[\mathbf{e^{-x^2}, x}\right]$

Out[•]= $-2\,e^{-x^2}\,x$

showing that $u(x)$ is the solution of a first-order differential equation

$$u'(x) + 2x\,u\,(x) = 0.$$

Differentiating this equation n times:

In[•]:= `Column[Table[Row[{D[u'[x] + 2 x u[x], {x, n}], "=0"}], {n, 1, 4}]] // TraditionalForm`

Out[•]//TraditionalForm=

$2\,x\,u'(x) + u''(x) + 2\,u(x) = 0$

$4\,u'(x) + 2\,x\,u''(x) + u^{(3)}(x) = 0$

$6\,u''(x) + 2\,x\,u^{(3)}(x) + u^{(4)}(x) = 0$

$8\,u^{(3)}(x) + 2\,x\,u^{(4)}(x) + u^{(5)}(x) = 0$

Defining the function $w_n(x) = u^{(n)}(x) = \frac{d^n u}{dx^n}$, we evidently have found the second-order differential equation

$$w_n''(x) + 2xw_n'(x) + 2(n+1)w_n(x) = 0.$$

Define the *Hermite polynomial*

$$H_n(x) = (-1)^n e^{x^2} \frac{d^n}{dx^n} e^{-x^2}$$

so that $w_n(x) = (-1)^n e^{-x^2} H_n(x)$

In[•]:= $\mathbf{w[x\_] := (-1)^n\ e^{-x^2}\ H[x]}$

In[•]:= `Simplify[w''[x] + 2 x w'[x] + 2 (n + 1) w[x]]`

Out[•]= $(-1)^n\,e^{-x^2}\,(2\,n\,H[x] - 2\,x\,H'[x] + H''[x])$

We arrive at *Hermite's differential equation*:

$$H''(x) - 2xH'(x) + 2nH(x) = 0,$$

In[•]:= `DSolve[H''[x] - 2 x H'[x] + 2 n H[x] == 0, H[x], x]`

Out[•]= $\left\{\left\{H[x] \rightarrow c_1 \text{ HermiteH}[n, x] + c_2 \text{ Hypergeometric1F1}\left[-\dfrac{n}{2}, \dfrac{1}{2}, x^2\right]\right\}\right\}$

The solutions we seek are Hermite polynomials $H_n(x)$:

In[•]:= `Column[Table[Row[{H`$_n$`[x], " = ", HermiteH[n, x]}], {n, 0, 4}]] // TraditionalForm`

Out[•]//TraditionalForm=

$H_0(x) = 1$
$H_1(x) = 2x$
$H_2(x) = 4x^2 - 2$
$H_3(x) = 8x^3 - 12x$
$H_4(x) = 16x^4 - 48x^2 + 12$

Following are plots:

In[•]:= `Manipulate[Plot[HermiteH[n, x], {x, -3, 3},`
`    PlotRange → {-2 (n + 1)`^{2}`, 2 (n + 1)`^{2}`}, GridLines → Automatic,`
`    PlotLabel → Style[With[{n = n}, TraditionalForm[HoldForm[HermiteH[n, x]]]]],`
`    {{n, 3, Style["n", Italic]}, Range[0, 5], Setter}]`

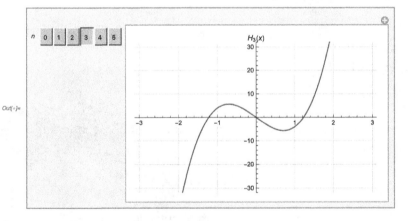

The Hermite polynomials form an orthogonal set with weight function e^{-x^2} over the interval $\{-\infty, \infty\}$:

In[•]:= `Table[`$\int_{-\infty}^{\infty}$`HermiteH[n1, x] HermiteH[n2, x] e`$^{-x^2}$` ⅆx, {n1, 0, 4}, {n2, 0, 4}]`

Out[•]= $\left\{\left\{\sqrt{\pi}, 0, 0, 0, 0\right\}, \left\{0, 2\sqrt{\pi}, 0, 0, 0\right\},\right.$
$\left.\left\{0, 0, 8\sqrt{\pi}, 0, 0\right\}, \left\{0, 0, 0, 48\sqrt{\pi}, 0\right\}, \left\{0, 0, 0, 0, 384\sqrt{\pi}\right\}\right\}$

Let's see if we can determine the normalization constants.

In[•]:= **data = {{0, 1}, {1, 2}, {2, 8}, {3, 48}, {4, 384}}**

Out[•]= **{{0, 1}, {1, 2}, {2, 8}, {3, 48}, {4, 384}}**

After some experimentation:

In[•]:= **Table$\left[\{n, 2^n\, n!\}, \{n, 0, 4\}\right]$**

Out[•]= **{{0, 1}, {1, 2}, {2, 8}, {3, 48}, {4, 384}}**

Thus we find the orthonormalized Hermite polynomials in $\{-\infty, \infty\}$:

$$(2^n n! \sqrt{\pi})^{-\frac{1}{2}} H_n(x).$$

2.14.2. *Laguerre Polynomials*

Next, we consider Laguerre polynomials, which in applications will usually be functions of a radial variable. Following the above strategy, we begin with the function

$$u(x) = x^n e^{-x}.$$

In[•]:= **Simplify$\left[D\left[x^n\, e^{-x}, x\right]\right]$**

Out[•]= $e^{-x}\ (n - x)\ x^{-1+n}$

This evidently satisfies the first-order differential equation $u'(r) - \frac{n-r}{r}u(r) = 0$ or

$$xu'(x) + (x-n)u(x) = 0.$$

Differentiate this equation $(n + 1)$ times using Leibniz's formula. For $n = 1, 2, \ldots$

In[•]:= **Column[Table[**
        Row[{"n = ", n, "   ", Simplify[D[x u'[x] + (x - n) u[x], {x, n + 1}]]}], {n, 1, 4}]]

Out[•]=

n = 1	$2\, u'[x] + (1 + x)\, u''[x] + x\, u^{(3)}[x]$
n = 2	$3\, u''[x] + (1 + x)\, u^{(3)}[x] + x\, u^{(4)}[x]$
n = 3	$4\, u^{(3)}[x] + (1 + x)\, u^{(4)}[x] + x\, u^{(5)}[x]$
n = 4	$5\, u^{(4)}[x] + (1 + x)\, u^{(5)}[x] + x\, u^{(6)}[x]$

We thereby arrive at:

$$xw_n''(x) + (x + 1)w_n'(x) + (n + 1)w_n(x) = 0,$$

where

$$w_n(x) = \frac{d^n}{dx^n}(x^n e^{-x}) = e^{-x}L_n(x),$$

in terms of Laguerre polynomials, conventionally defined by *Rodrigues' formula*:

$$L_n(x) = \frac{e^x}{n}\frac{d^n}{dx^n}(x^n e^{-x}).$$

Consider

In[•]:= `W[x_] := e^-x L[x]`

In[•]:= `Simplify[x w''[x] + (x + 1) w'[x] + (n + 1) w[x]]`

Out[•]= `e^-x (n L[x] - (-1 + x) L'[x] + x L''[x])`

We thus obtain *Laguerre's differential equation*:

$$xL_n''(x) + (1 - x)L_n'(x) + nL_n(x) = 0.$$

In[•]:= `DSolve[x L''[x] + (1 - x) L'[x] + n L[x] == 0, L[x], x]`

Out[•]= `{{L[x] → c_1 HypergeometricU[-n, 1, x] + c_2 LaguerreL[n, x]}}`

The first few Laguerre polynomials:

In[•]:= `Column[Table[Row[{L_n[x], " = ", LaguerreL[n, x]}], {n, 0, 4}]] // TraditionalForm`

$L_0(x)" = "1$
$L_1(x)" = "1 - x$
$L_2(x)" = "\frac{1}{2}(x^2 - 4x + 2)$
$L_3(x)" = "\frac{1}{6}(-x^3 + 9x^2 - 18x + 6)$
$L_4(x)" = "\frac{1}{24}(x^4 - 16x^3 + 72x^2 - 96x + 20)$

Plots:

```
In[•]:= Manipulate[
        Plot[LaguerreL[n, x], {x, 0, 8}, PlotRange → {-10, 10}, GridLines → Automatic,
         PlotLabel → Style[With[{n = n}, TraditionalForm[HoldForm[LaguerreL[n, x]]]]]],
        {{n, 3, Style["n", Italic]}, Range[0, 5], Setter}]
```

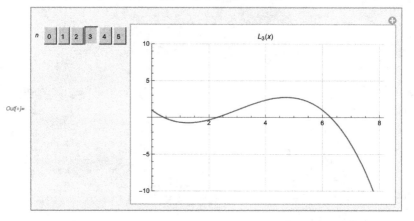

The Laguerre polynomials form an orthonormal set with weight function e^{-x} over the interval $\{0, \infty\}$:

```
In[•]:= Table[∫₀^∞ LaguerreL[n1, x] LaguerreL[n2, x] e^{-x} dx, {n1, 0, 4}, {n2, 0, 4}]
```

Out[•]= {{1, 0, 0, 0, 0}, {0, 1, 0, 0, 0}, {0, 0, 1, 0, 0}, {0, 0, 0, 1, 0}, {0, 0, 0, 0, 1}}

In physical applications we also require *associated Laguerre polynomials*, $L_n^k(r)$. These can be derived by differentiating the equation for $L_{n+k}(x)$ k times:

```
In[•]:= Column[Table[
        Row[{"k = ", k, "    ", Simplify[D[x L''[x] + (1 - x) L'[x] + (n + k) L[x], {x, k}]]}],
        {k, 1, 4}]]
```

```
         k = 1    n L'[x] - (-2 + x) L''[x] + x L^{(3)}[x]
         k = 2    n L''[x] - (-3 + x) L^{(3)}[x] + x L^{(4)}[x]
Out[•]=   k = 3    n L^{(3)}[x] - (-4 + x) L^{(4)}[x] + x L^{(5)}[x]
         k = 4    n L^{(4)}[x] - (-5 + x) L^{(5)}[x] + x L^{(6)}[x]
```

Defining $L_n^k(x) = (-1)^k \frac{d^k}{dr x^k} L_{n+k}(x)$, we deduce the defining differential equation

$$xL''(x) + (k + 1 - x)L'(x) + nL(x) = 0.$$

In[•]:= **DSolve[x L''[x] + (k + 1 - x) L'[x] + n L[x] == 0, L[x], x]**

Out[•]= {{L[x] → c_1 HypergeometricU[-n, 1 + k, x] + c_2 LaguerreL[n, k, x]}}

In[•]:= **Column[Table[**
    Row[{Style[With[{n = n, k = k}, TraditionalForm[HoldForm[LaguerreL[n, k, x]]]]],
    " = ", TraditionalForm[LaguerreL[n, k, x]]}],
    {n, 0, 3}, {k, 0, 3}]] // TraditionalForm

Out[•]//TraditionalForm=

$\{L_0^0(x)" = "1, L_0^1(x)" = "1, L_0^2(x)" = "1, L_0^3(x)" = "1\}$

$\{L_1^0(x)" = "1 - x, L_1^1(x)" = "2 - x, L_1^2(x)" = "3 - x, L_1^3(x)" = "4 - x\}$

$\{L_2^0(x)" = "\frac{1}{2}(x^2 - 4x + 2), L_2^1(x)" = "\frac{1}{2}(x^2 - 6x + 6), L_2^2(x)" = "\frac{1}{2}(x^2 - 8x + 12), L_2^3(x)" = "\frac{1}{2}(x^2 - 10x + 20)\}$

$\{L_3^0(x)" = "\frac{1}{6}(-x^3 + 9x^2 - 18x + 6), L_3^1(x)" = "\frac{1}{6}(-x^3 + 12x^2 - 36x + 24),$

$L_3^2(x)" = "\frac{1}{6}(-x^3 + 15x^2 - 60x + 60), L_3^3(x)" = "\frac{1}{6}(-x^3 + 18x^2 - 90x + 120)\}$

2.14.3. *Legendre Polynomials*

Finally we consider (again) the Legendre polynomials. Take

$$u(x) = (1 - x^2)^n,$$

In[•]:= **D[(1 - x²)ⁿ, x]**

Out[•]= $-2 n x (1 - x^2)^{-1+n}$

Thus we have the starting first-order differential equation $u'(x) + \frac{2nx}{1-x^2} u(x) = 0$ or

$$(1 - x^2) u'(x) + 2n x u(x) = 0.$$

Now differentiate $(n + 1)$ times:

In[•]:= **Column[Table[**
    Row[{"n = ", n, "   ", Simplify[D[(1 - x²) u'[x] + 2 n x u[x], {x, n + 1}]]}], {n, 1, 4}]]

Out[•]=

  n = 1 $2 u'[x] - 2 x u''[x] - (-1 + x^2) u^{(3)}[x]$

  n = 2 $6 u''[x] - 2 x u^{(3)}[x] - (-1 + x^2) u^{(4)}[x]$

  n = 3 $12 u^{(3)}[x] - 2 x u^{(4)}[x] - (-1 + x^2) u^{(5)}[x]$

  n = 4 $20 u^{(4)}[x] - 2 x u^{(5)}[x] - (-1 + x^2) u^{(6)}[x]$

Let $w_l(x) = \frac{d^n}{dx^n} u(x) = \frac{d^n}{dx^n}(1 - x^2)^n$. This is proportional to the Legendre polynomial of order n, which is defined by $P_n(x) = \frac{1}{2^n n!} \frac{d^n}{dx^n}(x^2 - 1)^n$:

$$(1 - x^2)P_n''(x) - 2xP_n'(x) + n(n + 1)P_n(x) = 0.$$

```
In[•]:= DSolve[(1 - x²) P''[x] - 2 x P'[x] + n (n + 1) P[x] == 0, P[x], x]
```

```
Out[•]= {{P[x] → c₁ LegendreP[n, x] + c₂ LegendreQ[n, x]}}
```

```
Column[Table[Row[{Pₙ[x], " = ", LegendreP[n, x]}], {n, 0, 4}]] // TraditionalForm
```

Out[•]//TraditionalForm=

$P_0(x) = 1$

$P_1(x) = x$

$P_2(x) = \frac{1}{2}(3x^2 - 1)$

$P_3(x) = \frac{1}{2}(5x^3 - 3x)$

$P_4(x) = \frac{1}{8}(35x^4 - 30x^2 + 3)$

The equation for the associated Legendre polynomials is

$$(1 - x^2)P''(x) - 2x\,P'(x) + \left[n(n+1) - \frac{m^2}{1 - x^2}\right]P(x) = 0.$$

The solutions are found to be

$$P_n^m(x) = (1 - x)^{m/2}\frac{d^m}{dx^m}P_n(x).$$

```
In[•]:= DSolve[(1 - x²) P''[x] - 2 x P'[x] + (n (n + 1) - m²/1 - x²) P[x] == 0, P[x], x]
```

```
Out[•]= {{P[x] → c₁ LegendreP[n, m, x] + c₂ LegendreQ[n, m, x]}}
```

```
In[•]:= Column[Table[
          Row[{Style[With[{n = n, m = m}, TraditionalForm[HoldForm[LegendreP[n, m, x]]]]],
               " = ", TraditionalForm[LegendreP[n, m, x]]}],
          {n, 0, 3}, {m, 0, n}]] // TraditionalForm
```

Out[•]//TraditionalForm=

$\{P_0^0(x) = 1\}$

$\{P_1^0(x) = x, P_1^1(x) = -\sqrt{1 - x^2}\}$

$\{P_2^0(x) = \frac{1}{2}(3x^2 - 1), P_2^1(x) = -3x\sqrt{1 - x^2}, P_2^2(x) = -3(x^2 - 1)\}$

$\{P_3^0(x) = \frac{1}{2}(5x^3 - 3x), P_3^1(x) = -\frac{3}{2}\sqrt{1 - x^2}(5x^2 - 1), P_3^2(x) = -15x(x^2 - 1), P_3^3(x) = -15(1 - x^2)^{3/2}\}$

2.15. Confluent Hypergeometric Functions

A geometric series is a function of whose terms constitute a geometric progression, in which the ratio of successive terms is equal. For example,

$$F(x) = 1 + ax + a^2x^2 + a^3x^3 + \cdots = \sum_{n=0}^{\infty} a^n x^n.$$

The series converges to the value $1/(1 - ax)$, provided that $|ax| < 1$. A certain generalization of a geometric series is known as a hypergeometric series or hypergeometric function. This has the form of a power series in x in which the coefficients a^n are replaced by ratios of rational functions of constants.

A rudimentary example of a hypergeometric function can be written

$$_1F_0(a; \_ ; x) = 1 + \frac{a}{1}x + \frac{a(a+1)}{2!}x^2 + \frac{a(a+1)(a+2)}{3!}x^3$$

$$+ \cdots = \sum_{n=0}^{\infty} \frac{(a)_n}{n!}x^n,$$

where $(a)_n$ are *Pochhammer symbols* defined by

$$(a)_0 = 1, (a)_1 = a, (a)_n = a(a+1)(a + 2) \ldots (a + n - 1)$$
$$= \Gamma(a + n)/\Gamma(a)$$

or

$$(a)_n = \frac{\Gamma(a + n)}{\Gamma(n)}.$$

In[ ]:= `Table[Pochhammer[a, n], {n, 0, 3}]`

Out[ ]= `{1, a, a (1 + a), a (1 + a) × (2 + a)}`

$_1F_0(a; \_ ; x)$ is a solution of the first-order differential equation

$$(1 - x)y'[x] - ay[x] = 0.$$

In[ ]:= `DSolve[(1 - x) y'[x] - a y[x] == 0, y[x], x]`

Out[ ]= `{{y[x] → (-1 + x)^-a c_1}}`

The confluent hypergeometric differential equation

$$xy'' + (c - x)y' - ay = 0$$

has a regular singular point at $x = 0$ and an essential singularity at $x = \infty$. Solutions analytic at $x = 0$ are confluent hypergeometric functions of the first kind (or Kummer functions):

$$
{}_1F_1(a,c,x) = \sum_{n=0}^{\infty} \frac{(a)_n}{(c)_n} \frac{x^n}{n!} = 1 + \frac{a}{c}x + \frac{a(a+1)}{c(c+1)} \frac{x^2}{2!}
$$

$$
+ \frac{a(a+1)(a+2)}{c(c+1)(c+2)} \frac{x^3}{3!} + \cdots .
$$

For $c = 0, -1, -2, \ldots$, the function becomes singular, unless a is an equal or smaller negative integer ($|a| \gg |c|$), and it is convenient to define the *regularized confluent hypergeometric function*

$$
{}_1\tilde{F}_1(a,c,x) = \frac{1}{\Gamma(c)} {}_1F_1(a,c,x)
$$

which is an entire function for all values of a, c and x.

In[ ]:= **Series[Hypergeometric1F1[a, c, x], {x, 0, 3}]**

Out[ ]= $1 + \dfrac{a\, x}{c} + \dfrac{a\,(1+a)\,x^2}{2\,c\,(1+c)} + \dfrac{a\,(1+a)\times(2+a)\,x^3}{6\,c\,(1+c)\times(2+c)} + O[x]^4$

The second, linearly independent solutions of the differential equation are confluent hypergeometric functions of the second kind (or Tricomi functions), defined by

$$
U(a,c,x) = x^{-a} {}_2F_0(a, 1 + a - c, - x^{-1}).
$$

This Demonstration shows plots of selectable confluent hypergeometric functions, with arguments $\pm x$ and $\pm ix$. For functions with complex values, the real and imaginary parts are shown as black and red curves, respectively.

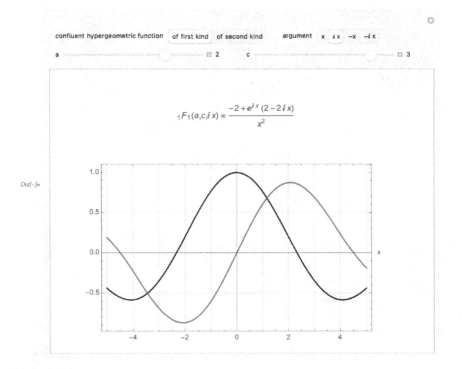

Demonstration 2.7: Confluent Hypergeometric Functions (https://demonstrations.
wolfram.com/ConfluentHypergeometricFunctions/)

For certain combinations of a, c and x, the confluent hypergeometric
function reduces to forms containing elementary or special functions.
Following are some examples:

In[ ]:= **Hypergeometric1F1[1, 1, x]**

Out[ ]= e^x

In[ ]:= **Hypergeometric1F1[1, 2, x]**

Out[ ]= $\dfrac{-1 + e^x}{x}$

In[ ]:= **Hypergeometric1F1$\left[\dfrac{1}{2}, \dfrac{3}{2}, -x^2\right]$**

Out[ ]= $\dfrac{\sqrt{\pi}\ \text{Erf}[x]}{2\,x}$

In[•]:= `FullSimplify[Hypergeometric1F1[-n, 1, x]]`

Out[•]= `LaguerreL[n, x]`

In[•]:= `Hypergeometric1F1[`$\frac{1}{2}$`, 1, 2 𝕚 x]`

Out[•]= $e^{i\,x}$ `BesselJ[0, x]`

In[•]:= `Hypergeometric1F1[`$\frac{3}{2}$`, 3, 2 𝕚 x]`

Out[•]= $\dfrac{2\,e^{i\,x}\ \text{BesselJ}[1,\ x]}{x}$

The general formula for a Bessel function is

$$J_v(x) = \frac{1}{\Gamma(v+1)} \left(\tfrac{x}{2}\right)^v {}_1F_1\left(v + \frac{1}{2}, 2v + 1, 2ix\right).$$

Hermite polynomials reduce to slightly different forms for even and odd orders of *n*. For $n = 0, 2, 4, \ldots$

$$H_n(x) = (-2)^{n/2}(n-1)!\, {}_1F_1\left(-\frac{n}{2}, \frac{1}{2}, x^2\right),$$

while for $n = 1, 3, 5, \ldots$

$$H_n(x) = -(-2)^{(n-1)/2} n!\, {}_1F_1\left(\frac{1-n}{2}, \frac{3}{2}, x^2\right).$$

In[•]:= `HypergeometricU[1, 1, x]`

Out[•]= e^x `Gamma[0, x]`

In[•]:= `HypergeometricU[1, 2, x]`

Out[•]= $\dfrac{1}{x}$

In[•]:= `HypergeometricU[1 - a, 1 - a, x]`

Out[•]= e^x `Gamma[a, x]`

2.16. Special Functions

Several of the special functions, as we have seen, can be represented by multiple derivatives of a simple elementary function, something of the form:

$$F_n(x) = g(x)\frac{d^n}{dx^n}f(x),$$

known as a Rodrigues' formula. Another useful representation makes use of a *generating function*. The special functions $F_n(x)$ is exhibited as the coefficient in an expansion such as

$$G(t, x) = \sum_n t^n F_n(x).$$

A generating function is a power series in a formal sense, which need not be convergent. Herbert Wilf: "A generating function is a clothesline on which we hang up a sequence of numbers for display."

This Demonstration exhibits some Rodrigues' formulas and generating functions for a few selected special functions.

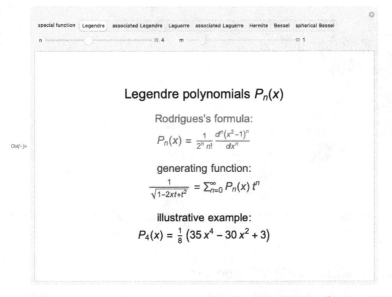

$Out[\circ]=$

special function Legendre associated Legendre Laguerre associated Laguerre Hermite Bessel spherical Bessel

n ———●————— ⊞ 4   m ——————————— ⊟ 1

Legendre polynomials $P_n(x)$

Rodrigues's formula:

$$P_n(x) = \frac{1}{2^n\,n!}\frac{d^n(x^2-1)^n}{dx^n}$$

generating function:

$$\frac{1}{\sqrt{1-2xt+t^2}} = \sum_{n=0}^{\infty} P_n(x)\,t^n$$

illustrative example:

$$P_4(x) = \tfrac{1}{8}\left(35\,x^4 - 30\,x^2 + 3\right)$$

Demonstration 2.8: Generating Functions and Rodrigues's Formulas for Special Functions Used in Quantum Mechanics (https://demonstrations.wolfram.com/Generating FunctionsAndRodriguessFormulasForSpecialFunctionsU/)

2.17. Expansions of Functions

Infinite series representations are of central importance for both elementary and special functions. The following Demonstrations illustrate some typical applications of series expansions.

Mathematica can explicitly evaluate a large number of infinite power series. This Demonstration gives some elementary examples with simple coefficients that sum to exponential, trigonometric, hyperbolic, and logarithmic functions. Not included are hypergeometric functions, binomial expansions, inverse trigonometric functions, or Dirichlet series such as the Riemann zeta function.

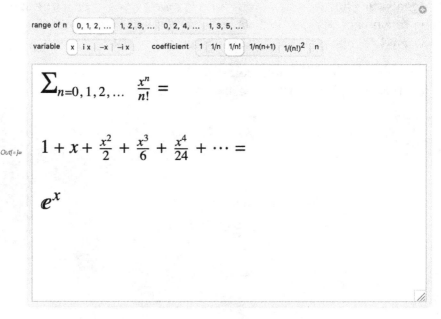

Demonstration 2.9: Infinite Series Explorer (https://demonstrations.wolfram.com/InfiniteSeriesExplorer/)

2.17.1. *Mittag-Leffler Expansions*

A meromorphic function $f(z)$ whose only singularities are simple poles at $z_1, z_2, z_3, \ldots$ ($0 < |z_1| \le |z_2| \le |z_3| \le \ldots$) with residues $r_1, r_2, r_3, \ldots$ at these poles can be represented by

$$f(z) = f(0) + \sum_{n=1}^{\infty} \left(\frac{r_n}{z - z_n} + \frac{r_n}{z_n} \right),$$

a result known as the Mittag-Leffler (M-L) expansion. This Demonstration considers M-L expansions for the gamma function and several trigonometric functions with poles in the complex plane. You can construct explicit approximations for up to eight pairs of positive and negative poles. A 3D plot of the function in the complex plane is also shown, with the poles appearing as spikes. The argument of the complex function is color-coded.

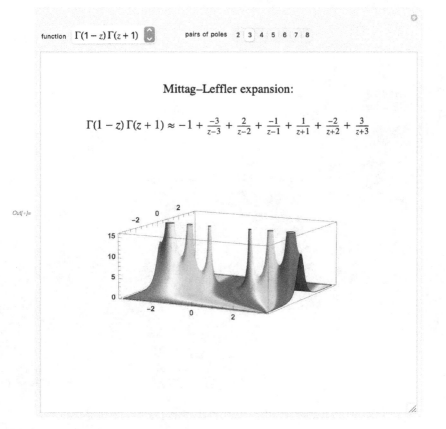

Demonstration 2.10: Mittag-Leffler Expansions of Meromorphic Functions (https://demonstrations.wolfram.com/MittagLefflerExpansionsOfMeromorphicFunctions/)

2.17.2. *Zeno's Paradox*

The Greek philosopher Zeno of Elea (ca. 490–430 BCE) is generally believed to have devised a group of paradoxes pertaining to motion over a finite distance during a finite interval of time. By Zeno's argument, an arrow shot at a target must first cover half the distance to the target, then half of the remaining distance, and so on. But this requires an infinite number of steps, so the arrow will never reach the target!

The distance traveled by the arrow toward the target can be represented by an infinite series $\frac{1}{2} + \frac{1}{4} + \frac{1}{8} + \frac{1}{16} + \ldots = \sum_{k=1}^{\infty} \frac{1}{2^k}$. It is now understood,

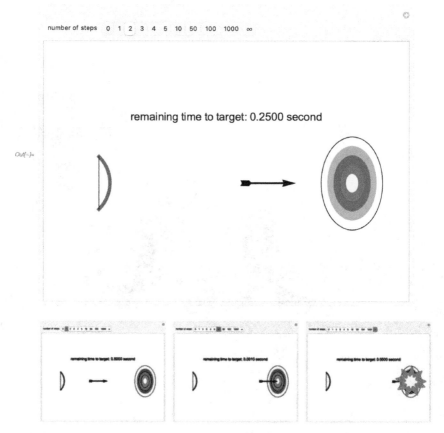

Demonstration 2.11: Zeno's Arrow Paradox and an Infinite Series (https://demonstrations.wolfram.com/ZenosArrowParadoxAndAnInfiniteSeries/)

of course, that an infinite series can converge to a finite limit. In the present case, $\sum_{k=1}^{\infty} \frac{1}{2^k} = 1$. Let us assume that in real life, the arrow hits the target 1 second after release. The time remaining after n steps, each halving the remaining distance, is then shown in the graphic.

It is tempting to conclude that Zeno's paradoxes were resolved after the introduction of the infinitesimal calculus and the understanding of convergent infinite series. In fact, the early 20th-century philosopher C. S. Peirce claimed that "this ridiculous little catch presents no difficulty at all to a mind adequately trained in mathematics and logic." However, some philosophical fine points are still under discussion, pertaining mainly to whether space and time are infinitely divisible, and to the exact meanings of a point in space and an instant in time. Recall that matter turned out *not* to be infinitely divisible.

2.18. Asymptotic Expansions

The asymptotic forms of special functions, usually as the argument $x \to \infty$, are useful in a variety of applications. The most common type of asymptotic expansion for a function $f(x)$ is a formal series that can be truncated after a finite number of terms to a sum that provides an approximation to the function for large values of x. This is usually written as

$$f(x) \sim \sum_{n=0}^{\infty} a_n x^{-n}.$$

Most often, the series diverges for any fixed x. But for fixed N, the truncated sum approaches the function $f(x)$ as $n \to \infty$

$$f(x) \approx \sum_{n=0}^{N} a_n x^{-n} = a_0 + \frac{a_1}{x} + \frac{a_2}{x^2} + \cdots + \frac{a_N}{x^N}.$$

Sometimes fewer terms can be used when the function is represented in the form

$$F(x) \left(1 + \sum_{n=0}^{N} A_n x^{-n} \right),$$

where $F(x)$ is the leading term of the asymptotic expansion. A well-known example is Stirling's asymptotic series for the gamma function:

$$\Gamma(x) \sim \sqrt{2\pi}\, e^{-x} x^{x-\frac{1}{2}} \left(1 + \frac{1}{12x} + \frac{1}{288x^2} - \frac{139}{51840x^3} - \cdots \right).$$

A common way of generating an asymptotic expansion is to apply repeated integration by parts, beginning with an integral representation for $f(x)$. Another approach makes use of Laplace's method of steepest descent.

This Demonstration shows an easier way to derive asymptotic expansions, using the capability of Mathematica to compute a power series

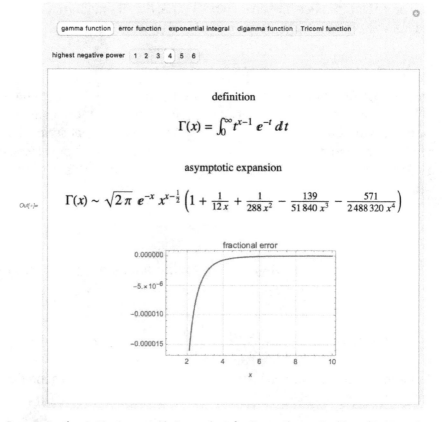

Demonstration 2.12: Asymptotic Expansions for Some Closest Packing of Spheres Special Functions (https://demonstrations.wolfram.com/AsymptoticExpansionsForSome SpecialFunctions/)

for a function about the point $x = \infty$ using Series[f[x],{x, ∞ , n}]. The function $F(x)$ can be determined using Series[f[x],{x, ∞ ,$\odot$}].

You can check the numerical accuracy of the asymptotic series. The fractional error is plotted for values of $1 \leq x \leq 10$.

2.19. Closest Packing of Spheres

According to legend, Sir Walter Scott posed a question to his mathematical assistant, Thomas Harriot, about the most efficient stacking of cannonballs on the decks of his ships. Around 1606, Harriot wrote about the problem to his colleague Johannes Kepler, best known for his work on planetary orbits. Kepler concluded that an arrangement known as face-centered cubic packing, a pattern well known to fruit sellers, is the optimal arrangement. This has become known as *Kepler's conjecture* or simply the *sphere packing problem*. This states that no packing arrangement of equally sized spheres in three-dimensional Euclidean space has a greater average density than that of either the face-centered cubic packing or the hexagonal close packing. In either of these packing arrangements, the spheres occupy approximately 74% of the space. The explicit value for the packing fraction is given by $f = \frac{\pi}{3\sqrt{2}} \approx$ 0.740480489 . . . .

Here is an optimally stacked pile of cannonballs:

$In[\cdot]:=$ points $= \left\{ \{0, 0, 0\}, \{1, 0, 0\}, \{2, 0, 0\}, \{3, 0, 0\}, \left\{\frac{1}{2}, \frac{\sqrt{3}}{2}, 0\right\}, \left\{\frac{3}{2}, \frac{\sqrt{3}}{2}, 0\right\}, \right.$

$\left\{\frac{5}{2}, \frac{\sqrt{3}}{2}, 0\right\}, \left\{1, \sqrt{3}, 0\right\}, \left\{2, \sqrt{3}, 0\right\}, \left\{\frac{3}{2}, \frac{3\sqrt{3}}{2}, 0\right\}, \left\{\frac{1}{2}, \frac{1}{2\sqrt{3}}, \sqrt{\frac{2}{3}}\right\},$

$\left\{\frac{3}{2}, \frac{1}{2\sqrt{3}}, \sqrt{\frac{2}{3}}\right\}, \left\{\frac{5}{2}, \frac{1}{2\sqrt{3}}, \sqrt{\frac{2}{3}}\right\}, \left\{1, \frac{1}{2\sqrt{3}} + \frac{\sqrt{3}}{2}, \sqrt{\frac{2}{3}}\right\},$

$\left\{2, \frac{1}{2\sqrt{3}} + \frac{\sqrt{3}}{2}, \sqrt{\frac{2}{3}}\right\}, \left\{\frac{3}{2}, \frac{1}{2\sqrt{3}} + \sqrt{3}, \sqrt{\frac{2}{3}}\right\}, \left\{1, \frac{1}{\sqrt{3}}, 2\sqrt{\frac{2}{3}}\right\},$

$\left\{2, \frac{1}{\sqrt{3}}, 2\sqrt{\frac{2}{3}}\right\}, \left\{\frac{3}{2}, \frac{1}{\sqrt{3}} + \frac{\sqrt{3}}{2}, 2\sqrt{\frac{2}{3}}\right\}, \left\{\frac{3}{2}, \frac{\sqrt{3}}{2}, \sqrt{6}\right\}\right\};$

Graphics3D[{GrayLevel[.25], Specularity[White, 10], Table[Sphere[points[[n]], .5],
{n, 1, 20}]}, Lighting → Automatic, Boxed → False, PlotRange →
{{-1, 3.5}, {-.5, 3}, {-2, 3}}, ViewAngle → 20 Degree, ImageSize → {250, 250}]

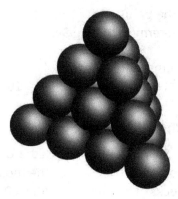

Following is an "experimental" verification of Kepler's conjecture. The lattice is defined by two angles α and β, with the second angle determining the relative displacement of successive planar layers. The spheres in each layer are placed directly over the cavities in the preceding layer. Since there are two possible sets of cavities, a regular arrangement of layers can be either a sequence like a b c a b c ... or an alternative sequence like a b a b a b . . . . In either case, the packing fraction is given by

$$f(\alpha, \beta) = \frac{\pi \sin \beta}{6 \sin \alpha(1 - \cos\beta)\sqrt{1 + 2\cos\beta}}.$$

Choosing $\alpha = \beta = 90°$ gives a simple cubic lattice with packing fraction $f = \frac{\pi}{6} \approx 0.5236$. Choosing $\alpha = \beta = 60°$ gives either the cubic closest packing (for a b c ...) or hexagonal closest packing (for a b a b ...). In either case, $f = \frac{\pi}{3\sqrt{2}} \approx 0.7405$. Kepler's conjecture claims that this is the maximum possible packing fraction for spheres in 3D. You can move the layers apart for a closer view of their structure.

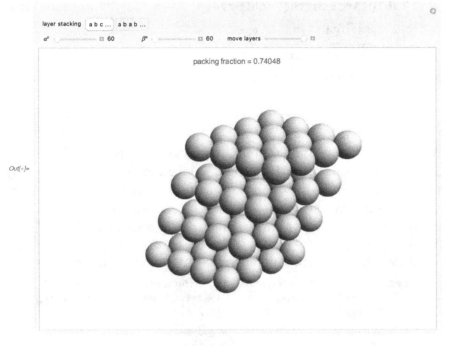

layer stacking a b c ... a b a b ...

α° 🔲 60 β° 🔲 60   move layers   🔲

packing fraction = 0.74048

Out[•]=

Demonstration 2.13: Closest Packing of Disks and Spheres; Kepler's Conjecture (https://demonstrations.wolfram.com/ClosestPackingOfDisksAndSpheresKeplersConjecture/)

2.20. Fractals

Fractals are complex patterns that are self-similar across different scales. They are created by recursively repeating a simple procedure over and over. For example the Koch curve:

```
In[•]:= GraphicsRow[Table[Graphics[KochCurve[n]], {n, 1, 5}]]
```

Out[•]=

This is produced by repeatedly replacing each segment of a generator shape with a smaller copy. At each iteration, the total length of the curve increases, eventually approaching infinity. This is much like the behavior of a coastline, with the length of the curve increasing as you measure it in finer detail. The arc lengths of the Koch curves above are found from:

In[ ]:= `Table[ArcLength[KochCurve[n]], {n, 5}] // Rationalize`

$$\left\{\frac{4}{3}, \frac{16}{9}, \frac{64}{27}, \frac{256}{81}, \frac{1024}{203}\right\}$$

In[ ]:= `FindSequenceFunction[%, n]`

Out[ ]= $\left(\dfrac{4}{3}\right)^{n}$

The *Hausdorff dimension D* of an object can be defined such that the increase in measure, such as length L, in successive steps is given by $L_{n+1} = L_n^D$, so that $D = \mathrm{Log}(L_{n+1})/\mathrm{Log}(L_n)$. Thus the Koch curve has a Hausdorff dimension $\frac{\mathrm{Log}\,4}{\mathrm{Log}\,3} = 1.26186$, intermediate between the dimensions of ordinary 1-dimensional and 2-dimensional objects.

An analogous sequence of iterations can produce a *Koch snowflake*:

In[ ]:= `GraphicsRow[Table[Graphics[GeometricTransformation[KochCurve[n],`
`      {RotationTransform[π, {1/2, 0}], RotationTransform[-π/3, {1, 0}],`
`      RotationTransform[π/3, {0, 0}]}]], {n, 0, 4}]]`

Out[ ]=

Another famous fractal is the Sierpinski triangle (or gasket or sieve), obtained by recursively subdividing an equilateral triangle into smaller equilateral triangles by removing triangular segments:

In[ ]:= `GraphicsRow[Table[SierpinskiMesh[n], {n, 0, 5}]]`

Out[ ]=

Here is the development of a 3-dimensional fractal known as a *Menger sponge*:

In[ ]:= `GraphicsRow[Table[MengerMesh[n, 3], {n, 0, 3}]]`

Out[ ]=

2.20.1. *The Mandelbrot Set*

Probably the most famous fractal object is the *Mandelbrot set*. For a given complex number c, select a point z_0 in the complex plane and compute the points in the iterated relations:

$$z_1 = z_0^2 + c, z_2 = z_1^2 + c, \ldots, z_{n+1} = z_n^2 + c.$$

This set of points is known as the *Julia set* for c. The Mandelbrot set is defined as the collection of points c in the complex plane for which this Julia set remains in a finite, simply connected region as $n \to \infty$. The Mandelbrot set, which has a fractal boundary, is shown in black on the graphic. The most prominent features are a cardioid and a circular disc tangent to one another. If $|z_n| \geq 2$ for any value of n, then the point cannot belong to the Mandelbrot set. Such points fall in a colored region, with different colors determined by the number of steps n it takes for an orbit to reach a value $|z| \geq 2$. Magnification of various regions of the complex plane reveals an incredible variety of fractal structures. The 2D slider centers the image on a desired region for magnification. The magnification should be increased stepwise for optimal control.

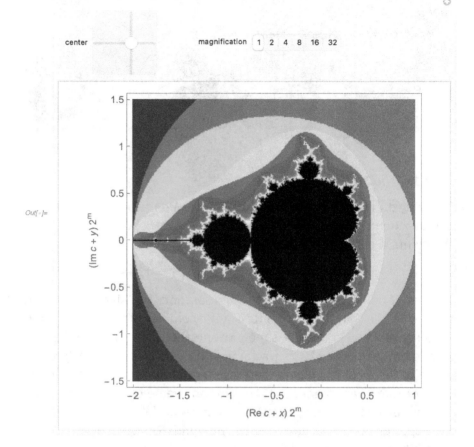

Some magnified views:

Snapshot 1: the region between the two main features is known as "seahorse valley"

Snapshot 2: each circular disk grows smaller circular disks; "baby Mandelbrot sets" also appear

Snapshot 3: one of many remarkably complex fractal patterns under higher magnification

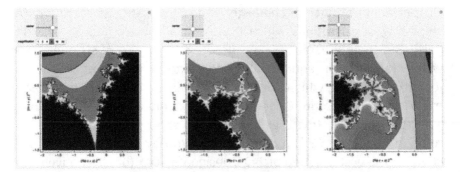

Demonstration 2.14: Magnified Views of the Mandelbrot Set (https://demonstrations.wolfram.com/MagnifiedViewsOfTheMandelbrotSet/)

2.21. Group Theory

Group theory deals with collections of objects which can be transformed among themselves by some appropriate operation. For example, the integers constitute a group (containing an infinite number of members) which can be transformed into one another by the operation of addition (which includes subtraction). Likewise, under the operation of multiplication, the four complex numbers $\{i, -1, -i, +1\}$ can be recycled among themselves. Two versions of the Yin and Yang symbol can be turned into one another by reversing the colors black and white or by rotating the figure by $180°$:

```
In[·]:= yy[x_] := Graphics[{EdgeForm[], GrayLevel[x], Disk[{0, 0}, 1, {π / 2, 3 π / 2}],
        GrayLevel[1 - x], Disk[{0, 0}, 1, {-π / 2, π / 2}], Disk[{0, -.5}, .5], GrayLevel[x],
        Disk[{0, .5}, .5], Thick, Black, Circle[], Circle[{0, .5}, .5, {-π / 2, π / 2}],
        Circle[{0, -.5}, .5, {π / 2, 3 π / 2}], EdgeForm[Black], GrayLevel[1 - x],
        Disk[{0, .5}, .125], GrayLevel[x], Disk[{0, -.5}, .125]},
      PlotRange → 1.25, ImageSize → {275, 150}];
    GraphicsRow[{yy[0], Graphics[{Thickness[.2],
        Arrowheads[.6], Arrow[{{-.25, 0}, {.25, 0}}]}], yy[1]}]
```

Out[·]=

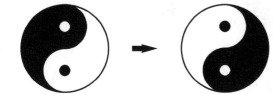

Of special importance in chemistry and physics are *symmetry groups*, consisting of operations which transform an object into an indistinguishable copy of itself. We consider here the group of six operations which transform an equilateral triangle into itself. Operation 1 is the identity element E, which does nothing. This is a necessary member of every symmetry group. Operation 2 is a counterclockwise rotation by $120°$, designated C (more generally C_3, to show that it is a three-fold rotation). Operation 3 is a clockwise rotation by $120°$, equivalent to a counterclockwise rotation of $240°$, designated C^{-1} (or alternatively C^2). Operations 4, 5 and 6 are reflections through the planes bisecting each of the angles of the triangle, designated σ_1, σ_2 and σ_3. This symmetry group is usually designated C_{3v}, indicating that it contains 3-fold axes, as well as 2 vertical mirror planes. The group is alternatively designated as the dihedral group D_3, the symmetry group of the regular polygon of 3 sides. It is isomorphic with the symmetric group S_3, the permutation group of 3 objects.

In this Demonstration, the sliders for operations 1, 2, and 3 perform actions of the symmetry group C_{3v}, as indicated by labels above the three arrows. You can explore the results of applying successive operations 1 and 2 of the symmetry group C_{3v} using tricolored equilateral triangles. The same result can be obtained in a single step using a single operation 3. For example, the operation C_3 followed by σ_1 gives the same result as the operation σ_2. In standard group theory notation, this is written right-to-left as the symbolic product $\sigma_1 C_3 = \sigma_2$. Note that $C_3 \sigma_1 = \sigma_3$, showing that symmetry operations do not, in general, commute. Certain products can still commute, for example, $CC^{-1} = C^{-1}C = E$. The triangle coloring enables the symmetry operations to be visualized. It should be understood, however, that all versions of the triangle are actually equivalent and indistinguishable.

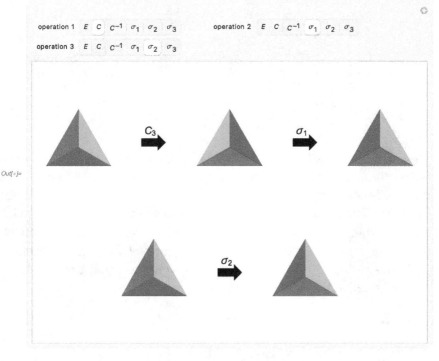

| operation 1 | E | C | C⁻¹ | σ₁ | σ₂ | σ₃ | | operation 2 | E | C | C⁻¹ | σ₁ | σ₂ | σ₃ |

| operation 3 | E | C | C⁻¹ | σ₁ | σ₂ | σ₃ |

Demonstration 2.15: C_{3v} Group Operations (https://demonstrations.wolfram.com/ C3vGroupOperations/)

The Wolfram Language has information about groups.

```
In[ ]:= FiniteGroupData[{"DihedralGroup", 3}, "ElementNames"]
```

$$Out[ ]= \left\{1, r, r^2, s, r \circ s, r^2 \circ s\right\}$$

These correspond to $\{E, C, C^{-1}, \sigma_1, \sigma_2, \sigma_3\}$ in our notation. The group multiplication table is found from

```
        FiniteGroupData[{"DihedralGroup", 3}, "MultiplicationTable"]
```

$$Out[ ]= \{\{1, 2, 3, 4, 5, 6\}, \{2, 3, 1, 6, 4, 5\}, \{3, 1, 2, 5, 6, 4\},$$
$$\{4, 5, 6, 1, 2, 3\}, \{5, 6, 4, 3, 1, 2\}, \{6, 4, 5, 2, 3, 1\}\}$$

In[•]:= **% // MatrixForm**

Out[•]//MatrixForm=

$$\begin{pmatrix} 1 & 2 & 3 & 4 & 5 & 6 \\ 2 & 3 & 1 & 6 & 4 & 5 \\ 3 & 1 & 2 & 5 & 6 & 4 \\ 4 & 5 & 6 & 1 & 2 & 3 \\ 5 & 6 & 4 & 3 & 1 & 2 \\ 6 & 4 & 5 & 2 & 3 & 1 \end{pmatrix}$$

Thus $\sigma_1 C = \sigma_2$ corresponds to g3 g4 = g5. A set of quantities which obeys the group multiplication table is called a *representation* of the group. We consider matrix representations of groups, which can include numbers. The group C_{3v} has three *irreducible representations*. A trivial, but nonetheless important, representation of every group is the *totally symmetric representation*, in which each group element is represented by 1. The multiplication table then simply reiterates that $1 \times 1 = 1$. For C_{3v} this is called the A_1 representation:

$$A_1 : E = 1, C = 1, C^{-1} = 1, \sigma_1 = 1, \sigma_2 = 1, \sigma_3 = 1$$

Slightly less trivial is the A_2 representation

$$A_2 : E = 1, C = 1, C^{-1} = 1, \sigma_1 = -1, \sigma_2 = -1, \sigma_3 = -1$$

Much more exciting is the E representation, which requires 2×2 matrices:

$$E = \begin{pmatrix} 1 & 0 \\ 0 & 1 \end{pmatrix}, \quad C = \begin{pmatrix} -1/2 & -\sqrt{3}/2 \\ -\sqrt{3}/2 & -1/2 \end{pmatrix},$$

$$C^{-1} = \begin{pmatrix} -1/2 & \sqrt{3}/2 \\ -\sqrt{3}/2 & -1/2 \end{pmatrix},$$

$$\sigma_1 = \begin{pmatrix} -1 & 0 \\ 0 & 1 \end{pmatrix}, \quad \sigma_2 = \begin{pmatrix} 1/2 & -\sqrt{3}/2 \\ -\sqrt{3}/2 & -1/2 \end{pmatrix},$$

$$\sigma_3 = \begin{pmatrix} 1/2 & \sqrt{3}/2 \\ \sqrt{3}/2 & -1/2 \end{pmatrix}.$$

The product $\sigma_1 C = \sigma_2$ corresponds to the matrix product

In[◦]:= `{{-1, 0}, {0, 1}}.`$\left\{\left\{-1/2, -\sqrt{3}\,/\,2\right\}, \left\{\sqrt{3}\,/\,2, -1/2\right\}\right\}$` // MatrixForm`

Out[◦]//MatrixForm=

$$\begin{pmatrix} \frac{1}{2} & \frac{\sqrt{3}}{2} \\ \frac{\sqrt{3}}{2} & -\frac{1}{2} \end{pmatrix}$$

Mathematica gives a 3×3 matrix representation:

In[◦]:= `FiniteGroupData[{"DihedralGroup", 3}, "MatrixRepresentation"]`

Out[◦]= `{{{1, 0, 0}, {0, 1, 0}, {0, 0, 1}}, {{0, 1, 0}, {0, 0, 1}, {1, 0, 0}},`
`{{0, 0, 1}, {1, 0, 0}, {0, 1, 0}}, {{0, 0, 1}, {0, 1, 0}, {1, 0, 0}},`
`{{0, 1, 0}, {1, 0, 0}, {0, 0, 1}}, {{1, 0, 0}, {0, 0, 1}, {0, 1, 0}}}`

In[◦]:= `Table[%[[n]] // MatrixForm, {n, 1, 6}]`

Out[◦]= $\left\{ \begin{pmatrix} 1 & 0 & 0 \\ 0 & 1 & 0 \\ 0 & 0 & 1 \end{pmatrix}, \begin{pmatrix} 0 & 1 & 0 \\ 0 & 0 & 1 \\ 1 & 0 & 0 \end{pmatrix}, \begin{pmatrix} 0 & 0 & 1 \\ 1 & 0 & 0 \\ 0 & 1 & 0 \end{pmatrix}, \begin{pmatrix} 0 & 0 & 1 \\ 0 & 1 & 0 \\ 1 & 0 & 0 \end{pmatrix}, \begin{pmatrix} 0 & 1 & 0 \\ 1 & 0 & 0 \\ 0 & 0 & 1 \end{pmatrix}, \begin{pmatrix} 1 & 0 & 0 \\ 0 & 0 & 1 \\ 0 & 1 & 0 \end{pmatrix} \right\}$

This is a reducible representation. There exists a similarity transformation SM_nS^{-1} which will transform each matrix in the 3×3 representation to a block-diagonal form containing the A_1 and E representations.

2.21.1. *Matrix Representation of the Addition Group*

The real numbers with the operation of addition are commonly cited as an elementary example of a group. The requirements of closure, associativity, and the existence of an inverse are all fulfilled. It is well known that groups can be represented by matrices, with the group structure reflected in the corresponding matrix multiplication. So how can one reconcile representing addition by multiplication?

The answer is provided by a simple relation involving multiplication of 2×2 matrices:

$$\begin{pmatrix} 1 & x \\ 0 & 1 \end{pmatrix} \begin{pmatrix} 1 & y \\ 0 & 1 \end{pmatrix} = \begin{pmatrix} 1 & x+y \\ 0 & 1 \end{pmatrix}.$$

In this Demonstration, values of x and y are limited to integers between -10 and 10 for neatness, but the result applies to all real and complex numbers.

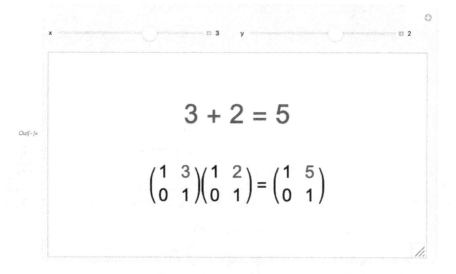

Out[⦁]=

Demonstration 2.16: Matrix Representation of the Addition Group (https://demonstrations.wolfram.com/MatrixRepresentationOfTheAdditionGroup/)

2.22. Prime Numbers

The prime numbers have been a source of endless fascination, dating back to the time of the ancient Greeks. Paul Erdös on prime numbers: "It will be millions of years before we'll have any understanding, and even then it won't be a complete understanding, because we're up against the infinite." The Wolfram Language implements state-of-the-art algorithms for dealing with primes and the advanced mathematics involving them, such as the Riemann zeta function. To find the nth prime number use the command Prime:

In[⦁]:= `Prime[5]`

Out[⦁]= 11

The first 100 prime numbers:

In[⦁]:= `Table[Prime[n], {n, 1, 100}]`

Out[⦁]= {2, 3, 5, 7, 11, 13, 17, 19, 23, 29, 31, 37, 41, 43, 47, 53, 59, 61, 67, 71, 73, 79, 83, 89, 97, 101, 103, 107, 109, 113, 127, 131, 137, 139, 149, 151, 157, 163, 167, 173, 179, 181, 191, 193, 197, 199, 211, 223, 227, 229, 233, 239, 241, 251, 257, 263, 269, 271, 277, 281, 283, 293, 307, 311, 313, 317, 331, 337, 347, 349, 353, 359, 367, 373, 379, 383, 389, 397, 401, 409, 419, 421, 431, 433, 439, 443, 449, 457, 461, 463, 467, 479, 487, 491, 499, 503, 509, 521, 523, 541}

Mathematica can very efficiently calculate the billionth prime and beyond. Let us check the CPU time required for some very large numbers. For the millionth prime:

In[∘]:= `Timing[Prime[10^6]]`

Out[∘]= {0.000015, 15 485 863}

the billionth prime:

In[∘]:= `Timing[Prime[10^9]]`

Out[∘]= {0.000012, 22 801 763 489}

the trillionth prime:

In[∘]:= `Timing[Prime[10^12]]`

Out[∘]= {0.000014`, 29 996 224 275 833}

the quadrillionth prime:

In[∘]:= `Timing[Prime[10^15]]`

Out[∘]= {42.411676`, 37 124 508 045 065 437}

This took about 42 seconds, pushing the limit of computation. (This also depends on your computer. I am using a powerful MacPro.)

It is interesting to see how the values of the 10^n th prime increases with n. Clearly we need a log scale:

In[∘]:= `primes = Table[N[Log[Prime[10^n]], 10], {n, 0, 14}]`

Out[∘]= {0.6931471806, 3.367295830, 6.293419279, 8.977020214, 11.55913134, 14.07765095, 16.55543810, 19.00526603, 21.43527145, 23.85010372, 26.25308295, 28.64651528, 31.03209263, 33.41108696, 35.78448188}

In[•]:= `ListPlot[primes]`

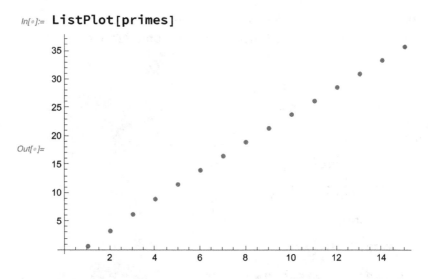

Out[•]=

Remarkably this shows a pretty accurate linear dependence.

In[•]:= `Clear[a, b]`

In[•]:= `FindFit[primes, a + b n, {a, b}, n]`

Out[•]= $\{a \to -1.178600616, b \to 2.488500108\}$

In[•]:= `Show[ListPlot[primes], Plot[-1.1786 + 2.4885 n, {n, 0, 15}]]`

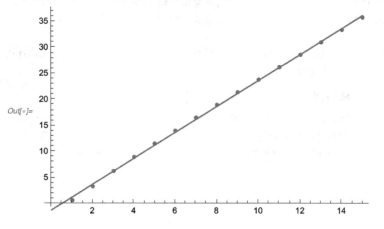

Out[•]=

The number of primes less than or equal to N is designated $\pi(N)$:

In[•]:= `PrimePi[10^6]`

Out[•]= 78 498

Note that

In[•]:= `Prime[78 498]`

Out[•]= 999 983

In[•]:= `Prime[78 499]`

Out[•]= 1 000 003

Thus $\pi(N) = P$ is essentially the inverse relation to Prime $(P) = N$. The *prime number theorem* describes the asymptotic distribution of the prime numbers among the positive integers. It states that

$$\lim_{N \to \infty} \pi(N) = \frac{N}{\log N} \quad \text{or} \quad \lim_{N \to \infty} \frac{\pi(N)}{N/\log N} = 1$$

also written

$$\pi(N) \sim \frac{N}{\log N},$$

A faster-converging asymptotic limit is given by

$$\pi(N) \sim li(N),$$

in terms of the logarithmic integral

$$li(x) = \int_0^x \frac{dz}{\log z}.$$

Let us test this for $N = 10^6$

In[•]:= $\dfrac{\texttt{PrimePi}[10^6]}{\texttt{LogIntegral}[10^6]}$ `// N`

Out[•]= 0.998352

For $N = 10^{12}$

$In[\bullet]:=$ $\dfrac{\text{PrimePi}\left[10^{12}\right]}{\text{LogIntegral}\left[10^{12}\right]}$ // N

$Out[\bullet]=$ 0.999999

Here is a plot of the prime-counting function, along with the two approximations:

```
In[•]:= Plot[{PrimePi[x], LogIntegral[x], x / Log[x]}, {x, 2, 100},
        PlotStyle → {Black, Red, Blue}, GridLines → Automatic,
        PlotLegends → Placed["Expressions", {{0, 0}, {-1, -2}}], ImageSize → {550, 425}]
```

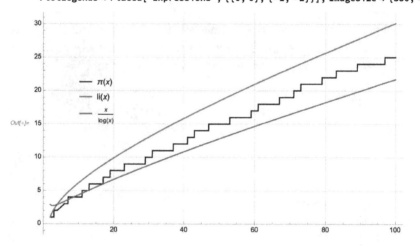

The probability that a randomly chosen number between 1 and N is prime is evidently given by $\pi(N)/N$. Thus for $N = 100$

$In[\bullet]:=$ $\dfrac{\text{PrimePi}[100]}{100}$ // N

$Out[\bullet]=$ 0.25

meaning 25%

$In[\bullet]:=$ $\dfrac{\text{PrimePi}\left[10^{6}\right]}{10^{6}}$ // N

$Out[\bullet]=$ 0.078498

and for $N = 100{,}000$, about 7.8%.

To test a number for primality:

In[∘]:= **PrimeQ[89]**

Out[∘]= True

In[∘]:= **PrimeQ[91]**

Out[∘]= False

To find the prime factors of an integer:

In[∘]:= **FactorInteger[100]**

Out[∘]= {{2, 2}, {5, 2}}

This means $100 = 2^2 \times 5^2$

In[∘]:= **FactorInteger[91]**

Out[∘]= {{7, 1}, {13, 1}}

$91 = 7 \times 13$

2.22.1. *RSA Encryption and Decryption*

The RSA algorithm for public-key encryption was originated by Ron Rivest, Adi Shamir, and Leonard Adleman at MIT in 1977. Several similar methods had been proposed by earlier workers. The algorithm is based on the fact that it is far more difficult to factor a product of two primes than it is to multiply the two primes. Even the most powerful modern supercomputers would require more time than the age of the universe to factor a 400-digit number, particularly if it has a few large, but not very close, prime factors. This might change if quantum computers ever become operational.

In this Demonstration, the RSA algorithm is simulated using much smaller randomly chosen prime numbers, p and q, both less than 100. The public key, which is made freely available to Alice and all other users, consists of the two numbers $N = p \times q$ and an exponent E, which is an odd integer relatively prime to $\phi(N)$ between 1 and $\phi(N) = (p-1)(q-1)$. (Here $\phi(N)$ is Euler's totient function, the number of positive integers less than N and relatively prime to N.) For simplicity, take $E = 17$ and also limit messages to three letters, such as XYZ. This constitutes the plaintext and is converted into an integer M using, for example, ASCII codes. The corresponding ciphertext C is computed using $C = M^E (\mathrm{mod}\, N)$.

Only the recipient Bob has access to the private key, which is an integer exponent D, a modular inverse to E such that $DE = 1(\mathrm{mod}\, \phi(N))$. To determine D, a codebreaker would need to find the prime factors of N, which, as noted earlier, is hopefully impossible. The plaintext is recovered using $M = C^D (\mathrm{mod}\, N)$. The method works since $M = M^{ED}(\mathrm{mod}\, N)$,

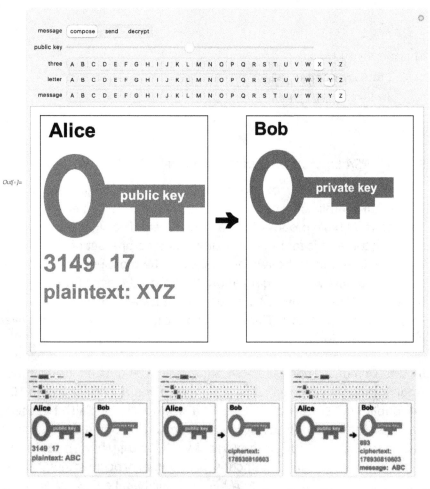

Demonstration 2.17: RSA Encryption and Decryption (https://demonstrations.wolf ram.com/RSAEncryptionAndDecryption/)

with application of Fermat's little theorem. The public and private keys can periodically be changed according to some prearranged schedule.

By inputting the public key (N, E) and the three-part ciphertext C, Bob can recover the plaintext message.

2.23. The Riemann Zeta Function

The zeta function is a generalization of the harmonic series

$$1 + \frac{1}{2} + \frac{1}{3} + \frac{1}{4} \cdots,$$

defined by the Dirichlet series

$$\zeta(s) = \sum_{n=1}^{\infty} \frac{1}{n^s} = \frac{1}{1^s} + \frac{1}{2^s} + \frac{1}{3^s} \cdots,$$

as a function of a complex variable usually denoted s. The series converges for real $s > 1$. The zeta function has proven to be of fundamental importance in the theory of prime numbers. For $s = 1$, the series reduces to the harmonic series

$$\zeta(1) = 1 + \frac{1}{2} + \frac{1}{3} \cdots,$$

which is known to be divergent.

In[•]:= **Zeta[1]**

Out[•]= ComplexInfinity

Well-known special cases are

In[•]:= **Zeta[2]**

Out[•]= $\dfrac{\pi^2}{6}$

and

In[•]:= **Zeta[4]**

Out[•]= $\dfrac{\pi^4}{90}$

In[ ]:= **Zeta[6]**

Out[ ]= $\dfrac{\pi^6}{945}$

A complex plot shows singularities at $s = 1$ and $s = 0$, as well as zeros at $s = -2, -4, -6, \ldots$.

In[ ]:= **ComplexPlot[Zeta[s], {s, -8 - 4 I, 2 + 4 I}, PlotPoints → 400]**

Out[ ]=

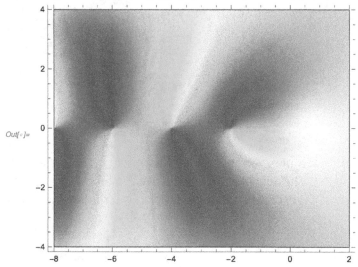

Of fundamental significance in prime number theory are the non-trivial zeros of the zeta function along the *critical line* with $s = \frac{1}{2} + ix$.

In[ ]:= **Table[N[ZetaZero[k]], {k, 1, 10}]**

```
{0.5` + 14.134725141734695` i, 0.5` + 21.022039638771556` i,
 0.5` + 25.01085758014569` i, 0.5` + 30.424876125859512` i,
 0.5` + 32.93506158773919` i, 0.5` + 37.586178158825675` i, 0.5` + 40.9187190121475` i,
 0.5` + 43.327073280915` i, 0.5` + 48.00515088116716` i, 0.5` + 49.7738320776723` i}
```

Since $\zeta\left(\frac{1}{2} + ix\right) = 0$ implies the complex conjugate relation $\zeta\left(\frac{1}{2} - ix\right) = 0$, all of the zeros actually occur in complex conjugate pairs. Thus we have, in addition to the above list:

In[ ]:= **Table[N[ZetaZero[-k]], {k, 1, 10}]**

```
{0.5` - 14.134725141734695` i, 0.5` - 21.022039638771556` i,
 0.5` - 25.01085758014569` i, 0.5` - 30.424876125859512` i,
 0.5` - 32.93506158773919` i, 0.5` - 37.586178158825675` i, 0.5` - 40.9187190121475` i,
 0.5` - 43.327073280915` i, 0.5` - 48.00515088116716` i, 0.5` - 49.7738320776723` i}
```

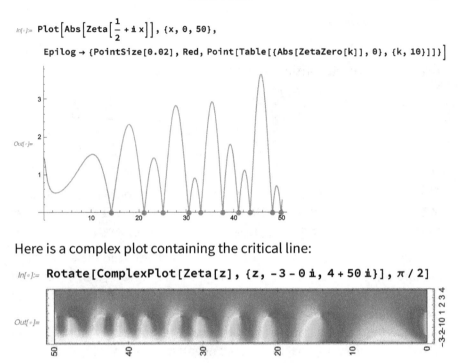

Here is a complex plot containing the critical line:

In[•]:= `Rotate[ComplexPlot[Zeta[z], {z, -3 - 0 i, 4 + 50 i}], π / 2]`

Out[•]=

The celebrated *Riemann hypothesis* conjectures that the non-trivial zeros all lie on the critical line. This is known to be true for the first 10^{13} zeros but a rigorous proof is yet to be found. Many consider this to be the most important unsolved problem in pure mathematics. It is one of the Clay Mathematics Institute's Millennium Prize Problems, for which a $1 million prize awaits a verified solution.

2.23.1. Euler Product for the Zeta Function

Euler in 1737 proved a remarkable connection between the zeta function and an infinite product containing the prime numbers:

$$\zeta(s) \prod_{n=1}^{\infty} \left(1 - \frac{1}{p(n)^s} \right) = 1$$

where $p(n)$ is the nth prime. This represents a very suggestive relationship between prime numbers and the Riemann zeta function. It has been called "The Golden Key" (J. Derbyshire, *Prime Obsession: Bernhard*

Riemann and the Greatest Unsolved Problem in Mathematics, New York: Penguin, 2004).

To prove this result consider the product $\zeta(s)\left(1 - \frac{1}{2^s}\right)$:

$$\zeta(s)\left(1 - \frac{1}{2^s}\right) = 1 + \frac{1}{2^s} + \frac{1}{3^s} + \frac{1}{4^s} + \frac{1}{5^s}\cdots - \left(\frac{1}{2^s} + \frac{1}{4^4} + \frac{1}{6^s}\right.$$

$$\left. + \frac{1}{8^s}\cdots\right) = 1 + \frac{1}{3^s} + \frac{1}{5^s} + \frac{1}{7^s} + \frac{1}{9^s}\cdots$$

This has removed the term $\frac{1}{2^s}$, as well as every term containing a multiple of 2, from the summation. Analogously, $\zeta(s)(1 - \frac{1}{2^s}) \times (1 - \frac{1}{3^s})$ removes every multiple of 3, and so on, for each successive prime.

We have found this derivation to be an excellent student exercise in manipulating infinite sums and products. The following Demonstration enables the stepwise evaluation of the product as the number of prime factors is increased. The deviation of each partial result from 1 is shown on a log-log plot as a function of s and the number of factors. The difference rapidly approaches a large negative power of 10.

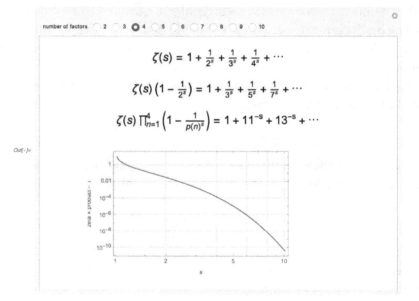

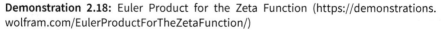

Demonstration 2.18: Euler Product for the Zeta Function (https://demonstrations. wolfram.com/EulerProductForTheZetaFunction/)

Riemann derived an expression for the prime-counting function $\pi(x)$ based on the zeros of the zeta function, the values ρ where $\zeta(\rho) = 0$:

$$\pi(x) = R(x) - \sum_{\rho} R(x^\rho) - \frac{1}{\log x} + \frac{1}{\pi}\arctan\left(\frac{\pi}{\log x}\right),$$

where the last two terms account for the "trivial" zeros at $\rho = -2, -4, \ldots$.

The Riemann R function is defined by

$$R(x) = \sum_{k=1}^{\infty} \frac{\mu(k)}{k} \mathrm{Ei}\left(\frac{\log x}{k}\right),$$

where $\mu(k)$ is the Möbius function and $\mathrm{Ei}(x)$ the exponential integral. In the following, we consider an approximation to Riemann's formula, denoted $\Pi(n, x)$, in which we take account of just n pairs of zeta zeros on the critical line, of the form $\rho = \frac{1}{2} + i\sigma$. The terms $R(X^\rho)$ introduce wiggles into the smooth function $R(x)$ to approximate the stepwise behavior of $\pi(x)$. The more zeros we use, the closer the approximation to $\pi(x)$.

```
Manipulate[Show[Plot[PrimePi[x], {x, 2, 50}, PlotStyle → Black,
    GridLines → Automatic, ImageSize → {600, 500}, Epilog →
      {Text[Style[TraditionalForm[π[x]], 20, Black, FontFamily → "Times"], {20, 15}],
        Text[Style[TraditionalForm[Π[x]], 20, Red, FontFamily → "Times"], {30, 15}]}],
    Plot[Π[n, x], {x, 2, 50}, PlotStyle → Red, PerformanceGoal → "Speed"]],
  {{n, 10, Row[{"number of zeta zero pairs ", Style["n", Italic]}]},
   0, 50, 1, Appearance → "Labeled"},
```

$$\text{Initialization} \rightarrowtail \Big(\Pi[0, x\_] := \text{RiemannR}[x];$$

$$\rho = \text{Table}[N[\text{ZetaZero}[k]], \{k, 50\}];$$

$$\Pi[n\_, x\_] := \text{RiemannR}[x] - 2\,\text{Re}\Big[\sum_{p=1}^{n}\sum_{k=1}^{20}\frac{\text{MoebiusMu}[k]}{k}$$

$$\text{ExpIntegralEi}\Big[\Big(\frac{\rho[\![p]\!]}{k}\Big)\text{Log}[x]\Big]\Big] - \frac{1}{\text{Log}[x]} + \frac{1}{\pi}\,\text{ArcTan}\Big[\frac{\pi}{\text{Log}[x]}\Big];\Big),$$

```
  TrackedSymbols ⤻ {n}, ControlPlacement → Top]
```

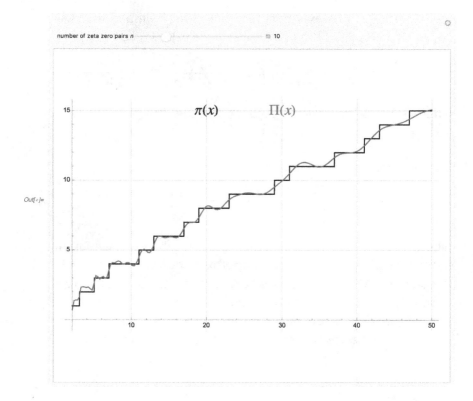

2.24. Topology

2.24.1. *Coffee Mug to Donut*

A topologist is a mathematician who can't tell the difference between a coffee mug and a donut — both are surfaces of genus 1. This Demonstration shows a continuous deformation — known as a homeomorphism — of a coffee mug into a donut, then back to a coffee mug.

Demonstration 2.19: Coffee Mug to Donut (https://demonstrations.wolfram.com/CoffeeMugToDonut/)

2.24.2. *Topological Spaces*

A topological space can be defined as a pair (S, T), where S is a set of points and T (a topology) is a collection of subsets of S that satisfy the following axioms:

1. The empty set $\emptyset$ and the set S itself belong to T.
2. Any finite or infinite union of members of T also belongs to T.
3. The intersection of any finite number of members of T also belongs to T.

Topological spaces are, of course, usually associated with infinite sets of points. But it is amusing to apply topology to a finite set of points. This Demonstration considers a space $S = \{1, 2, 3\}$, with T selected from the power set of three points: $\{\} = \emptyset, \{1\}, \{2\}, \{3\}, \{1, 2\}, \{2, 3\}, \{1, 3\}$ and $\{1, 2, 3\}$. The set T is a topological space only if the three conditions listed are satisfied.

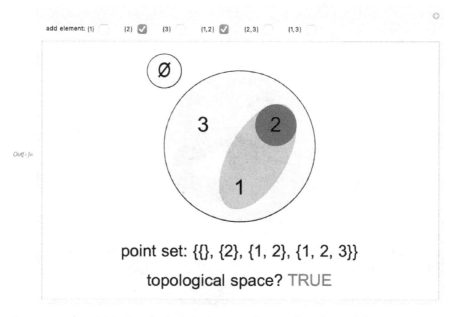

Out[ ]=

point set: {{}, {2}, {1, 2}, {1, 2, 3}}

topological space? TRUE

Demonstration 2.20: Topological Spaces on Three Points (https://demonstrations. wolfram.com/TopologicalSpacesOnThreePoints/)

2.25. Los Alamos Chess

This is not exactly applied mathematics, but it is something created by mathematicians: a simplified version of chess, played on a 6 × 6 (rather than 8 × 8) board without bishops. Pawns can move only one space forward, and there is consequently no *en passant* capture. In this modified version, castling is allowed, along with pawn promotion to a previously lost piece. There is no automation in this Demonstration. Players must make moves manually, by dragging a piece. Captured pieces must be dragged to the gray sideline. Just as in a non-computerized board game, players are responsible for making only legal moves and declaring "king in check", "checkmate", or "stalemate" when appropriate.

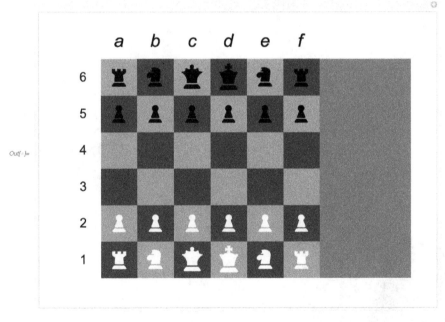

Demonstration 2.21: Los Alamos Chess (https://demonstrations.wolfram.com/Los AlamosChess/)

Back in 1956, I was a summer student at Los Alamos National Laboratory. This was the home of the MANIAC I, back then one of the most powerful computers in the world. Its main function was to perform intricate calculations of thermonuclear processes. Some of the resident computer scientists became interested in programming computers to play chess. Since even the MANIAC lacked the computational power to play a standard game, some simplified variations were considered. This was when I invented the 6×6 version of chess described in this Demonstration. After I left my summer job, a chess-playing program for MANIAC I was written by Stanislaw Ulam and colleagues. The program was successively improved for several years thereafter.

Chapter 3

Physics: Electromagnetism

Many of the principles and applications of electricity and magnetism can be described in Mathematica Demonstrations.

3.1. Electrical Circuits

3.1.1. *Ohm's Law*

Let us begin with Ohm's law, the most elementary description of electric circuits. Input the voltage *V* in volts and the resistance *R* in ohms to obtain the current *I* in amperes.

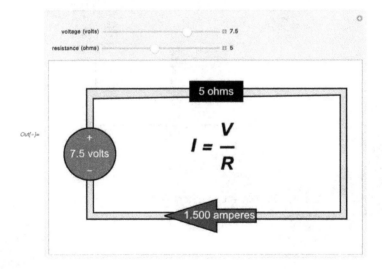

Demonstration 3.1: Ohm's Law (https://demonstrations.wolfram.com/OhmsLaw/)

3.1.2. *Parallel-Plate Capacitor*

The capacitance of a parallel-plate capacitor (or condenser) is given in SI units by $C = \varepsilon_0 \kappa_e A/d$, where A is the area of each plate, d is the spacing between plates, κ_e is the dielectric constant (relative permittivity), and ε_0 is the permittivity of free space, 8.85×10^{-12} farad/meter. If A is expressed in m^2 and d in mm, then $C = 8.85 \times 10^{-3}\kappa_e A/d$ microfarads (μF). Capacitance determines the quantity of positive and negative charges Q that can be held on the plates by a voltage V, such that $C = Q/V$. In an air-gap capacitor, in which there is no dielectric layer, $\kappa_e \approx 1$.

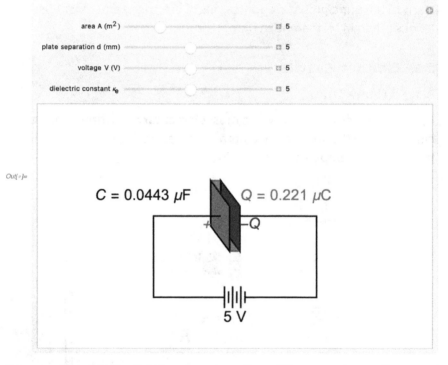

Out[ ]=

Demonstration 3.2: Parallel-Plate Capacitors (https://demonstrations.wolfram.com/ParallelPlateCapacitors/)

3.1.3. *Galvanometer*

In a D'Arsonval galvanometer, a disk wound with many turns of fine wire can rotate in the field of a permanent magnet, its deflection proportional to the current through the wire. A coil spring (not shown) provides a restoring torque to the disk. As part of an appropriate circuit, the galvanometer can function as a DC multimeter, measuring the voltage, current, or resistance of a connected circuit element, shown as a black rectangle. Depending on the mode selected — voltmeter, ammeter, or ohm-meter — the branch of the circuit shown in red is operative. As an illustration, let the resistance of the galvanometer R_G equal 20 Ω, while $R_V = 9980$ Ω and $R_A = 0.02$ Ω. This will enable the galvanometer to read voltages in the range -100 to 100 V and currents in the range -10 to 10 A. With an appropriate choice of R_0 and E_0, resistances in the range

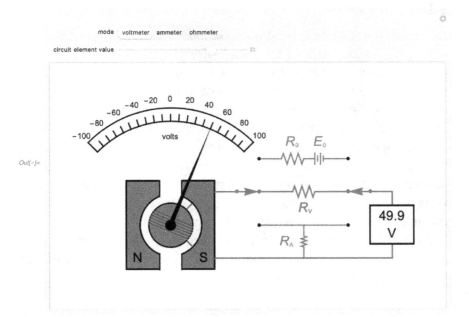

Demonstration 3.3: Galvanometer as a DC Multimeter (https://demonstrations. wolfram.com/GalvanometerAsADCMultimer/)

5 to 1000 Ω can likewise be measured. Note that the current through the galvanometer is inversely proportional to the resistance, thus the ohmmeter scale is linear in $1/R$.

The "circuit element value" slider controls the value of voltage, current or resistance, as shown in the box in the graphic. (Its numerical value corresponds to the angular displacement of the needle in radians.) The ranges of the three scales are adjusted by additional circuit elements, not shown in the diagram.

The rudimentary setup shown in this Demonstration is intended to show the general principles involved in the functioning of a multimeter. Modern instruments are based on solid-state components and can be adjusted for several different ranges of voltage, current and resistance. They can also handle AC, as well as DC, circuits.

3.1.4. *Transformer*

An electrical transformer is a device to change the voltage and amperage of alternating currents. In the simple design shown here, N_P primary wire coils (blue) and N_S secondary coils (red) are wound around a ferromagnetic core. An alternating current in the primary circuit creates a time-dependent magnetic field in the core, which, in turn, induces an alternating current in the secondary circuit, via Faraday's law of electromagnetic induction. The respective rms voltages are in the same ratio as the numbers of turns: $V_S/V_P = N_S/N_P$. If $N_S < N_P$, this acts as a step-down transformer. Long-distance transmission lines use high voltage and low currents to minimize energy losses. A sequence of step-down transformers then reduces the voltage to household levels (120 volts in the U.S.). If the secondary resistance and induction are negligibly small (simplified model), the primary and secondary currents are given by the reciprocal relation $i_P/i_S = N_S/N_P$.

If the load resistance R and inductance L_S are taken into account, the secondary current is affected by the impedance of the circuit. Details of the magnitude of i_S are omitted in this elementary discussion, except to note that the secondary voltage and current are no longer in phase, the current leading the voltage by the phase angle arctan $(2\pi f L_S/R)$.

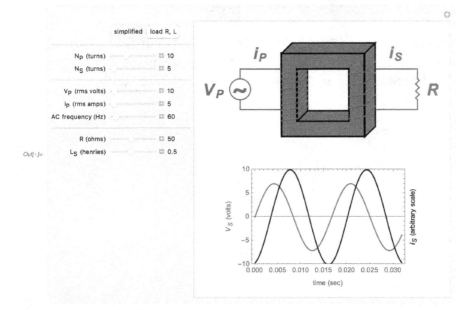

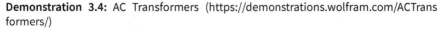

Demonstration 3.4: AC Transformers (https://demonstrations.wolfram.com/ACTransformers/)

3.1.5. *Lemon Batteries*

A rudimentary electrochemical cell can be constructed from two dissimilar metals immersed in an electrolyte. The lemon battery is a popular demonstrative example, with the highly acidic juicy insides providing an excellent electrolyte. The potential difference, usually of the order of a fraction of a volt, can be measured by a voltmeter connected to the two electrodes. The values shown in this Demonstration were determined by experiments in the author's laboratory. Combinations of three electrodes were tested: galvanized nails, pennies, and dimes, with compositions approximating those of zinc, copper, and silver, respectively. A positive voltage will be obtained if the left-hand electrode is the more electropositive metal. Reversing the electrodes (or voltmeter connections) gives the negative of the original reading. Two or more lemons can be connected in series to give multicell batteries.

The combinations Zn/Cu, Zn/Ag, Cu/Ag gave readings of 0.60, 0.73 and 0.13 V, respectively; if the corresponding pure metals under standard conditions were used, the values should be 1.10, 1.56 and 0.46 V.

Out[ ]=

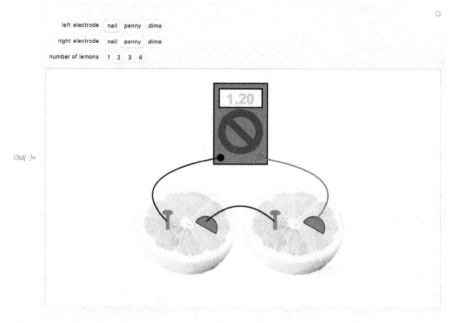

Demonstration 3.5: Lemon Batteries (https://demonstrations.wolfram.com/Lemon Batteries/)

3.1.6. *Electromagnetic Field Energies in Capacitors and Inductors*

A capacitor with square plates of width *a* separated by a distance *d* with a filler of dielectric constant (relative permittivity) κ has a capacitance given by $C = \kappa \varepsilon_0 a^2 / d$. Typical values are in the range of picofarads (pF). A voltage V can hold positive and negative charges $q = \pm CV$ on the plates of the capacitor while producing an internal electric field $E = V/d$. Assuming idealized geometry, the energy of a charged capacitor equals $\frac{1}{2}CV^2$. This energy can be considered to be stored in the electric

circuit element	capacitor	inductor
capacitor		
plate width a (cm)		2.5
plate separation d (cm)		4
dielectric constant κ		2
voltage V (volts)		5
inductor		
number of turns		10
radius r (cm)		2
length ℓ (cm)		6
resistance R (ohms)		0.5
voltage V (volts)		5

$Out[\circ]=$

$$C = 0.2767 \text{ pF}$$
$$E = 125. \text{ volts/m}$$
$$\rho_{elec} = 1.383 \times 10^{-7} \text{ joules/m}^3$$

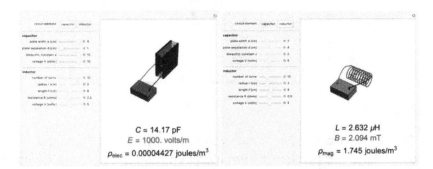

$C = 14.17$ pF
$E = 1000.$ volts/m
$\rho_{elec} = 0.00004427$ joules/m^3

$L = 2.632\ \mu H$
$B = 2.094$ mT
$\rho_{mag} = 1.745$ joules/m^3

Demonstration 3.6: Electromagnetic Field Energies in Capacitors and Inductors (https://demonstrations.wolfram.com/ElectromagneticFieldEnergiesInCapacitorsAnd Inductors/)

field, which implies a corresponding energy density $\rho_{elec} = \frac{1}{2}\varepsilon E^2$ (with $\varepsilon = \kappa\varepsilon_0$).

Next consider an air-core inductor, again assuming idealized geometry. The relative permeability κ_m is approximated as 1. The inductance of a helical conducting coil, as shown in the graphic, is then given by $L = \mu_0 n^2 \pi r^2/\ell$, where n is the number of turns. Typical values can be in the range of microhenries (μH). Considered as a solenoid, the inductor produces a magnetic field $B = \mu_0 n I/\ell$, when carrying a current $I = V/R$. The energy of the inductor equals $\frac{1}{2}LI^2$, which implies a magnetic-field energy density $\rho_{mag} = \frac{1}{2\mu_0}B^2$.

Combining the above results gives the well-known formula for the energy density of an electromagnetic field in a vacuum: $\rho_{em} = \frac{1}{2}(\varepsilon_0 E^2 + \mu_0^{-1}B^2)$. This is valid for electric and magnetic fields from any sources, notably for electromagnetic radiation.

3.2. AC Circuits

A number of important applications of differential equations involve alternating current (AC) circuits containing resistance R, inductance L, capacitance C and an oscillating voltage source V. A simple circuit is conventionally drawn like this:

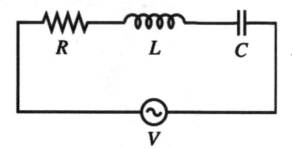

The simplest case is a circuit with resistance R and voltage V (or emf $\mathcal{E}$). The current I is then determined by Ohm's law $\mathcal{I} = \frac{\mathcal{E}}{R}$. We use the script symbols $\mathcal{I}$ and $\mathcal{E}$ for current and emf since the letters I and E are reserved in Mathematica. The standard units are amperes for $\mathcal{I}$, volts for $\mathcal{E}$, and ohms for R. The other relevant units are henrys for L and farads for *C*. Ohm's law is true even for an AC circuit, in which the voltage varies sinusoidally with time, say

$$\mathcal{E}(t) = \mathcal{E}_0 \cos \omega t.$$

The current is then given by

$$\mathcal{I}(t) = \frac{\mathcal{E}(t)}{R} = \frac{\mathcal{E}_0}{R} \cos \omega t = \mathcal{I}_0 \cos \omega t.$$

Thus the current through a resistance oscillates in phase with the voltage. The frequency ω is expressed in units of rad/s. It is also common to measure frequency ν in cycles/s, a unit called the hertz (Hz). Since one cycle traces out 2π radians, the two measures of frequency are related by $\omega = 2\pi\nu$. Thus the common US 60 Hz household voltage has an angular frequency of $\omega = 2\pi \times 60 \approx 377$ rad/s. The voltage change across an inductance is given by $Ld\mathcal{I}/dt$. Thus for a circuit with inductance, but negligible resistance, the analog of Ohm's law is

$$L\frac{d\mathcal{I}}{dt} = \varepsilon(t).$$

With an oscillating voltage $\mathcal{E}(t)$ above an initial current $\mathcal{I}(0) = 0$, this equation is easily integrated:

In[•]:= `DSolve[{L I'[t] == ε0 Cos[ω t], I[0] == 0}, I[t], t]`

Out[•]= $\left\{\left\{I[t] \to \dfrac{\varepsilon 0\ \text{Sin}[t\ \omega]}{L\ \omega}\right\}\right\}$

This can be written

$$\mathcal{I}(t) = \frac{\mathcal{E}_0}{X_L} \cos(\omega t - \pi/2),$$

where the *inductive reactance* $X_L = \omega L$ has the same units as *R*. For a DC voltage ($\omega = 0$), an inductor behaves just like an ordinary conductor. Note that the current is 90° out of phase with the voltage $\mathcal{E}(t) = \mathcal{E}_0 \cos \omega t$.

Specifically, for a pure inductance, the current *lags* the voltage by $\pi/2$. Alternatively stated, the voltage *leads* the current by $\pi/2$. Physically, this reflects the fact that the inductor builds up an opposing emf (by Lenz's law) in response to an increase in current.

For a circuit with capacitance C, the relevant relation is $\mathcal{E} = \frac{q}{C}$, where q (in coulombs) is the charge on the capacitor. In a DC circuit, no current can pass through a capacitor. For an AC circuit, however, with the current being given by $\mathcal{I} = dq/dt$, we find $\frac{d\mathcal{E}}{dt} = \frac{\mathcal{I}(t)}{C}$. Using the same oscillating voltage, we find (doing a derivative in our head!)

$$\mathcal{I}(t) = -\omega_C \mathcal{E}_0 \sin\omega t = \frac{\mathcal{E}_0}{X_C}\cos(\omega t + \pi/2),$$

where the *capacitive reactance* is defined by $X_C = 1/\omega C$. This shows that for a pure capacitance, the current *leads* the voltage by $\pi/2$. The mnemonic "ELI the ICEman" summarizes the phase relationships for inductance and capacitance: for L, $\mathcal{E}$ leads $\mathcal{I}$, while for C, $\mathcal{I}$ leads $\mathcal{E}$. This is shown graphically in the following plot, where $\mathcal{E}(t)$ represents the voltage, $\mathcal{I}(t)$ the current through an inductance and $\mathcal{I}_C(t)$ the current through a capacitance.

```
In[·]:= Manipulate[Plot[{ε0 Cos[ω t], ε0/(ω L) Cos[ω t - π / 2], ω C ε0 Cos[ω t + π / 2]},
        {t, 0, 10}, PlotTheme → "Scientific", GridLines → Automatic,
        PlotStyle → {Black, Red, Blue}, FrameLabel → {Style["t", Italic], "",
          Row[{Style[TraditionalForm[ε[t]], Black], Spacer[50], Style[TraditionalForm[
              Iₗ[t]], Red], Spacer[50], Style[TraditionalForm[I_C[t]], Blue]}]}],
      {{ε0, 1, "ε0"}, .5, 2, Appearance → "Labeled"},
      {{ω, 2, "ω"}, 1.5, 3, Appearance → "Labeled"},
      {{L, .5, Style["L", Italic]}, .25, 2, Appearance → "Labeled"},
      {{C, .5, Style["C", Italic]}, 0, 1.5, Appearance → "Labeled"}]
```

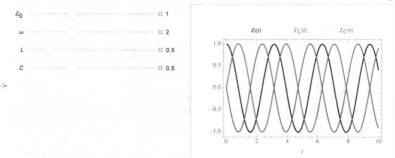

In an electrical circuit with both resistance and inductance, the current and voltage are related by

$$L\frac{d\mathcal{I}}{dt} + R\mathcal{I}(t) = \mathcal{E}(t).$$

Suppose that at time $t = 0$, while the current has the value $\mathcal{I}_0$, the voltage $\mathcal{E}$ is suddenly turned off. We can then solve:

In[∘]:= **DSolve[{L $\mathcal{I}$'[t] + R $\mathcal{I}$[t] == 0, $\mathcal{I}$[0] == $\mathcal{I}$0}, $\mathcal{I}$[t], t]**

Out[∘]= $\left\{\left\{ \mathcal{I}[t] \to e^{-\frac{Rt}{L}} \mathcal{I}0 \right\}\right\}$

Evidently the current decays exponentially: $\mathcal{I}(t) = \mathcal{I}_0 e^{-kt}$, with $k = R/L$. Now suppose the circuit is powered by an AC voltage $\mathcal{E}(t) = \mathcal{E}_0 \cos \omega t$. For convenience, assume $\mathcal{I}(0) = 0$. We now have an inhomogeneous differential equation:

In[∘]:= **DSolve[{L $\mathcal{I}$'[t] + R $\mathcal{I}$[t] == $\mathcal{E}$0 Cos[ω t], $\mathcal{I}$[0] == 0}, $\mathcal{I}$[t], t]**

Out[∘]= $\left\{\left\{ \mathcal{I}[t] \to \dfrac{e^{-\frac{Rt}{L}} \mathcal{E}0 \left(-R + e^{\frac{Rt}{L}} R \cos[t\,\omega] + e^{\frac{Rt}{L}} L\,\omega \sin[t\,\omega] \right)}{R^2 + L^2\,\omega^2} \right\}\right\}$

In[∘]:= **Expand[%]**

Out[∘]= $\left\{\left\{ \mathcal{I}[t] \to -\dfrac{e^{-\frac{Rt}{L}} R\,\mathcal{E}0}{R^2 + L^2\,\omega^2} + \dfrac{R\,\mathcal{E}0 \cos[t\,\omega]}{R^2 + L^2\,\omega^2} + \dfrac{L\,\mathcal{E}0\,\omega \sin[t\,\omega]}{R^2 + L^2\,\omega^2} \right\}\right\}$

The first term represents a transient current, which damps out as t increases. The remaining *steady state* current can be expressed as

$$\mathcal{I}(t) = \frac{\mathcal{E}_0}{R^2 + \omega^2 L^2}(R \cos \omega t + \omega L \sin \omega t) = \frac{\mathcal{E}_0}{R^2 + \omega^2 L^2}\cos(\omega t - \delta),$$

having written $R = \cos\delta$, $\omega L = \sin\delta$ and using $\cos\delta \cos\omega t + \sin\delta \sin\omega t = \cos(\omega t - \delta)$, so that $\delta = \arctan(\omega L / R)$. Following is a plot showing both the transient and steady state currents:

In[•]:= `Manipulate[Plot[` $\dfrac{\mathcal{E}0\,R}{R^2 + \omega^2\,L^2}$ `e`$^{-R\,t/L}$ `+` $\dfrac{\mathcal{E}0}{R^2 + \omega^2\,L^2}$ `Cos[` ω `t - ArcTan[` ω `L / R]],`

    `{t, 0, 15}, PlotTheme → "Scientific", GridLines → Automatic,`

    `FrameLabel → {Style["t", Italic], TraditionalForm[`I`[t]]}],`

    `{{`$\mathcal{E}0$`, 1, "`$\mathcal{E}_0$`"}, .5, 2, Appearance → "Labeled"},`

    `{{`ω`, 2, "`ω`"}, 1.5, 3, Appearance → "Labeled"},`

    `{{R, 1, Style["R", Italic]}, .5, 2, Appearance → "Labeled"},`

    `{{L, 1, Style["L", Italic]}, .25, 2, Appearance → "Labeled"}]`

Out[•]=

A very useful strategy when dealing with quantities having sinusoidal dependence takes advantage of Euler's theorem, in the form $e^{i\omega t} = \cos\omega t + i\sin\omega t$. Exponentials are much simpler to differentiate and integrate than sines and cosines. At the end of a computation, we extract the physically significant results from the real (and sometimes the imaginary) part of the result. For example,

$$\mathbf{Re}\ e^{i\omega t} = \cos\omega t, \quad \mathbf{Im}\ e^{i\omega t} = \sin\omega t.$$

Suppose the AC voltage above is replaced by the complex form $\mathcal{E}(t) = \mathcal{E}_0 e^{i\omega t}$. The equation for the driven RL circuit above is then written in the form:

$$L\frac{d\mathcal{I}}{dt} + R\mathcal{I}(t) = \mathcal{E}_0 e^{i\omega t}.$$

In[•]:= `DSolve[{L `I`'[t] + R `I`[t] == `$\mathcal{E}0$` e`$^{i\,\omega\,t}$`, `I`[0] == 0}, `I`[t], t]`

Out[•]= $\left\{\left\{I[t] \rightarrow \dfrac{e^{-\frac{R\,t}{L}}\left(-1 + e^{\frac{t\,(R+i\,L\,\omega)}{L}}\right)\mathcal{E}0}{R + i\,L\,\omega}\right\}\right\}$

In[•]:= **Expand[%]**

Out[•]= $\left\{\left\{\mathcal{I}[t] \to -\dfrac{e^{-\frac{Rt}{L}} \, \mathcal{E}0}{R + i\,L\,\omega} + \dfrac{e^{-\frac{Rt}{L} + \frac{t\,(R + i\,L\,\omega)}{L}} \, \mathcal{E}0}{R + i\,L\,\omega}\right\}\right\}$

Defining the *complex impedance*

$$Z = R + i\omega L = R + iX_L,$$

this can be simplified to

$$\mathcal{I}(t) = \frac{V_0}{Z}e^{-Rt/L} + \frac{V_0}{Z}e^{i\omega t}.$$

This can be compacted even further, if we wish, by defining a complex frequency $\Omega = \omega + i\frac{R}{L}$ with a generalized complex voltage $\mathcal{E}(t) = \mathcal{E}_0 e^{i\Omega t}$. We then have $\mathcal{I}(t) = \frac{\varepsilon(t)}{Z}$, which is a complex generalization of Ohm's law $\mathcal{I} = \frac{\mathcal{E}}{R}$.

Circuits containing R, L, and C involve second-order differential equations, which we consider next.

3.3. AC Circuits (Continued)

The behavior of an RLC circuit is closely analogous to that of an oscillating spring. The circuit equation can be written

$$L\frac{d\mathcal{I}}{dt} + R\mathcal{I} + \frac{q}{C} = \mathcal{E}.$$

Since $\mathcal{I} = \frac{dq}{dt}$, the time derivative of the equation leads to a more useful form:

$$L\frac{d^2\mathcal{I}}{dt^2} + R\frac{d\mathcal{I}}{dt} + \frac{I}{C} = \frac{d\mathcal{E}}{dt}.$$

Let us use the complex exponential form for the driving voltage $\mathcal{E}(t) = \mathcal{E}_0 e^{i\omega t}$.

In[ ]:= `DSolve[L I''[t] + R I'[t] + `$\frac{I[t]}{C}$` == i ω ε0 e`^{iωt}`, I[t], t]`

Out[ ]= $\left\{\left\{I[t] \rightarrow \left(2 C L \varepsilon 0 \omega \left(\sqrt{C} e^{\frac{1}{2}\left(-\frac{R}{L}+\frac{\sqrt{-4L+CR^2}}{\sqrt{C}L}\right)t+\frac{t\left(R-\frac{\sqrt{-4L+CR^2}}{\sqrt{C}}+2iL\omega\right)}{2L}} \middle/ R - \right.\right.\right.\right.$

$\sqrt{C} e^{\frac{1}{2}\left(-\frac{R}{L}-\frac{\sqrt{-4L+CR^2}}{\sqrt{C}L}\right)t+\frac{t\left(R+\frac{\sqrt{-4L+CR^2}}{\sqrt{C}}+2iL\omega\right)}{2L}} \middle/ R + e^{\frac{1}{2}\left(-\frac{R}{L}+\frac{\sqrt{-4L+CR^2}}{\sqrt{C}L}\right)t+\frac{t\left(R-\frac{\sqrt{-4L+CR^2}}{\sqrt{C}}+2iL\omega\right)}{2L}} \sqrt{-4L+CR^2} +$

$e^{\frac{1}{2}\left(-\frac{R}{L}-\frac{\sqrt{-4L+CR^2}}{\sqrt{C}L}\right)t+\frac{t\left(R+\frac{\sqrt{-4L+CR^2}}{\sqrt{C}}+2iL\omega\right)}{2L}} \sqrt{-4L+CR^2} + 2i\sqrt{C} e^{\frac{1}{2}\left(-\frac{R}{L}+\frac{\sqrt{-4L+CR^2}}{\sqrt{C}L}\right)t+\frac{t\left(R-\frac{\sqrt{-4L+CR^2}}{\sqrt{C}}+2iL\omega\right)}{2L}} L\omega -$

$\left. 2i\sqrt{C} e^{\frac{1}{2}\left(-\frac{R}{L}-\frac{\sqrt{-4L+CR^2}}{\sqrt{C}L}\right)t+\frac{t\left(R+\frac{\sqrt{-4L+CR^2}}{\sqrt{C}}+2iL\omega\right)}{2L}} L\omega \right) \middle/$

$\left(\sqrt{-4L+CR^2}\left(i\sqrt{C}R+i\sqrt{-4L+CR^2}-2\sqrt{C}L\omega\right)\left(-\sqrt{C}R+\sqrt{-4L+CR^2}-2i\sqrt{C}L\omega\right)\right) +$

$\left.\left.e^{\frac{1}{2}\left(-\frac{R}{L}-\frac{\sqrt{-4L+CR^2}}{\sqrt{C}L}\right)t} c_1 + e^{\frac{1}{2}\left(-\frac{R}{L}+\frac{\sqrt{-4L+CR^2}}{\sqrt{C}L}\right)t} c_2 \right\}\right\}$

In[ ]:= `Simplify[%]`

Out[ ]= $\left\{\left\{I[t] \rightarrow \frac{1}{-i + C\omega(R + iL\omega)} e^{-\frac{\left(R+\frac{\sqrt{-4L+CR^2}}{\sqrt{C}}\right)t}{2L}}\right.\right.$

$\left.\left.\left(-i\left(c_1 + e^{\frac{\sqrt{-4L+CR^2}t}{\sqrt{C}L}} c_2\right) + C\omega\left(e^{\frac{\left(R-\frac{\sqrt{-4L+CR^2}}{\sqrt{C}}\right)t}{2L}+it\omega}\varepsilon0 + (R+iL\omega)c_1 + e^{\frac{\sqrt{-4L+CR^2}t}{\sqrt{C}L}}(R+iL\omega)c_2\right)\right)\right\}\right\}$

Setting c_1 and c_2 equal to 0 removes the transients, leaving the the steady state solution,

In[ ]:= `% /. {c`$_1$` → 0, c`$_2$` → 0}`

Out[ ]= $\left\{\left\{I[t] \rightarrow \frac{C e^{it\omega} \varepsilon0\ \omega}{-i + C\omega(R+iL\omega)}\right\}\right\}$

This can be written more compactly, as a generalization of Ohm's law

$$\mathcal{I}(t) = \frac{\mathcal{E}(t)}{Z},$$

where Z is the complex impedence

$$Z = R + iX = R + i(X_L + X_C) = R + i\left(\omega L - \frac{1}{\omega C}\right).$$

This can be expressed in polar form as $Z = \sqrt{R^2 + X^2}e^{i\delta}$, with $\delta = \arctan\frac{X}{R}$.

3.4. Electric and Magnetic Fields

3.4.1. *Point Charges*

In an earlier Demonstration, two-dimensional equipotential contours $\phi(x, y)$, representing cross sections of equipotential surfaces, were plotted for two point charges of variable magnitude and location. It was also possible to make a vector plot of the corresponding electric field $\mathbf{E}(x, y)$. It is much trickier to plot the lines of force emanating from a positive point charge and converging on a negative point charge. These are everywhere tangent to the electric field vectors and form a set of contours $\Psi(x, y)$, shown as red curves, everywhere orthogonal to the equipotentials $\Phi(x, y)$, shown in gray.

Derivation of $\psi(x, y)$ is quite complicated in either Cartesian or spherical coordinates. It is, however, straightforward in prolate ellipsoidal coordinates defined by the variables $\xi = (r_1 + r_2)/R$ and $\eta = (r_1 - r_2)/R$. Here r_1 and r_2 are the distances from the field point to charges q_1 and q_2,

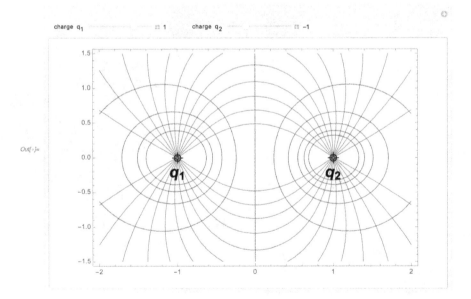

Demonstration 3.7: Lines of Force for Two Point Charges (https://demonstrations. wolfram.com/LinesOfForceForTwoPointCharges/)

respectively, and R is the distance between the two charges. Expressed in the Cartesian coordinates of the graphic: $r_1 = \sqrt{(x - x_1)^2 + (y - y_1)^2}$, $r_2 = \sqrt{(x - x_2)^2 + (y - y_2)}$, $R = \sqrt{(x_2 - x_1)^2 + (y_2 - y_1)^2}$. The equipotentials are given by $\phi(\xi, \eta) = \frac{q_1}{2R(\xi+\eta)} + \frac{q_2}{2R(\xi-\eta)}$. The function $\psi(\xi, \eta)$ representing the orthogonal network of lines of force must then satisfy the equation $\nabla\phi(\xi, \eta) \cdot \nabla\psi(\xi, \eta) = 0$. The solution $\psi(\xi, \eta) = \frac{1}{\xi^2-\eta^2}[q_1(\xi - \eta + \xi^2\eta - \xi\eta^2) + q_2(-\eta + \xi^2\eta + -\xi + \xi\eta^2)]$, transformed back to Cartesian coordinates, is represented by the red contour plot shown in the graphic.

3.4.2. *Electric Fields for Three Point Charges*

The electric field of a point charge q at r_0 is given (in Gaussian units) by $E(r) = q(r - r_0)/|r - r_0|^3$. The lines of force representing this field radiate outward from a positive charge and converge inward toward a

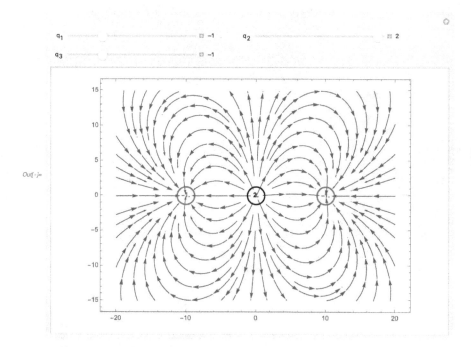

Demonstration 3.8: Electric Fields for Three Point Charges (https://demonstrations.wolfram.com/ElectricFieldsForThreePointCharges/)

negative charge. The composite field of several charges is the vector sum of the individual fields. In this Demonstration, you can move the three charges, shown as small circles, and vary their electric charges to generate a stream plot of the electric field.

3.4.3. *Parallel Line Charges*

The electrostatic potential in an $x - y$ plane for an infinite line charge in the z direction with linear density λ is given by $\phi(x, y) = -2\lambda\log(x^2 + y^2)$. We use Gaussian units for compactness. The zero of potential is evidently the value on the circle $x^2 + y^2 = 1$. For two parallel line charges, with linear densities λ_1 and λ_2, intersecting the plane at $(-R, 0)$ and $(R, 0)$, respectively, the potential function generalizes to: $\phi(x, y) = -2\lambda_1\log((x+R)^2 + y^2) - 2\lambda_2\log((x - R)^2 + y^2)$.

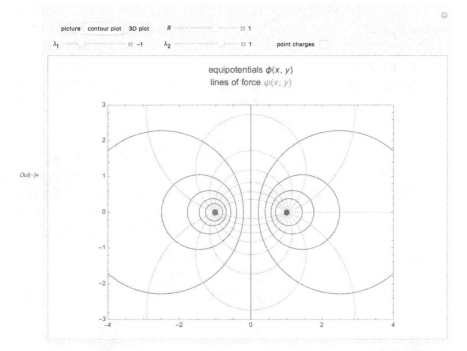

Demonstration 3.9: Potential and Lines of Force for Two Parallel Infinite Line Charges (https://demonstrations.wolfram.com/PotentialAndLinesOfForceForTwoParallelInfinite LineCharges/)

For selected values of R, λ_1 and λ_2, selecting "contour plot" shows the equipotentials of $\phi(x, y)$. For $\lambda_1 = \lambda_2$, the equipotentials have the form of Cassini ovals. Also shown as green contours are the orthogonal trajectories $\psi(x, y)$, which represent the electrostatic lines of force. These are given by $\psi(x, y) = -4\lambda_1 \arctan\left(\frac{Y}{X+R}\right) - 4\lambda_2 \arctan\left(\frac{Y}{X-R}\right)$.

A 3D plot of the potential contours is also available. Click the checkbox to display, for purposes of comparison, the analogous equipotentials and lines of force for two point charges q_1 and q_2 replacing the line charges.

3.4.4. *Method of Images*

The potential of a point charge in the neighborhood of a grounded conductor is given by a solution of Laplace's equation $\nabla^2\phi = 0$, subject to the boundary condition that $\phi = 0$ on the surface of the conductor. This solution is unique in the region enclosed by the conductor. Adding charges outside that region, which reproduce the same boundary conditions, can alternatively lead to a valid solution to the original problem. Under certain favorable conditions, it is possible to apply the method of images, in which one or more image charges of specified magnitude can be strategically placed to enable the Laplace equation with the given boundary conditions to be more easily solved.

Two classic examples are considered in this Demonstration. A point charge q located at r_0 near an infinite grounded plane conductor at $x = 0$ has the same potential distribution as a pair of charges q and $-q$ symmetrically placed with respect to the plane. The potential is then given by $\phi(r) = \frac{q}{4\pi\varepsilon_0}\left(\frac{1}{|r-r_0|} - \frac{1}{|r+r_0|}\right)$. The labeled equipotentials in the contour plot can be multiplied by $\frac{q}{4\pi\varepsilon_0}$ to give their actual values. A point charge q at r_0 either inside or outside a grounded spherical conductor of radius r, centered at the origin, can be solved by placing an image charge $-q' = -\frac{r}{|r_0|}q$ at $r' = \frac{r^2}{(|r_0|)^2}r_0$.

You can drag the locator to move the point charge q. A checkbox enables you to see the image charge q'. It will go off-scale if the locator is too close to the center of the sphere, but it still contributes to the potential.

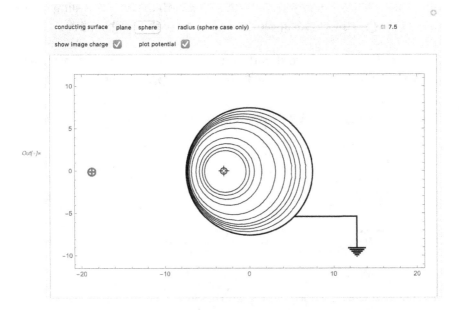

conducting surface   plane   sphere   radius (sphere case only) .... 🔲 7.5

show image charge ✅   plot potential ✅

Out[ ]=

Demonstration 3.10: Method of Images in Electrostatics (https://demonstrations. wolfram.com/MethodOfImagesInElectrostatics/)

3.4.5. *Potential of a Charged Spheroid*

This Demonstration shows the electrostatic potential of a uniformly charged spheroid. We consider both prolate spheroids, with $a = b < c$, and oblate spheroids, with $a = b > c$. Here a, b, c are the semi-axes, with the c axis oriented horizontally. The potential is cylindrically symmetrical and it suffices to show just the plane containing the c axis. The potential external to the spheroid is given by $\Phi(\mathbf{r}) = \frac{q}{4\pi\varepsilon_0} \int \frac{1}{|\mathbf{r}-\mathbf{r}'|} d^3 \mathbf{r}' = \frac{1}{4\pi\varepsilon_0} \left(\frac{q}{r} + \frac{1}{4}Q\frac{3Z^2-r^2}{r^5} + \ldots \right)$, the sum representing a multipole expansion over the charge distribution. For an oblate or prolate spheroid, the monopole contribution is dominant, with only the quadrupole term making a significant additional contribution to the potential. The quadrupole moment of a charged spheroid is given by $Q = Q_{zz} = \frac{2}{5}q(a^2 - c^2)$.

You can select the semi-axes a and c to display a scaled contour plot of the potential. Multiply by $q/4\pi\varepsilon_0$ to find the actual potential. The same result pertains to a gravitational potential, with *GM* as the scaling factor. You can isolate the quadrupole contribution with the checkbox.

The potential of a spheroid with unit charge $q = 1$, thus density $\varrho = 1/\frac{4}{3}\pi a^2 c$, expressed in cylindrical coordinates ρ, z, is given by

$$\frac{4}{3}\Phi(\rho, z) = \left(1 + \frac{\rho^2 - 2z^2}{2(c^2 - a^2)}\right)\sinh^{-1}\sqrt{\frac{c^2 - a^2}{a^2 + k}}$$

$$-\frac{\sqrt{c^2 + k\rho^2}}{(c^2 - a^2)(a^2 + k)} + \frac{2z^2}{(c^2 - a^2)\sqrt{c^2 + k}},$$

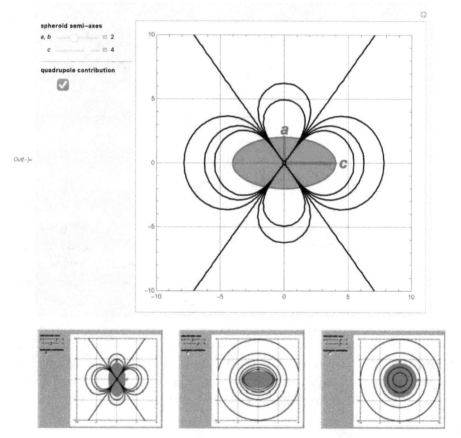

Demonstration 3.11: Potential of a Charged Spheroid (https://demonstrations. wolfram.com/PotentialOfAChargedSpheroid/)

where κ is determined by the quadratic equation $\frac{\rho^2}{a^2+k} + \frac{z^2}{c^2+k} = 1$, taking the positive sign of the square root.

3.4.6. *Magnetic Field of a Current Loop*

An electrical current I moving around a circular loop of radius a, shown in yellow from a lateral point of view, produces a magnetic field, with lines of force shown as blue loops. For clarity, only lines of force in the vertical plane bisecting the ring $(y = 0)$ are shown.

The strength of the magnetic field is indicated by the density of the lines of force. The magnitude is expressed in units of $\mu_0/4\pi$. The field is cylindrically symmetrical about the axis of the ring. By a right-hand rule, a counter-clockwise current produces magnetic lines of force that point upward inside the ring, downward outside the ring. At distances $r \gg a$,

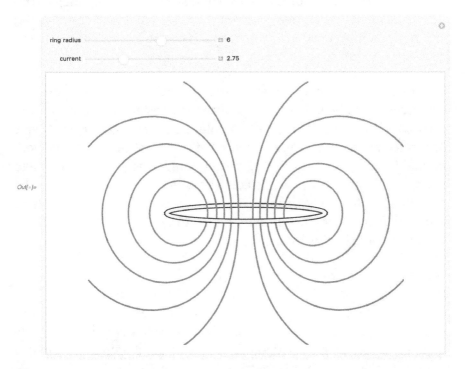

Demonstration 3.12: Magnetic Field of a Current Loop (https://demonstrations.wolfram.com/MagneticFieldOfACurrentLoop/)

the ring behaves like a magnetic dipole $\mathbf{m} = \pi a^2 \mathbf{I}$, with vector potential $\mathbf{A} = \frac{\mu_0}{4\pi} \frac{\mathbf{m} * \mathbf{r}}{r^3}$. As $a \to 0$ (with $a^2 I$ constant), this approaches the field of a point magnetic dipole.

The contour plot of the vector potential $A_\phi(x, z)$ in the $y = 0$ plane coincides with the magnetic lines of force.

3.4.7. *Magnetic Field of a Bar Magnet*

A bar magnet is often approximated simply as a magnetic dipole with north and south magnetic poles separated by a distance L. This is not accurate when the magnet has a significant size, so that magnetic lines of force also emanate from the central portion of the magnet. In this Demonstration, we consider a cylindrical bar magnet of length L, radius a, and magnetization M — the magnetic moment per unit volume, which is characteristic of the ferromagnetic material. The magnetization is assumed to be uniform throughout the volume of the magnet, which neglects slight inhomogeneities and possible deviations from the assumed relation $dB/dH = $ constant.

The magnetic induction outside the magnet can conveniently be expressed as the negative gradient of a magnetostatic potential: $\mathbf{B}(\mathbf{r}) = -\nabla \Phi_m(\mathbf{r})$. For a point magnetic dipole $\mathbf{m}$, $\Phi_m(\mathbf{r}) = \frac{\mu_0}{4\pi} \mathbf{m} \cdot \mathbf{r}/r^3$. This is integrated over the volume of the magnet. It is most convenient to work in cylindrical coordinates: R, Φ, Z for the source and ρ, ϕ, z for the field point (ϕ can arbitrarily be set equal to 0, in view of the anticipated cylindrical symmetry). A simplifying feature is that integration over Z shows that the problem can be reduced to two magnetic monopolar disks separated by the distance L.

For ease of visualization, only the field lines in the medial plane of the magnet are shown. The three-dimensional field can easily be pictured by virtue of the cylindrical symmetry about the Z axis. The lines of force originate from the north pole on the right and terminate at the south pole on the left. Magnetic-induction magnitudes are not emphasized in this Demonstration, only the geometry of field lines.

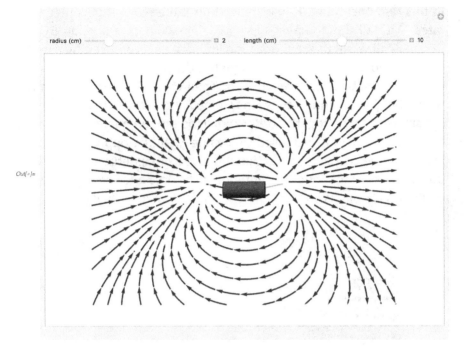

Demonstration 3.13: Magnetic Field of a Cylindrical Bar Magnet (https://demonstra
tions.wolfram.com/MagneticFieldOfACylindricalBarMagnet/)

3.4.8. *Magnetic Hysteresis*

Ferromagnetic materials exhibit hysteresis, meaning dependence of
magnetization on the history of the applied magnetic field. A ferromag-
net can thus be described as exhibiting memory of its previous magnetic
states. A sample of iron is comprised of domains, microscopic regions
in which the atomic magnets are locally aligned. These are represented
in the graphic by blue arrows. In the unmagnetized state, the domains
are randomly oriented. When an external magnetic field H, expressed
in units of amperes/meter (A/m), is applied, the domains begin to align
themselves in the direction of the magnetic field. The iron becomes
magnetized, acquiring a magnetic flux density (or magnetic induction)
B, expressed in units of tesla (T).

In this Demonstration, H is increased until the magnet becomes saturated, with all the domains aligned for a maximum induction B_S. The iron bar will retain its magnetization indefinitely, even after the external field is removed. In order to demagnetize the bar, a magnetic field in the opposite direction must be applied. The iron resists demagnetization, with B lagging behind changes in H. When H is reduced to zero, the flux density is reduced slightly to B_R, known as the remanence. Only when the magnetic field is increased to a value H_C in the opposite direction, known as the coercivity, does the iron lose its magnetization and do its domains return to random orientations. The area enclosed by one cycle on the B vs. H plot is equal to the energy dissipated as heat.

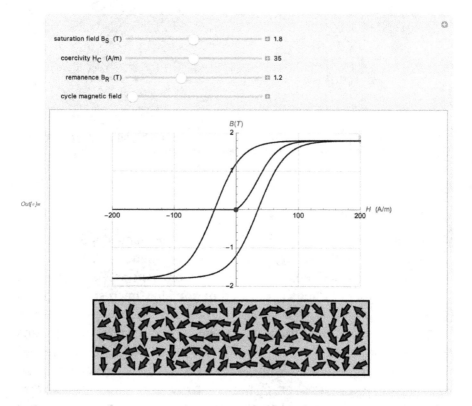

Demonstration 3.14: Magnetic Hysteresis (https://demonstrations.wolfram.com/MagneticHysteresis/)

The parameters in this Demonstration are representative of many iron alloys (including steels). Other magnetic materials, including rare-earth elements such as neodymium, are capable of much higher magnetic fluxes. The slider that cycles the magnetic field represents possible physical behavior only when moved from left to right.

3.4.9. *Ampère's Force Law*

Ampère's force law for parallel currents can be regarded as an analog of Coulomb's law for charges. The force per unit length between two current elements separated by a distance r is given by $\frac{dF}{dL} = -2\frac{\mu_0}{4\pi}\frac{I_1 I_2}{r} = -2 \times 10^{-7}\frac{I_1 I_2}{r}$, where μ_0 is the permeability of free space. In contrast to Coulomb's law, parallel current elements attract (signified by the minus sign) while opposing currents repel. The formal SI definition of the ampere is "the constant current which will produce an attractive force

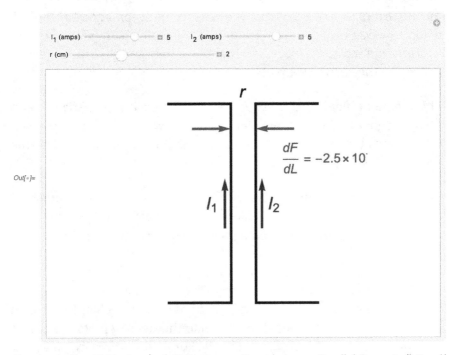

Demonstration 3.15: Ampère's Force Law — Force between Parallel Currents (https://demonstrations.wolfram.com/AmperesForceLawForceBetweenParallelCurrents/)

of 2×10^{-7} newtons per meter of length between two straight, parallel conductors of infinite length and negligible circular cross section placed one meter apart in a vacuum."

Ampère's force law is a consequence of the Lorentz force on the moving charge in each current element acted upon by the magnetic field produced by the other current element: $\mathbf{F} = q\mathbf{v} \times \mathbf{B}$.

3.4.10. *Fields of Magnet Array*

This Demonstration shows the magnetic fields produced by five 1 cm cubic magnets in a linear array. The magnets are held together by a copper axle (not shown), which keeps them from repelling one another but still allows each magnet to be rotated independently. (It is determined in advance which magnets can rotate with their dipoles parallel or normal to the axis.) The magnets have a field strength B (more precisely, a magnetic remanence B_r) that can be selected between 1 and 10 T. Strong fields can be produced by "rare earth" magnets such as neodymium or samarium-cobalt. Since these are extremely brittle and subject to corrosion, they are nickel-plated.

The magnetic field of a small cube is quite well approximated as a point magnetic dipole located at its center, with one of six specified orientations along the coordinate axes, $\pm\mathbf{i}, \pm\mathbf{j}, \pm\mathbf{k}$, designated by the symbols $\rightarrow, \leftarrow, \uparrow, \downarrow, \odot, \otimes$, respectively.

The magnetic induction can be expressed in terms of a magnetostatic potential $\Phi(\mathbf{r})$, using $\mathbf{B}(\mathbf{r}) = -\mu_0 \nabla \Phi(\mathbf{r})$. For our array of dipoles, $\Phi(\mathbf{r}) = \sum_{i=1}^{5} \frac{\mathbf{m}_i \cdot (\mathbf{r} - \mathbf{r}_i)}{4\pi(\mathbf{r} - \mathbf{r}_i)^3}$, where $\mathbf{m}_i$ is the magnetic moment of the ith cube.

You can choose a graphic showing a stream plot for the magnetic lines of force or a density plot giving the magnitude of the magnetic field, with higher field intensity represented by regions of darker blue. The stream plots are scaled proportional to μ_0, while the density plots are scaled for maximum variation in color intensity. For visual simplicity, only the x and y components in the medial plane are included, representing a cross section in the $z = 0$ plane.

One particularly interesting array was created by Klaus Halbach (ca. 1980) for possible application in particle accelerators. With the sequence of orientations $\{\rightarrow, \otimes, \leftarrow, \odot, \rightarrow\}$, or, rotated by 90°, $\{\rightarrow, \uparrow, \leftarrow, \downarrow, \rightarrow\}$, the magnetic field is large on one side of the array and close to zero on the opposite side.

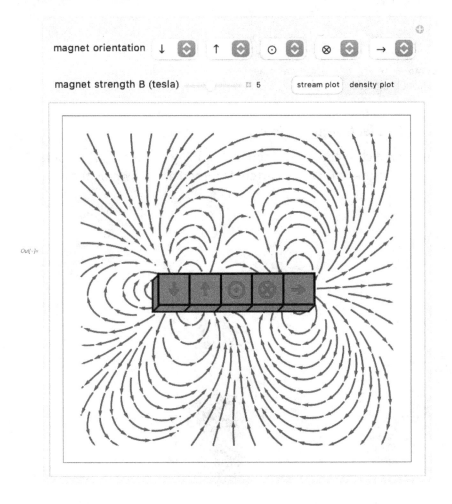

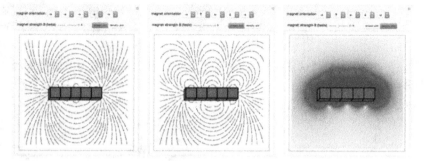

Demonstration 3.16: Fields of Magnet Array (https://demonstrations.wolfram.com/FieldsOfMagnetArray/)

3.4.11. *Electromagnetic Ring Toss*

Suppose a copper (or other conducting) ring is resting on one pole of an electromagnet. When the current is turned on (shown by the red circuit

Demonstration 3.17: Electromagnetic Ring Toss (https://demonstrations.wolfram.com/ElectromagneticRingToss/)

coloring), the ring will fly off the magnet. This is a consequence of Faraday's law of electromagnetic induction. A time-varying magnetic field will induce a circulating current in the ring. The magnetic field thereby produced will cause the ring to be repelled by the electromagnet. This will not happen if a radial slit is cut through the ring, thus preventing any current circulation. For purposes of visualization, the action is shown in slow motion and the disk is stopped in midair before it falls back to the ground.

3.5. Maxwell's Equations

To anyone versed in science, the immense range of physical phenomena that can be encoded in Maxwell's four relatively compact equations is breathtaking. Added to this is the remarkable symmetry between electric and magnetic variables and the fundamental underlying symmetry inherent in the special theory of relativity. One suggested measure of elegance is whether the equations can fit nicely on a T-shirt.

This Demonstration exhibits several formulations of Maxwell's equations. The least compact form is written as eight partial differential equations for the components of the electric and magnetic fields. These can be compacted to the familiar set of four vector equations. Even greater compactness can be achieved by transformation to four-vector or tensor notation, and the ultimate reduction, using spacetime algebra, expresses the theory as a single equation, written $\nabla \mathbf{F} = \mu_0 c \mathbf{j}$.

The equations will be exhibited in both SI and Gaussian forms. Beauty aside, this Demonstration can provide a convenient reference for the various versions of Maxwell's equations. For the component and vector forms, the forms of the equations in material media are also displayed. The physical significance of the four Maxwell equations are: (1) Gauss's law; (2) nonexistence of magnetic monopoles; (3) Faraday's law of induction; and (4) Ampère's law augmented by Maxwell's displacement current.

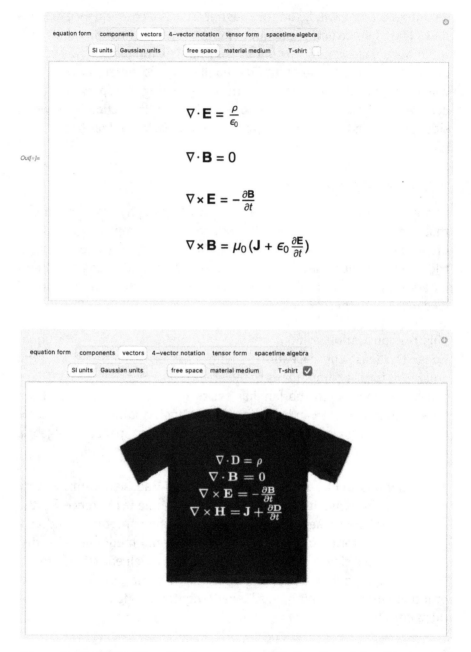

Demonstration 3.18: Alternative Forms of Maxwell's Equations (https://demonstrati ons.wolfram.com/AlternativeFormsOfMaxwellsEquations/)

3.5.1. *Maxwell's Displacement Current*

According to Ampere's law, the line integral of the magnetic field **H** around a closed loop equals the total free current passing through the loop: $\oint \mathbf{H} \cdot d\mathbf{s} = I_{free}$. In the Demonstration graphic, magnetic lines of force are shown as blue loops while the free electric current is shown as a red arrow. Ampere's law can be expressed in differential form as $\nabla \times \mathbf{H} = \mathbf{J}_{free}$, where **J** is the current density. The vector identity $\nabla \cdot \nabla \times \mathbf{H} = 0$ implies the steady-state limit of the equation of continuity: $\nabla \cdot \mathbf{J} = 0$. Maxwell recognized that the more general form of the equation of continuity $\nabla \cdot \mathbf{J} + \frac{\partial \rho}{\partial t} = 0$, where ρ is the charge density, requires a modification of Ampere's law. Substituting from the first of Maxwell's equations, $\nabla \cdot \mathbf{D} = \rho$, Ampere's law can be generalized to $\nabla \times \mathbf{H} = \mathbf{J} + \frac{\partial \mathbf{D}}{\partial t}$, which becomes the third of Maxwell's equations. The added term is known as the displacement current since it involves the rate of change of the dielectric displacement **D**. This provides a mechanism whereby a

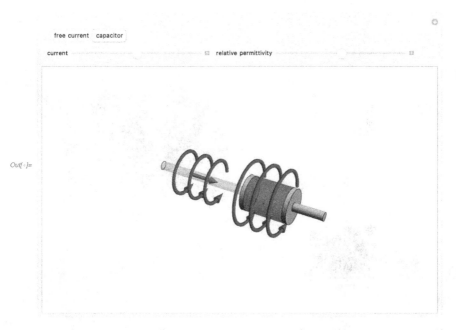

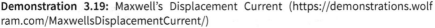

Demonstration 3.19: Maxwell's Displacement Current (https://demonstrations.wolf ram.com/MaxwellsDisplacementCurrent/)

time-varying electric field can create a magnetic field, complementary to Faraday's law, in which a time-varying magnetic field can produce an electric field. What Maxwell called the "mutual embrace" of electric and magnetic fields can produce propagating electromagnetic waves. This would not be possible without the displacement current.

3.5.2. *Faraday's Law*

According to Faraday's law of electromagnetic induction, an electro-motive force (emf) is induced in a conducting coil by a time-varying magnetic flux through the coil. This can be written $\mathcal{E} = -\frac{d\Phi}{dt}$, where the magnetic flux through the coil is given by $\Phi = \int \mathbf{B} \cdot d\sigma$. For a circular search coil of radius R wound with N turns of wire, $\Phi = \pi R^2 N B \cos\theta$, where θ is the angle of the coil to the magnetic induction $\mathbf{B}$, which is assumed uniform over its cross section, although variable over time.

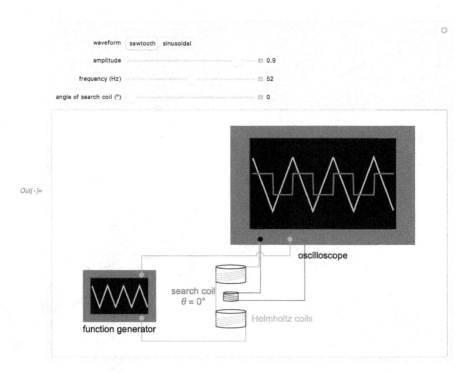

Demonstration 3.20: Showing Faraday's Law with an Oscilloscope (https://demonstrati ons.wolfram.com/ShowingFaradaysLawWithAnOscilloscope/)

The function generator varies the voltage through the Helmholtz coils, which produces a time-dependent magnetic induction $B(t)$ mirroring the signal profile. The induced signal is then proportional to the time derivative of the input signal, thus depending linearly on both its amplitude and frequency. Both the function generator and oscilloscope show stroboscopic plots of voltage versus time. The dual-trace oscilloscope can show both signals simultaneously, and we have taken the liberty of coloring the search-coil signal red.

3.5.3. *Magnetic Monopoles*

To date, there is no conclusive experimental evidence for the existence of magnetic monopoles, the magnetic analog of electric charges. All known magnetic effects arise from magnetic dipoles or from electrical currents. Much of the interest in magnetic monopoles started with a proposal by P. A. M. Dirac in 1931 that if even one magnetic monopole exists in the Universe, a necessary consequence is the quantization of electric charge. Several theories beyond the Standard Model, proposed by 't Hooft, Polyakov, and others, also predict the existence of monopoles. Magnetic monopoles added to Maxwell's equations would create a theory of higher symmetry than the present version of electrodynamics.

This Demonstration is concerned with the interaction between a classical electric charge and a magnetic monopole. The problem was actually solved a long time ago by Poincaré. For historical continuity, we use Gaussian electromagnetic units. The field of a point monopole of magnetic charge g is given by $\mathbf{B} = g\mathbf{r}/r^3$, in complete analogy with Coulomb's law for an electric charge. The Lorentz force on an electron of mass m and charge $-e$ moving with velocity $\mathbf{v}$ is then $\mathbf{F} = -\frac{e}{c}\mathbf{v} \times \mathbf{B}$, leading to Newton's equation of motion $m\ddot{\mathbf{r}} = -\frac{ge}{c}\frac{\dot{\mathbf{r}} \times \mathbf{r}}{r^3}$.

The equations of motion can be completely solved with a few vector operations. Taking the scalar product with $\dot{\mathbf{r}}$, we have $\dot{\mathbf{r}} \cdot \ddot{\mathbf{r}} = 0 = \frac{1}{2}\frac{d}{dt}(\dot{\mathbf{r}} \cdot \dot{\mathbf{r}})$; therefore $\dot{\mathbf{r}} \cdot \dot{\mathbf{r}} = 0 = v^2 = \text{const}$, so that the speed of the electron v is a constant (for $t > 0$). Taking the scalar product with $\mathbf{r}$ gives $\mathbf{r} \cdot \ddot{\mathbf{r}} = 0$, so that $\frac{d}{dt}(\mathbf{r} \cdot \dot{\mathbf{r}}) == v^2$, with the solution $r(t) = \sqrt{r_0^2 + v^2 t^2}$, where $r(0) = r_0$, the initial separation of the electron and monopole and $\dot{r}(0) = 0$.

Taking the vector product of **r** with Newton's equation, we find $m\mathbf{r} \times \ddot{\mathbf{r}} = \frac{d}{dt}(m\mathbf{r} \times \dot{\mathbf{r}}) = \frac{d\mathbf{L}}{dt} = -\frac{d}{dt}\left(\frac{eg}{\hat{r}}\right)$. The orbital angular momentum **L** is evidently not a constant of the motion (although its magnitude L^2 is). Note also that $\mathbf{L} = m\mathbf{r_0} \times \mathbf{v}$. Instead, the appropriate constant of the motion is the vector $\mathbf{J} \equiv \mathbf{L} + \frac{eg}{c}\hat{\mathbf{r}}$ (somewhat reminiscent of the Runge–Lenz vector for the Coulomb problem). The angular momentum of the electromagnetic field can be calculated from $\frac{1}{4\pi c}\int \mathbf{r} \times (\mathbf{E} \times \mathbf{B})d^3r = \frac{eg}{c}\hat{\mathbf{r}}$, a result first obtained by J. J. Thomson. Thus the vector **J**, sometimes called the Poincaré vector, represents the total angular momentum: mechanical plus electromagnetic. It is shown by a blue arrow. Since **L** is perpendicular to **r**, $J^2 = L^2 + \left(\frac{eg}{c}\right)^2$. Also, $\mathbf{J}\cdot\hat{\mathbf{r}} = \frac{eg}{c}$, thus the trajectory of the position vector **r** is evidently confined to the surface of a right circular cone (the Poincaré cone) with constant slant angle $\theta = \cos^{-1}\left(\frac{eg/c}{J}\right)$ with respect to the axis **J**.

The motion of $\hat{\mathbf{r}}$ about the origin with an angular velocity ω determines the ϕ-dependence of the trajectory. We have $\omega = \dot{\phi}(t) = \frac{J}{mr^2}$, so that integration gives $\phi(t) = \frac{J}{\sqrt{J^2-1}}\arctan(vt/r_0)$.

The electron spin is, in its lowest energy state, parallel everywhere to the magnetic field **B** and does not contribute to the motion.

In the graphic, all variables are scaled relative to eg/c. The monopole is marked with a blue cross, while the electron's trajectory is shown in red. The trajectory is actually a geodesic on the surface of the cone, which would follow a straight line if the cone were unrolled. To keep within the scale of the diagram, the values of J are limited to be between 1.001 and 1.005 (multiples of eg/c).

The existence of magnetic monopoles would imply the quantization of electric charge. As a major implication in Dirac's paper, this is perhaps the most intriguing aspect of magnetic monopoles. The electromagnetic vector potential **A** is related to the magnetic induction by $\mathbf{B} = \nabla \times \mathbf{A}$. With $\mathbf{B} = g\mathbf{r}/r^3$ for a magnetic monopole, two possible forms of the vector potential are $\mathbf{A_1} = \frac{g(1-\cos\theta)}{r\sin\theta}\hat{\phi}$ and $\mathbf{A_2} = \frac{g(1+\cos\theta)}{r\sin\theta}\hat{\phi}$. The first form is singular for $\theta = \pi$ along the negative z axis, while the second is singular for $\theta = 0$ along the positive z axis. For values of $\theta \neq 0$ or π, either form is valid and they must be related by a gauge condition: $\mathbf{A}_1 - \mathbf{A}_2 = \nabla\chi$, where $\chi = 2g\phi$.

Gauge invariance in quantum mechanics requires that alternative representations of the wavefunction ψ differ by a phase factor $\exp(ie\chi/\hbar c)$, in the present case $\exp(i2eg\phi/\hbar c)$. Comparing the wavefunctions for $\phi = 0$ and $\phi = 2\pi$, we should find $\exp(i4\pi eg/\hbar c) = \exp(i2n\pi) = 1$. This implies that $2eg/\hbar c = n$, $n = 0, \pm 1, \pm 2, \ldots$, so that the electric charge e (as well as the magnetic pole strength g) must therefore occur as integral multiples of some elementary magnitude.

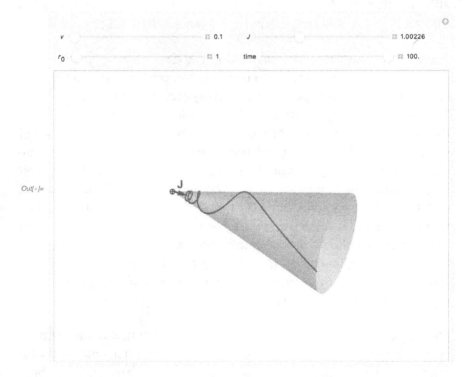

Demonstration 3.21: Classical Electron in the Field of a Magnetic Monopole (https://demonstrations.wolfram.com/ClassicalElectronInTheFieldOfAMagneticMonopole/)

3.6. Electromagnetic Radiation

J. J. Thomson first suggested a pictorial representation of how an instantaneously accelerated point charge can produce a pulse of electromagnetic radiation. An electron, with charge e, moving at a constant speed v, even when at a significant fraction of the speed of light c, produces an electric field of magnitude $E(\mathbf{r}, t) = \frac{1}{\sqrt{1 - v^2/c^2}} \frac{e}{|\mathbf{r}(t) - \mathbf{r}_0(t)|^2}$, (add factor $1/4\pi\varepsilon_0$ if you cannot live without SI units), where $\mathbf{r}_0(t)$ represents the *projected* position of the source charge at time t, assuming that it continues to move at constant speed v from its position $\mathbf{r}_0(t')$ at the retarded time t'. This is derived most lucidly in the Feynman Lectures. Thus a uniformly moving point source emits a spherical longitudinal electric field, although its magnitude does vary with direction. This is represented in the graphic by a series of 12 uniformly spaced radial spokes.

The electron is assumed to move initially at a speed $v_1 = \frac{1}{2}c$ until time $t = 10$, when it reaches the red dot at the center of the figure. The charge is then, in concept, instantaneously accelerated to speed $v_2 > v_1$. For $t > 10$, the charge emits a longitudinal electric field characteristic of the speed v_2. On a sphere of radius $c(t - 10)$, shown in red (a ring of fire?), the v_2 field catches up with the v_1 field, which still behaves as if the electron were moving at its original speed. Since electric-field lines must be continuous in charge-free space, the two sets of field lines connect with transverse segments along the ring of fire, with an angular intensity proportional to $\sin\theta$. Transverse magnetic field lines $\mathbf{B}$, perpendicular to the $\mathbf{E}$ lines (not shown on the graphic) are also created by the moving charge. The lengthening of the segments by a factor $r\sin\theta$ implies the long-range radial dependence of the radiation fields as r^{-1}, rather than r^{-2}, as for electrostatic fields.

Thus, it has been shown that pulses of electromagnetic radiation consist of transverse electric and magnetic fields moving radially outward with the speed of light from the point of instantaneous charge acceleration.

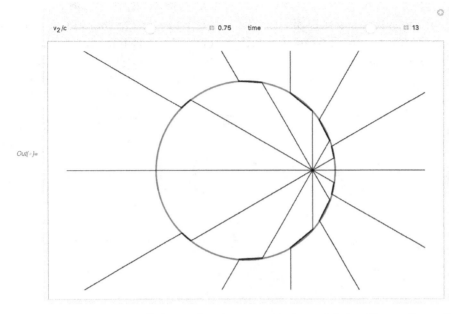

v_2/c ⬚ 0.75   time ⬚ 13

Out[ ]=

Demonstration 3.22: Radiation Pulse from an Accelerated Point Charge (https:// demonstrations.wolfram.com/RadiationPulseFromAnAcceleratedPointCharge/)

3.6.1. *Absorption Spectroscopy*

This Demonstration shows some general qualitative features of absorption spectroscopy, common to all types of spectroscopy. Given a stack of quantized energy levels — atomic, molecular or nuclear — radiation will be absorbed when its frequency v matches one of the energy level differences, according to the Bohr condition $h\nu = E_n - E_m$, assuming the transition is allowed by the appropriate selection rules.

The upper slider allows you to simulate a spectrometer sweeping across the relevant frequency range. You will observe a transition, shown by a red arrow, near the resonance frequency for each transition. No arrows will appear if the frequency is not close to one of the transition frequencies.

The quality of spectrometers is limited by their frequency resolution, which the second slider allows you to vary. At low resolution, the spectral peaks are broadened and the energy levels can be determined with less accuracy. It is the task of the spectroscopist to assign the peaks of the spectrum to specific transitions. If you check the "assignments" box, the results are given.

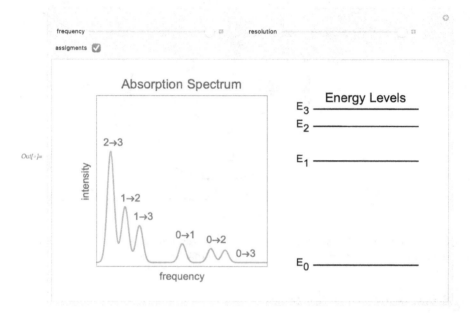

Demonstration 3.23: Absorption Spectroscopy (https://demonstrations.wolfram.com/AbsorptionSpectroscopy/)

3.6.2. *The Casimir Effect*

According to quantum electrodynamics, the vacuum, even in the absence of photons, is filled with zero-point energy (ZPE) from all modes λ of the electromagnetic field, given by $E_0 = \sum_{\lambda=0}^{\infty} \frac{1}{2}\hbar\omega_\lambda$. The ZPE of the vacuum is infinite unless regularized by frequency cutoffs or other stratagems. In most electromagnetic phenomena, the ZPE can be canceled out or renormalized away. Casimir and Polder in 1948 proposed a physical situation in which the effects of ZPE might be directly observable. They considered two perfectly conducting parallel plates, with area L^2, separated by a distance d of the order of microns. The electric field inside a perfect conductor equals zero, so this gives boundary values of zero for all modes at the surface. This perturbs the zero-point modes of the electromagnetic field, since modes with horizontal wavelength components greater than d will be excluded from the region between the plates. They will lie in the ultraviolet and beyond and are shown as black waves. Modes outside the plates can belong to a continuum of frequencies. The result is a net attractive force $-\frac{\pi^2 \hbar c L^2}{240 d^4}$.

In the above formulas $\hbar$ is the reduced Planck's constant $(h/2\pi)$, c is the speed of light and ω_λ is the frequency of the mode λ. Note that this force is a purely quantum effect since it vanishes for $\hbar = 0$. It is also independent of the electric charge e. Measurement of the Casimir–Polder force involves very delicate experiments, but its validity has been successfully verified to better than 1% accuracy.

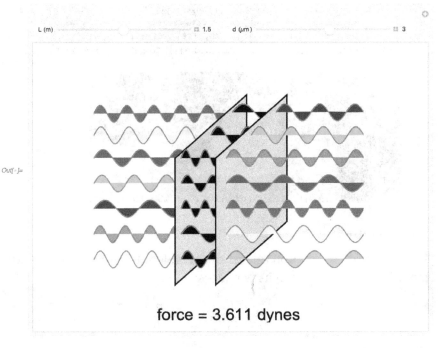

force = 3.611 dynes

Demonstration 3.24: The Casimir Effect (https://demonstrations.wolfram.com/The CasimirEffect/)

In the graphic, the relative scale of d has been greatly exaggerated compared to L, the edge length of each square plate. Conducting plates of area $1\,m^2$ separated by 1 micron (10^{-6} m) experience an attractive force of 130 dynes (1.30×10^{-3}N).

3.7. Optics

Isaac Newton's classic experiment (ca. 1672) showed that white light incident on a glass prism could be separated into its constituent colors. The refracted beam exhibits a continuum of colors, usually designated red, orange, yellow, green, blue, indigo, violet. The shortest wavelength violet is refracted by the largest angle.

```
λ[0] = 430; λ[1] = 450; λ[2] = 470; λ[3] = 500; λ[4] = 580; λ[5] = 595; λ[6] = 650;
Graphics[{Black, Rectangle[{-1.5, -.25}, {1.5, 1}],
  LightGray, Polygon[{{0, √3 / 2}, {-1/2, 0}, {1/2, 0}}], Table[
  {ColorData["VisibleSpectrum"][λ[n]], EdgeForm[], Polygon[{{-.220, .500 + .001 n},
    {.222 - .008 n, .465 + .01 n}, {1.5, -.13 + .0625 n}, {1.5, -.20 + .0625 n},
    {.230 - .008 n, .455 + .01 n}, {-.220, .500 - .001 n}}]]}, {n, 0, 6}],
  Thick, White, Line[{{-1.5, 0}, {-.220, .500}}]}, ImageSize → {500, 225}]
```

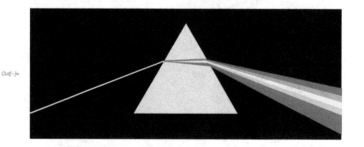

3.7.1. *Lenses*

The lensmaker's equation relates the focal length of a simple lens with the spherical curvature of its two faces:

$$\frac{1}{f} = (n - 1)\left(\frac{1}{R_1} - \frac{1}{R_2} + \frac{(n-1)d}{nR_1R_2}\right),$$

where R_1 and R_2 represent the radii of curvature of the lens surfaces closest to the light source (on the left) and the object (on the right). The sign of R_i is determined by the location of the center of curvature along the optic axis, with the origin at the center of the lens. Thus for a doubly convex lens, R_1 is positive while R_2 is negative.

The focal length f is positive for a converging lens but negative for a diverging lens, giving a virtual focus, indicated by a cone of gray rays. The lens index of refraction is given by n. Optical quality glass has n in the vicinity of 2.65. The top slider enables you to vary n between 1.0008, the value for air, and 3.42, the refractive index of diamond. The width d represents the distance between the faces of the lens along the optical axis. The value of R_2 is restrained by the slider so that the lens faces never intersect anywhere. The parameters d, R_1, R_2, and f are to be expressed in the same length units, often cm. The reciprocal $1/f$ is known as the optical power of the lens, expressed in diopters (m^{-1}). A converging lens can serve as a simple magnifying glass.

In the thin-lens approximation, the lens width d is small compared to the other lengths and the lensmaker's equation can be simplified to $\frac{1}{f} = (n-1)\left(\frac{1}{R_1} - \frac{1}{R_2}\right)$.

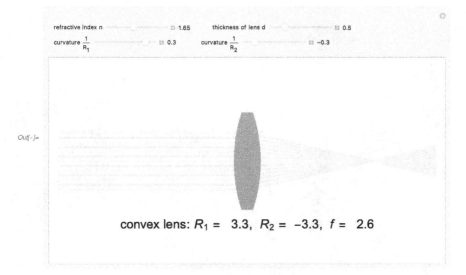

convex lens: $R_1 = 3.3$, $R_2 = -3.3$, $f = 2.6$

Demonstration 3.25: Lensmaker's Equation (https://demonstrations.wolfram.com/LensmakersEquation/)

3.7.2. *Light Beams through Multiple Polarizers*

A polarizer (or polaroid) is a thin plastic sheet that produces a high degree of linear (or plane) polarization in light passing through it. This Demonstration shows a beam of unpolarized light reduced in intensity by 50% after passing through a polarizer oriented at an angle θ_1. (Angles are measured counter-clockwise from the horizontal, looking into the beam from the screen.) A second polarizer oriented at angle θ_2 will further reduce the intensity by a factor of $\cos^2(\theta_2 - \theta_1)$. In particular, if the

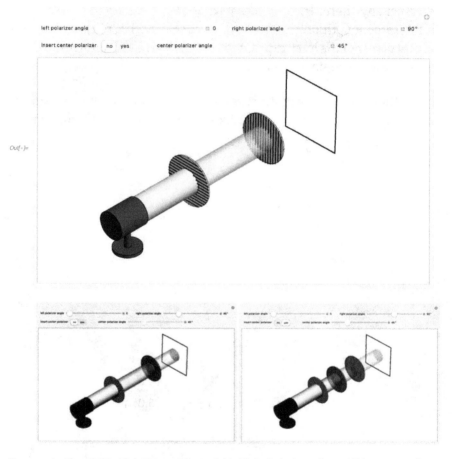

Demonstration 3.26: Light Beams through Multiple Polarizers (https://demonstrations.wolfram.com/LightBeamsThroughMultiplePolarizers/)

two polarizers are parallel ($\theta_2 = \theta_1$), there is no reduction in intensity. However, if the two polarizers are "crossed", with $\theta_2 - \theta_1 = 90°$, no light will pass through.

A remarkable effect occurs when a third polarizer is inserted between two crossed polarizers: up to one quarter of the light intensity can then be transmitted. This is a consequence of the quantum nature of light. Photons linearly polarized at angle θ_1 are transformed into a superposition of two linear polarizations parallel and perpendicular to a new angle θ_2 with probabilities $\cos^2(\theta_2 - \theta_1)$ and $\sin^2(\theta_2 - \theta_1)$, respectively.

In this Demonstration, you can observe the changes in intensity of a light beam as you vary the angles of two or three polarizers.

3.8. Dielectrics

The index of refraction n is often described as an apparent decrease in the speed of light from c to c/n as it passes through a dielectric medium. In fact, light photons do not actually slow down, but the effect is simulated by a retarding phase shift in the emerging electromagnetic waves. This is caused by superposition of the incident wave with a retarded wave produced by radiation from the electrons in the medium.

3.8.1. *Lorentz Oscillator Model*

This Demonstration describes a highly idealized and simplified classical atomic model for the refractive index. Using the sliders, you can vary the wavelength of the incident light, $\lambda = 2\pi c/\omega$, over the visible region 400–700 nm. You can also vary the natural frequency of the electron oscillators, $\lambda_0 = 2\pi c/\omega_0$, which generally lies in the ultraviolet, and N, the number of oscillating electrons per unit volume. The lower half of the graphic shows the phase retardation of the amplitude for the transmitted radiation compared to the incident radiation. The parameters approximate those of glass, with $n \approx 1.5$.

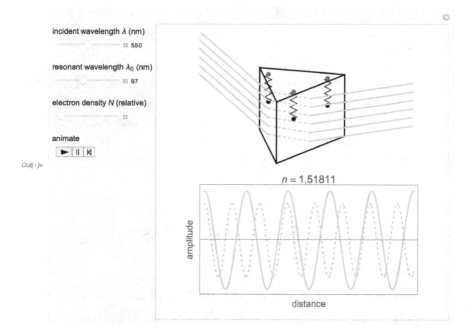

incident wavelength λ (nm)

⊞ 550

resonant wavelength λ_0 (nm)

⊞ 97

electron density *N* (relative)

⊞

animate

▶ ‖ ◁

Out[ ]=

$n = 1.51811$

amplitude

distance

Demonstration 3.27: Lorentz Oscillator Model for Refractive Index (https://demonstra tions.wolfram.com/LorentzOscillatorModelForRefractiveIndex/)

3.8.2. *Drude-Lorentz Model*

Drude and Lorentz (ca. 1900) developed a classical theory to account for the complex index of refraction and dielectric constant of materials, as well as their variations with the frequency of light. The model is based on treating electrons as damped harmonically bound particles subject to external electric fields. A highly simplified version of the model is given in this Demonstration, with results limited to a qualitative level. Still, the phenomena of normal and anomalous dispersion and their relation to the absorption of radiation can be quite reasonably accounted for. The classical parameters of the theory transform simply to their quantum analogs, so that the results remain valid in modern theories of materials science.

Usually the dielectric constant increases slowly with frequency — normal dispersion. However, in the neighborhood of an atomic transition the material exhibits anomalous dispersion, in which the dielectric constant decreases sharply with frequency, accompanied by absorption of light.

In this Demonstration, you can vary the parameters ω_0 and γ. A checkbox highlights the region of anomalous dispersion.

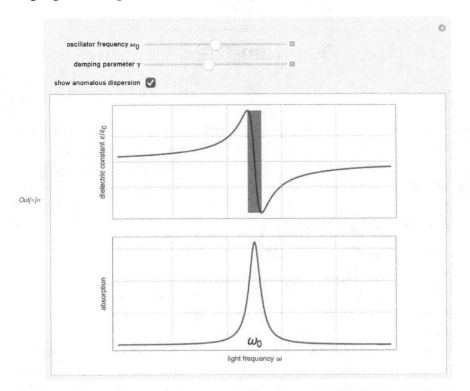

Demonstration 3.28: Drude-Lorentz Model for Dispersion in Dielectrics (https://demonstrations.wolfram.com/DrudeLorentzModelForDispersionInDielectrics/)

Chapter 4

Physics: Quantum Theory I, Principles

There are over 500 Wolfram Demonstrations on various aspects of quantum theory, ranging from elementary accounts of the fundamental principles to advanced topics, such as elementary particle physics and quantum computers.

4.1. Fundamental Principles

4.1.1. *Wave-Particle Duality*

The "central mystery" of quantum mechanics is the wave-particle duality, as exemplified by the famous double-slit experiment. In this idealized Demonstration, a special laser (not yet on the market!) can be tuned to any wavelength of visible light and triggered to emit pulses of up to 3500 photons. Small numbers of photons (or individual photons), after passing through the slits, produce scintillations at apparently random points on the screen. But as the number of photons per pulse is increased, a pattern of light and dark bands gradually emerges, with spacings determined by the wavelength and slit separation, which you can control with sliders.

The intensities, in fact, trace out a classical diffraction pattern, first observed in Young's double-slit experiment. The trajectories of individual photons cannot be predicted. But each photon somehow "knows" about the entire diffraction pattern, which is exhibited only in the statistical behavior of a large number of photons. Remarkably, electrons

slit separation		1
wavelength of light/nm		550
photons per pulse		2500

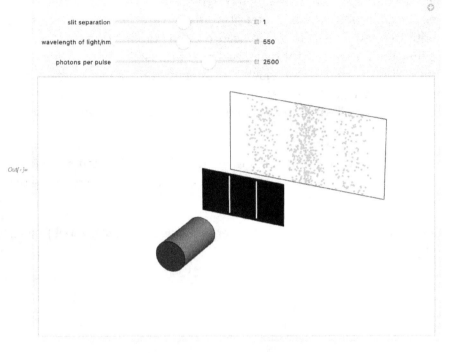

Demonstration 4.1: Wave-Particle Duality in the Double-Slit Experiment (https://demonstrations.wolfram.com/WaveParticleDualityInTheDoubleSlitExperiment/)

and other particles behave analogously, in accord with their de Broglie wavelengths. This constitutes the fundamental basis for the quantum theory of matter.

4.1.2. *Franck-Hertz Experiment*

This experiment carried out by James Franck and Gustav Ludwig Hertz in 1914 was intended to support Niels Bohr's model of the atom, according to which electrons occupy discrete energy levels that can absorb or emit energy in only certain quantized amounts.

In a tube containing mercury vapor at low pressure, a heated cathode emits electrons, which are accelerated by a positively charged grid and collected at the anode. The anode is at a slightly negative potential relative to the grid, so that electrons require a small amount of kinetic energy to reach it after passing through the grid. The electrons undergo elastic collisions with the mercury atoms and are detected at the anode until the grid potential is increased to approximately 4.9 volts. At this point, the anode current decreases precipitously. This is attributed to the collisions becoming inelastic, as the electron kinetic energy excites mercury atoms to the lowest available excited state. This energy difference agrees well with the 254 nm transition in the emission spectrum of mercury.

As the grid potential is further increased, this behavior recurs at 9.8 and 14.7 volts, multiples of 4.9 volts, as the electrons are able to excite two or more mercury atoms.

James Franck and Gustav Hertz were awarded the 1925 Nobel Prize in Physics for this work.

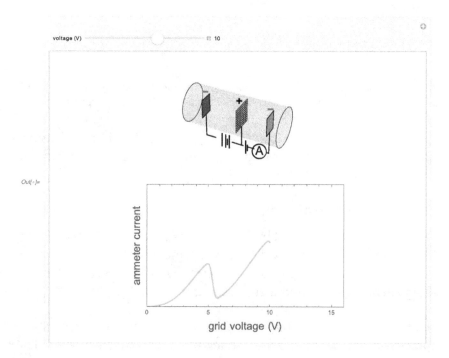

Demonstration 4.2: Franck-Hertz Experiment (https://demonstrations.wolfram.com/ FranckHertzExperiment/)

4.1.3. *The Photoelectric Effect*

The photoelectric effect is a quantum-mechanical phenomenon in which light impinging on the surface of a metal can cause electrons to be ejected. Only light with wavelengths shorter than some threshold value λ_0, characteristic of each metal, can cause emission of photoelectrons, no matter how intense the radiation. Einstein explained this in 1905 by proposing that light is composed of discrete photons, each carrying energy $E = h\nu = \frac{hc}{\lambda}$. Only when the photon energy exceeds the work function Φ of the metal, a measure of how strongly the outermost electrons are bound, can photoelectrons be emitted. The relevant equation is $\frac{hc}{\lambda} = \Phi + KE_{max}$, where the last term represents the maximum kinetic energy of the ejected electrons. Once the threshold wavelength is attained, the current of electrons increases linearly with the radiation intensity. This can be monitored by an ammeter in the circuit shown.

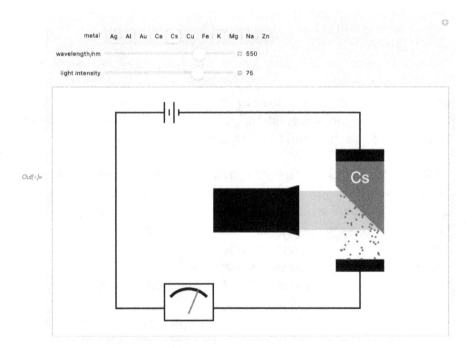

Demonstration 4.3: The Photoelectric Effect (https://demonstrations.wolfram.com/ThePhotoelectricEffect/)

The light source covers the entire visible range 400–700 nm. In the ultra-violet region, the light ray appears as black. Einstein was awarded the 1922 Nobel Prize in Physics for his theory of the photoelectric effect, rather than for his discoveries of the special and general theories of relativity.

4.1.4. *Bell's Theorem*

The Einstein-Podolsky-Rosen (EPR) *Gedankenexperiment* sought to demonstrate that quantum mechanics, although invariably predicting results in agreement with experiment, was an incomplete theory. In particular, the desirable philosophical feature of objective reality was lacking. According to the widely accepted Copenhagen interpretation, certain variables in a quantum system do not acquire definite values until they are measured. Thus they have no physical meaning in the absence of observation. Einstein disagreed vehemently. As he put it so succinctly, "Is the Moon still there when nobody looks?" Bohm reformulated the EPR experiment in terms of a pair of entangled spin-$\frac{1}{2}$ particles (also applicable to polarized photons) emitted from a compact source. It is a known fact that measurement of the polarization of one particle unambiguously determines the polarization of the other. From the viewpoint of objective realism, the states of both particles is assumed to exist independent of observation, perhaps as hidden variables not yet incorporated into the formalism of quantum mechanics.

John Stuart Bell in 1964 devised a statistical test that could distinguish between the worldviews of quantum mechanics and objective realism. Subsequent experiments using correlated photons, notably those of Clauser, Horne, Shimony, and Holt and, most definitively, by Alain Aspect and coworkers, demonstrate convincingly that quantum mechanics is correct. This result can be summarized as Bell's theorem: No physical theory of local hidden variables can ever reproduce all the predictions of quantum mechanics. Henry Stapp regards Bell's theorem as the most significant development in science (not just physics) of the 20th century.

This Demonstration describes a simplified version of Aspect's experiment. The little cube in the center emits pairs of correlated photons in opposite directions toward two polarizers, oriented at angles θ_1 and θ_2. A coincidence counter at the bottom monitors the number of photon pairs that get through both polarizers and are detected. The counter tabulates the coincidence fraction for several hundred or several thousand emitted photon pairs for a given setting of the polarizers and displays this result. The upper part of the diagram shows the actual experimental results while the lower part, enclosed in a gray philosophical haze, shows the expectations of objective reality. Except for a few special orientations, these results differ.

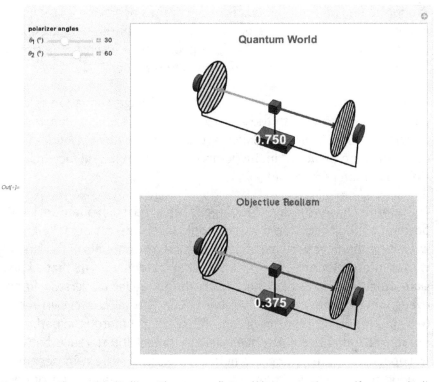

Demonstration 4.4: Bell's Theorem (https://demonstrations.wolfram.com/Bells Theorem/)

4.1.5. *Schrödinger's Cat*

Schrödinger in 1935 proposed a *gedankenexperiment* questioning whether the worldview of the Copenhagen interpretation of quantum mechanics might apply also to phenomena on a macroscopic scale. In the version of the experiment described in this Demonstration, a cat is enclosed in an opaque box and a spray of catnip is released. Initially, the cat is in a perturbed state, resentful of being cooped up in a dark box. But, as the catnip begins to act, the cat will eventually relax into a blissful state. According to the Copenhagen interpretation, the time-dependent quantum state of the cat might be described by a wavefunction $\Psi(t) = t \odot + \sqrt{1 - t^2} \odot$, $(0 \leq t \leq 1)$. However, the instantaneous state of the cat cannot be known until the box is opened, thus achieving a "reduction of the wavefunction" to one of two observable "pure" cat states, $\odot$ or $\odot$ with probabilities t^2 and $1 - t^2$, respectively. In a sense, the state is "created" only after an actual measurement is made.

In stark contrast, the time-dependent Schrödinger equation is completely determinate, with the superposition $\Psi(t)$ explicitly known as a function of time. This can, in concept, be exhibited by selecting "show quantum superposition" in the Demonstration, but it is, in fact, inaccessible to human perception!

The current consensus on Schrödinger's cat is that such quantum superposition cannot occur on a macroscopic level (the cat actually knows what is happening) because of decoherence. (Proponents of the "many-worlds interpretation" of quantum mechanics would argue that all possible outcomes do occur, thereby creating parallel universes.) In any event, on an atomic level, possibly within the feline's catnip receptors, quantum superposition can still occur. Numerous experiments on atomic ions have since been able to detect interference between wavepackets representing a single microscopic system in separated regions of space. (Inevitably, some such entities have been dubbed Schrödinger's cations.)

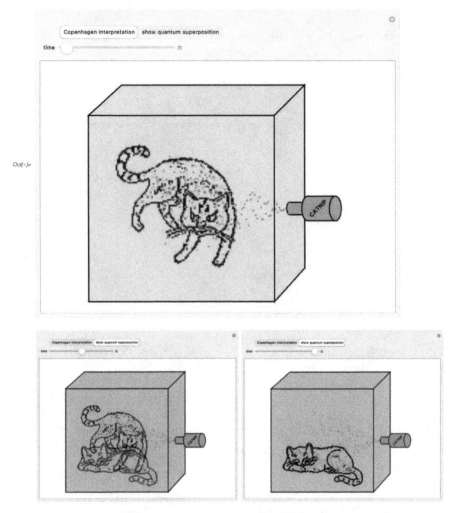

Demonstration 4.5: Schrödinger's Cat on Catnip (https://demonstrations.wolfram. com/SchroedingersCatOnCatnip/)

4.1.6. *Fundamental Commutation Relations*

All the fundamental quantum-mechanical commutators involving the Cartesian components of position, momentum, and angular momentum are enumerated. Commutators of sums and products can be derived

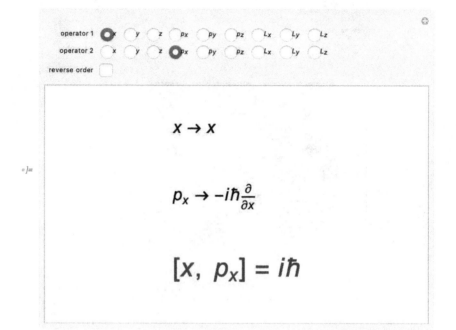

Demonstration 4.6: Fundamental Commutation Relations in Quantum Mechanics (https://demonstrations.wolfram.com/FundamentalCommutationRelationsInQuantum Mechanics/)

using relations such as $[A, B + C] = [A, B] + [A, C]$ and $[A, BC] = B[A, C] + [A, B]C$. For example, the operator $L^2 = L^2_x + L^2_y + L^2_z$ obeys the commutation relations $[L^2, L_x] = [L^2, L_y] = [L^2, L_z] = 0$.

4.1.7. Momentum Eigenstates

This Demonstration shows the motions of non-relativistic one-dimensional momentum eigenfunctions. The time-dependent Schrödinger equation for a free particle in one dimension is given by $\frac{-\hbar^2}{2m}\frac{\partial^2}{\partial x^2}\Psi(x, t) = -i\hbar\frac{\partial}{\partial t}\Psi(x, t)$. The eigenfunctions are $\Psi_k(x, t) = \frac{1}{\sqrt{2\pi}} e^{-ik\hbar x} e^{-i(k^2\hbar^2/2m)t}$, with a continuum of momentum eigenvalues $p_k = k\hbar$, $-\infty < k < \infty$ and energy eigenvalues $E_k = k^2\hbar^2/2m$. The energy eigenvalues are two-fold degenerate except for $k = 0$. The degeneracy corresponds to left-to-right motion when $k > 0$ and right-to-left motion when $k < 0$.

For simplicity, we set $\hbar = m = 1$. Plots are shown for the real and imaginary parts of $\Psi_k(x,t) = \frac{1}{\sqrt{2\pi}}e^{i(kx - k^2 t/2)}$ as blue and purple sinusoidal curves, respectively. A three-dimensional representation is also shown.

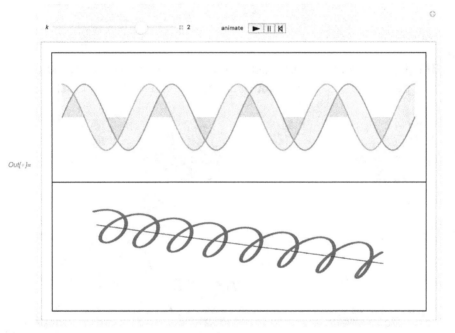

Demonstration 4.7: Momentum Eigenstates (https://demonstrations.wolfram.com/MomentumEigenstates/)

4.1.8. *Evolution of a Gaussian Wave Packet*

A Gaussian wave packet centered around $x = 0$ at time $t = 0$ with an average initial momentum p_0 can be represented by the wavefunction $\psi(x,0) = (\sqrt{2\pi}\sigma_0)^{-1/2} \exp(-\frac{x^2}{4\sigma_0^2} + ip_0 x)$. (For convenience, we take $\hbar = m = 1$.) The solution of the free-particle Schrödinger equation with this initial condition works out to $\psi(x,t) = \left(\frac{\sigma_0}{\sqrt{2\pi}}\right)^{1/2} (\sigma_0^2 + \frac{it}{2})^{-1/2} \exp\left(-\sigma_0^2 p_0^2\right) \exp\left(-\frac{(x - 2i\sigma_0^2 + p_0)^2}{4(\sigma_0^2 + it/2)}\right)$. The probability density is then given by $\rho(x, t) = |\psi(x, t)|^2 = (\sqrt{2\pi}\sigma(t))^{-1} \exp\left(-\frac{(x-p_0 t)^2}{2\sigma(t)^2}\right)$, where $\sigma(t) = \sigma_0(1 + \frac{t^2}{4\sigma_0^4})^{1/2}$, shown as a black curve. The wave packet remains Gaussian as it spreads out, with its center moving to $x = p_0 t$, thereby following the classical trajectory of the particle. The corresponding momentum probability distribution is given by $\rho(p, t) = |\phi(p, t)|^2 = \sqrt{\frac{2}{\pi}\sigma_0}e^{-2\sigma_0^2(p-p_0)^2}$, shown in red. The rms uncertainties are given by $\Delta x = \sqrt{\int x^2 \rho(x, t)dx} = \sigma(t), \Delta p = \sqrt{\int (p - p_0)^2 \rho(p, t)dp} = \frac{1}{2\sigma_0}$, which is independent of t.

This is consistent with the fact that p is a constant of the motion for a free particle. Thus, with $\hbar$ put back in, the uncertainty product is given

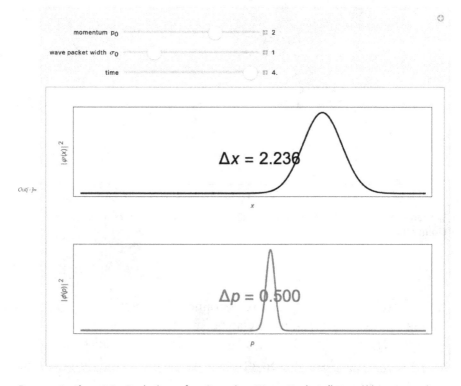

Out[ ]=

Demonstration **4.8:** Evolution of a Gaussian Wave Packet (https://demonstrations. wolfram.com/EvolutionOfAGaussianWavePacket/)

by $\Delta x \Delta p = \frac{\hbar}{2}(1 + \frac{t^2}{4\sigma_0^4})^{1/2} \geq \frac{\hbar}{2}$, in accord with Heisenberg's uncertainty principle. At $t = 0$, the Gaussian probability distribution represents a *minimum uncertainty* wave packet with $\Delta x \Delta p = \hbar/2$, but the product increases when $t > 0$.

In this Demonstration, you can drag the time slider to simulate the simultaneous time evolution of the probability and momentum distributions. Note that the x distribution broadens with time while the p distribution maintains its original width. The numerical values of x, p, and t are illustrative only and have no absolute significance.

4.1.9. *Space Quantization of Angular Momentum*

The commutation relations for angular momentum in quantum mechanics are given by $[J_x, J_y] = i\hbar J_z$, $[J^2, J_z] = 0$, with cyclic permutations. From these, the allowed values of quantized angular momentum can be derived, namely, $J^2 = j(j+1)\hbar^2$ and $J_z = m\hbar$, with $m = -j, -j+1, \ldots, j$, $j = 0, \frac{1}{2}, 1, \frac{3}{2}, 2, \ldots$ Customarily, the z component is singled out, with the other two components retaining indefinite or fluctuating values (except when $j = 0$). The definite magnitude and direction of one component of angular momentum is known as "space quantization". Restriction of m to integer values was exploited in Bohr's model of the hydrogen atom. When spin is involved, m and j can also take half-integer values. The vector model of angular momentum pictures the total angular momentum vector as precessing about its constant z component. This is also consistent with the fluctuating values of J_x and J_y.

The fact that the quantized value of J^2 equals $j(j+1)$, rather than j^2, can be rationalized by the fact that the average value of the sum of the squares of the three J components is given by $\frac{3}{2j+1} \sum_{m=-j}^{j} m^2 = j(j+1)$.

4.1.10. *Addition of Angular Momenta*

Angular momentum in quantum mechanics is a quantized vector with magnitude $|\mathbf{J}| = \sqrt{j(j+1)}\hbar$ and component $J_z = m\hbar$ in any direction,

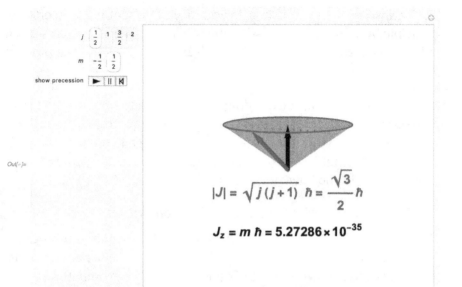

Demonstration 4.9: Space Quantization of Angular Momentum (https://demonstra tions.wolfram.com/SpaceQuantizationOfAngularMomentum/)

conventionally chosen as the z axis. The quantum numbers are restricted to integer or half-integer values: $j = 0, \frac{1}{2}, 1, \frac{3}{2}, 2, \ldots$, with $m = -j, -j + 1, \ldots, j$. Vector addition of two angular momenta $\mathbf{J} = \mathbf{J}_1 + \mathbf{J}_2$ is restricted by a triangle inequality $|j_1 - j_2| \leqslant j \leqslant j_1 + j_2$ with $m = m_1 + m_2$. Although quantum formalism is indifferent to such interpretations, the addition of angular momentum in the absence of any electric or magnetic field can be pictured by a vector model in which $\mathbf{J}_1$ and $\mathbf{J}_2$ precess about $\mathbf{J}$, which itself precesses about a z axis. The amplitude for addition of $\mathbf{J}_1$ and $\mathbf{J}_2$ to give $\mathbf{J}$ with component $J_z = m\hbar$ can be expressed in terms of Clebsch–Gordan coefficients as $|j_1 j_2 j m > \geqslant \sum_{m_1 m_2} < j_1 m_1 j_2 m_2 | j_1 j_2 j m > |j_1 m_1 j_2 m_2 >$ with the sum restricted by $m = m_1 + m_2$. You can set the precession into motion with the trigger control. To choose a new set of j and m values, pause and reset the trigger.

Demonstration 4.10: Addition of Angular Momenta in Quantum Mechanics (https://demonstrations.wolfram.com/AdditionOfAngularMomentaInQuantumMechanics/)

4.1.11. *Hanbury Brown and Twiss Experiment*

In 1956, British astronomers Robert Hanbury Brown and Richard Q. Twiss measured the stellar radius of Sirius by making use of a new type of interferometer. This was based not on the usual amplitude interference but rather on radiation *intensity*, exploiting the fact that photons emitted by the star are governed by Bose–Einstein statistics. In contrast to fermions, such as electrons or neutrons, which tend to avoid one another (the basis of the Pauli exclusion principle), bosons, such as photons or pions, prefer to "bunch" together.

This Demonstration describes a simplified Hanbury Brown and Twiss apparatus that detects the coincidence counts of two detectors, both receiving incoherent radiation from two sources with a controllable delay, emitting either bosons or fermions. It is observed that boson coincidence counts reach a maximum when the delay time is reduced to zero. By contrast, fermion counts are reduced as the delay time is decreased. These are shown in the graphic as simulated oscilloscope traces, showing signal versus time. You can control the efficiency of the apparatus. For lower efficiencies, the response curve becomes flatter as the maximum or minimum is suppressed.

The amplitudes of the four pictured boson or fermion trajectories are designated: $\langle a|A\rangle$, $\langle b|B\rangle$, $\langle a\,|\,B\rangle$, $\langle b\,|\,A\rangle$. The total amplitude of the process in which two particles are incident on each of the two detectors is given by $\Psi = \langle a\,|\,A\rangle\langle b\,|\,B\rangle \pm \langle a\,|\,B\rangle\langle b\,|\,A\rangle$, where the plus sign applies to bosons and the minus sign to fermions. The corresponding intensity is then equal to $I = \Psi^*\Psi =$

$$|\langle a\,|\,A\rangle|^2|\langle b\,|\,B\rangle|^2 + |\langle a\,|\,B\rangle|^2|\langle b\,|\,A\rangle|^2 \pm \langle a\,|\,A\rangle^*\langle b\,|\,B\rangle^*\langle a\,|\,B\rangle\langle b\,|\,A\rangle$$
$$\pm \langle a\,|\,B\rangle^*\langle b\,|\,A\rangle^*\langle a\,|\,A\rangle\langle b\,|\,B\rangle$$

We assume simple approximations to the amplitudes:

$$\langle a\,|\,A\rangle = \langle b\,|\,B\rangle = Ce^{i\omega t}, \langle a\,|\,B\rangle = \langle b\,|\,A\rangle = Ce^{i\omega(t+\Delta t)},$$

where Δt is the time delay in the crossed paths. The radiation frequency ω and the time delay depend on the types of particles and the specifics of the experiment. Their magnitudes are left unspecified, so that our results are completely general.

Using the preceding amplitudes, the two-detector correlation intensities work out to $I = 4|C|^2[1 \pm \cos(2\omega\Delta t)]$ for bosons and fermions, respectively.

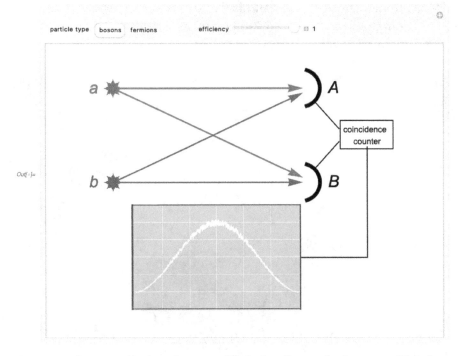

Demonstration 4.11: Hanbury Brown and Twiss Interference for Bosons and Fermions (https://demonstrations.wolfram.com/HanburyBrownAndTwissInterferenceForBosons AndFermions/)

4.1.12. *Pauli Spin Matrices*

The Pauli spin matrices σ_1, σ_2, and σ_3 represent the intrinsic angular momentum components of spin-$\frac{1}{2}$ particles in quantum mechanics. Their matrix products are given by $\sigma_i \sigma_l = \delta_{ij}I + i\epsilon_{ijk}\sigma_k$, where I is the 2×2 identity matrix, O is the 2×2 zero matrix and ϵ_{ijk} is the Levi-Civita permutation symbol. These products lead to the commutation and anticommutation relations $[\sigma_i, \sigma_l] = \sigma_i \sigma_l - \sigma_j \sigma_i = i\epsilon_{ijk}\sigma_k$ and $\{\sigma_i, \sigma_l\} = \sigma_i \sigma_l + \sigma_j \sigma_i = 2\delta_{ij}I$. The Pauli matrices transform as a 3-dimensional pseudovector (axial vector) $\vec{\sigma}$ related to the angular-momentum operators for spin-$\frac{1}{2}$ by $\vec{S} = \frac{\hbar}{2}\vec{\sigma}$. These, in turn, obey the canonical commutation relations $[S_i, S_j] = i\hbar\epsilon_{ijk}S_k$. The three Pauli spin matrices are generators for the Lie group SU(2).

In this Demonstration, you can display the products, commutators, or anti-commutators of any two Pauli matrices. It is instructive to explore the combinations $\sigma^{\pm} = \sigma_1 \pm i\sigma_2$ that represent spin-ladder operators.

first σ [σ_1] σ_2 σ_3 second σ [σ_1] σ_2 σ_3

matrix product   commutator   anticommutator

Out[ ]=

$$\sigma_1 = \begin{pmatrix} 0 & 1 \\ 1 & 0 \end{pmatrix} \qquad \sigma_2 = \begin{pmatrix} 0 & -i \\ i & 0 \end{pmatrix}$$

$$\sigma_3 = \begin{pmatrix} 1 & 0 \\ 0 & -1 \end{pmatrix} \qquad \mathcal{I} = \begin{pmatrix} 1 & 0 \\ 0 & 1 \end{pmatrix}$$

$$[\sigma_1, \sigma_2] = 2i\,\sigma_3$$

Demonstration 4.12: Pauli Spin Matrices (https://demonstrations.wolfram.com/Pauli SpinMatrices/)

4.1.13. *The Fine Structure Constant from the Old Quantum Theory*

The fine structure constant, $\alpha = e^2/\hbar c = 0.00729735 \approx 1/137$, measures the relative strength of the electromagnetic coupling constant in quantum field theory. Its small magnitude enables very accurate predictions in the perturbation expansions of quantum electrodynamics. This famous dimensionless parameter was first introduced by Arnold Sommerfeld in 1916 in a relativistic generalization of Bohr's atomic theory. As its simplest physical realization, the fine structure constant α is equal to the ratio of the speed of the electron in the first Bohr orbit to the speed of light.

In Sommerfeld's first modification of the original atomic theory, the circular Bohr orbits were generalized so that elliptical orbits could also occur, in analogy with Kepler's laws of planetary motion. Bohr energy levels above the $n = 1$ ground state were thereby shown to be degenerate, involving two quantum numbers, n_ϕ and n_r. Sommerfeld later used the relativistic kinetic energy formula to introduce corrections to the electronic orbits. This caused some of the degenerate levels to split, thereby accounting for the "fine structure" of atomic spectral lines. Classically, the perturbation causes the relativistic elliptical orbits to precess about their major axes, although slowly compared to the electron's orbital speed.

The more general significance of the fine structure constant emerged only several years after Sommerfeld introduced it. Eddington promoted the integer approximating its reciprocal (136, and later 137, as measurements became more accurate) to a near-mystical quantity, which he claimed was central to the structure of the entire universe. Pauli, for many years, sought its origin from some deeper physical principle. Today we understand that the Standard Model (SM) contains some 20 or so coupling constants, masses and mixing angles, including the fine structure constant, which can only be experimentally determined. It is hoped that some future successor to the SM will come closer to predicting the values of these constants.

The graphics in this Demonstration show electron orbits for the principal quantum numbers $n = 1, 2, 3$, for both the non-relativistic and relativistic theories. The quantum number $k = n - n_r$ determines the eccentricity via $\epsilon = \sqrt{1 - k^2/n^2}$. Note that increasing k corresponds to more circular orbits, in contrast to the more familiar angular momentum quantum number l, for which decreasing values give more circular orbits.

The selected orbit is shown as a red curve, while the other orbits are lighter curves. For clarity, the $n = 1$ and $n = 2$ orbits are shown simultaneously, while the $n = 3$ orbits are in a separate graphic. The precessional rates are exaggerated for purposes of visualization.

The non-relativistic version of the old quantum theory was most succinctly expressed by the Sommerfeld–Wilson quantum conditions: $\oint p_i dq_i = n_i h$, for each periodic degree of freedom in the system. For example, the Keplerian orbital motion of a bound state of the electron in a hydrogen atom, an ellipse confined to a plane, has two degrees of freedom. The Hamiltonian can be written $H = \frac{p_r^2}{2\mu} + \frac{p_\varphi^2}{2\mu r^2} - \frac{Ze^2}{r}$, where $\mu = \frac{m_e m_p}{m_e + m_p} \approx m_e$ is the reduced mass and Z is the nuclear charge ($Z = 1$ for H, $Z = 2$ for He$^+$, etc.). For simplicity, we use atomic units $\hbar = e = \mu = 1$ and assume infinite nuclear mass. Thus the Bohr radius is $a_0 = \hbar^2/me^2 = 1$. The two quantum conditions are the phase integrals $J_\phi = \oint p_\phi d\phi = n_\phi h$ and $J_r = \oint p_r dr = n_r h$. The first is simple, since the Hamiltonian is independent of ϕ, so that p_ϕ is a constant. Thus $J_\phi = 2\pi p_\phi = n_\phi h$ or $p_\phi = n_\phi \hbar$, with $n_\phi = 1, 2, 3, \ldots$ This represents, in fact, the quantization of angular momentum. The integral J_r is a bit more challenging: $J_r = 2 \int_{r_1}^{r_2} \sqrt{2E + \frac{2z}{r} - \frac{n_\phi^2}{r^2}}\, dr$, where r_1 and r_2 are the periapsis and apoapsis of the orbit. This works out to $\frac{Z}{\sqrt{-2E}} - n_\varphi = n_r$, with $n_r = 0, 1, 2, \ldots$ The energy, in atomic units, reduces to the familiar Bohr formula $E_n = -\frac{Z^2}{2n^2}$, where the principal quantum number $n = n_\phi + n_r = 1, 2, 3, \ldots$, and the azimuthal quantum number n_ϕ, usually written as k, has the allowed values $k = 1, 2, \ldots, n$. The elliptical orbits are given by the polar equations $r = ka_0/(1 - \epsilon \cos\phi)$, with the eccentricity $\epsilon = \sqrt{1 - \frac{k^2}{n^2}}$.

In the relativistic generalization of Sommerfeld's orbits, the radial and angular momenta of the electron are given by $p_r = m\dot{r}/\sqrt{1 - \beta^2}$, $p_\phi = mr^2\dot{\phi}/\sqrt{1 - \beta^2}$, where $\beta = v/c$. These contain essentially relativistic generalizations of the components of kinetic energy. The Hamiltonian takes the form $H = \sqrt{m^2c^4 + c^2 p_r^2 + \frac{c^2}{r^2}p_\phi^2} - \frac{Ze^2}{r}$. Evaluation of the phase integrals is more complicated, and the interested reader is directed to the references. The relativistic energy works out to

$$E = mc^2 \left[1 + \left(\frac{\alpha Z}{n - k + \sqrt{k^2 - \alpha^2 Z^2}} \right)^2 \right]^{-1/2} \approx mc^2 - \frac{Z^2}{2n^2} - \frac{\alpha^2 Z^4}{n^4} \left(\frac{n}{k} - \frac{3}{4} \right) + \cdots$$

The third term in the expansion represents the fine structure splitting, which removes the degeneracy in n for $n > 1$. In the relativistic theory, the elliptical orbits precess about their major axes.

Remarkably, Sommerfeld's formula agrees exactly with the result obtained by solution of the Dirac equation for the hydrogen atom in relativistic quantum mechanics. To be blunt, this is really "dumb luck", since Sommerfeld was, at the time, unaware of electron spin, whereas the Dirac formula actually takes account of the electron's spin-orbit coupling. And, of course, the angular momenta in the old quantum theory are too large by one unit of $\hbar$.

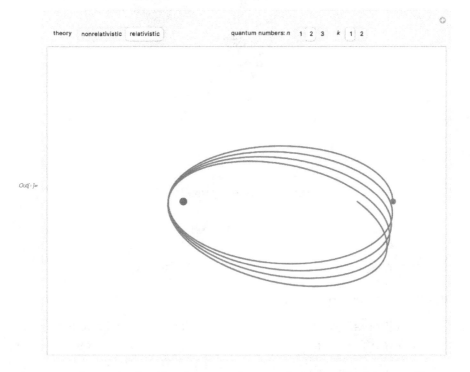

Demonstration 4.13: The Fine Structure Constant from the Old Quantum Theory (https://demonstrations.wolfram.com/TheFineStructureConstantFromTheOldQuantum Theory/)

4.2. The Harmonic Oscillator

4.2.1. *Semiclassical Solution*

It was shown in Chapter 2 that a mass m acted upon a Hooke's law spring with force constant k oscillates harmonically with an angular frequency $\omega = \sqrt{\frac{k}{m}}$. The energy can therefore be written $E = \frac{p^2}{2m} + \frac{1}{2}m\omega^2 x^2$. The WKB method determines the energy levels from $\oint p\,dx = (n + \frac{1}{2})h$. Explicitly, for the harmonic oscillator, $2\int_{-A}^{A}\sqrt{2m(E - \frac{1}{2}m\omega^2 x^2)}\,dx = (n + \frac{1}{2})h$, where $\pm A$ are endpoints of oscillation, given by $A = \sqrt{\frac{2E}{m\omega^2}}$. Evaluating the integral:

$In[\circ]:= $ **A =** $\sqrt{\dfrac{2\ \epsilon}{m\ \omega^2}}$; **2** $\sqrt{2\ m}\ \displaystyle\int_{-A}^{A}\sqrt{\epsilon - \dfrac{1}{2}\,m\ \omega^2\ x^2}\ \mathbb{d}x$

$Out[\circ]= $ $\boxed{2\ \sqrt{m}\ \pi\ \sqrt{\epsilon}\ \sqrt{\dfrac{\epsilon}{m\ \omega^2}}\quad \text{if}\quad \boxed{\textit{condition}\ \ \textcolor{gray}{+}}}$

$In[\circ]:= $ **PowerExpand** $\left[2\ \sqrt{m}\ \pi\ \sqrt{\epsilon}\ \sqrt{\dfrac{\epsilon}{m\ \omega^2}}\ \right]$

$Out[\circ]= $ $\dfrac{2\ \pi\ \epsilon}{\omega}$

We find therefore the quantized energy levels

$$E_n = \left(n + \frac{1}{2}\right)\hbar\omega, \quad 0, 1, 2, \ldots,$$

which is in agreement with the quantum-mechanical result.

4.2.2. *Ladder Operators*

The Hamiltonian for the linear harmonic oscillator can be written $H = -\frac{1}{2}\frac{d^2}{dx^2} + \frac{1}{2}\omega^2 x^2$, in units with $\hbar = m = 1$. The eigenstates are given by $E_n = (n + \frac{1}{2})\omega$, $\psi_n(x) = (2^n n!)^{-1/2}(\omega/\pi)^{1/4}e^{-\omega x^2/2}H_n(\sqrt{\omega}x)$, $n = 0, 1, 2, \ldots$, where H_n is a Hermite polynomial. An alternative reformulation of the problem can be based on the representation $H = (a^\dagger a + \frac{1}{2})\omega$ in terms of ladder operators $a = \sqrt{\frac{\omega}{2}}x + \frac{i}{\sqrt{2\omega}}p = \sqrt{\frac{\omega}{2}}x + \frac{1}{\sqrt{2\omega}}\frac{d}{dx}$

and $a^\dagger = \sqrt{\frac{\omega}{2}}x - \frac{i}{\sqrt{2\omega}}p = \sqrt{\frac{\omega}{2}}x - \frac{1}{\sqrt{2\omega}}\frac{d}{dx}$. The step-down or annihilation operator a acts on the eigenfunctions according to $a\,\psi_n(x) = \sqrt{n}\,\psi_{n-1}(x)$, with $a\,\psi_0(x) = 0$. The step-up or creation operator $a^\dagger$ satisfies $a^\dagger\,\psi_n(x) = \sqrt{n+1}\,\psi_{n+1}(x)$.

In this Demonstration, the eigenfunction $\psi_n(x)$ is plotted in black. Also shown is either $a\psi_n(x)$ in red or $a^\dagger\psi_n(x)$ in blue.

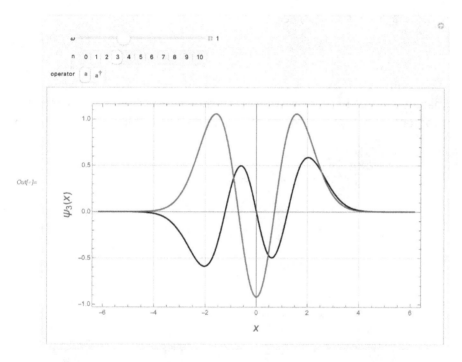

Demonstration 4.14: Ladder Operators for the Harmonic Oscillator (https://demonstrations.wolfram.com/LadderOperatorsForTheHarmonicOscillator/)

4.2.3. *Charged Harmonic Oscillator in Electric Field*

For an electron (mass m, charge $-e$) bound by a harmonic potential $\frac{1}{2}m\omega^2 x^2$ and acted upon by a constant external electric field E, the Schrödinger equation can be written as

$$\frac{-\hbar}{2m}\psi_n''(x) + \left(\frac{1}{2}m\omega^2 x^2 - eEx\right)\psi_n(x) = E_n\psi_n(x).$$

An exact solution can be obtained by completing the square in the potential energy:

$$V(x) = \frac{1}{2}m\omega^2\left(x - \frac{eE}{m\omega^2}\right)^2 - \frac{e^2E^2}{2m\omega^2} = \frac{1}{2}m\omega^2\xi^2 - \frac{e^2E^2}{2m\omega^2}.$$

Introducing the new variable $\xi = x - \frac{eE}{m\omega^2}$, the Schrödinger equation can be written as

$$-\frac{\hbar^2}{2m}\Psi_n''(\xi) + \frac{1}{2}m\omega^2\xi^2\Psi_n(\xi) = \left(E_n + \frac{e^2E^2}{2m\omega^2}\right)\Psi_n(\xi)$$

$$= \left(n + \frac{1}{2}\right)\hbar\omega\Psi_n(\xi), n = 0, 1, 2, \ldots,$$

making use of the known solution of the standard harmonic oscillator problem, expressed in terms of ξ. The perturbed energies are shifted

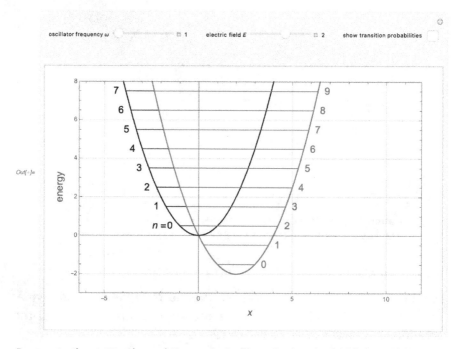

Demonstration 4.15: Charged Harmonic Oscillator in Electric Field (https://demonstrations.wolfram.com/ChargedHarmonicOscillatorInElectricField/)

downward by a constant term:

$$E_n = \left(n + \frac{1}{2}\right)\hbar\omega - \frac{e^2 E^2}{2m\omega^2}.$$

The graphic shows the potential energy and energy levels for the unperturbed (in black) and perturbed (in red) oscillator, for selected values of ω and E. For simplicity, atomic units, $\hbar = m = e = 1$, are used. If the electric field is turned on during a time interval Δt that is short compared to the oscillation period $2\pi/\omega$, the *sudden approximation* in perturbation theory can be applied. Accordingly, the transition probability from state n to a state m is given by $P(n \to m) = |\langle \psi_m | \psi_n \rangle|^2$. These results can be seen by selecting "show transition probabilities" and the initial state n.

4.2.4. *Three-Dimensional Oscillator*

The isotropic three-dimensional harmonic oscillator is described by the Schrödinger equation $-\frac{1}{2}\nabla^2\Psi + \frac{1}{2}\omega^2 r^2\Psi = E\Psi$, in units such that $\hbar = m = 1$. The wavefunction is separable in Cartesian coordinates, giving a product of three one-dimensional oscillators with total energies $E_{n_1 n_2 n_3} = (n_1 + n_2 + n_3 + \frac{3}{2})\hbar\omega$. More interesting is the solution separable in spherical polar coordinates: $\psi_{nlm}(r, \theta, \phi) = R_{nl}(r)Y_{lm}(\theta, \phi)$, with the radial function $R_{nl}(r =)N_{nl}r^l e^{-\omega r^2/2} L_{(n-l)/2}^{l+1/2}(\omega r^2)$. Here, L is an associated Laguerre polynomial, Y a spherical harmonic and N a normalization constant. The energy levels are then given by $E_n = (n + \frac{3}{2})\hbar\omega$, being $\frac{1}{2}(n+1)(n+2)$-fold degenerate. For a given angular momentum quantum number l, the possible values of n are $l, l + 2, l + 4, \ldots$. The conventional code is used to label angular momentum states, with $s, p, d, f, \ldots$ representing $l = 0, 1, 2, 3, \ldots$.

This Demonstration shows contour plots in the x-z plane for the lower-energy eigenfunctions with $l = 0$ to 3. For $m > 0$, the eigenfunctions are complex. In all cases, the real parts of $\psi_{nlm}(r, \theta, \phi)$ are drawn. The wavefunctions are positive in the blue regions and negative in the white regions. The radial functions are also plotted, as well as an energy level diagram, with each dash representing the degenerate set of $2l + 1$ eigenstates for a given l.

The pattern of degeneracies for a three-dimensional oscillator implies invariance under an SU(3) Lie algebra, the same as the gauge group describing the color symmetry of strong interactions.

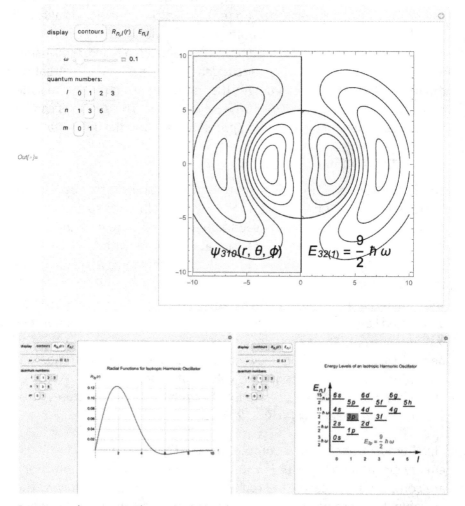

Demonstration 4.16: Three-Dimensional Isotropic Harmonic Oscillator (https://demonstrations.wolfram.com/ThreeDimensionalIsotropicHarmonicOscillator/)

4.2.5. *Two-Dimensional Oscillator in Magnetic Field*

The two-dimensional problem of a charged isotropic harmonic oscillator in a constant magnetic field can be solved exactly. You can choose to display: (1) a contour plot of the solutions; (2) the radial distribution function in cylindrical coordinates; or (3) an energy level diagram. You can select the oscillator frequency ω, the magnetic field B and the quantum numbers n and m. In the contour plots, positive and negative regions are colored blue and yellow, respectively.

For a charged particle (charge q, mass μ) in a magnetic field, the canonical form for the non-relativistic Hamiltonian is given by

$$H = \frac{1}{2\mu}\left(\mathbf{p} - \frac{q}{c}\mathbf{A}\right)^2 + V,$$

where $\mathbf{A}$ is the vector potential. The magnetic field is given by $\mathbf{B} = \nabla \times \mathbf{A}$. We consider an electron ($q = -e$) confined to the x-y plane, bound by an isotropic harmonic-oscillator potential and subjected to a constant magnetic field B in the z direction. This field can be represented by the vector potential $\mathbf{A} = \frac{1}{2}\mathbf{r} \times \mathbf{B}$, such that

$$A_x = \frac{1}{2}yB, \quad A_y = -\frac{1}{2}xB, \quad A_z = 0.$$

The Schrödinger equation, in Cartesian coordinates, can then be written

$$\frac{1}{2\mu}\left(-i\hbar\frac{\partial}{\partial x} + \frac{e}{2c}yB\right)^2 \psi(x,y) + \frac{1}{2\mu}\left(-i\hbar\frac{\partial}{\partial y} - \frac{e}{2c}xB\right)^2 \psi(x,y)$$
$$+ \frac{1}{2}\mu\omega^2(x^2 + y^2)\psi(x,y) = E\psi(x,y).$$

Expanding the squares, we obtain

$$-\frac{\hbar^2}{2\mu}\left(\frac{\partial^2}{\partial x^2} + \frac{\partial^2}{\partial y^2}\right)\psi(x,y) + \frac{1}{2}\mu\left(\omega^2 + \frac{e^2B^2}{4\mu^2c^2}\right)(x^2 + y^2)\psi(x,y)$$
$$+ \frac{eB}{2\mu c}i\hbar\left(x\frac{\partial}{\partial y} - y\frac{\partial}{\partial x}\right)\psi(x,y) = E\psi(x,y).$$

Note now that $L_z = -i\hbar(x\frac{\partial}{\partial y} - y\frac{\partial}{\partial x})$, the z component of angular momentum, and that $\omega_L = \frac{eB}{2\mu c}$, the Larmor frequency for an electron. It is convenient now to transform to cylindrical coordinates (ρ, θ, z), such that $\psi(x, y) = \Psi(\rho, \theta) = P_{(\rho)} \frac{1}{\sqrt{2\pi}} e^{im\theta}$, which is an eigenfunction of L_z with eigenvalues $m\hbar, m = 0, \pm 1, \pm 2, \ldots$. The radial function $P(\rho)$ satisfies the equation

$$-\frac{\hbar^2}{2\mu}\left[\frac{1}{\rho}\frac{d}{dp}\left(\rho\frac{d}{dp}\right) - \frac{m^2}{\rho^2}\right]P(\rho) + \frac{1}{2}\mu^2\Omega^2\rho^2 P(\rho) = (E + m\,\hbar\omega_L)P(\rho),$$

where $\Omega^2 = \omega^2 + \omega_L^2$. This has the form of the unperturbed two-dimensional oscillator and has the solutions (unnormalized, using

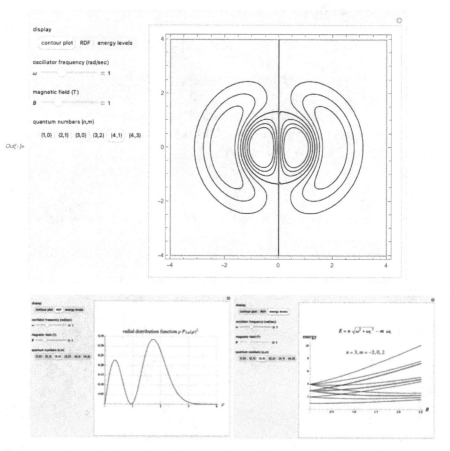

Demonstration 4.17: Two-Dimensional Oscillator in Magnetic Field (https://demonstra tions.wolfram.com/TwoDimensionalOscillatorInMagneticField/)

atomic units $\hbar = \mu = e = 1$):

$$P_{nm}(\rho) = \rho^{|m|}e^{-\Omega\rho^2/2}L^{|m|}_{(n-|m|-1)/2}(\Omega\rho^2), \quad m = 0, \pm1, \pm2, \ldots,$$

$$n = |m| + 1, \quad |m| + 3, \quad |m| + 5, \ldots,$$

where L^{α}_{β} is an associated Laguerre polynomial. The corresponding energies are

$$E_{nm} = n\hbar\Omega - m\hbar\omega_L = n\hbar\sqrt{\omega^2 + \omega_L^2} - m\hbar\omega_L.$$

Using atomic units and expressing B in teslas (T), $\omega_L \to B/2$. The energy, expanded in powers of the magnetic field, is then given by

$$E_{nm} = n\omega - \frac{mB}{2} + \frac{nB^2}{4\omega} - \frac{nB^4}{32\omega^3} + \cdots$$

4.2.6. Coherent States of the Harmonic Oscillator

Coherent states of a harmonic oscillator are wavepackets that have the shape of the ground state probability distribution but undergo the motion of a classical oscillator of arbitrary energy. Schrödinger first considered these in the context of minimum-uncertainty wavepackets. More recently (1963), Roy Glauber exploited coherent states in quantum-mechanical descriptions of oscillating electromagnetic fields in quantum optics and in connection with the Hanbury-Brown and Twiss experiment. Glauber shared the 2005 Nobel Prize in Physics for this work.

A coherent state, also known as a Glauber state or a "squeezed quantum state", is an eigenfunction of the harmonic oscillator annihilation operator $a = \frac{1}{\sqrt{2\omega}}(\omega x + ip)$, where $\hbar = m = 1$ for simplicity. The eigenstates of a (a non-Hermitian operator) are given by $|\lambda\rangle = e^{-\lambda^2/2}\sum_{n=0}^{\infty}\frac{\lambda^n}{\sqrt{n!}}|n\rangle$, where $|n\rangle$ are the harmonic oscillator eigenstates. These coherent states are solutions of the eigenvalue equation $a|\lambda\rangle = \lambda|\lambda\rangle$ with energy expectation values $\langle E\rangle = (\lambda^2 + \frac{1}{2})\omega$. The eigenvalues λ can be complex numbers but we restrict them here to real values. This average energy has a form analogous to the harmonic oscillator eigenvalues $E_n = (n + \frac{1}{2})\omega$. The latter are represented by horizontal lines within the potential energy parabola. The probability density for the wavepacket representing $|\lambda\rangle$

works out to $\rho(x,t) = \sqrt{\frac{\omega}{\pi}}\exp\left[-\omega\left(x - \sqrt{\frac{2}{\omega}}\lambda\cos(\omega t)\right)^2\right]$, shown as a blue Gaussian. As the time variation is run, the wavepacket oscillates so that its peak moves between the classical turning points. The wavepacket remains localized in the lowest energy state, when $\lambda = 0$.

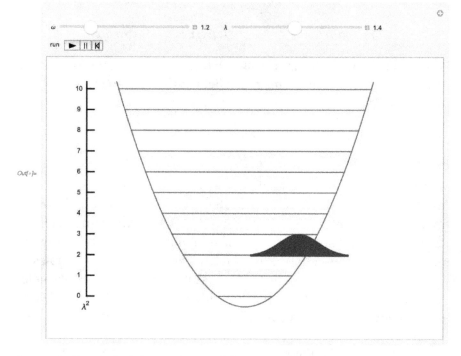

Demonstration 4.18: Coherent States of the Harmonic Oscillator (https://demonstrations.wolfram.com/CoherentStatesOfTheHarmonicOscillator/)

4.2.7. *Damped Harmonic Oscillator*

The quantum theory of the damped harmonic oscillator has been considered a simple model for a dissipative system, usually coupled to another oscillator that can absorb energy or to a continuous heat bath. This Demonstration treats a quantum damped oscillator as an isolated non-conservative system, which is represented by a time-dependent

Schrödinger equation. It is conjectured that spontaneous transition to a lower state will occur when the energy is reduced to that of the lower state, and this recurs sequentially, down to the ground state, which asymptotically disappears as the energy approaches zero. Within this model, the obtained result is an exact solution of the time-dependent Schrödinger equation.

The time-dependent wavefunction is given by

$$\psi_n(x, t) = \frac{1}{\sqrt{2^n n!}} \left(\frac{\omega}{\pi}\right)^{1/4} e^{-(\omega - i\gamma)x^2/2} H_n\left(\sqrt{\omega}x\right) e^{-i(n+1/2)\omega t} e^{-\gamma t/2},$$

$$n = 0, 1, 2, \ldots,$$

where H_n is a Hermite polynomial, and

$$\omega = \omega_0^2 - \gamma^2,$$

where ω_0 is the natural frequency of the undamped oscillator and γ is the damping constant. Atomic units $\hbar = m = 1$ are used. The real part of the expectation value of the Hamiltonian is assumed for the time-dependent energy, which gives

$$\epsilon_n(t) \approx \left(n + \frac{1}{2}\right) \omega e^{-\gamma t}.$$

The graphic shows the probability density $\rho_n(x, t) = \psi_n^*(x, t)\psi_n(x, t)$ and energy $\epsilon_n(t)$ as functions of t for $n = 0, 1, 2$. The inset shows the energy, as downward transitions occur, asymptotically decreasing to 0.

The classical damped harmonic oscillator is described by the well-known equation

$$m\ddot{x} + \eta\dot{x} + kx = 0,$$

where m is the mass of the oscillating particle, k is the Hooke's law force constant and η is a damping constant. It is convenient to define the modified damping constant

$$\gamma = \frac{\eta}{2m}$$

and the natural frequency of the undamped oscillator

$$\omega_0 = \sqrt{\frac{k}{m}},$$

which reduces the first equation to

$$\ddot{x} + 2\gamma\dot{x} + \omega_0^2 x = 0.$$

The solution of the equation of motion can be expressed in the form

$$x(t) = x_0 e^{-\gamma t}\cos(\omega t + \varphi).$$

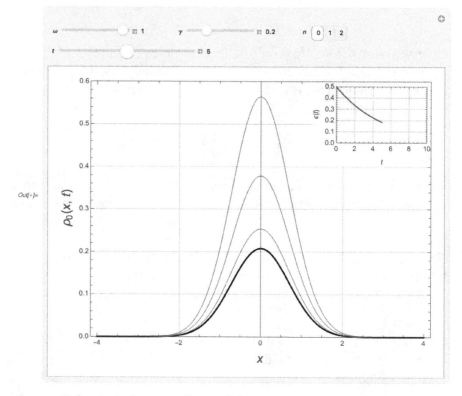

Demonstration 4.19: Quantum Theory of the Damped Harmonic Oscillator (https://demonstrations.wolfram.com/QuantumTheoryOfTheDampedHarmonicOscillator/)

For the quantum analog of the damped oscillator, we propose the Hamiltonian

$$H = \frac{p^2}{2} - \gamma xp + \frac{\omega^2 x^2}{2},$$

which is *non-Hermitian* but accounts nicely for the decay of the system. The corresponding time-dependent Schrödinger equation for $\psi n(x, t)$ is given by

$$-\frac{1}{2}\frac{\partial^2 \psi}{\partial x^2} + i\gamma x\frac{\partial \psi}{\partial x} + \frac{\omega^2 x^2}{2}\psi = i\frac{\partial \psi}{\partial t},$$

with the solutions given above.

4.2.8. *Landau Levels in a Magnetic Field*

This Demonstration considers the quantum-mechanical system of a free electron in a constant magnetic field, with definite values of the linear and angular momentum in the direction of the field. The wavefunction is plotted in a plane normal to the magnetic field. The corresponding energies are the equally spaced Landau levels, similar to the energies of a harmonic oscillator. These results find application in the theory of the quantum Hall effects.

You can select a 3D plot of the wavefunction, a plot of the radial function or an energy level diagram. The first slider varies the magnetic field strength B. You can then select n and m, the radial and angular quantum numbers, respectively.

The non-relativistic Hamiltonian for an electron in a magnetic field $B = \nabla \times A$, where A is vector potential, is given by

$$H = \frac{1}{2m_e}(p + eA)^2 = -\frac{\hbar^2}{2m_e}\nabla^2 - \frac{i\hbar e}{m_e}A \cdot \nabla + \frac{e^2 A^2}{2m_e},$$

where m_e and $-e$ are the mass and charge of the electron, respectively. We also make use of the Coulomb gauge condition $\nabla \cdot A = 0$. For a constant field in the z direction, $B = \hat{z}B$, it is convenient to work in cylindrical coordinates, r, θ, z. With a convenient choice of gauge, the vector

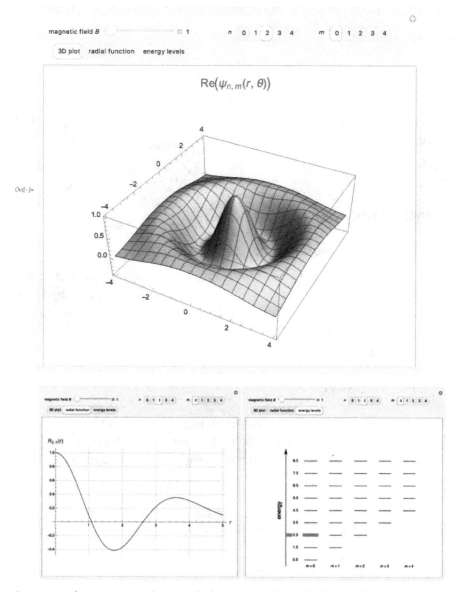

Demonstration 4.20: Landau Levels in a Magnetic Field (https://demonstrations. wolfram.com/LandauLevelsInAMagneticField/)

potential can be represented by

$$A_\theta = \frac{1}{2}Br, \quad A_r = A_z = 0.$$

This gives $\mathbf{B} = \nabla \times \mathbf{A} = \frac{1}{r}\frac{\partial}{\partial r}(rA_\theta)\hat{\mathbf{z}} = B\hat{\mathbf{z}}$.

The Schrödinger equation for $\psi(r, \theta, z)$ is given by

$$-\frac{\hbar^2}{2m_e}\left(\frac{1}{r}\frac{\partial}{\partial r}\left(r\frac{\partial\psi}{\partial r}\right) + \frac{1}{r^2}\frac{\partial^2\psi}{\partial\theta^2} + \frac{\partial^2\psi}{\partial z^2}\right) - \frac{ie\hbar B}{2m_e}\frac{\partial\psi}{\partial\theta} + \frac{e^2B^2}{8m_e}r^2\psi = E\psi.$$

The equation is separable in cylindrical coordinates, and we can write

$$\psi(r, \theta, z) = R(r)e^{im\theta}e^{ikz}, \quad m = 0, 1, 2, \ldots, -\infty < k < \infty,$$

for definite values of the angular and linear momenta. We consider only angular momentum anti-clockwise about the z axis. We set $k = 0$ and consider only motion in a plane perpendicular to the magnetic field. Introducing atomic units $\hbar = m_e = e = 1$, the radial equation reduces to

$$-\frac{1}{2}\left(R''(r) + \frac{1}{r}R'(r) - \frac{m^2}{r^2}R(r)\right) + \left(\frac{B^2}{8}r^2 + \frac{m}{2}B\right)R(r) = ER(r).$$

The solution with the correct boundary conditions as $r\to\infty$ is given by $R_{nm}(r) = r^m e^{-Br^2/4}L_n^m\left(\frac{Br^2}{2}\right)$, where L_n^m is an associated Laguerre polynomial. The corresponding energy eigenvalues are $E_{nm} = (n + m + \frac{1}{2})B$. These are the well-known Landau levels, which are equivalent to the levels of a two-dimensional harmonic oscillator with $\omega = \frac{e\hbar B}{2m_e}$. Recall that $\omega_c = \frac{e\hbar B}{m_e}$ is the cyclotron frequency for an electron in a magnetic field.

4.2.9. *Schwinger's Oscillator Model for Angular Momentum*

In an internal Atomic Energy Commission document published in 1952, Julian Schwinger developed the quantum theory of angular momentum from the commutation relations for a pair of independent harmonic oscillators. This work has since been subsequently quoted many times. This Demonstration shows the angular momentum states j, m derived from the quantum numbers n_a, n_b for a pair of harmonic oscillators, with $n_a, n_b = 0, 1, 2, \ldots.$

A pair of uncoupled harmonic oscillators, designated a and b, can be defined by raising and lowering operators with commutation relations

$$[a, a^\dagger] = [b, b^\dagger] = 1, \quad [a, b] = [a, b^\dagger] = [a^\dagger, b] = [a^\dagger, b^\dagger] = 0.$$

It can then be shown that the operators

$$J_1 = \frac{a^\dagger b + b^\dagger a}{2}, \quad J_2 = \frac{a^\dagger b - b^\dagger a}{2i}, \quad J_3 = \frac{a^\dagger a - b^\dagger b}{2}$$

obey the canonical commutation relations for angular momentum:

$$[J_1, J_2] = iJ_3, \quad [J_2, J_3] = iJ_1, \quad [J_3, J_1] = iJ_2, \quad [J_{1,2,3}, J^2] = 0.$$

The number operators for the two oscillators are given by

$$N_a = a^\dagger a, \quad N_b = b^\dagger b, \quad N = N_a + N_b = a^\dagger a + b^\dagger b,$$

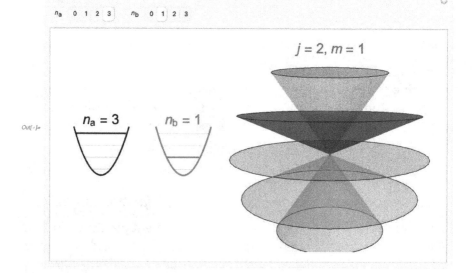

Out[ ]=

Demonstration 4.21: Schwinger's Oscillator Model for Angular Momentum (https://demonstrations.wolfram.com/SchwingersOscillatorModelForAngularMomentum/)

with corresponding eigenvalues n_a, n_b, n, each equal to an integer $0, 1, 2, \ldots$.

In terms of the number operators, relevant angular momentum operators can be expressed as

$$J^2 = \frac{N}{2}\left(\frac{N}{2}+1\right), \quad M = \frac{N_a - N_b}{2}.$$

The quantum number j evidently can be identified with $\frac{n}{2} = \frac{n_a+n_b}{2}$, with possible values $0, \frac{1}{2}, 1, \frac{3}{2}, \ldots$. Analogously, $m = \frac{n_a-n_b}{2}$, running from $-j$ to j in integer steps.

4.2.10. *Propagators for Free Particle and Harmonic Oscillator*

The time evolution of a one-dimensional quantum system from an initial state $\psi(x, 0)$ can be represented, in terms of the propagator, by

$$\psi(x, t) = \int \psi(x', 0) K(x, x', t) dx'.$$

For the free particle,

$$K_{FP}(x, x', t) = \left(\frac{m\omega}{2\pi i \hbar t}\right)^{1/2} e^{-\frac{m(x-x')^2}{2i\hbar t}},$$

while for the harmonic oscillator,

$$K_{HO}(x, x', t) = \left(\frac{m\omega}{2\pi i \hbar \sin \omega t}\right)^{1/2}$$
$$\times \exp\left(-\frac{m\omega[(x^2 + x'^2)\cos \omega t - 2xx']}{2i\hbar \sin \omega t}\right).$$

For compactness, we use units with $\hbar = m = \omega = 1$. For the initial state, we consider the Gaussian wave packet and the rectangular pulse. The plots, for selected cases, show the probability densities $|\psi(x, 0)|^2$ and $|\psi(x, t)|^2$.

For the free particle with initial Gaussian wave packet $\psi(x,0) = \left(\frac{\alpha}{\pi}\right)^{1/4} e^{-\alpha x^2/2}$, we find

$$\psi(x,t) = \int_{-\infty}^{\infty} \psi(x',0)K_{FP}(x,x',t)dx' = \left(\frac{a}{\pi}\right)^{1/4}(1+i\alpha t)^{-1/2}$$

$$\times \exp\left(-\frac{x^2\alpha}{2 \times (1+i\alpha t)}\right).$$

For initial rectangular pulse $\psi(x,0) = \alpha^{1/2}, -\frac{\alpha}{2} \leq x \leq \frac{\alpha}{2}$,

$$\psi(x,t) = \int_{-\alpha/2}^{\alpha/2} \alpha^{1/2}K_{FP}(x,x',t)dx'$$

$$= \frac{\sqrt{\alpha}}{2}\left(\mathrm{erf}\left[\frac{2\alpha x+1}{2\alpha\sqrt{2it}}\right] - \mathrm{erf}\left[\frac{2\alpha x-1}{2\alpha\sqrt{2it}}\right]\right).$$

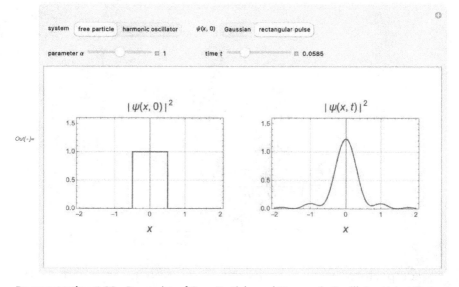

Demonstration 4.22: Dynamics of Free Particle and Harmonic Oscillator Using Propagators (https://demonstrations.wolfram.com/DynamicsOfFreeParticleAndHarmonicOscillatorUsingPropagators/)

For the harmonic oscillator with initial Gaussian wave packet,

$$\psi(x,t) = \int_{-\infty}^{\infty} \psi(x',0)K_{HO}(x,x',t)dx' = \left(\frac{\alpha}{\pi}\right)^{1/4}(\cos t + i\alpha \sin t)^{-1/2}$$

$$\times \exp\left(-\frac{x^2(\alpha \cos t + i \sin t)}{2(\cos t + i\alpha \sin t)}\right).$$

(For $\alpha = 1$, this reduces to the time-dependent ground-state eigenfunction $\psi_0(x,t) = \pi^{-1/4}e^{-x^2/2}e^{-it/2}$.)

For initial rectangular pulse,

$$\psi(x,t) = \int_{-\alpha/2}^{-\alpha/2} \alpha^{1/2}K_{HO}(x,x',t)dx' = \frac{\sqrt{\alpha}\sec t\sqrt{\sin 2t}}{2\sqrt{2}\sqrt{\sin t}}$$

$$\times e^{-\frac{1}{2}ix^2\tan t}\left(\text{erf}\left[\frac{x+\frac{\cos t}{2\alpha}}{\sqrt{i\sin 2t}}\right] - \text{erf}\left[\frac{x-\frac{\cos t}{2\alpha}}{\sqrt{i\sin 2t}}\right]\right).$$

4.2.11. Hydrogen Atom and Harmonic Oscillator

The bound states of the hydrogen atom are governed by the geometrical symmetry SO(3) (not considering the full dynamical symmetry SO(4)). Similarly, the two-dimensional isotropic harmonic oscillator exhibits the symmetry SU(2). To anyone versed in the theory of Lie groups, it would not be surprising that there might be an explicit connection between these two problems, in view of the local isomorphism between the corresponding Lie algebras so(3) and su(2).

The radial Schrödinger equation for a hydrogen-like system, in atomic units, is given by

$$-\frac{1}{2r^2}\frac{d}{dr}\left(r^2\frac{dR}{dr}\right) + \frac{l(l+1)}{2r^2}R(r) - \frac{Z}{r}R(r)$$

$$= -\frac{Z^2}{2n^2}R(r), \quad l = 0,1,2,\ldots, n = l+1, l+2, \ldots,$$

with the unnormalized solutions $R_{nl}(r) = r^l e^{-Zr/n}L_{n-l-1}^{2l+1}\left(\frac{2Zr}{n}\right)$, where L is an associated Laguerre polynomial. Consider now a two-dimensional isotropic harmonic oscillator, expressed in polar coordinates. The associated radial Schrödinger equation takes the form

$$-\frac{1}{2\rho}\frac{d}{d\rho}\left(\rho\frac{dP}{d\rho}\right) + \frac{m^2}{2\rho^2}P(\rho) + \frac{1}{2}\omega^2\rho^2 P(\rho) = n_{osc}\omega P(\rho),$$

$m = 0, \pm1, \pm2, \dots, n_{osc} = |m| + 1, |m| + 3, |m| + 5, \dots$

Using DSolve, we find the unnormalized solutions: $P_{mn_{osc}}(\rho) = \rho^m e^{-\omega\rho^2/2} L^m_{(n_{osc}-m-1)/2}(\omega\rho^2).$

The solutions of the two problems can be made equivalent by the substitutions: $r \to \frac{\eta\omega}{2Z}\rho^2, m \to 2l + 1, n_{osc} \to 2n.$

For selected values of n and l, the graphic shows plots of the radial wavefunctions $R(r)$ and $P(\rho)$, as well as the corresponding radial distribution functions (RDFs) $r^2 R(r)^2$ and $\rho P(\rho)^2$.

Julian Schwinger, in his quantum mechanics course, suggested a very clever method to solve the hydrogen-atom problem by converting it into

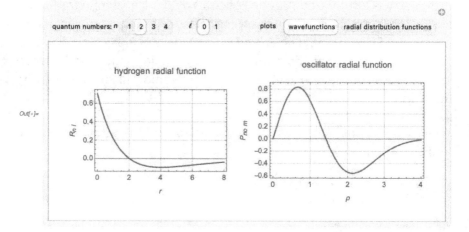

Demonstration 4.23: Connection between Quantum-Mechanical Hydrogen Atom and Harmonic Oscillator (https://demonstrations.wolfram.com/ConnectionBetweenQuant umMechanicalHydrogenAtomAndHarmonicOsc/)

the equation for a two-dimensional isotropic harmonic oscillator. To do this, let $r = \lambda\rho^2/2$ and $R_{nl}(r) = P(\rho)/\rho$. Then $P(\rho)$ turns out to obey the radial equation for the oscillator.

4.3. The Hydrogen Atom

The Schrödinger equation for the hydrogen-like atom (arbitrary Z) in atomic units ($\hbar = m = e = 1$) and spherical coordinates:

$$\left\{ -\frac{1}{2}\left(\frac{1}{r^2}\frac{\partial}{\partial r}r^2\frac{\partial}{\partial r} + \frac{1}{r^2\sin\theta}\frac{\partial}{\partial \theta}\sin\theta\frac{\partial}{\partial \theta} + \frac{1}{r^2\sin^2\theta}\frac{\partial^2}{\partial \phi^2} \right) - \frac{Z}{r} \right\}$$
$$\times \psi(r, \theta, \varphi) = E\psi(r, \theta, \phi).$$

The normalized eigenfunctions are given by

$$\psi_{nlm}(r, \theta, \phi) = R_{nl}(r)Y_l^m(\theta, \phi)$$

where $Y_l^m(\theta, \phi)$ are spherical harmonics and

$$R_{nl}(r) = \sqrt{\left(\frac{2Z}{n} \right)^3 \frac{(n-l-1)!}{2n(n+l)!}} \left(\frac{2Zr}{n} \right)^l e^{-Zr\ln}L_{n-l-1}^{2l+1}(2Zr\ln),$$
$$n = 1, 2, 3, \ldots, l = 0, 1, 2, \ldots, n-1,$$

where L is an associated Laguerre polynomial. The energy eigenvalues are

$$E_n = -\frac{Z^2}{2n^2},$$

independent of l. Following are plots of the radial functions for $n = 1, 2, 3$, designated 1s, 2s, 2p, 3s, 3p, 3d.

In[•]:= $R[n\_, l\_, r\_] := \sqrt{\left(\dfrac{2}{n}\right)^3 \dfrac{(n-l-1)!}{2n(n+l)!}} \left(\dfrac{2r}{n}\right)^l e^{-r/n}$ LaguerreL[n - l - 1, 2 l + 1, 2 r / n]

In[•]:= g[n_, l_] := Plot[R[n, l, r], {r, 0, 5 n}, Frame → True,
    GridLines → Automatic, PlotLabel → R$_{n,l}$[r], ImageSize → {180, 120}]

In[∘]:= `Grid[{{g[1, 0], g[2, 0], g[2, 1]}, {g[3, 0], g[3, 1], g[3, 2]}}]`

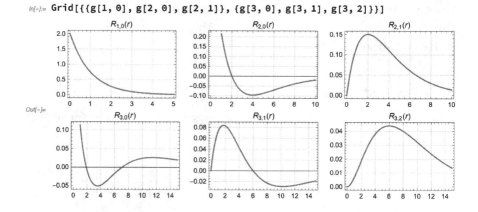

Out[∘]=

4.3.1. *Radial Functions*

An application of supersymmetric quantum mechanics enables all the bound-state radial functions for the hydrogen atom to be evaluated using first-order differential operators, without any explicit reference to Laguerre polynomials.

The non-relativistic hydrogen-like system with atomic number Z and assumed infinite nuclear mass satisfies the Schrödinger equation $\left(-\frac{1}{2}\nabla^2 - \frac{Z}{r} + \frac{Z^2}{2n^2}\right)\,\psi_{nlm}(r, \theta, \phi) = 0$, in atomic units $\hbar = m = e = 1$. Separation of variables in spherical polar coordinates gives $\psi_{nlm}(r, \theta, \phi) = R_{nl}(r)Y_{lm}(\theta, \phi)$.
Defining the reduced radial function $P(r) = rR(r)$, the radial equation can be expressed as $\left(-\frac{d^2}{dr^2} + \frac{l(l+1)}{r^2} - \frac{2Z}{r} + \frac{Z^2}{n^2}\right)P_{nl}(r) = 0$. For the case $l = n-1$ (the $1s, 2p, 3d, 4f, \ldots$ states) the radial function has the nodeless form $P_{n,n-1}(r) = \text{const}\, r^n e^{-Zr/n}$.

The operators A_{l+1} and A_l^+ are defined with the effect of lowering or raising the quantum number l by 1, respectively, when applied to the radial function $P_{nl}(r)$, namely, $A_{l+1}P_{n,l}(r) = \text{const}\, P_{n,l+1}(r)$ and $A_l^+ P_{nl}(r) = \text{const}\, P_{n,l-1}(r)$. The constants are most easily determined after the fact by the normalization conditions $\int_0^\infty P_{nl}(r)^2 dr = 1$.

In this Demonstration, you can plot any radial function with $n = 1$ to 4 and show the result of applying A_l (red curve) or A_l^+ (blue curve). The plots pertain to the case $Z = 1$. You can also choose to view the results as formulas (with variable Z) or on an energy level diagram.

Supersymmetric quantum mechanics can be applied to the solution of the hydrogenic radial equation, treated as a pseudo-one-dimensional problem in the variable r with effective Hamiltonians denoted h. There exist two partner Hamiltonians for each value of l, which can be written $h_l^{(1)} = -\frac{d^2}{dr^2} + v_l^{(1)}(r) = A_l^+ A_l$ and $h_l^{(2)} = \frac{d^2}{dr^2} + v_l^{(2)}(r) = A_l A_l^+$, with $A_l = \frac{d}{dr} + W_l(r)$ and $A_l^+ = -\frac{d}{dr} + W_l(r)$. The superpotential $W_l(r)$ is given

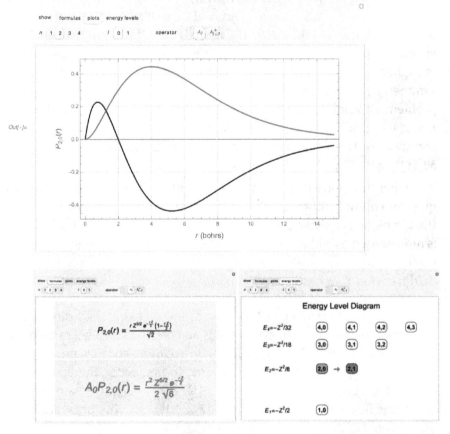

Demonstration 4.24: Hydrogenic Radial Functions via Supersymmetry (https://demonstrations.wolfram.com/HydrogenicRadialFunctionsViaSupersymmetry/)

by $W_l(r) = -P'_{l+1,l}(r)/P_{l+1,l}(r)$. With $P_{nl}(r)$ as defined above, $Wl(r) = -\frac{l+1}{r} + \frac{Z}{l+1}$. The lowest-energy eigenstate of $h_l^{(1)}$ has no partner eigenstate, but all higher-energy eigenstates have degenerate supersymmetric partners. These can be labeled by increasing values of the principal quantum number n, beginning with $n = l + 1$. The composite pattern for all l-values leads to the characteristic degeneracies for n in a pure Coulomb field, associated with a higher symmetry than would be implied by spherical invariance alone.

4.3.2. *The Hydrogen Atom in Parabolic Coordinates*

The Schrödinger equation for the hydrogen atom, $-\frac{1}{2}\nabla^2\psi(\mathbf{r}) - \frac{1}{r}\psi(\mathbf{r}) = E\psi(\mathbf{r})$ (in atomic units $\hbar = m = e = 1$), can be separated and solved in parabolic coordinates (ξ, η, ϕ) as well as in the more conventional spherical polar coordinates (r, θ, ϕ). This is an indication of degeneracy in higher eigenstates and is connected to the existence of a "hidden symmetry", namely the SO(4) Lie algebra associated with the Coulomb problem. Parabolic coordinates can be defined by $\xi = r(1+\cos\theta) = r+z$, $\eta = r(1 - \cos\theta) = r - z$, with the same $\phi = \arctan(y/x)$ as in spherical coordinates. The wavefunction is separable in the form $\psi_{n_1 n_2 m}(\xi, \eta, \phi) = Nf_1(\xi)f_2(\eta)e^{im\phi}$ with $f_{1,2}(\zeta) = \zeta^{-1/2}M_{n,\frac{1}{2}+\frac{|m|+1}{2},\frac{|m|}{2}}(\zeta/n)$. Here M is a Whittaker function and $n = n_1 + n_2 + |m| + 1$, equal to the principal quantum number. Contour plots for the real part of the wavefunctions in the x, z-plane are shown, including the values $\phi = 0$ and π. The nucleus is represented as a black dot. The corresponding energy eigenvalues are given by $E_n = -\frac{1}{2n^2}$, independent of other quantum numbers (in the field-free non-relativistic case).

The hydrogen atom in a constant electric field $\mathcal{E}$ along the z direction is also separable in parabolic coordinates and can thus be used to treat the Stark effect. The functions $f_1(\xi)$ and $f_2(\eta)$ are more complicated but can be obtained by perturbation expansions. To first order, the Stark effect energies are given by $E_{nn_1n_2} \approx -\frac{1}{2n^2} + \frac{3}{2}\mathcal{E}n(n_1 - n_2)$. One atomic unit of electric field $\mathcal{E}$ is equivalent to 5.142×10^{11} V/m. The presence of an electric field is shown by a red arrow.

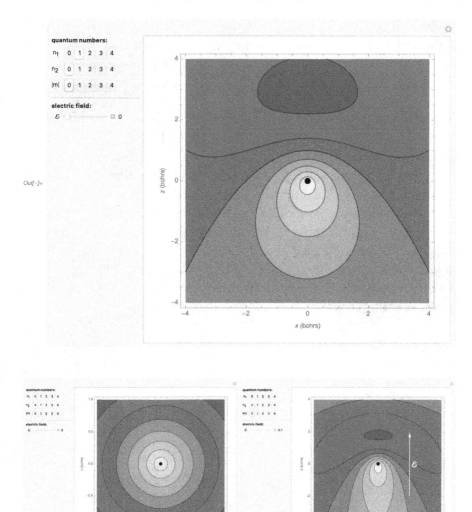

Demonstration 4.25: The Hydrogen Atom in Parabolic Coordinates (https://demon strations.wolfram.com/TheHydrogenAtomInParabolicCoordinates/)

4.3.3. *Continuum Eigenstates*

The positive-energy continuum states of a hydrogen-like system are described by the eigenfunctions $\psi_{klm}(r, \theta, \phi) = R_{k\ell}(r)Y_{\ell m}(\theta, \phi)$ with corresponding eigenvalues $E_k = \frac{k^2}{2}$, $(0 \le k < \infty)$. $Y_{\ell m}(\theta, \phi)$ are the same spherical harmonics that occur for the bound states. In atomic units $\hbar = \mu = e = 1$, the radial equation can be written $-\frac{1}{2}R''_{k\ell}(r) - \frac{1}{r}R'_{k\ell}(r) + \left[\frac{\ell(\ell+1)}{2r^2} - \frac{Z}{r}\right]R_{k\ell}(r) = \frac{k^2}{2}R_{k\ell}(r)$. The solutions with the appropriate analytic and boundary conditions have the form $R_{k\ell}(r) = \frac{2k e^{\pi Z/2k}}{(2\ell+1)!}|\Gamma(\ell+1+iZ/k)|(2kr)^\ell e^{-ikr}{}_1F_1(\ell+1+iZ/k, 2\ell+2, 2ikr)$. These functions are delta function-normalized, such that $\int_0^\infty R_{k\ell}(r)R_{k'\ell}(r)r^2 dr = \delta(k - k')$. They have the same functional forms (apart from normalization constants) as the discrete eigenfunctions under the substitution $n \to -iZ/k$. You can plot the continuum function for various choices of Z, ℓ, and k. The asymptotic form for large r approaches a spherical wave of the form $R_{k\ell}(r) \approx \frac{1}{r}\cos[kr+\frac{Z}{k}\ln 2kr-\frac{\pi}{2}(\ell+1)-\arg\Gamma(\ell+1+iZ/k)]$. The terms in the argument of cos, in addition to kr, represent the phase shift with respect to the free particle. Coulomb scattering generally involves a significant number of partial waves.

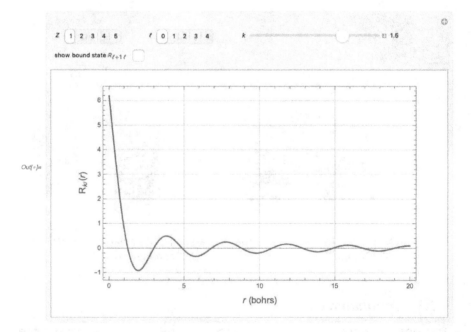

Out[ ]=

Demonstration 4.26: Hydrogen-Like Continuum Eigenstates (https://demonstrations. wolfram.com/HydrogenLikeContinuumEigenstates/)

A checkbox lets you compare the lowest-energy bound state with the same ℓ, that is, the wavefunctions for 1s, 2p, 3d, ... (magnified by a factor of $2\ell+2$ for better visualization). The $E = 0$ solution, obtained as the limit of the discrete function as $n \rightarrow \infty$ or of the continuum function as $k \rightarrow 0$, has the form of a Bessel function: $R_{0\ell}(r) = \text{const} J_{2\ell+2}(\sqrt{8Zr})/\sqrt{2Zr}$.

4.3.4. *Zero-Energy Limit of Coulomb Wavefunctions*

In the limit of zero energy, the Coulomb–Schrödinger equation in atomic units simplifies to

$$-\frac{1}{2}\nabla^2\psi - \frac{Z}{r}\psi = 0,$$

with the radial function satisfying

$$-\frac{1}{2}R''(r) - \frac{1}{r}R'(r) + \frac{\ell(\ell+1)}{2r^2}R(r) - \frac{Z}{r}R(r) = 0.$$

This can be solved exactly, giving a compact form for the radial function for angular momentum l:

$$R_\ell(r) = \frac{J_{2\ell+1}(\sqrt{8Zr})}{\sqrt{2Zr}},$$

where J is a Bessel function. This Demonstration shows that the given limiting form is obtained, both for the discrete eigenfunctions in the limit $n \rightarrow \infty$ and for the continuum eigenfunctions as $k \rightarrow 0$. The eigenfunctions are shown in black, while the Bessel-function limit is drawn in red.

It is also amusing to see the behavior of the radial distribution function for larger values of n.

The hydrogenic eigenfunctions can be expressed in terms of confluent hypergeometric functions $_1F_1$. The normalization constants are trimmed so as to coincide with the Bessel function limit as $n \rightarrow \infty$ for the discrete eigenfunctions and $k \rightarrow 0$ for the continuum. Thus we take

$$R_{n,l}(r) = \frac{1}{(2l+1)!}(2Zr)^l e^{-Zr/n} {}_1F_1(1 + l - n, 2l + 2, 2Zr/n)$$

and

$$F_{k,l}(r) = Re\left(\frac{1}{(2l+1)!}\frac{ke^{\frac{\pi z}{2k}}}{\sqrt{2\pi Zk}}\left|\Gamma\left(1+i\frac{Z}{k}\right)\right|(2kr)^l e^{-ikr}\right.$$

$$\left. \times\ _1F_1(1+l+iZ/k, 2l+2, 2ikr)\right),$$

for the discrete and continuum eigenfunctions, respectively.

The limiting behavior as $n \to \infty$ or $k \to 0$ can be deduced from the asymptotic limit:

$$_1F_1(a, b, z) \sim \Gamma(b)e^{z/2}\left(\left(\frac{b}{2}-a\right)z\right)^{\frac{1}{2}-\frac{b}{2}}$$

$$\times J_{b-1}\left(\sqrt{2(b-2a)z}\right) \text{ as } a \to -\infty.$$

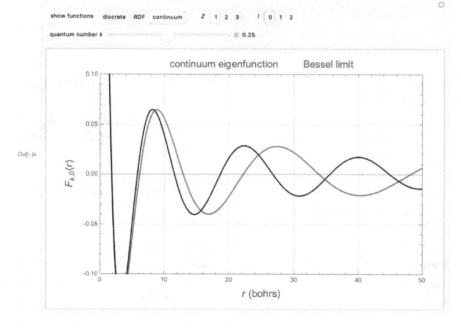

Demonstration 4.27: Zero-Energy Limit of Coulomb Wavefunctions (https://demonstrations.wolfram.com/ZeroEnergyLimitOfCoulombWavefunctions/)

4.3.5. *Hydrogen Atom in Curved Space*

In 1940, Schrödinger considered the hypothetical problem of a hydrogen atom in a space of positive curvature. The actual curvature of space is far too feeble to have any detectable physical effect on an atomic scale, but this might become relevant in the neighborhood of a black hole or neutron star. Schrödinger was able to derive an exact solution with a remarkably simple energy spectrum:

$$E_n = -\frac{Z^2}{2n^2} + \frac{n^2 - 1}{2R^2},$$

in atomic units with curvature parameter R. In this model, the continuum is replaced by a closely spaced discrete spectrum, resembling the eigenvalues of the particle-in-a-box. The system is described by hyperspherical coordinates in four-dimensional Euclidean space, such that the Cartesian coordinates are given by

$$x^1 = R\sin\chi\sin\theta\cos\phi, \quad x^2 = R\sin\chi\sin\theta\sin\phi,$$
$$x^3 = R\sin\chi\cos\theta, \quad x^4 = R,\cos\chi,$$

with

$$0 \le \phi \le 2\pi, \quad 0 \le \theta \le \pi, \quad 0 \le \chi \le \pi.$$

The Coulomb potential is given by

$$V = -\frac{Z}{r} = -\frac{Z\cot\chi}{R},$$

while the Laplacian can be written

$$\nabla^2 = \frac{1}{R^2\sin^2\chi}\left(\frac{\partial}{\partial\chi}\left(\sin^2\chi\frac{\partial}{\partial\chi}\right) - \Lambda^2\right),$$

where Λ^2 is the usual three-dimensional angular momentum operator. The Schrödinger equation can be solved exactly. The radial equation reduces to

$$\left(\frac{d^2}{d\chi^2} - \frac{l(l+1)}{\sin^2\chi} + 2ZR\cot\chi + 2R^2E + 1\right)\mathcal{P}(\chi) = 0.$$

The (unnormalized) solutions are given by

$$\mathcal{P}_{nl}(\chi) = \sin^n \chi e^{-ZR\chi/n} P_{n-l-1}^{(\alpha,\beta)}(-i \cot \chi), \quad \begin{Bmatrix} \alpha \\ \beta \end{Bmatrix} = -n \mp iZR/n,$$

where $P_n^{(\alpha,\beta)}(z)$ is a Jacobi polynomial.

The left graphic shows plots of the radial function $\mathcal{P}_{nl}(\chi)$ for selected values of Z, n, l and R. The right graphic shows the corresponding hydrogenic functions $P_{nl}(r)$ in Euclidean space, which represent the limit as the curvature approaches 0, or $R \to \infty$.

The canonical partition function for the hydrogen atom had long presented a paradox since the summation over just the bound states

$$q = \sum_{n=1}^{\infty} 2n^2 e^{\beta Z^2/2n^2} \quad (\beta = 1/kT)$$

is divergent. However, by using the curved-space energies

$$E_n = -\frac{Z^2}{2n^2} + \frac{n^2 - 1}{2R^2},$$

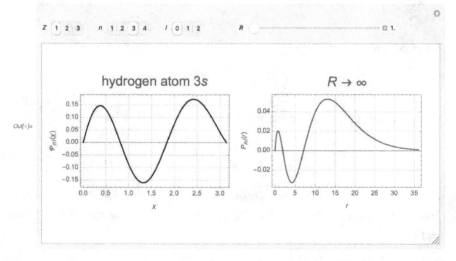

Demonstration 4.28: Hydrogen Atom in Curved Space (https://demonstrations.wolfram.com/HydrogenAtomInCurvedSpace/)

a finite result can be derived, with the radius of curvature of the four-dimensional hypersphere serving as a "metaphor" for the volume in three-dimensional space, with the correspondence

$$R = \left(\frac{V}{2\pi^2}\right)^{1/3}.$$

4.3.6. *Polarizability of the Hydrogen Atom*

An electric field $\mathcal{E}$ distorts the charge distribution of an atom. For s states, the energy is decreased by $-\frac{1}{2}\alpha\mathcal{E}^2$ to second order in the field strength. The parameter α is known as the (electric) polarizability. We consider the 1s and 2s states of the hydrogen atom, making use of perturbation theory. The graphic shows a contour plot of the wavefunction as the electric field is increased. The wavefunction is positive in the blue region and negative in the yellow region. A similar distortion of the initially spherical charge density occurs in the formation of chemical bonds.

For the 1s ground state,

$$\psi_1^{(0)} = \frac{1}{\sqrt{\pi}}e^{-r} \quad \text{and} \quad E_1^{(0)} = -\frac{1}{2},$$

in atomic units. The unperturbed Hamiltonian is

$$H^{(0)} = -\frac{1}{2}\nabla^2 - \frac{1}{r},$$

while the perturbation due to an electric field (in the z direction) is

$$H^{(1)} = -\mathcal{E}r\cos\theta.$$

The first-order perturbation equation for the $n = 1$ ground state is given by

$$(H^{(0)} - E_1^{(0)})\psi_1^{(1)} + (H^{(1)} - E_1^{(1)}) = 0.$$

The first-order energy $E_1^{(1)} = 0$. We obtain thereby an inhomogeneous differential equation

$$\left(-\frac{1}{2}\nabla^2 - \frac{1}{r} + \frac{1}{2}\right)\psi_1^{(1)} = \frac{1}{\sqrt{\pi}}\mathcal{E}re^{-r}\cos\theta.$$

Writing $\psi_1^{(1)} = \mathcal{E}f(r)\cos\theta$, the differential equation reduces to

$$f''(r) + \frac{2}{r}f'(r) - \frac{2}{r^2}f(r) + \frac{2}{r}f(r) - f(r) = \frac{2}{\sqrt{\pi}}re^{-r}.$$

The solution that is finite for all r is

$$f[r] = -\frac{1}{\sqrt{\pi}}\left(r + \frac{1}{2}r^2\right)e^{-r}.$$

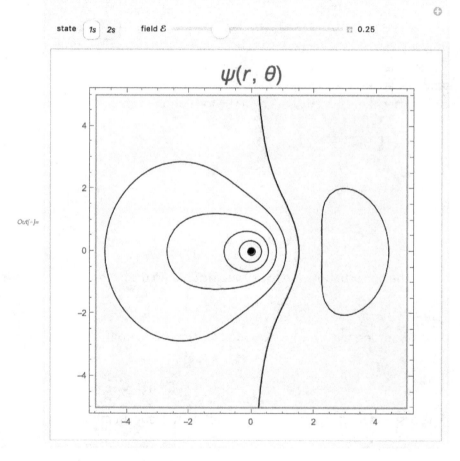

Demonstration 4.29: Polarizability of the Hydrogen Atom (https://demonstrations. wolfram.com/PolarizabilityOfHydrogenAtom/)

Thus the ground state eigenfunction to first order is given by

$$\psi_1(r,\theta) = \frac{1}{\sqrt{\pi}}e^{-r}\left(1 - \mathcal{E}\left(r + \frac{1}{2}r^2\right)\cos\theta\right).$$

The second-order energy is obtained from

$$E_1^{(2)} = \langle \psi_1^{(1)}|H^{(1)}|\psi_1^{(0)}\rangle = -\frac{1}{2}\alpha\mathcal{E}^2,$$

giving a polarizability $\alpha_{1s} = 4.5\,\text{bohr}^3$.

An analogous treatment for the 2s state results in the following approximation:

$$\psi_2(r,\theta) = \frac{1}{4\sqrt{2\pi}}(2-r)e^{-r/2} - \mathcal{E}\frac{1}{10\sqrt{2\pi}}r^4 e^{-r/2}\cos\theta,$$

with a polarizability $\alpha_{2s} = 120\,\text{bohr}^3$.

Chapter 5

Physics: Quantum Theory II, Applications

5.1. Exact Solutions of the Schrödinger Equation

In addition to the free particle, harmonic oscillator and hydrogen atom, there is a small number of additional problems for which the Schrödinger equation can be solved in closed form. Such solutions are of importance since physical systems can often be treated as perturbations of an exact solution.

5.1.1. *Delta Function Potential*

After the free particle, the most elementary example of a one-dimensional time-independent Schrödinger equation is conceptually that of a particle in a delta function potential: $-\frac{1}{2}\psi''(x) + \lambda\delta(x)\psi(x) = E\psi(x)$ (in units with $\hbar = m = 1$). For an attractive potential, with $\lambda < 0$, there is exactly one bound state, with $E_0 = -\frac{\lambda^2}{2}$ and $\psi_0(x) = |\lambda|\, e^{-|\lambda x|}$. Note that $\frac{d}{dx}|x| = \text{sign}(x)$ and $\frac{d^2}{dx^2}|x| = 2\delta(x)$. Since the delta function has dimensions of $1/|x|$, this solution is considered the one-dimensional analog of a hydrogen-like atom. The bound state, in fact, resembles a cross section of a 1s orbital e^{-Zr}.

For $E > 0$, free particles are scattered by a delta function potential. The positive-energy solutions can be written $\psi_k^{\pm}(x) = \frac{1}{\sqrt{2\pi}}(e^{\pm ikx} + \frac{\lambda}{ik-\lambda}e^{ik|x|})$, with $E = k^2/2$. The amplitudes of the transmitted and reflected waves are accordingly given by $\frac{k^2}{k^2+\lambda^2}$ and $\frac{\lambda^2}{k^2+\lambda^2}$, respectively. Note that these are the same for attractive and repulsive delta function potentials, independent of the sign of λ.

For continuum states, the graphic shows a wave incident from the left. The transmitted wave is shown on the right in blue and the reflected wave on the left in red, with opacities indicating relative wave amplitudes.

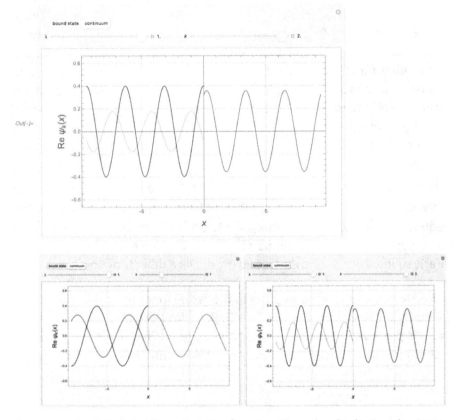

Demonstration 5.1: Schrödinger Equation for a One-Dimensional Delta Function Potential (https://demonstrations.wolfram.com/SchroedingerEquationForAOneDimensional DeltaFunctionPotential/)

5.1.2. *Dirac Bubble Potential*

The Schrödinger equation has been solved in closed form for about 20 quantum-mechanical problems. This Demonstration describes one such example published some time ago. A particle moves in a potential that is zero everywhere except on a spherical bubble of radius r_0, drawn as a red circle in the contour plots. This result has been applied to model the buckminsterfullerene molecule C_{60} and also to approximate the interatomic potential in the helium van der Waals dimer He_2.

The relevant Schrödinger equation is given by $-\frac{1}{2}\nabla^2\psi + \frac{\lambda}{r_0}\delta(r - r_0)\psi = E\psi$, in units with $\hbar = m = 1$, r and r_0 in bohrs, and E in hartrees. For $E = k^2/2 > 0$, the equation has separable continuum solutions $\psi(r, \theta, \phi) = R_l(r)Y_{lm}(\theta, \phi)$, where the Y_{lm} are spherical harmonics. The radial function has the form $R_l(r) = \text{const} j_l(kr)$ for $r \leq r_0$ and const $[j_l(kr)\cos\delta_l - y_l(kr)\sin\delta_l]$ for $r \geq r_0$. Here j_l and y_l are spherical Bessel functions and the δ_l are phase shifts. For each value of l, a single bound state will exist, provided that $\lambda \leq -(2l + 1)$. If no bound state exists, the plot will remain blank. The bound-state radial function is $R_l(r) = -\lambda\kappa r_0 R_l(r_0)j_l(i\kappa r_<)h_l^{(1)}(i\kappa r_>)$, where $r_>$ and $r_<$ are the greater and lesser of r and r_0, and $h_l^{(1)}$ is a Hankel function. The energy is given by $E = -\kappa^2/2$, with κ determined by the transcendental equation $-\lambda\kappa r_0 j_l(i\kappa r_0)h_l^{(1)}(i\kappa r_0) = 1$. Both the bound and continuum wavefunctions are continuous at $r = r_0$ but have discontinuous first derivatives. The second derivative produces a delta function.

This Demonstration shows plots of the radial functions $R_l(r)$ and a cross section of the density plots of Re $\psi(r, \theta, \phi)$ for $l = 0, 1, 2$. The wavefunction is positive in the blue regions and negative in the white regions. Be cautioned that the density plots might take some time to complete.

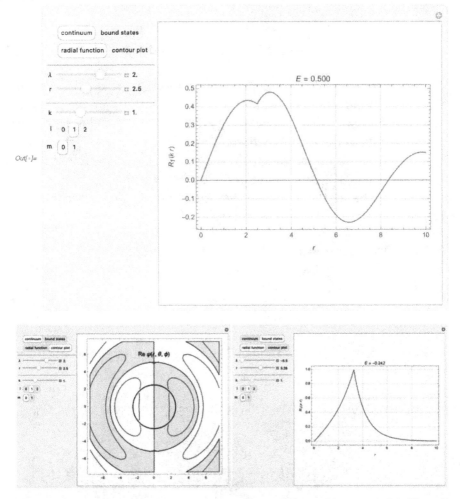

Demonstration 5.2: Schrödinger Equation for a Dirac Bubble Potential (https://demonstrations.wolfram.com/SchroedingerEquationForADiracBubblePotential/)

5.1.3. *Particle in a Finite Spherical Well*

This Demonstration considers a particle bound to a finite spherical well in three dimensions. The potential energy is given by

$$V(r) = \begin{cases} -V_0 & r \le r_0 \\ 0 & r > r_0. \end{cases}$$

The Schrödinger equation is given by

$$-\frac{\hbar^2}{2m}\nabla^2\psi + V(r)\psi = E\psi.$$

For selected values of V_0 and the angular momentum quantum number l, the bound-state eigenvalues and eigenfunctions are determined. You may choose to display the energy diagram, the radial functions or contour plots of the eigenfunctions. The potential energy includes the centrifugal contribution. For either $l = 0$ or 1, radial functions for the first three states $n = 1, 2, 3$ are plotted, with the vertical blue line marking the radius r_0. In the contour plots, the wavefunctions are positive in the blue regions, negative in the white regions.

For simplicity, set $\hbar = m = 1$ (atomic units) and represent the energy by $E = -\frac{\kappa^2}{2}$. Clearly the Schrödinger equation is separable in spherical polar coordinates and we can write

$$\psi(r, \theta, \phi) = R(r)Y_{lm}(\theta, \phi),$$

where Y is a spherical harmonic. The radial functions then obey the equations:

$$R_1''(r) + \frac{2}{r}R_1'(r) - \frac{l(l+1)}{r^2}R_1(r) - (\kappa^2 + 2V_0)R_1(r) = 0 \quad \text{for } r \leq r_0$$

and

$$R_2''(r) + \frac{2}{r}R_2'(r) - \frac{l(l+1)}{r^2}R_2(r) - \kappa^2 R_2(r) = 0 \quad \text{for } r > r_0.$$

The solutions are spherical Bessel and Hankel functions:

$$R_1(r) = aj_l(kr) \quad \text{for} \quad r \leq r_0 \quad \text{and} \quad R_2(r) = bh_l^{(1)}(i\kappa r) \quad \text{for } r > r_0,$$

where $\kappa = \sqrt{-2E}$ and $k = \sqrt{2(E + V_0)} = \sqrt{2V_0 - \kappa^2}$.

The eigenfunctions are determined by the continuity conditions on the wavefunctions and their derivative at $r = r_0$: $R_1(r_0) = R_2(r_0)$ and $R_1'(r_0) = R_2'(r_0)$. This can be simplified to $\frac{R_1'(r_0)}{R_1(r_0)} = \frac{R_2'(r_0)}{R_2(r_0)}$.

For $l = 0$, this leads to a transcendental equation $k \cot(kr_0) = -\kappa$.

For $l = 1$, the corresponding relation is $k^{-2}[1 - kr_0 \cot(kr_0)] = -\kappa^{-2}(1 + \kappa r_0)$.

Solutions for real k correspond to one of the finite number of bound states (with $E < 0$).

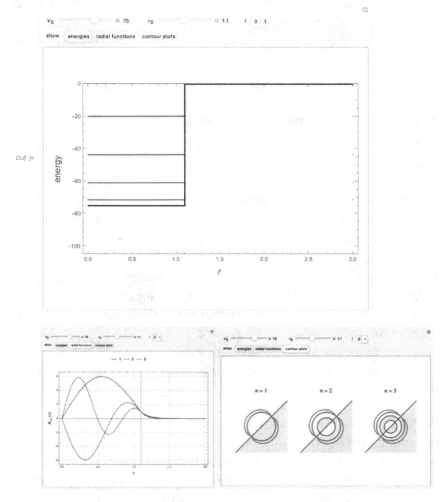

Demonstration 5.3: Solutions of Schrödinger Equation for a Particle in a Finite Spherical Well (https://demonstrations.wolfram.com/SolutionsOfSchroedingerEquationForAParticleInAFiniteSpherica/)

5.1.4. *Supersymmetry and the Square-Well Potential*

The most elementary problem in quantum mechanics considers a particle of mass m in a one-dimensional infinite square well of width a ("particle in a box"). The Schrödinger equation can conveniently be written in the modified form $-\frac{\hbar^2}{2m}\psi_n''(x) - \frac{\pi^2\hbar^2}{2ma^2}\psi_n(x) = E_n\psi_n(x)$ in $0 \leq x \leq a$, such that the ground state energy is rescaled to $E_0 = 0$. The eigenstates are then given by $E_n = \frac{\pi^2\hbar^2}{2ma^2}[(n+1)^2 - 1]$, $\psi_n(x) = \sqrt{\frac{2}{a}}\sin[(n+1)\pi x/a]$. The quantum number n is now equal to the number of nodes in the wavefunction. For simplicity, let $\frac{\hbar}{2m} = 1$ and $a = \pi$. The Schrödinger equation then simplifies to $H\psi_n(x) = E_n\psi_n(x)$ with $H = -\frac{d^2}{dx^2} - 1$, $E_n = n(n+2)$, $\psi_n(x) = \sqrt{2/\pi}\sin[(n+1)x]$, $n = 0, 1, 2, \ldots$.

The first step is to define the superpotential $W(x) = -\frac{\psi_0'(x)}{\psi_0(x)} = -\cot x$ and two ladder operators $A = \frac{d}{dx} + W(x)$ and $A^+ = -\frac{d}{dx} + W(x)$. The original Hamiltonian is then given by $H \equiv H_1 = A^+A$. The operator obtained by reversing A and A^+, $H_2 = AA^+$, is called the supersymmetric partner Hamiltonian. More explicitly, $H_1 = -\frac{d^2}{dx^2} + V_1(x)$ and $H_2 = -\frac{d^2}{dx^2} + V_2(x)$, where $V_1(x) = W(x)^2 - W'(x)$ and $V_2(x) = W(x)^2 + W'(x)$. It can then be shown that if $\psi_n(x)$ is an eigenfunction of H_1 with eigenvalue E_n then $A\psi_n(x)$ is an eigenfunction of H_2 with the same eigenvalue: $H_2 A\psi_n(x) = E_n A\psi_n(x) \equiv \text{const}\,\varepsilon_n\phi_n(x)$. We denote the eigenfunction of H_2 by $\phi_n(x)$ and its eigenvalue ε_n. For unbroken supersymmetry, $\varepsilon_n = E_n$. Note that $A\psi_0(x) = 0$, meaning that the ground state of H_1 has no superpartner. Correspondingly, we find $H_1 A^+\phi_n(x) = \text{const}\,E_n\psi_n(x)$. (The constants provide normalization factors.) Note that the operator A removes one of the nodes of the wavefunction $\psi_n(x)$ as it converts it into $\phi_n(x)$. Conversely, A^+ adds a node.

In this Demonstration, you can plot any of the lowest four square-well eigenfunctions $\psi_n(x) = \sqrt{2/\pi}\sin[(n+1)x]$, $n = 0, 1, 2, 3$ on a scale with each origin at the corresponding eigenvalue $E_n = n(n+2)$. On the right are the corresponding eigenfunctions of the supersymmetric partner Hamiltonian H_2, moving in the potential well $V_2(x) = 2\cot^2 x + 1$ (compared to $V_1(x) = -1$). The first three normalized supersymmetric eigenstates are given by $\phi_1(x) = \sqrt{8/3\pi} \sin^2 x$, $\varepsilon_1 = E_1$; $\phi_2(x) = \sqrt{16/\pi} \cos x \sin^2 x$, $\varepsilon_2 = E_2$; $\phi_3(x) = \sqrt{32/15\pi} (2 + 3 \cos 2x) \sin^2 x$, $\varepsilon_3 = E_3$.

In particle physics, supersymmetry has been proposed as a connection between bosons and fermions. Although this is a beautiful theory, there is, as yet, no experimental evidence that Nature contains supersymmetry. If it does exist, it must be a massively broken symmetry. It is possible that the Large Hadron Collider will find supersymmetric partners of some known particles.

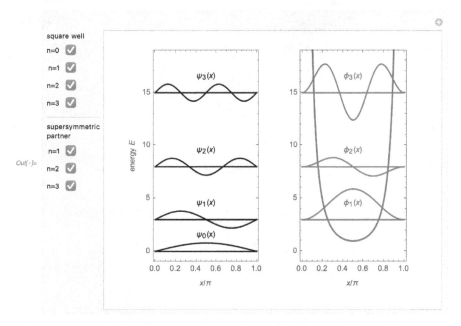

Demonstration 5.4: Supersymmetry for the Square-Well Potential (https://demonstrations.wolfram.com/SupersymmetryForTheSquareWellPotential/)

5.1.5. Double-Well Potential

It is possible to derive exact solutions of the Schrödinger equation for an infinite square well containing a finite rectangular barrier, thus creating a double-well potential. The problem was previously approached using perturbation theory. We consider the potential $V(x) = \infty$ for $x < 0$ and

$x > \pi$, $V(x) = V_0$ for $\frac{\pi}{2} - \frac{a}{2} \leqslant x \leqslant \frac{\pi}{2} + \frac{a}{2}$, and $V(x) = 0$ elsewhere. We set $\hbar = m = 1$ for convenience. Solutions of the Schrödinger equation $-\frac{1}{2}\psi''(x) + V(x)\psi(x) = E\psi(x)$ have the form of particle-in-a-box eigenfunctions in three connected segments. For the unperturbed problem, the normalized eigenstates are $\psi_n(x) = (2/\pi)^{1/2} \sin nx$ with $E_n = n^2/2$, for $n = 1, 2, 3, \ldots$ You can display eigenvalues and eigenfunctions up to $n = 8$. As the barrier increases in height and width, the $n = 1$ and $n = 2$ levels approach degeneracy. The linear combinations $\psi_1 + \psi_2$ and $\psi_1 - \psi_2$ then approximate the localized states $|L\rangle$ and $|R\rangle$, respectively.

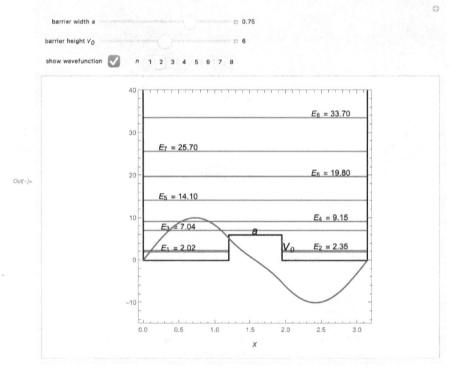

Demonstration 5.5: Exact Solution for Rectangular Double-Well Potential (https://demonstrations.wolfram.com/ExactSolutionForRectangularDoubleWellPotential/)

5.1.6. *Pöschl–Teller Potentials*

It has been long known that the Schrödinger equation for a class of potentials of the form $V_\lambda(x) = -\frac{\lambda(\lambda+1)}{2} \operatorname{sech}^2 x$, usually referred to as

Pöschl–Teller potentials, is exactly solvable. The eigenvalue problem

$$-\frac{1}{2}\psi''(x) - \frac{\lambda(\lambda+1)}{2}\operatorname{sech}^2 x\psi(x) = E\psi(x)$$

(in units with $\hbar = m = 1$) has physically significant solutions for $\lambda = 1, 2, 3, \ldots$, for both bound and continuum states. For $\lambda = 1$, we find the solution $\psi(x) = \operatorname{sech} x$, $E = -1/2$, which follows simply from

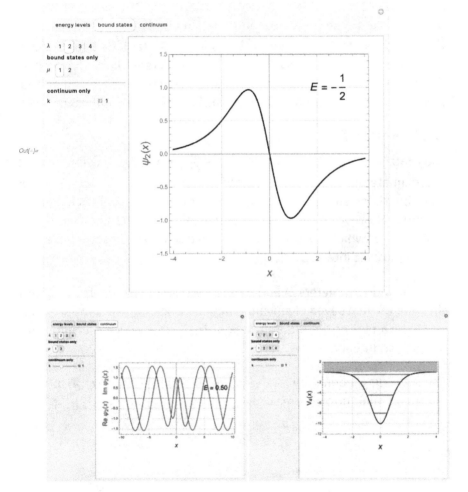

Demonstration 5.6: Eigenstates for Pöschl–Teller Potentials (https://demonstrations. wolfram.com/EigenstatesForPoeschlTellerPotentials/)

the derivative relation $\partial_{x,x} \operatorname{sech} x = \operatorname{sech} x - 2 \operatorname{sech}^3 x$. More generally, the Schrödinger equation has the bound state solutions

$$\psi_{\lambda,\mu} = P_\lambda^\mu(\tanh x), \quad E_{\lambda,\mu} = \frac{\mu^2}{2}, \quad \lambda = 1, 2, 3, \ldots, \mu = \lambda, \lambda - 1, \ldots, 1,$$

where the P_λ^μ are associated Legendre polynomials.

The Schrödinger equation has, in addition, continuum positive-energy eigenstates with $E_{\lambda,k} = k^2/2$. The trivial case $\lambda = 0$ gives a free particle $\psi_{0,k}^+(x) = e^{ikx}$. The first two non-trivial solutions are $\psi_{1,k}^+(x) = (1 + \frac{i}{k}\tanh x)e^{ikx}$ and $\psi_{2,k}^+(x) = (1 + k^2)^{-1}(1 + k^2 + 3ik\tanh x - 3\tanh^2 x)e^{ikx}$. These represent waves traveling left to right. A remarkable property of Pöschl–Teller potentials is that they are "reflectionless", meaning that waves are 100% transmitted through the barrier with no reflected waves.

5.1.7. *Kratzer Potential*

The Kratzer potential $V(r) = -2D\left(\frac{a}{r} - \frac{a^2}{2r^2}\right)$ was originally intended to approximate the interatomic interaction in diatomic molecules. This has long since been superseded by superior alternatives, such as the Morse potential. However, the Kratzer potential belongs to the small number of problems for which the Schrödinger equation is exactly solvable, and is thus of intrinsic interest.

For selected parameters D and a, you can display an energy diagram, showing the first seven eigenvalues superposed on the potential energy curve, or a plot of the radial function $P_n(r)$ for a selected value of the quantum number n.

The Schrödinger equation for the radial function $P(r) = rR(r)$, in the case of zero angular momentum, is given by

$$-\frac{1}{2}\frac{d^2 P}{dr^2} + V(\rho)P(r) = \epsilon P(r).$$

The eigenfunctions for bound states are found to be $P_n(r) = M_{\kappa,\mu}\left(\frac{4aD}{\kappa}r\right)$, where $M_{\kappa,\mu}$ is a Whittaker function, $\mu = \frac{1}{2}\sqrt{1 + 8a^2D}$ and $\kappa = -\frac{i\sqrt{2aD}}{\sqrt{\epsilon}}$. The quantization is determined by the condition that the eigenfunctions must approach 0 as $r \to \infty$. The asymptotic behavior of the Whittaker functions is given by:

$$M_{\kappa,\mu}(x) \sim \frac{\Gamma(1+2\mu)}{\Gamma\left(\frac{1}{2}+\mu-\kappa\right)} x^{-\kappa} e^{x/2} \quad \text{as } x \to \infty.$$

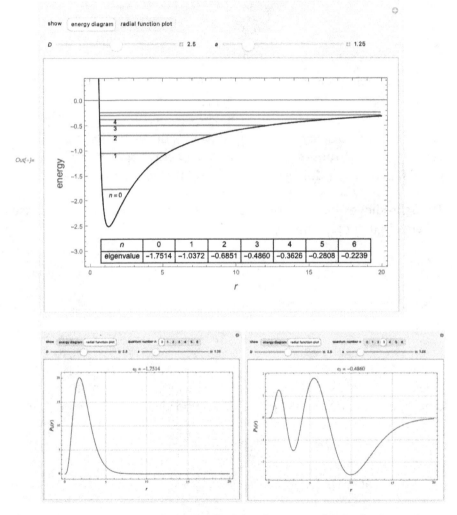

Demonstration 5.7: Exact Solutions of the Schrödinger Equation for the Kratzer Potential (https://demonstrations.wolfram.com/ExactSolutionsOfTheSchroedingerEquation ForTheKratzerPotential/)

Clearly this is divergent as $x \rightarrow \infty$, unless the parameters μ and κ produce a singularity in the gamma function of the denominator, which requires $\frac{1}{2} + \mu - \kappa = -n$, with $n = 0, 1, 2, \ldots$.

The corresponding eigenvalues are thereby determined:

$$\epsilon_n = -\frac{2a^2D^2}{\left(n + \mu + \frac{1}{2}\right)^2}.$$

5.1.8. *Pseudoharmonic Potential*

The pseudoharmonic potential $V(r) = V_0 \left(\frac{r}{a} - \frac{a}{r}\right)^2$ belongs to the small number of problems for which the Schrödinger equation is exactly solvable and is thus of intrinsic interest. For selected parameters V_0 and a, you can either display an energy diagram, showing the first several eigenvalues superposed on the potential energy curve, or a plot of the radial function $P_n(r)$ for a selected value of the quantum number n.

The Schrödinger equation for the radial function $P(r) = rR(r)$, in the case of zero angular momentum, is given by

$$-\frac{1}{2}\frac{d^2P}{dr^2} + V(p)P(r) = \epsilon P(r).$$

The eigenfunctions for bound states are found to be

$$P_n(r) = r^{\beta + \frac{1}{2}} e^{-\frac{\sqrt{2V_0}}{2a}r^2} L_n^\beta \left(\frac{\sqrt{2V_0}}{a}r^2\right),$$

where L_n^β is an associated Laguerre polynomial. The solution of the differential equation initially gave associated Laguerre functions L_α^β, with

$$\alpha = -\frac{1}{4V_0}\left(2V_0 - 2\sqrt{2}aV_0^{3/2} + V_0\sqrt{1 + 8a^2V_0} - a\sqrt{2V_0}\epsilon\right)$$

$$\text{and} \quad \beta = \frac{1}{2}\sqrt{1 + 8a^2V_0}.$$

The quantization is determined by the condition that the eigenfunctions must approach 0 as $r \rightarrow \infty$. The asymptotic behavior of Laguerre

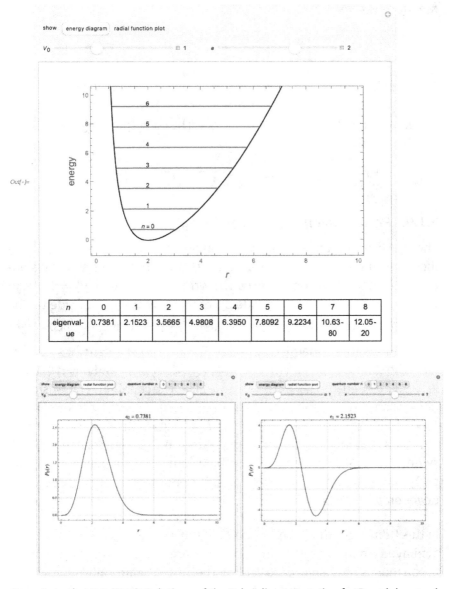

n	0	1	2	3	4	5	6	7	8
eigenvalue	0.7381	2.1523	3.5665	4.9808	6.3950	7.8092	9.2234	10.63-80	12.05-20

Demonstration 5.8: Exact Solutions of the Schrödinger Equation for Pseudoharmonic Potential (https://demonstrations.wolfram.com/ExactSolutionsOfTheSchroedingerEquationForPseudoharmonicPote/)

functions is given by:

$$L_\alpha^\beta(x^2) \sim \frac{\Gamma[1+\alpha+\beta]}{\Gamma[1+\alpha] \times \Gamma[-\alpha]} x^{-2(\alpha+\beta+1)} e^{x^2} \quad \text{as } x \to \infty.$$

This would overtake the converging factor $e^{-x^2/2}$ in the solution as $x \to \infty$, unless α is an integer n, which would then produce a singularity in a gamma function of the denominator. The corresponding eigenvalues are thereby determined:

$$\epsilon_n = \frac{\sqrt{V_0}}{\sqrt{2a}}(2+4n-2a\sqrt{2V_0}+\sqrt{1+8a^2V_0}) \quad \text{with } n = 0, 1, 2, \ldots.$$

5.1.9. *Particle in an Equilateral Triangle*

The particle in an equilateral triangle is the simplest quantum-mechanical problem that has a non-separable but exact analytic solution. The Schrödinger equation can be written $-\frac{\hbar^2}{2m}\nabla^2\psi\{x,y\} = E\psi(x,y)$ with $\psi(x,y) = 0$ on and outside an equilateral triangle of side a. The ground-state solution $\psi_0(x,y) = \sin\left(\frac{4\pi y}{\sqrt{3}a}\right) - 2\sin\left(\frac{2\pi y}{\sqrt{3}a}\right)\cos\left(\frac{2\pi x}{a}\right)$ corresponds to an energy eigenvalue $E_0 = \frac{2h^2}{3ma^2}$. The general solutions have the form $\psi_{p,q}(x,y\}$ with $q = 0, \frac{1}{3}, \frac{2}{3}, 1, \frac{4}{3}, \frac{5}{3}, 2, \ldots$ and $p = q+1, q+2, \ldots$, with energies $E_{p,q} = (p^2+pq+q^2)E_0$. The Hamiltonian transforms under the symmetry group C_{3v} so eigenfunctions belong to one of the irreducible representations A_1, A_2, or E. The states labeled by quantum numbers $p, 0$, including the ground state $1, 0$, are non-degenerate with symmetry A_1. All other integer combinations p, q give degenerate pairs of A_1 and A_2 states. Non-integer quantum numbers belong to two-fold degenerate E levels.

In this Demonstration, contour plots of the wavefunctions $\psi_{p,q}(x,y)$ are displayed when you select the quantum numbers p and q. (If you change q, you must also change p.) Except for the ground state, only the contours $\psi = 0$, representing the nodes of the wavefunction, are drawn. The contour plots might take a few seconds to generate.

Vibration of an equilateral triangular plate with fixed edges gives a classical analog of this problem with the same solutions.

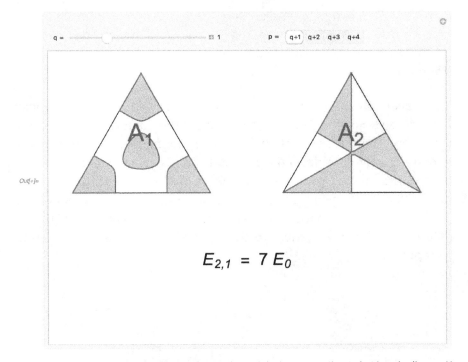

$$E_{2,1} = 7 E_0$$

Demonstration 5.9: Quantum-Mechanical Particle in an Equilateral Triangle (https://demonstrations.wolfram.com/QuantumMechanicalParticleInAnEquilateralTriangle/)

5.1.10. *Scattering by a Symmetrical Eckart Potential*

The Schrödinger equation for scattering of a monoenergetic beam of particles of mass m from a symmetric Eckart potential can be written $-\frac{\hbar^2}{2m}\psi''(x) + V_0 \operatorname{sech}^2\left(\frac{x}{a}\right)\psi(x) = \frac{\hbar^2\kappa^2}{2m}\psi(x)$, where V_0 is the potential height, a is a measure of its width, and $\hbar k$ is the particle momentum. The equation can be solved exactly in terms of Gauss hypergeometric functions. In contrast to a classical scattering problem, particles have a finite probability of penetrating the barrier even if their kinetic energy is less than the barrier height — this is an instance of the quantum-mechanical tunnel effect. For an incident beam of unit intensity $I = 1$, the transmitted and reflected beams have intensities $T = \sinh^2(\pi ka)/[\sinh^2(\pi ka) + \cosh^2(\pi/2\sqrt{|8mV_0a^2/\hbar^2 - 1|})]$ and $R = I - T$, respectively. The tunneling probability decreases with increasing barrier height and width and drops precipitously for more massive incident particles. Tunneling increases with particle energy, however. Another feature that contrasts with classical behavior is the partial reflection of the wave, even for kinetic energies greater than the barrier height $(\hbar^2 k^2/2m > V_0)$.

The wavenumber k is determined by the mass and energy of the incident particle by $E = \hbar^2 k^2/2m$. In this Demonstration, units based on $\hbar = 1$ are used. The top figure shows the potential barrier and the particle kinetic energy as a dashed horizontal line. The black, blue, and red arrows are labeled with the magnitudes of the incident, transmitted, and reflected waves, respectively. The lower figure shows a plot of the real and imaginary parts of the wavefunction. The amplitudes to the left and right of the barrier are closely related to the three scattering components.

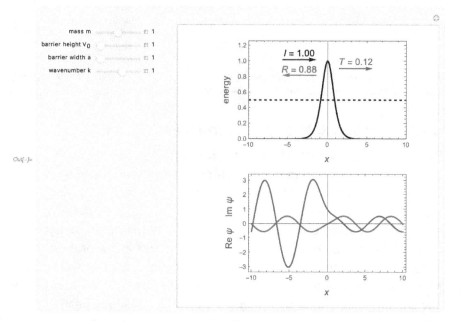

Demonstration 5.10: Scattering by a Symmetrical Eckart Potential (https://demonstra tions.wolfram.com/ScatteringByASymmetricalEckartPotential/)

5.1.11. *Quasi-Exact Solutions of the Schrödinger Equation*

Quasi-exact solutions to a Schrödinger equation pertain to limited regions of a spectrum of eigenstates for which closed-form eigenfunctions and eigenvalues can be derived, whereas the remainder of the spectrum can only be approximated. These occur for certain potentials with parameters in some limited range. The sextic anharmonic oscillator is the only one-dimensional polynomial potential that can be quasi-exactly solved if its parameters are appropriately chosen. Depending on the parameters, the system can be a single-, double- or triple-well potential.

Consider solutions of the time-independent one-dimensional Schrödinger equation, in atomic units:

$$-\frac{1}{2}\psi''(x) + V(x)\psi(x) = E\psi(x).$$

One trick for finding quasi-exact solutions is to assume some appropriately behaved function $\psi(x)$ and to use the relation

$$-\frac{1}{2}\frac{\psi''(x)}{\psi(x)} = E - V(x)$$

to identify a potential function $V(x)$. For example, the simplest case of a quasi-exact sextic anharmonic oscillator follows from

$$\psi(x) = e^{-\beta x^4/4}e^{\alpha x^2/2},$$

which gives $V(x) = \frac{1}{2}(\alpha^2 - 3\beta)x^2 - \alpha\beta x^4 + \frac{\beta^2}{2}x^6$, with $E = -\frac{\alpha}{2}$. More generally, it can be shown that the potential can have the form

$$V(x) = \frac{1}{2}(\alpha^2 - 3\beta - 2n\beta)x^2 - \alpha\beta x^4 + \frac{\beta^2}{2}x^6, \quad n = 0, 1, 2, \dots.$$

For the cases $n = 0, 1$ and 2, we show plots of the quasi-exact eigenfunctions and of the potential functions $V(x)$, with superposed eigenvalues shown in red.

For simplicity, set $\beta = 1$. For $n = 0$, $V(x) = \frac{1}{2}(\alpha^2 - 3)x^2 - \alpha x^4 + \frac{1}{2}x^6$.

The ground state $\psi_0(x)$ is quasi-exactly soluble: $\psi_0(x) = |A_{00}|^{-1/2}$ $e^{-x^4/4}e^{\alpha x^2/2}$, $E_0 = -\frac{\alpha}{2}$,

$$A_{00} = e^{\alpha^2/4}\sqrt{\frac{-\alpha}{2}}K_{-1/4}\left(\frac{\alpha^2}{4}\right).$$

For $n = 1$, $V(x) = \frac{1}{2}(\alpha^2 - 5)x^2 - \alpha x^4 + \frac{1}{2}x^6$.

The first excited state $\psi_1(x)$ is quasi-exactly soluble:

$$\psi_1(x) = |A_{11}|^{-1/2}xe^{-x^4/4}e^{\alpha x^2/2}, \quad E_1 = -\frac{3\alpha}{2},$$

$$A_{11} = \frac{\pi}{4\sqrt{-\alpha}}e^{\alpha^2/4}\left[\alpha^2/_{-1/4}\left(\frac{\alpha^2}{4}\right) - (2 + \alpha^2)/_{1/4}\left(\frac{\alpha^2}{4}\right)\right.$$

$$\left. + \alpha^2/_{3/4}\left(\frac{\alpha^2}{4}\right) - \alpha^2/_{5/4}\left(\frac{\alpha^2}{4}\right)\right].$$

For $n = 2$, $V(x) = \frac{1}{2}(\alpha^2 - 7)x^2 - \alpha x^4 + \frac{1}{2}x^6$.

The ground state $\psi_0(x)$ and the second excited state $\psi_2(x)$ are quasi-exactly soluble:

$$\psi_0(x) = |A_{20}|^{-1/2}\left(x^2 + \frac{1}{\alpha + \sqrt{\alpha^2 + 2}}\right)e^{-x^4/4}e^{\alpha x^2/2},$$

$$E_0 = -\frac{3\alpha}{2} - \sqrt{2 + \alpha^2},$$

$$\psi_2(x) = |A_{22}|^{-1/2}\left(x^2 + \frac{1}{\alpha - \sqrt{\alpha^2 + 2}}\right)e^{-x^4/4}e^{\alpha x^2/2},$$

$$E_2 = -\frac{3\alpha}{2} + \sqrt{2 + \alpha^2},$$

$$\left.\begin{matrix}A_{20}\\A_{22}\end{matrix}\right\} = \frac{1}{2\sqrt{-2\alpha}}e^{\alpha^2/4}\left[\mp(2\alpha + \alpha^3 \pm 2\sqrt{2 + \alpha^2})K_{1/4}\left(\frac{\alpha^2}{4}\right)\right.$$

$$\left. + \alpha^2\sqrt{2 + \alpha^2}K_{5/4}\left(\frac{\alpha^2}{4}\right)\right].$$

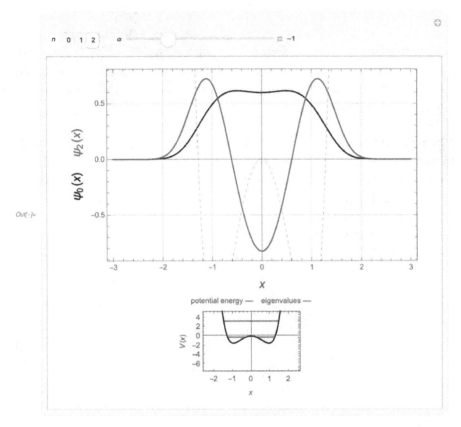

Demonstration 5.11: Quasi-Exact Solutions of Schrödinger Equation — Sextic Anharmonic Oscillator (https://demonstrations.wolfram.com/QuasiExactSolutionsOfSchro edingerEquationSexticAnharmonicOsc/)

5.2. Approximate Solutions of the Schrödinger Equation

5.2.1. *Rayleigh–Ritz Method*

The Rayleigh–Ritz variational method has been well known in mathematics for well over a century. Its application to quantum mechanics was definitively described by J. K. L. MacDonald in *Phys. Rev.* **43**(10), 1933 pp. 830–833. The eigenfunctions of a quantum-mechanical Hamiltonian can be approximated by a linear combination of n basis functions. This gives an $n \times n$ secular equation with n roots, approximating the n lowest eigenvalues. Two interleaving theorems can be proven: (1) between each pair of successive roots of the secular equation, augmented by $+\infty$ and $-\infty$, there occurs at least one exact eigenvalue; (2) if n is increased to $n+1$, then the new approximate roots will be interleaved by the previous ones. As a corollary to (1), often called simply "the" variational principle, the lowest approximate eigenvalue provides an upper bound to the exact ground state eigenvalue.

In this Demonstration, the Rayleigh–Ritz method is applied to two simple quantum-mechanical problems — the hydrogen atom and the linear harmonic oscillator. For the hydrogen atom, the energy scale is distorted from the actual rapidly converging spectrum. These are somewhat artificial problems in the sense that exact ground-state eigenvalues can be obtained with the exponential coefficients $\alpha = 1$. But for $\alpha \neq 1$, one can pretend that exact solutions are not available.

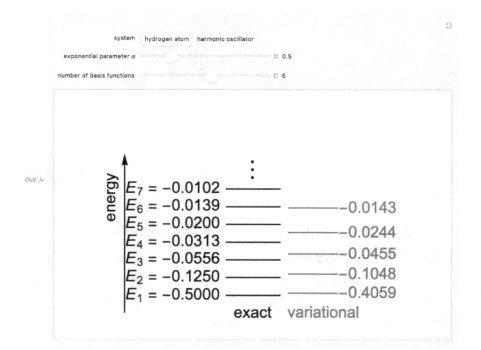

Demonstration 5.12: Interleaving Theorems for the Rayleigh–Ritz Method in Quantum Mechanics (https://demonstrations.wolfram.com/InterleavingTheoremsForTheRayle ighRitzMethodInQuantumMechani/)

5.2.2. *Quartic Oscillator*

The oscillator with a quartic anharmonicity, with Hamiltonian

$$H = \frac{p^2}{2\mu} + \frac{1}{2}kx^2 + \frac{1}{4}\lambda x^4$$

has been extensively treated in the literature. Consider the *pure quartic oscillator*, in which the quadratic term is missing: $k = 0$. For simplicity, take $\mu = \lambda = 1$. The Schrödinger equation thus reduces to $-\frac{1}{2}\psi''(x) + \frac{1}{4}x^4\psi(x) = E\psi(x)$.

No analytic solution has been found, but accurate numerical computations have been carried out. This Demonstration applies the operator method, a generalization of the canonical operator formulation for the harmonic oscillator, for potential energies that are functions of even powers of x. For larger values of the matrix dimension, the results obtained here are comparable with the published results.

The computation results in a secular equation for the eigenvalues, which are plotted as red lines on the graph superposed on the potential energy curve. The number of eigenvalues shown is equal to the selected matrix dimension. For comparison, the first eight eigenvalues according to the WKB method are shown as thin gray lines.

The ladder operators can be defined by

$$a = \sqrt{\frac{\omega}{2}}x + i\sqrt{\frac{i}{2\omega}}p,$$

$$a^\dagger = \sqrt{\frac{\omega}{2}}x - i\sqrt{\frac{i}{2\omega}}p,$$

with an adjustable parameter ω introduced. The non-vanishing matrix elements of the Hamiltonian can then be computed, giving

$$H_{n,n} = \frac{\omega}{4}(2n + 1) + \frac{1}{16\omega^2}(6n^2 + 6n + 3),$$

$$H_{n+2,n} = H_{n,n+2} = -\frac{\omega}{4}\sqrt{(n + 1)(n + 2)} + \frac{1}{8\omega^2}\sqrt{(n + 1)(n + 2)(2n + 3)},$$

$$H_{n+4,n} = H_{n,n+4} = \frac{1}{16\omega^2}\sqrt{(n+1)(n+2)(n+3)(n+4)}.$$

The eigenvalues are then determined using the built-in Wolfram Language function `Eigenvalues` for selected dimensions 1 to 8.

The WKB method determines the eigenvalues using the integral $\sqrt{2\mu}\oint\sqrt{E - \frac{\lambda}{4}x^4}\, dx = \left(n+\frac{1}{2}\right)h$. The resulting energies are given by $E_n = 0.867145\left(n+\frac{1}{2}\right)^{4/3}$. These are shown in gray.

A classical realization of a quartic oscillator can be approximated by a particle attached to two Hooke's law springs.

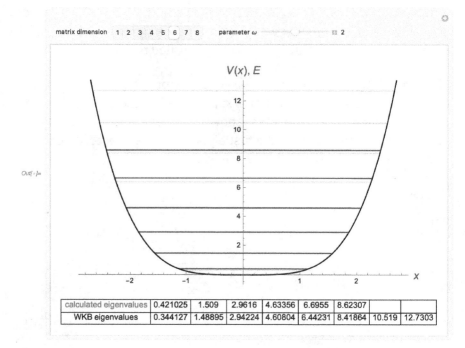

| matrix dimension | 1 | 2 | 3 | 4 | 5 | 6 | 7 | 8 | parameter ω | | 2 |

calculated eigenvalues	0.421025	1.509	2.9616	4.63356	6.6955	8.62307		
WKB eigenvalues	0.344127	1.48895	2.94224	4.60804	6.44231	8.41864	10.519	12.7303

Demonstration 5.13: Eigenvalues for a Pure Quartic Oscillator (https://demonstrations.wolfram.com/EigenvaluesForAPureQuarticOscillator/)

5.2.3. *Heaviside-Lambda Potential Well*

This Demonstration calculates the bound energy levels of a particle in an inverted Heaviside-lambda (vee-shaped) potential well of depth V_0 and width $2a$, using the semiclassical Wentzel–Kramers–Brillouin (WKB) method. The numerical results are within 1% of the values that would be obtained from the exact solutions of the corresponding Schrödinger equation. The energies are determined by the Sommerfeld–Wilson quantization conditions $\oint \sqrt{2m[E - V(x)]}dq = \left(n + \frac{1}{2}\right)h$. With $\hbar = m = 1$, the integral reduces to $4\int_0^{a(1+E/V_0)} \sqrt{E + V_0 - \frac{V_0}{a}x}dx$, noting that $x = \pm a\left(1 + \frac{E}{V_0}\right)$ are the classical turning points. This can be solved for the energy levels: $E_n = -V_0 + \frac{2^{1/3}}{4}\left(\frac{3\pi V_0}{a}\right)^{2/3}\left(n + \frac{1}{2}\right)$, $n = 0, 1, 2, \ldots, n_{max}$. The highest bound state is given by $n_{max} = \left[-\frac{1}{2} + \frac{4a\sqrt{2V_0}}{3\pi}\right]$, where $[]$ is the integer part of the number.

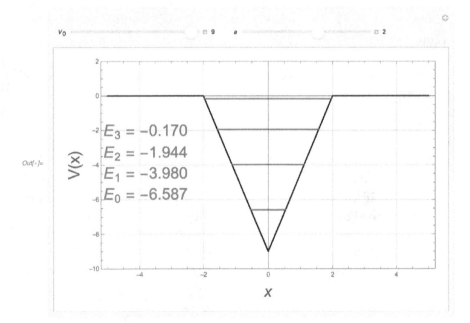

Out[∘]=

$E_3 = -0.170$
$E_2 = -1.944$
$E_1 = -3.980$
$E_0 = -6.587$

Demonstration 5.14: Energies for a Heaviside-Lambda Potential Well (https://demonstrations.wolfram.com/EnergiesForAHeavisideLambdaPotentialWell/)

5.2.4. *Quantum Pendulum*

For an idealized classical pendulum consisting of a point mass m attached to a massless rigid rod of length L attached to a stationary pivot, in the absence of friction and air resistance, the energy is given by

$$E = \frac{1}{2}mL^2\dot{\theta}^2 + mgL(1 - \cos\theta),$$

where θ is the angular displacement from the vertical direction. The oscillation is presumed to occur between the limits $\theta = \pm\theta_0$, where $\theta_0 < \pi$ to avoid the transition to a spherical pendulum. The exact solution for this classical problem is known and turns out to be very close to the behavior of a linear oscillator, for which $1 - \cos\theta$ can be approximated by $\frac{\theta^2}{2}$. The natural frequency of oscillation is given by the series

$$\omega = \omega_0 \left(1 + \frac{1}{16}\theta_0^2 + \frac{1}{3072}\theta_0^4 \cdots \right),$$

where $\omega_0 = \sqrt{\frac{g}{L}}$, the limiting linear approximation for the natural frequency (a result of great historical significance).

The non-linear pendulum can be formulated as a quantum-mechanical problem represented by the Schrödinger equation

$$-\frac{1}{2}\psi''(\theta) + \omega_0^2(1 - \cos\theta)\psi(\theta) = \varepsilon\psi(\theta),$$

where $\varepsilon = E/mL^2$. This has the form of Mathieu's differential equation, and its solutions are even and odd Mathieu functions of the form $ce_{2n}(2\theta)$ and $se_{2n+2}(2\theta)$. However, we describe a more transparent solution, which uses the Fourier series used to compute the Mathieu functions.

Accordingly, the solution of the Schrödinger equation is represented by a Fourier expansion

$$\psi(\theta) = \sum_{n=0}^{\infty} \left(a_n \cos\left(\frac{2n\pi\theta}{\theta_0}\right) + b_n \sin\left(\frac{(2n+2)\pi\theta}{\theta_0}\right)\right).$$

This can be put in a more compact form:

$$\psi(\theta) = \sum_{n=0}^{\infty} c_n \sin\left(\frac{(n+1)\pi}{2\theta_0}(\theta_0 - \theta)\right).$$

The matrix elements of the Hamiltonian are given by

$$H_{mn} = \int_{-\theta_0}^{\theta_0} \Phi_m(\theta) \left(-\frac{1}{2}\Phi_n''(\theta) + \omega_0(1 - \cos\theta)\Phi_n(\theta) \right) d\theta,$$

in terms of a set of normalized basis functions

$$\Phi_n(\theta) = \frac{1}{\sqrt{\theta_0}} \sin\left(\frac{(n+1)\pi}{2\theta_0}(\theta_0 - \theta) \right), \quad n = 0, 1, 2, \ldots$$

The built-in Mathematica function `Eigensystem` is then applied to compute the eigenvalues and eigenfunctions for $n = 0, 1, 2, 3, 4$, which are then displayed in the graphic.

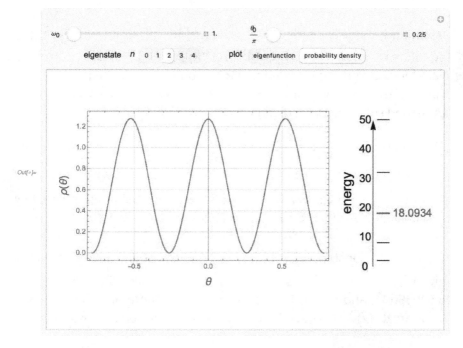

Demonstration 5.15: Quantum Pendulum (https://demonstrations.wolfram.com/QuantumPendulum/)

5.2.5. *Bouncing Ball*

The Schrödinger equation can be written $-\frac{\hbar^2}{2m}\psi''(z)+mgz\psi(z) = E\psi(z)$, where m is the mass of the ball (idealized as a point mass), g is the acceleration of gravity, and z is the vertical height (with ground level taken as $z = 0$). For perfectly elastic collisions, the potential energy at $z = 0$ can be assumed infinite: $V(0) = \infty$, leading to the boundary condition $\psi(0) = 0$. Also, we should have $\psi(z) \rightarrow 0$ as $z \rightarrow \infty$.

The problem, as stated, is not physically realistic on a quantum level, given Earth's value of g, because m would have to be much too small. But an analogous experiment with a charge in an electric field is possibly more accessible. We will continue to refer to the gravitational parameters, however.

Redefining the independent variable as $x = \left(\frac{2m^2g}{\hbar^2}\right)^{1/3}\left(z - \frac{E}{mg}\right)$, the equation reduces to the simpler form $\psi''(x) - x\psi(x) = 0$. (The form of the variable is suggested by running DSolve on the original equation.) The solution that remains finite as $x \rightarrow \infty$ is found to be $\psi(x) = \text{const} \, \text{Ai}(x)$. (A second solution, $\text{Bi}(x)$, diverges as $x \rightarrow \infty$.)

The eigenvalues E_n can be found from the zeros of the Airy function: $\text{Ai}\left[-\left(\frac{2m^2g}{\hbar^2}\right)^{1/3}\frac{E}{mg}\right] = 0$, using N[AiryAiZero[n]]. The roots lie on the negative real axis, the first few being approximately $-2.33811, -4.08795, -5.52056, -6.78671, -7.94413, -9.02265, \ldots$.

Defining the constant $\alpha = \left(\frac{2m^2g}{\hbar^2}\right)^{1/3}$, the lowest eigenvalues are thus given by $E_0/mg = 2.33811\alpha^{-1}$, $E_1/mg = 4.08795\alpha^{-1}$, $E_2/mg = 5.52056\alpha^{-1}$, and so on. The corresponding (unnormalized) eigenfunctions are $\psi_n(z) = \text{Ai}[\alpha(z - E_n/mg)]$. These are plotted on the graphic.

The semiclassical phase integral gives quite accurate values of the energies. Evaluate these using $\oint \sqrt{2m(E_n - V(z))}dz = \left(n + \frac{3}{4}\right)h$ (the added fraction is $\frac{3}{4}$, rather than the more common $\frac{1}{2}$, because one turning point is impenetrable). The integral is explicitly given by $2\sqrt{2m}\int_0^{E_n/mg}\sqrt{E_n-mgz}\,dz=\left(n+\frac{3}{4}\right)2\pi\hbar$, leading to $E_n/mg=$ $\left(\frac{9\pi^2}{4}\right)^{1/3}\left(n+\frac{3}{4}\right)^{2/3}\alpha$. The first six numerical values are $\{2.32025,$ $4.08181, 5.51716, 6.78445, 7.94249, 9.02137\}$, compared with the corresponding exact results from the Schrödinger equation $\{2.33811,$ $4.08795, 5.52056, 6.78671, 7.94413, 9.02265\}$.

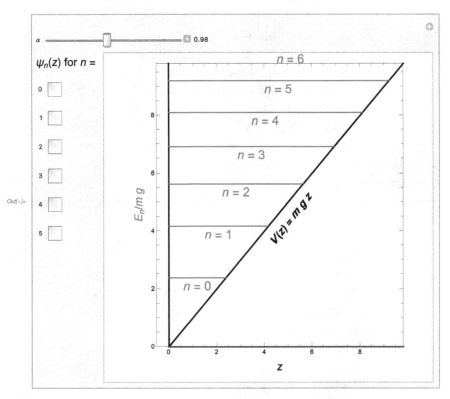

Demonstration 5.16: Quantum Mechanics of a Bouncing Ball (https://demonstrations. wolfram.com/QuantumMechanicsOfABouncingBall/)

5.2.6. *Scattering by a Rigid Sphere*

Consider the quantum-mechanical treatment of scattering in three dimensions by a spherically symmetrical potential centered at the origin.

A standard problem is scattering by a rigid sphere, defined by the potential-energy function: $V(r) = \infty$ for $r \leq a$, $V(r) = 0$ for $r > a$. For any spherically symmetrical potential, the asymptotic behavior of the wavefunction can be represented by the Faxen–Holzmark formula $\psi(r, \theta) \approx e^{ikz} + f(\theta)\frac{e^{ikr}}{r}$, where the first term represents an incoming plane wave in the positive z direction ($z = r\cos\theta$) and the second term is an outgoing spherical wave from the scattering center. The scattering amplitude $f(\theta)$ determines the angular distribution of the outgoing wave. The differential scattering cross section is given by $\frac{d\sigma}{d\Omega} = \sigma(\theta) = |f(\theta)|^2$. A spherical-harmonic expansion of the plane wave, $e^{ikr\cos\theta} = \sum_{l=0}^{\infty}(2l+1)i^l j_l(kr) P_l(\cos\theta)$, reduces the outgoing wave to a sum of partial waves, the so-called partial wave expansion. The $l = 0$ component is known as the s-wave, the $l = 1$ component, the p-wave, and so on. In practice, only small number of partial waves need be considered for a sufficiently accurate representation of the scattering, at least at low energies. The defining parameter of a partial wave is its phase shift δ_l. For scattering by a rigid sphere, $\tan\delta_l = j_l(ka)/y_l(ka)$. In the preceding formulas, j_l and y_l are spherical Bessel functions of the first and second kind, while P_l is a Legendre polynomial.

It can be shown that $f(\theta) = \frac{1}{2ik}\sum_{l=0}^{\infty}(2l + 1)(e^{2i\delta_l} - 1)P_l(\cos\theta)$. From this it follows that the total cross section is given by $\sigma_T = \frac{4\pi}{k^2}\sum_{l=0}^{\infty}(2l+1)\sin^2\delta_l = \frac{4\pi}{k}Im\, f(0)$, a result known as the optical theorem. For rigid-sphere scattering at low energies ($k \to 0$), the scattering cross sections are approximated by $\sigma(\theta) \approx a^2$ and $\sigma_T \approx 4\pi a^2$, four times the classical value.

This Demonstration shows a pictorial representation of the spherical wavefronts in the Faxen–Holzmark formula, which you can animate. (The angular dependence of these amplitudes is not shown.) The checkbox produces a plot of the differential scattering cross section $\sigma(\theta)$, shown in red, which changes as k and a are varied.

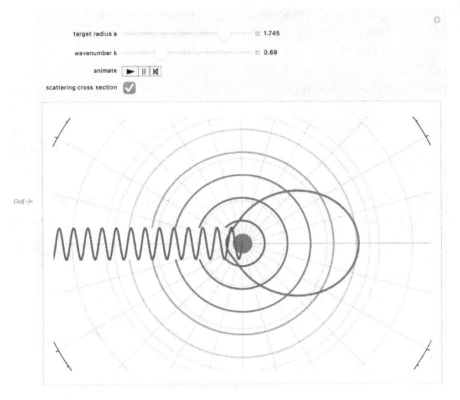

target radius a ‹·················· › ⌗ 1.745

wavenumber k ‹·················· › ⌗ 0.69

animate ► ‖ K

scattering cross section ✓

Out[ ]=

Demonstration 5.17: Quantum Scattering by a Rigid Sphere (https://demonstrations. wolfram.com/QuantumScatteringByARigidSphere/)

5.3. Nuclear and Particle Physics

5.3.1. *Rutherford Scattering*

This Demonstration outlines a quantum-mechanical computation for the scattering of alpha particles from heavy atoms, known as Rutherford scattering. Quite remarkably, the result for the differential cross section $\frac{d\sigma}{d\Omega} = |f(\theta)|^2$ agrees perfectly with that computed using classical scattering theory, although the complex scattering amplitude $f(\theta)$ does contain a complex factor.

The Faxen–Holtzmark representation for scattering from a spherically symmetrical potential assumes a wavefunction $\psi(r, \theta) = e^{ikz} + f(\theta)\frac{e^{ikr}}{r}$.

The first term represents an incoming plane wave (note that $z = r\cos\theta$), while the second term is an outgoing spherical wave, modulated by the scattering amplitude $f(\theta)$. We consider the scattering potential $V(r) = ZZ'\frac{e^{-\beta r}}{r}$, where $Z(Z = 79$ for Au, used in Rutherford's original experiments) is the atomic number of the target atom, $Z' = 2$ for the alpha particles, and β is a shielding constant due to the atomic electrons, with an approximate value $\beta \approx me^2 Z^{1/3}/\hbar^2$ based on the Thomas–Fermi statistical model. The potential, incidentally, has the same form as a Yukawa potential for nucleon-nucleon interaction.

The (first-order) Born approximation is adequate for this problem. The Schrödinger equation is given by $\{-\frac{\hbar^2}{2\mu}\nabla^2 + V(r)\}\Psi(\mathbf{r}) = \frac{\hbar^2 k^2}{2\mu}\Psi(\mathbf{r})$, where

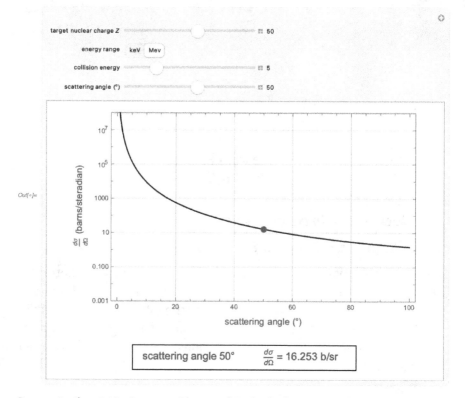

Demonstration 5.18: Quantum Theory of Rutherford Scattering (https://demonstrati ons.wolfram.com/QuantumTheoryOfRutherfordScattering/)

$\mu \approx m_\alpha$, the alpha particle mass, and $E = \frac{\hbar^2 k^2}{2\mu}$. Where $\mathbf{K} = \mathbf{k'} - \mathbf{k}$, we then find $f(\theta) = -\frac{\mu}{2\pi\hbar^2} \int V(r')e^{i\mathbf{K}\cdot\mathbf{r'}}\,d^3r'$ is the difference between the scattered and incident propagation vectors. The scattering amplitude is then given by $f(\theta) = -\frac{2\mu z z' e^2}{\hbar^2}\frac{1}{\beta^2 + K^2}$. Using $K = 2k\sin\frac{\theta}{2}$ and $E = \frac{\hbar^2 k^2}{2\mu}$, we obtain the cross section $\frac{d\sigma}{d\Omega} = \left(\frac{z z' e^2}{4E}\right)\left[\frac{e^4 m^2 z^{2/3}}{8\mu\hbar^2 E} + \sin^2\frac{\theta}{2}\right]^{-2}$. With $\beta = 0$, for a pure Coulomb field, this reduces to the famous Rutherford scattering formula $\frac{d\sigma}{d\Omega} = \left(\frac{z z' e^2}{4E}\right)^2 \mathrm{cosec}^4\frac{\theta}{2}$. We use Gaussian cgs units for historical continuity. Because of the long range of the Coulomb potential, the scattering cross sections vary over many orders of magnitude and the total (integrated) cross section diverges.

5.3.2. *Nuclear Shell Model*

The nuclear shell model is an analog of the Aufbau principle, which describes the electronic structure of atoms. It was developed independently in 1949 by Maria Goeppert-Mayer and by J. Hans D. Jensen and coworkers. Goeppert-Mayer and Jensen shared the 1963 Nobel Prize in physics. According to the shell model, nuclear energy levels, individually for neutrons and protons, are filled successively, in conformity with the Pauli exclusion principle. Just as in the atomic case, there are certain "magic numbers" in the occupancy of nucleon shells: 2, 8, 20, 28, 50, 82, and 126, which confer enhanced stability to nuclei. (This is analogous to the atomic magic numbers 2, 10, 18, 36, 54, 86.)

To a first approximation, the energy levels of nucleons begin with those of an isotropic three-dimensional harmonic oscillator. A second approximation lowers each level slightly by an amount proportional to l^2, where l is the orbital angular momentum quantum number. The code used to designate the values $l = 0, 1, 2, 3, \ldots$ is $s, p, d, f, g, h, i, k, \ldots$ (sober physicists don't find giraffes hiding in kitchens). In contrast to the convention used in atoms, the integer quantum number labels the ordering of levels of a given angular momentum. Thus you will find levels labeled $1p, 2d$, etc. The left side of the graphic gives the nl designations of the levels. It was suggested by Enrico Fermi that spin-orbit coupling plays an important role in determining nucleon energies. Each l-level, except $l = 0$, is accordingly split into two states, with $j = l \pm \frac{1}{2}$. This leads finally to the spectrum of nucleon energy levels shown on the right, with appropriate gaps determining the magic numbers. Neutrons are represented by blue dots and protons by red dots. The diagram is highly schematic since the magnitudes and even the ordering of the nl_j levels differ from nucleus to nucleus.

Following is a partial listing of nuclides with magic numbers N and/or Z:

$N = 2$: $^4_2$He;

$N = 8$: $^{15}_7$N, $^{16}_8$O;

$N = 20$: $^{36}_{16}$S, $^{37}_{17}$Cl, $^{38}_{18}$Ar, $^{39}_{19}$K, $^{40}_{20}$Ca;

$N = 28$: $^{48}_{20}$Ca, $^{50}_{22}$Ti, $^{51}_{23}$V, $^{52}_{24}$Cr, $^{54}_{26}$Fe;

$N = 50$: $^{86}_{36}$Kr, $^{88}_{38}$Sr, $^{89}_{39}$Y, $^{92}_{42}$Mo;

$N = 82$: $^{136}_{54}$Xe, $^{138}_{56}$Ba, $^{139}_{57}$La, $^{140}_{58}$Ce, $^{141}_{59}$Pr, $^{142}_{60}$Nd, $^{144}_{62}$Sm;

$N = 126$: $^{208}_{82}$Pb.

$Z = 2$: $^3_2$He, $^4_2$He;

$Z = 8$: $^A_8$O with $A = 16, 17, 18$;

$Z = 20$: $^A_{20}$Ca with $A = 40, 42, 43, 44, 46, 48$;

$Z = 28$: $^A_{28}$Ni with $A = 58, 60, 61, 62, 64$;

$Z = 50$: $^A_{50}$Sn with $A = 112, 114, 115, 116, 118, 120, 122, 124$;

$Z = 82$: $^A_{82}$Pb with $A = 204, 206, 208$.

Of special interest are the doubly-magic nuclei: $^4_2$He, $^{16}_8$O, $^{40}_{20}$Ca, $^{48}_{20}$Ca, and $^{208}_{82}$Pb.

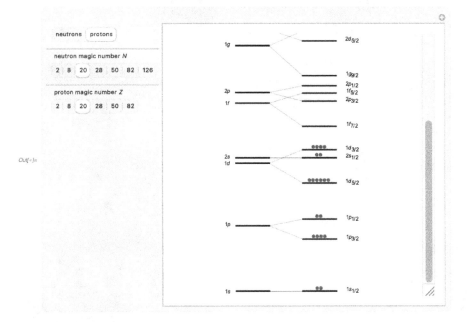

Demonstration 5.19: Magic Numbers in the Nuclear Shell Model (https://demons trations.wolfram.com/MagicNumbersInTheNuclearShellModel/)

5.3.3. *Alpha Decay*

Alpha emission is a radioactive process involving two nuclei X and Y, which has the form $^A_Z X \longrightarrow ^{A-4}_{Z-2} Y + ^4_2 He$, the helium-4 nucleus being known as an alpha particle. All nuclei heavier than Pb ($Z = 82$) exhibit alpha activity. Geiger and Nuttall (1911) found an empirical relation between the half-life $t_{1/2}$ of alpha decay and the energy Q of the emitted alpha particles. Using more recent data, the Geiger–Nuttall law can be written $\log_{10} t_{1/2} \approx -46.83 + 1.454 Z/\sqrt{Q}$, where t is in seconds, Q in MeV, and Z is the atomic number of the daughter nucleus. The observed range of half-lives is huge, varying from 2×10^{15} years for $^{144}_{60}$ Nd to 3×10^{-7} sec for $^{212}_{84}$ Po. We limit our consideration to even-even nuclei. Slightly different values of the parameters pertain when odd Z or A nuclei are involved.

George Gamow in 1928, just two years after the invention of quantum mechanics, proposed that the process involves tunneling of an alpha particle through a large barrier. The barrier is created by the Coulomb repulsion between the alpha particle and the rest of the positively

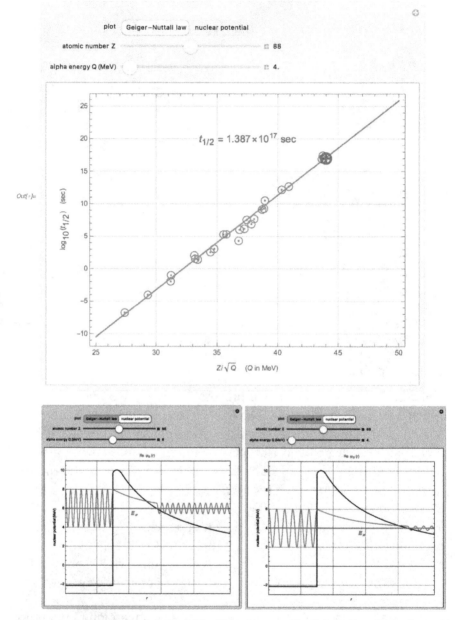

Demonstration 5.20: Gamow Model for Alpha Decay — The Geiger–Nuttall Law (https://demonstrations.wolfram.com/GamowModelForAlphaDecayTheGeigerNuttallLaw/)

charged nucleus, in addition to breaking the strong nuclear forces acting on the alpha particle. Gurney and Condon independently proposed a similar mechanism. A plot of the nuclear potential also shows the alpha particle wavefunction $\psi_\alpha(r)$. The amplitude of the transmitted wave is highly magnified.

The tunneling amplitude can be approximated by the WKB formula $T \approx \exp\left[-\frac{\sqrt{2\mu}}{\hbar} \int_R^{R_\alpha} \sqrt{V(r) - E_\alpha}\, dr\right]$, where $V(r) = \frac{2Ze^2}{4\pi\epsilon_0 r}$ is the repulsive Coulomb potential energy between the α-particle (charge $+2e$) and the daughter nucleus (charge $+Ze$). The energy of the emitted α-particle is given by $E_\alpha = \frac{2Ze^2}{4\pi\epsilon_0 R_\alpha}$, where R_α is the distance from the center of the nucleus at which the α becomes a free particle, while R is the approximate radius of the nuclear potential well in which the α is originally bound. The integral $\int_R^{R_\alpha} \sqrt{1/r - 1/R_\alpha}\, dr$ can be done exactly to give $\cos^{-1}\sqrt{\frac{R}{R_\alpha}} - \sqrt{\frac{R}{R_\alpha}\left(1 - \frac{R}{R_\alpha}\right)}$. For $R_\alpha \gg R$, a sufficiently good approximation is $\frac{\pi}{2} - 2\sqrt{\frac{R}{R_\alpha}}$, so that $T \approx \exp\left[-\frac{2\mu}{\hbar}\sqrt{\frac{Ze^2}{2\pi\epsilon_0 R_\alpha}}\left(\frac{\pi}{2} - 2\sqrt{\frac{R}{R_\alpha}}\right)\right]$. The transition probability per unit time approximates the reciprocal of the half-life for α-decay, thus $t_{1/2} \approx \frac{1}{|T|^2}$. The Geiger–Nuttall formula introduces two empirical constants to fudge for the various approximations and is commonly written in the form $\log_{10} t_{1/2} \approx a - bZ/\sqrt{Q}$, where Q, measured in MeV, is often used in nuclear physics in place of E_α.

5.3.4. *Nuclear Liquid-Drop Model and Radioactive Decay*

The liquid-drop model in nuclear physics was originally proposed by George Gamow and developed by Hans Bethe and Carl von Weizsäcker in the 1930s. It treats the nucleus as an incompressible fluid of protons and neutrons bound together by the strong nuclear force. For a nuclide $^A_Z X_N$ containing Z protons and $N = A - Z$ neutrons Weizsäcker's semi-empirical formula for the mass of a nucleus has the form

$$M(Z, A) = Zm_p + (A - Z)m_n - E_B/c^2$$

with

$$E_B = a_V A - a_S A^{2/3} - a_C \frac{Z(Z-1)}{A^{1/3}} - a_A \frac{(A - 2Z)^2}{A} + a_P \frac{\delta}{A^{1/2}}.$$

Here m_p and m_n are the rest mass of the proton and neutron, respectively, in atomic mass units (amu) and E_B is the total binding energy, expressed in MeV. The latter is approximated as a sum of five contributions, in the order written: a volume term proportional to A, a surface tension term proportional to the area $A^{2/3}$, a Coulomb repulsion term, an asymmetry term, and a pairing term. The coefficients a_x are empirically determined, with best current values given here. In the pairing term, $\delta = +1$ for even-even nuclei, -1 for odd-odd nuclei, and 0 for odd-even nuclei, or whenever A is odd.

In this Demonstration, theoretical values of nuclear masses for all observed nuclides from $Z = 4$ to 94, calculated to 0.001 amu, are displayed in the boxes. To further extend the liquid drop model, any

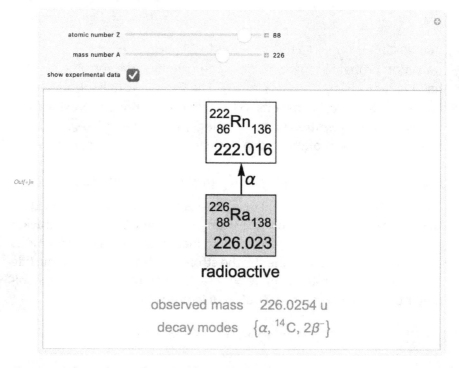

Demonstration 5.21: Nuclear Liquid-Drop Model Applied to Radioactive Decay Modes (https://demonstrations.wolfram.com/NuclearLiquidDropModelAppliedToRadioactive DecayModes/)

possible α, β^-, or β^+ radioactive decay modes are predicted. Results from the liquid-drop model can be compared with experimental isotope data sources accessible from the Wolfram website. Nuclear masses are generally accurate within .01 amu of experimental values while decay modes are usually about 80% correct. Particularly for heavier nuclei, decay modes including spontaneous fission (SF), cluster emission (of ^{20}Ne, ^{28}Mg, etc.), and double beta decay ($2\beta^-$) are not accounted for by this version of the liquid-drop model.

5.3.5. *Evolution of Matter from a Quark-Gluon Plasma*

The Relativistic Heavy Ion Collider (RHIC) at Brookhaven National Laboratory is able to smash gold ions together to create conditions under which individual protons and neutrons melt into a plasma consisting of quarks and gluons, at temperatures in excess of 4 trillion K. This is believed to approximate the state of the universe approximately 10^{-6} seconds after the Big Bang, 13.7 billion years ago. By about 10^{-3} seconds the quarks have combined into color-neutral hadrons, most notably protons and neutrons. Also, by a process not yet fully understood, almost all the antimatter particles have been annihilated, leaving our universe composed almost exclusively of matter. By the first three minutes, all the protons and neutrons have combined into the lighter elements deuterium, helium, and lithium, but with hydrogen (protons) still remaining the predominant species. After stars and their supernovas evolve, nucleosynthesis accounts for all the heavier elements.

When the universe is about 350,000 years old, nuclei have captured most of the free electrons to produce electrically neutral atoms. Space becomes transparent to photons, which are still detected as the cosmic microwave background radiation today. In the past three billion or so years, molecules of increasing complexity have been able to assemble themselves. Molecular evolution eventually led to Darwinian evolution, which brings us to the present state of affairs with advanced lifeforms. The time scale of the slider and animation are extremely nonlinear.

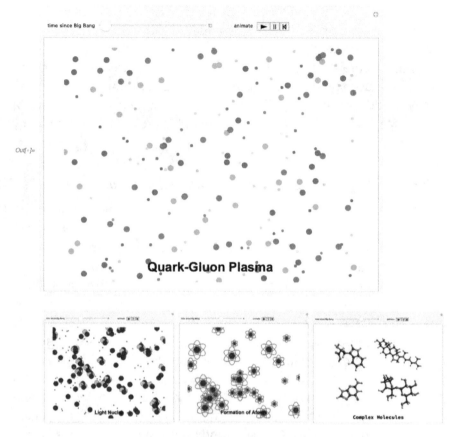

Demonstration 5.22: Evolution of Matter from a Quark-Gluon Plasma (https://demons trations.wolfram.com/EvolutionOfMatterFromAQuarkGluonPlasma/)

5.3.6. *Feynman Diagrams*

Feynman diagrams are symbolic representations for interactions among elementary particles. An interaction occurs when particle trajectories intersect at a vertex. The fundamental vertex in quantum electrodynamics involves a photon γ, represented by a wavy line, and two electrons e, entering and exiting the vertex, represented by solid lines. Arrows oriented in the positive time direction identify the particles as negatively charged electrons e^-. Arrows oriented in the negative time directions represent antiparticles, positrons e^+ propagating forward in time. Each

Feynman diagram can be interpreted as an integral which contributes to the quantum-mechanical amplitude of a process, via a set of Feynman rules. Remarkably, different orientations of a Feynman diagram can represent alternative sequences of spacetime events. You can rotate an eeγ vertex into eight different orientations, each describing a completely different physical process. Included are electron-positron creations and

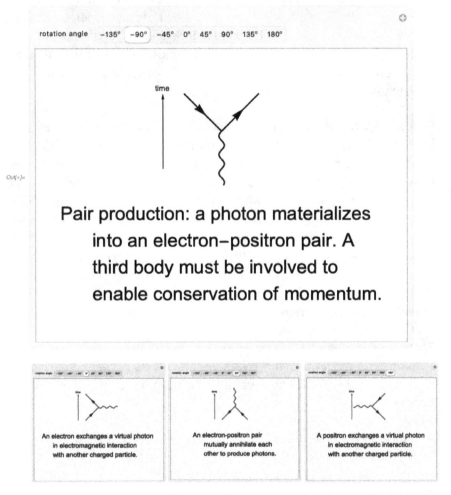

Demonstration 5.23: Rotation of Feynman Diagrams around an Electron-Photon Vertex (https://demonstrations.wolfram.com/RotationOfFeynmanDiagramsAroundAnElectronPhotonVertex/)

annihilations, which contain the essence of Einstein's mass-energy relation $E = mc^2$.

5.3.7. *Magnetic Monopoles and Free Quarks*

A bar magnet is a magnetic dipole with a north pole and a south pole at its opposite ends. Can you cut the magnet to create isolated magnetic monopoles? Nobody has been able to do this yet: each part of the cut magnet develops new north and south poles, regenerating a new dipole. (However, some speculative extensions of the standard model do propose the existence of magnetic monopoles.) Moving the "separate monopoles or quarks" slider on the magnet graphic shows what happens when you pull a magnet apart.

Free quarks, the building blocks of hadrons, have a somewhat analogous behavior. The charges responding to the strong interaction come in three "colors", conventionally designated as red, green, and blue. There also exist the corresponding "anticolors": anti-red, anti-green, and anti-blue. Carrying further the analogy with chromatic colors, these are sometimes called cyan, magenta, and yellow, respectively. (Compare magnetic and electric charges, in which just one "color" and one "anticolor" suffice.) Only color-neutral hadrons have been found in nature, consisting of color-anticolor pairs in mesons or red-green-blue triplets in baryons. The quarks are bound by gluons, shown as helices, and are continually interchanging colors in their dynamical interactions.

Each colored quark has six possible "flavors", not shown in this Demonstration. The most common quark flavors are up (u) and down (d). Of higher energies are the strange (s), charm (c), bottom (b), and top (t) quarks.

If, usually in a scattering process, one attempts to remove a quark from a hadron, the quark bond will stretch until enough energy is available to create a new quark-antiquark pair; the new antiquark cancels the color of the departing quark, while the new quark reconstitutes the original hadron. This is shown in the meson and baryon graphics.

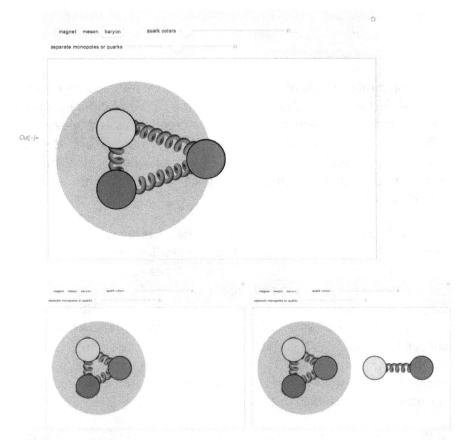

Demonstration 5.24: Magnetic Monopoles and Free Quarks (https://demonstrations. wolfram.com/MagneticMonopolesAndFreeQuarks/)

5.3.8. *Combining Colored Quarks*

Quarks, the building blocks of hadrons (baryons and mesons), exist in six different flavors, namely up (u), down (d), strange (s), charm (c), bottom (b), and top (t), along with their corresponding antiquarks. For each flavor, there exist three possible colors, designated red, blue, and green. These have nothing to do with actual visible colors but, as you will see, the ways in which they combine is highly suggestive of the behavior of colored lights. The corresponding antiquarks have colors designated as anti-red, anti-green, and anti-blue. These behave, in fact, quite analogously to cyan, magenta, and yellow, respectively, the associated complementary colors in conventional optics.

Color constitutes a type of "charge" for the strong interactions responsible for nuclear forces. You can imagine that quarks of different colors attract while those with the same color repel. (This is a gross simplification since quark interactions are highly complex and depend also on spins and energies.) The theory of quark color interactions is called "quantum chromodynamics", in analogy with quantum electrodynamics.

Free quarks have never been isolated, despite years of heroic experimental efforts. This can be restated in terms of quantum chromodynamics as the proposition that only color-neutral particles can exist. A color-neutral combination of red, green, and blue quarks can be assembled into a baryon. Alternatively, the combination of a given color and its anticolor, for example red and anti-red, produces a meson. Quarks continually change colors through their interaction with gluons, the gauge particles for the strong interaction. The quark in a meson actually contains a linear combination of red, green, and blue. The companion antiquark correspondingly exhibits an admixture of anticolors.

In this Demonstration, you can assemble hadrons by various combinations of the six colored quarks and antiquarks. Three quarks will produce a color-neutral baryon, which displays as white. Three antiquarks will give you a color-neutral antibaryon, which displays as black. Any combination of quarks with their antiquarks (one, two, or three pairs) produces a color-neutral meson, which displays as gray. The additive color behavior is precisely the same as that involving red, green, blue, cyan, magenta, and yellow.

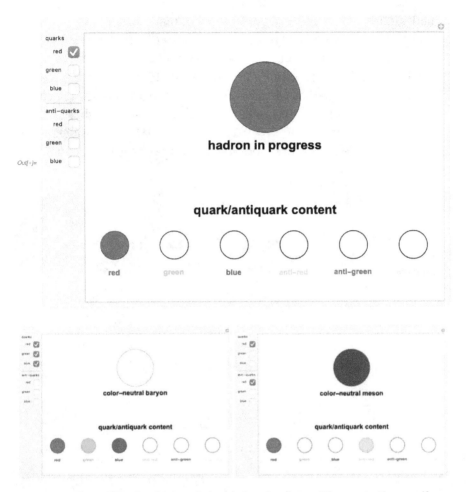

Demonstration 5.25: Combining Colored Quarks (https://demonstrations.wolfram.com/CombiningColoredQuarks/)

5.3.9. *Combining Quarks into Hadrons*

The "particles" setter summarizes the component particles of the Standard Model: quarks, leptons, gauge bosons, and the Higgs particle. The fact that isolated quarks have never been observed is referred to as "quark confinement". Baryons and mesons, known collectively as hadrons, exist as combinations of quarks. Baryons, including the proton and neutron, consist of quark triplets. Mesons combine a quark with an antiquark. There also exist antibaryons, made of antiquark triplets. All mesons and baryons, with the exception of the proton and the neutron (when part of a nucleus) are unstable and decay into more stable particles with lifetimes ranging in order from 10^{-23} to 10^{-10} seconds. The six flavors of quarks are named up (u), down (d), strange (s), charm (c), bottom (b), and top (t). Quarks have fractional electric charges, with $Q = 2/3$ for u, c, and t, and $Q = -1/3$ for d, s, and b (in multiples of the electron charge e). The corresponding antiquarks have charges with the opposite sign.

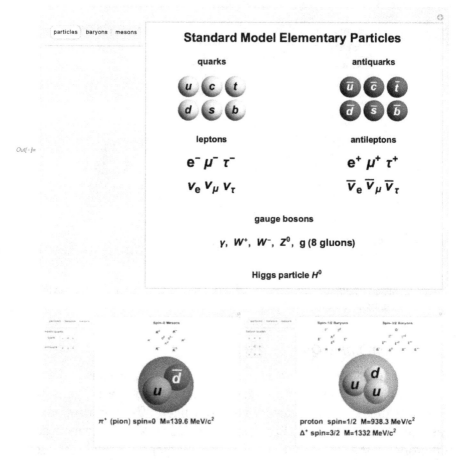

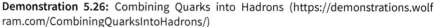

Demonstration 5.26: Combining Quarks into Hadrons (https://demonstrations.wolf ram.com/CombiningQuarksIntoHadrons/)

All quarks (and antiquarks) have spin 1/2, like the electron. They therefore behave as fermions. As a consequence, all baryons have odd half-integer spins (1/2, 3/2, etc.) and are fermions, while mesons have integer spins (0, 1, etc.) and are bosons.

In this Demonstration, you can create combinations of u, d, and s quarks and antiquarks to synthesize some of the lower-mass baryons and mesons. Since, in the domain of elementary particles, mass and energy are essentially equivalent ($E = mc^2$), quark and hadron masses are conventionally expressed in units of MeV/c^2.

Each quark and antiquark flavor comes in three colors, which serve as the "charges" for the strong interaction. Baryons are "color neutral" combinations of red, blue and green quarks. Mesons achieve color neutrality by combining a color with its "anticolor". If not for color, combinations such as uuu with total spin 3/2 could not exist without violating the Pauli exclusion principle. Quark color is not otherwise considered in this Demonstration.

5.3.10. *Proton and Neutron Masses*

Nucleons (protons and neutrons) are complex structures, whose primordial ingredients are three "valence quarks": *uud* for the proton and *udd* for the neutron. The electric charges of the up quark *u* and the down quark *d* are $+\frac{2}{3}e$ and $-\frac{1}{3}e$, respectively, which add up to a proton charge of $+e$ and a neutron charge of 0. Each quark flavor exists in three possible charge states, commonly designated as red, green, and blue. The quark colors are continually exchanged by absorption and emission of gluons. This is the mechanism of the strong interaction, described by a theory known as quantum chromodynamics (QCD). Hadrons can exist only in color-neutral combinations: either three colored quarks for a baryon or a color-anticolor pair for a meson. This implies perpetual quark confinement, negating the possibility of observing free isolated quarks.

High-energy scattering from nucleons confirms their composite structure. Detailed analysis of momentum transfer in scattering experiments implies that the intrinsic masses of the *u* and *d* quarks are approximately $1.9 \pm 0.2 \text{MeV}/c^2$ and $4.6 \pm 0.2 \text{MeV}/c^2$, respectively. (Recall that the electron has a mass of $0.511 \text{MeV}/c^2$.) Thus the combined mass of three quarks can account for only about 1% of the proton or neutron mass, $938.3 \text{MeV}/c^2$ and $939.6 \text{MeV}/c^2$, respectively.

It is now understood that the preponderance of nucleon mass originates from the energy of gluons exchanged between quarks and also interacting among themselves. (Unlike photons, which carry no charge,

Out[ ]=

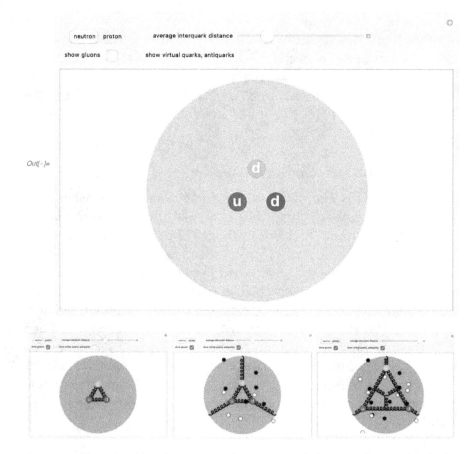

Demonstration 5.27: How the Proton and Neutron Got Their Masses (https://demonstrations.wolfram.com/HowTheProtonAndNeutronGotTheirMasses/)

gluons carry color charges and interact strongly with one another.) Frank Wilczek calls the relation $m = E/c^2$, showing how energy can create mass, "Einstein's second law", or "mass without mass". The gluon field also can produce virtual quarks and antiquarks, shown as gray and white disks. Because of the strength of the interactions in QCD, perturbation theory will not suffice (as it does in QED). The masses of the proton and neutron can be approximated using lattice gauge theory. With the most powerful supercomputers in current use, masses accurate to about 2% have been obtained. In this Demonstration, you can go through a conceptual stepwise sequence to build up the complex structure of a nucleon.

5.3.11. *The Higgs Particle*

The Higgs particle was identified at the Large Hadron Collider (LHC) at CERN in 2013, after many years of searching, in what has been the biggest and most expensive scientific experiment in history. The Higgs was considered the last missing piece of the Standard Model, providing a mechanism for giving mass to the weak-interaction gauge bosons.

This Demonstration gives a highly simplified account of the Higgs mechanism which produces the neutral scalar Higgs boson H^0. The motivation was a puzzle arising in a unification of electromagnetic and weak interactions as a SU(2) × U(1) "electroweak" gauge group mediated by four massless vector bosons, according to a theory developed by Sheldon Glashow, Steven Weinberg and Abdus Salam (they shared the 1979 Nobel Prize in Physics). Whereas electromagnetic interactions are carried by massless photons γ, weak interactions, such as radioactive decays, involve interchange of massive W bosons, with masses of the order of 80 GeV. However, putting these masses in "by hand" would spoil the symmetry and gauge invariance of the theory. It is important to note that massless vector bosons have two possible transverse polarization states, such as the right- and left-handed polarizations of photons. Massive vector bosons have *three* polarization states, with a longitudinal mode added.

Peter Higgs and several others proposed that all of space is permeated by an invisible Higgs field $\phi = \{\phi^1, \phi^2, \phi^3, \phi^4\}$, with four scalar components (actually a doublet of complex scalars). The symmetry of the Higgs field is spontaneously broken when its (four-dimensional)

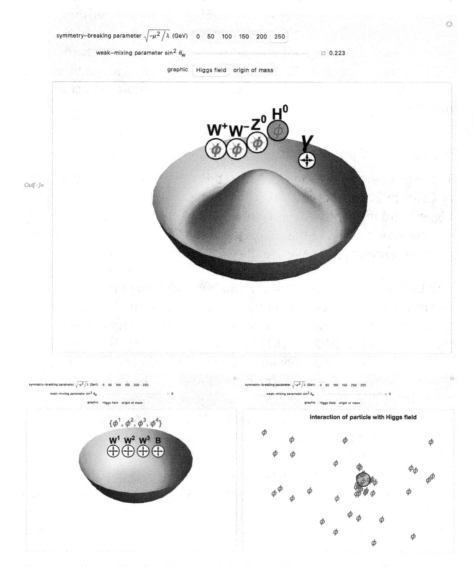

Demonstration 5.28: The Higgs Particle (https://demonstrations.wolfram.com/TheHiggsParticle/)

potential energy surface is distorted into the shape of a "Mexican hat", of the form $V(\phi^\dagger\phi) = \mu^2\phi^\dagger\phi + \lambda(\phi^\dagger\phi)^2$, with μ^2 negative. The Higgs field thereby acquires a vacuum expectation value expressed by the parameter $v = \sqrt{-\mu^2/\lambda}$, estimated as 250 GeV. Three of the scalar components are thereby "gauged away" — more picturesquely described as being "eaten" — by three of the massless electroweak bosons, to turn into their third polarization states. This produces three massive vector bosons, designated W^+, W^-, and W^0. The remaining electroweak boson B remains massless. At the same time, the remaining Higgs field component turns into the putative massive Higgs boson H^0.

The neutral bosons W^0 and B form linear combinations $\gamma = \cos\theta_w B + \sin\theta_w W^0$ and $Z^0 = -\sin\theta_w B + \cos\theta_w W^0$, such that only the Z^0 experiences the weak interaction while γ remains the massless photon. The weak mixing angle or Weinberg angle θ_w is estimated to have a value such that $\sin^2\theta_w \approx 0.223$. The Higgs mechanism predicts the masses $M(W^\pm) = \frac{ve}{2\sin\theta_w} \approx 80.4$ GeV and $M(Z^0) = \frac{ve}{2\sin\theta_w\cos\theta_w} \approx 91.2$ GeV (e, the electron charge, represents the electromagnetic coupling constant with $\alpha = \frac{e^2}{4\pi} \approx \frac{1}{137}$). The Higgs mass is given by $M(H^0) = \sqrt{-2\mu^2}$, with the observed value of 125 GeV. Peter Higgs and François Englert were awarded the Nobel Prize in Physics in 2013 for their prediction of the particle. Supersymmetric extensions of the Standard Model predict the possibility of multiplets of Higgs bosons.

5.3.12. *The Planck Scale*

It is speculated that the most natural units of mass, length, and time can be related to the fundamental physical constants associated with the theories of relativity, quantum mechanics, and gravitation. This originated from a proposal (ca. 1900) of Max Planck and is consequently designated as the Planck scale. The speed of light, $c = 2.99792458 \times 10^8$ m s^{-1}, is inextricably associated with electromagnetism and the special theory of relativity. Likewise, Planck's constant, most conveniently expressed as $\hbar = h/2\pi = 1.05457148 \times 10^{-34}$ m^2 kg s^{-1}, is the essential parameter in quantum theory, while the gravitational constant $G = 6.67300 \times 10^{-11}$m^{3}kg^{-1}s^{-2} is fundamental in both Newtonian gravity and the general theory of relativity.

A product containing the three fundamental constants of the form $c^{n_1} \hbar^{n_2} G^{n_3}$ will have the dimensions $kg^{n_2-n_3} \ m^{n_1+2n_2+3n_3} \ s^{-n_1-n_2-2n_3}$. Your task is to find appropriate choices of the exponents n_1, n_2, n_3 to give natural units of mass, length, and time in terms of c, $\hbar$, and G. The so-called Planck mass M_P, Planck length L_p, and Planck time T_P differ by many orders of magnitude from any currently accessible experimental realization. They are objects on the scale of the proposed fundamental entities of superstring theories, M-theory, loop quantum gravity, and other speculative attempts to create a "theory of everything".

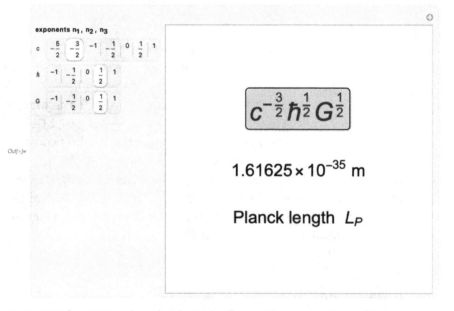

Demonstration 5.29: The Planck Scale (https://demonstrations.wolfram.com/The PlanckScale/)

5.4. Quantum Computers

5.4.1. *Stern–Gerlach Simulations on a Quantum Computer*

In the Stern–Gerlach experiment, an unpolarized beam of neutral particles of spin 1/2 is directed through an inhomogeneous magnetic field (blue and red magnet), which produces separated beams of spin-up and spin-down particles. For simplicity, only the outgoing spin-up beam is shown in the graphic. This beam is then directed through a second magnet, for which the polarization can be rotated by an angle θ from the original. This further splits the beam (except when $\theta = 0$ or π) into spin-up and spin-down beams with respect to the new polarization direction. Again, only the spin-up component is shown. The probability for a particle to emerge with spin-up ($\uparrow$) or spin-down ($\downarrow$) is given by $\cos^2(\theta/2)$ and $\sin^2(\theta/2)$, respectively. The resulting probabilities of $\uparrow$ and $\downarrow$ are shown for five selected angles.

The results of the Stern–Gerlach experiment can be simulated by a quantum computer. The qubits $|0\rangle$ and $|1\rangle$ correspond to the spin states $\uparrow$ and $\downarrow$, respectively. The initial state $0\rangle$ corresponds to the polarized beam leaving the first magnet. By an appropriate sequence of quantum gates, the results of the beam passing through the second magnet, with polarization angle θ, can be simulated. The statistical results are verified after a large number of runs on the quantum computer.

The action of the single-qubit quantum gates can be represented by 2×2 unitary matrices acting on the qubit $\begin{pmatrix} \alpha \\ \beta \end{pmatrix} = \alpha|0\rangle + \beta|1\rangle$: identity (or IDLE): $\boxed{I} = \begin{pmatrix} 1 & 0 \\ 0 & 1 \end{pmatrix}$, Hadamard gate: $\boxed{H} = \begin{pmatrix} 1 & 1 \\ 1 & -1 \end{pmatrix}$, Pauli X (or NOT) gate: $\boxed{X} = \begin{pmatrix} 0 & 1 \\ 1 & 0 \end{pmatrix}$, phase (or $\pi/4$) gate: $\boxed{S} = \begin{pmatrix} 1 & 0 \\ 0 & i \end{pmatrix}$, $\pi/8$ gate: $\boxed{T} = \begin{pmatrix} 1 & 0 \\ 0 & e^{\frac{i\pi}{4}} \end{pmatrix}$.

For example, the $\theta = \pi/4$ rotation is produced by the sequence

$$\boxed{H}\,\boxed{T}\,\boxed{H}\,|0\rangle = \begin{pmatrix} 1 & 1 \\ 1 & -1 \end{pmatrix}\begin{pmatrix} 1 & 0 \\ 0 & e^{\frac{i\pi}{4}} \end{pmatrix}\begin{pmatrix} 1 & 1 \\ 1 & -1 \end{pmatrix}\begin{pmatrix} 1 \\ 0 \end{pmatrix} = \begin{pmatrix} \frac{1}{2} + \frac{1}{2}e^{\frac{i\pi}{4}} \\ \frac{1}{2} - \frac{1}{2}e^{\frac{i\pi}{4}} \end{pmatrix}.$$

The probability of a result $|0\rangle$ in the subsequent measurement is then given by $|\frac{1}{2} + \frac{1}{2}e^{\frac{i\pi}{4}}|^2 = 0.853553$, or about 85% spin-up.

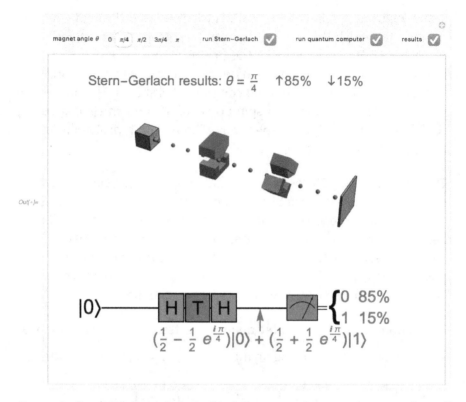

Demonstration 5.30: Stern–Gerlach Simulations on a Quantum Computer (https://demonstrations.wolfram.com/SternGerlachSimulationsOnAQuantumComputer/)

5.4.2. *Deutsch's Algorithm*

In 1985, David Deutsch proposed a highly contrived but simple algorithm to explore the potentially greater computational power of a quantum computer as compared to a classical computer. Consider four possible functions of a single-bit (or basis qubit) $x = 0$ or 1, which produce a single-bit result $f(x) = 0$ or 1, as follows: $f_1(x) = 0, f_2(x) = 1, f_3(x) = x$, $f_4(x) = 1 - x$. The first two functions are classified as "constant" (with $f(0) = f(1)$), while the latter two are described as "balanced" (with $f(0) \neq f(1)$). Suppose now that a classical computer, idealized as a "black box", can perform the computation $x \rightarrow \boxed{f} \rightarrow (x)$.

To determine whether $f(x)$ is constant or balanced on a classical computer, it is necessary to run the program *twice*, with inputs $x = 0$ and $x = 1$, respectively. For example, with the input $x = 0$, suppose we find $f(x) = 1$. Then f can be either f_2 or f_4. We need a second run with $x = 1$ to determine which alternative is correct. By contrast, a 2-qubit quantum computer can find the result in a *single* operation — one shot instead of two.

As shown in the graphic, a black box performing one of the four functions is built into the quantum computer circuit. Our objective is to determine whether this function is constant or balanced. The two qubits $|0\rangle$ and $|1\rangle$ (which can be abbreviated as the quantum state $|01\rangle$) are input, and the program is executed. The first exit qubit is measured, which collapses it to a classical bit 0 or 1. Very directly, 0 indicates that f is constant while 1 indicates that it is balanced. The second exit qubit can be discarded. You can select one of the four possible functions and run the quantum computer program. The quantum state of the two-qubit system at each stage of the computation is exhibited, colored in red.

The Hadamard gate $\boxed{H}$ transforms the basis qubits into superpositions as follows: $H|0\rangle = (|0\rangle + |1\rangle)/\sqrt{2}, H|1\rangle = (|0\rangle - |1\rangle)/\sqrt{2}$. The Deutsch gate carries out the following action, showing the incoming and outgoing qubits:

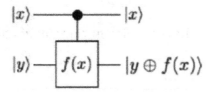

Here $\oplus$ represents the exclusive or (XOR) Boolean operation on the bits y and $f(x)$. The above would be a CNOT gate if $f(x) = x$.

In a generalization to n qubits, known as the Deutsch–Jozsa algorithm, a single query on a quantum computer can find a result that would require up to the order of 2^n queries on a classical computer. Similar fragmentary

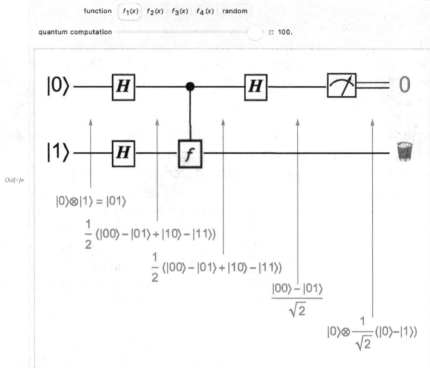

Demonstration 5.31: Deutsch's Algorithm on a Quantum Computer (https://demo nstrations.wolfram.com/DeutschsAlgorithmOnAQuantumComputer/)

results show promise of possible exponential gains in computational power using a quantum machine.

5.4.3. *Quantum Gates on a Bloch Sphere*

Using the Bloch sphere, a cubit $|\psi\rangle = \alpha|0\rangle + \beta|1\rangle = \cos(\theta/2)|0\rangle + \sin(\theta/2)e^{i\phi}|1\rangle$ can be represented as a unit vector (shown in red) from the origin to the point on the unit sphere with spherical coordinates (θ, ϕ). A single-qubit quantum gate G_1 operating on $|\psi\rangle$ produces a rotated qubit $G_1|\psi\rangle = |\psi_1\rangle$, represented by the green vector. Check the box for "add gate 2?" to perform a second operation using gate G_2. This produces another qubit $G_2G_1|\psi\rangle = |\psi_2\rangle$, which is represented by the blue vector. You can choose from the gates H, X, Y, Z, S and T.

The action of the single-qubit quantum gates can be represented by 2×2 unitary matrices acting on the qubit $\begin{pmatrix} \alpha \\ \beta \end{pmatrix} = \begin{pmatrix} \cos(\theta/2) \\ \sin(\theta/2)\, e^{i\phi} \end{pmatrix}$: Hadamard gate: $H = \begin{pmatrix} 1 & 1 \\ 1 & -1 \end{pmatrix}$, Pauli X gate: $X = \begin{pmatrix} 0 & 1 \\ 1 & 0 \end{pmatrix}$, Pauli Y gate: $Y = \begin{pmatrix} 0 & -i \\ i & 0 \end{pmatrix}$, Pauli Z gate: $Z = \begin{pmatrix} 1 & 0 \\ 0 & -1 \end{pmatrix}$, phase (or $\pi/4$) gate: $S = \begin{pmatrix} 1 & 0 \\ 0 & i \end{pmatrix}$, $\pi/8$

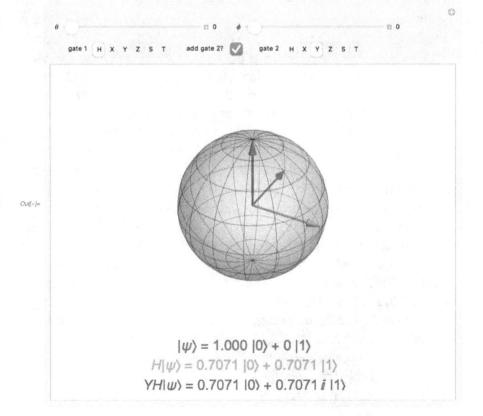

$|\psi\rangle = 1.000\ |0\rangle + 0\ |1\rangle$
$H|\psi\rangle = 0.7071\ |0\rangle + 0.7071\ |1\rangle$
$YH|w\rangle = 0.7071\ |0\rangle + 0.7071\ i\ |1\rangle$

Demonstration 5.32: Single-Qubit Quantum Gates on a Bloch Sphere (https://demo nstrations.wolfram.com/SingleQubitQuantumGatesOnABlochSphere/)

gate: $T = \begin{pmatrix} 1 & 0 \\ 0 & e^{\frac{i\pi}{4}} \end{pmatrix}$. In general, the operation $G \begin{pmatrix} \alpha \\ \beta \end{pmatrix}$ gives a qubit of the form $\begin{pmatrix} \cos(\theta_1/2)\, e^{iX} \\ \sin(\theta_1/2)\, e^{i(\phi_1 + X)} \end{pmatrix}$, with an overall phase factor e^{iX} of no physical significance. Multiplication by e^{-iX} removes this factor and reduces the qubit to the canonical form $\begin{pmatrix} \cos(\theta_1/2) \\ \sin(\theta_1/2)\, e^{i\phi_1} \end{pmatrix}$.

5.4.4. *Quantum Computer Simulation of GHZ Experiment*

An entangled state of three photons in a superposition, either with all horizontally polarized (HHH) or with all vertically polarized (VVV), is known as a Greenberger–Horne–Zeilinger (GHZ) state. It is repressented by the state vector $\Psi = \frac{1}{\sqrt{2}}(|\,HHH\rangle + |\,VVV\rangle)$. A measurement on any one of the photons, using a two-channel polarizer, would give 50% probability for either H or V. Measurements on the other two photons would then be found to show the same polarization. In the canonical GHZ experiment, measurements are performed on the three entangled photons using two-channel polarizers D1, D2 and D3 set to orientations different from the original H and V, which we denote by X and Y. The X polarizations are at angles of $\pm 45°$ with respect to the original polarizations, such that $X = \frac{1}{2}(|\,H\rangle \pm |\,V\rangle)$. The Y polarizations are left and right circular polarizations, represented by $Y = \frac{1}{\sqrt{2}}(|\,H\rangle \pm i\,|\,V\rangle)$. The polarization detectors are set in one of four possible combinations: XXX, XYY, YXY or YYX. We use binary notation, 0 and 1, to label the two possible polarizations for either the X or Y orientation. For the XYY, YXY or YYX configuration, we observe four equally probable results, which we designate 001, 010, 001 and 111. For XXX, we again observe four equally probable results, but now 000, 011, 101 or 110. In all of these cases, any two detector readings, say those of D1 and D2, unambiguously determine the reading of D3. For example, for configuration XYY, if the first two detectors read 01 or 10, the third would then show 0. In this Demonstration, a GHZ experiment is simulated using a three-qubit quantum computer. The GHZ state $\Psi = \frac{1}{\sqrt{2}}(|\,000\rangle + |\,111\rangle)$ is produced by a circuit using one Hadamard (*H*) and two CNOT gates.

The polarization detectors are simulated by a combination of *H* and *S* gates. The output state, for example, $\Psi = \frac{1}{2}(|001\rangle + |010\rangle + |100\rangle + |111\rangle)$, implies that the final bit measurements give the results 001, 010, 100 and 111 with equal probability. Also shown is an illustration of Mermin's *Gedankenexperiment*, which is a simplification of the actual GHZ experiment. The results shown are those corresponding to local realism, with the selected "presets", which can be compared with the quantum mechanics results.

The results of all reproducible experiments agree with the predictions of quantum mechanics and are contrary to those of *local realism*, which would entail the existence of hidden variables. According to local realism, each photon would be presumed to carry an "instruction set" that

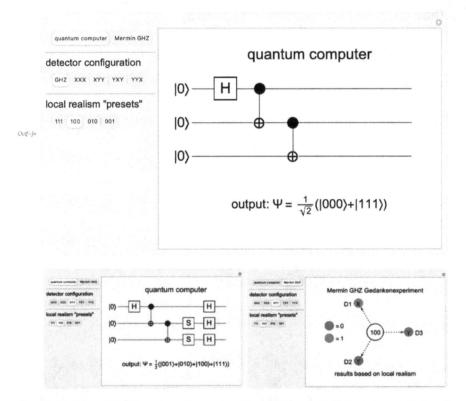

Demonstration 5.33: Quantum Computer Simulation of GHZ Experiment (https://demonstrations.wolfram.com/QuantumComputerSimulationOfGHZExperiment/)

determines, in advance, its polarization in any X or Y measurement. The result that any two readings unambiguously determine the third itself negates the possibility of local realism, since the third photon cannot "communicate" with the other two once they leave the source. In contrast to Bell's inequalities, in which this conclusion is reached by statistical analysis of a multitude of experimental results, the GHZ experiment requires only a single run.

The Hadamard gate H (not to be confused with the horizontal polarization, also called H) acts on a qubit in one of the basis states to produce a linear combination of the two basis states. Specifically $H|0\rangle = \frac{1}{\sqrt{2}}(|0\rangle + |1\rangle)$ and $H|1\rangle = \frac{1}{\sqrt{2}}(|0\rangle - |1\rangle)$. As a unitary operator, $H = \frac{1}{\sqrt{2}}\begin{pmatrix} 1 & 1 \\ 1 & -1 \end{pmatrix}$. The $\pi/2$-phase shift gate S is represented by $S = \begin{pmatrix} 1 & 0 \\ 0 & i \end{pmatrix}$.

Chapter 6

Physics: Further Topics

6.1. Relativity

6.1.1. *Minkowski Spacetime*

Minkowski spacetime provides a lucid pictorial representation for the special theory of relativity. An *event* occurring at a time t at the location (x, y, z) in three-dimensional space is described by a point $(x_0, x_1, x_2, x_3) \equiv (ct, x, y, z)$ in a four-dimensional manifold known as Minkowski spacetime. The factor $c = 2.9979 \times 10^8$ m/s, the speed of light, gives $x_0 = ct$ the dimensions of length, to match those of x_1, x_2, x_3. The fundamental principle of special relativity can be expressed as the invariance of the *interval $ds^2 = dx_0^2 - dx_1^2 - dx_2^2 - dx_3^2$* as measured by observers in *all* inertial frames. This differs dramatically from Galilean relativity, the foundational postulate of Newtonian mechanics, in that both time and space intervals become *relative*, or dependent on the velocity of the observer.

For simplicity, this Demonstration considers just a single space dimension x that, along with the time variable ct, gives a two-dimensional projection of Minkowski space. A stationary observer measures variables denoted x and ct, while an observer in another inertial frame moving at a constant speed v measures variables denoted x' and ct'. For ease of visualization, the primed variables are shown in red. These alternative variables are related by a *Lorentz transformation*, $x' = x \cosh \theta - ct \sinh \theta$ and $ct' = -x \sinh \theta + ct \cosh \theta$. Here θ is the *rapidity*, defined by $\theta = \operatorname{arctanh}(v/c)$. The velocity can also be expressed in dimensionless

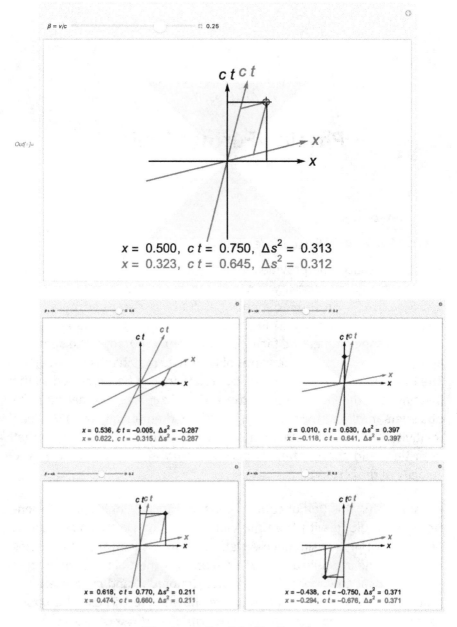

Out[ ]=

$x = 0.500, \ ct = 0.750, \ \Delta s^2 = 0.313$
$x = 0.323, \ ct = 0.645, \ \Delta s^2 = 0.312$

$x = 0.536, \ ct = -0.005, \ \Delta s^2 = -0.287$
$x = 0.622, \ ct = -0.315, \ \Delta s^2 = -0.287$

$x = 0.010, \ ct = 0.630, \ \Delta s^2 = 0.397$
$x = -0.118, \ ct = 0.641, \ \Delta s^2 = 0.397$

$x = 0.618, \ ct = 0.770, \ \Delta s^2 = 0.211$
$x = 0.474, \ ct = 0.660, \ \Delta s^2 = 0.211$

$x = -0.438, \ ct = -0.750, \ \Delta s^2 = 0.371$
$x = -0.294, \ ct = -0.676, \ \Delta s^2 = 0.371$

Demonstration 6.1: *(Continued)*

Snapshot 1: This spacelike interval could represent the length of a rod. The stationary observer measures a length that is shorter than that measured by the moving observer. This is called the *Lorentz-FitzGerald contraction*, given by $L = L_0\sqrt{1 - v^2/c^2}$.

Snapshot 2: The interval here could represent time measured in the moving frame. The black and red axes might interchange to represent the moving and stationary observers, respectively (it's all relative!). The time interval in the moving frame, $t = 0.740/c$, represents the *proper time*. The longer time measured by the moving observer shows *time dilation*.

Snapshot 3: The event marked by the locator lies in the future lightcone. This means that this event could possibly be caused by an event at the origin.

Snapshot 4: The event lies in the *past* lightcone, meaning that it might possibly be the cause of the event at the origin.

Demonstration 6.1: Minkowski Spacetime (https://demonstrations.wolfram.com/Min kowskiSpacetime/)

form as $\beta = v/c$. In accordance with this hyperbolic transformation, the primed (red) coordinate axes are skewed at angles θ relative to the stationary axes. The origin represents an event in which $x = ct = 0$ momentarily for *both* observers. You can move the locator to determine another event, for which the two observers no longer agree on values of x and ct. The two sets of values of x and ct are represented by the black and red projections on their respective axes. Their numerical values are given at the bottom of the graphic. The constancy of the interval is shown by the relation $\Delta s^2 = (ct)^2 - x^2 = (ct')^2 - (x')^2$. In the cases $\Delta s^2 > 0$, $\Delta s^2 < 0$, and $\Delta s^2 = 0$, the interval is called *timelike, spacelike*, or *lightlike* (or *null*), respectively. Timelike intervals lie within the future or past lightcones, projected as yellow triangles in the graphic. The red lines meeting at the event point are parallel to their respective red axes. Note that time is not ordered in a spacelike event: past and future are not invariant; nor is space ordered in a timelike event: left and right are not invariant.

6.1.2. *Einstein's Velocity Addition Formula*

According to the special theory of relativity, the composition of two collinear velocities u and v is given by a well-known formula derived by Einstein: $u \oplus v = \frac{u+v}{1+uv/c^2}$, where c is the speed of light, 2.9979×10^8 m/sec. For $u, v \ll c$, this reduces to the simple Galilean formula $u \oplus v = u + v$. The result can be derived by successive application of collinear Lorentz boosts, but it can be shown more intuitively by an argument outlined in the détails. In the Demonstration the speeds are scaled as v/c (also known as β) to keep the two rocket ships within the graphic. Einstein's formula is analogous to the law of addition for hyperbolic tangents, $\tanh(r_1 + r_2) = \frac{\tanh r_1 + \tanh r_2}{1 + \tanh r_1 + \tanh r_2}$, where r corresponds to the rapidity, defined by $\beta = \tanh r$.

Suppose a baseball team is traveling on a train moving at 60 mph. The star fastball pitcher needs to tune up his arm for the next day's game. Fortunately, one of the railroad cars is free, and its full length is available. If his 90 mph pitches are in the same direction the train is moving, the ball will actually be moving at 150 mph relative to the ground. The law of addition of velocities in the same direction is relatively straightforward, $V = u + v$. But according to Einstein's special theory of relativity, this is only approximately true and requires that u and v be small fractions of the speed of light, $c \approx 3 \times 10^8$ m/sec (or 186,000 miles/sec). Expressed mathematically, we can write $V(u, v) \approx u + v$ if $u, v \ll c$. According to special relativity, the speed of light, when viewed from any frame of reference, has the same constant value c. Thus, if an atom moving at velocity v emits a light photon at velocity c, the photon will still be observed to move at velocity c, not $c + v$.

Our problem is to deduce the functional form of $V(u, v)$ consistent with these facts. It is convenient to build in the known asymptotic behavior for $v \ll c$ by defining $V(u, v) = f(u, v)(u + v)$. When $u = c$, we evidently have $V = c$, so $f(c, v) = \frac{c}{c+v} = \frac{1}{1+v/c}$, and likewise $f(u, c) = \frac{c}{c+u} = \frac{1}{1+u/c}$. If both u and v equal c, $f(c, c) = \frac{c}{c+c} = \frac{1}{1+1}$. A few moments' reflection should convince you that a function consistent with these properties is

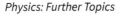

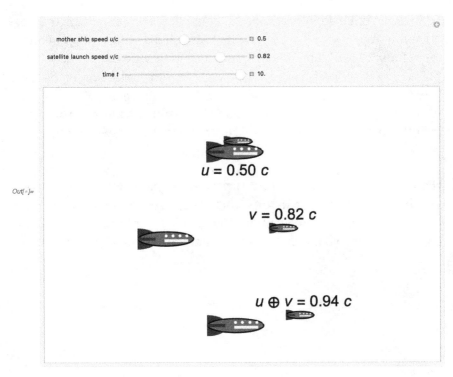

mother ship speed u/c ▦ 0.5

satellite launch speed v/c ▦ 0.82

time t ▦ 10.

Out[ ]=

$u = 0.50\ c$

$v = 0.82\ c$

$u \oplus v = 0.94\ c$

Demonstration 6.2: Einstein's Formula for Adding Velocities (https://demonstrations. wolfram.com/EinsteinsFormulaForAddingVelocities/)

$f(u, v_2) = \frac{1}{1+uv/c^2}$, which gives Einstein's velocity addition law $V(u, v) = \frac{u+v}{1+uv/c^2}$.

6.1.3. *Time Dilation*

According to Einstein's special theory of relativity, a clock moving at a significant fraction of the speed of light with respect to an observer runs more slowly than the observer's own clock. This implies that time must be flowing more slowly in a moving frame of reference, which is referred to as *time dilation*. If a process (such as the decay of an unstable particle) occurs with an average lifetime of τ_0 in the rest frame, the lifetime τ of the particle moving at speed v is given by $\tau = \tau_0/\sqrt{1 - \frac{v^2}{c^2}}$, where c is the speed of light, 2.9979×10^8 m/sec. The decay of muons has provided verification of Einstein's formula to a high degree of accuracy. The negative muon μ^-, with a mass of 105.7 MeV/c^2, is the second-generation lepton analogous to the electron e^-. The antiparticles μ^+ and e^+ (the positron) are similarly related. The mean lifetime of free muon decay is 2.197 µsec in the rest frame. The decay processes are $\mu^- \rightarrow e^- \bar{v}_e v_\mu$ and $\mu^+ \rightarrow e^+ v_e \bar{v}_\mu$. Here v is a neutrino and $\bar{v}$ an antineutrino, each occurring in both electron and muon flavors. In finer detail, these weak-interaction processes involve $W^{\pm}$ bosons as intermediates.

High-energy collisions of protons produce copious numbers of pions, which, in turn, decay into muons. This all happens within the blue square in the graphic. The beam of muons thus produced is injected into a circular synchrotron, which can accelerate them to energies up to 10,000 MeV

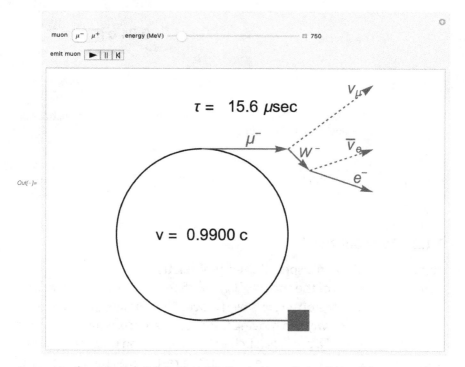

Demonstration 6.3: Relativistic Time Dilation in Muon Decay (https://demonstrations. wolfram.com/RelativisticTimeDilationInMuonDecay/)

(10 GeV). The lifetimes τ are then determined as a function of energy. Muons accelerated to 750 MeV already travel at 99% the speed of light and have average lifetimes enhanced by an order of magnitude. At the maximum energy available in this Demonstration, speeds of 0.9999 c are achieved and the muon lifetime is increased by a factor of 100.

Earlier experiments on muons produced by cosmic rays found their half-lives to be dependent on distance traveled through the atmosphere; they also exhibited relativistic time dilation.

6.1.4. *Curved Spacetime*

According to Newton's law of universal gravitation, two masses M and m attract one another with a force varying as the inverse square of the distance between them: $F = -\frac{GMm}{r^2}$, where G is Newton's constant of gravitation. Orbits of attracting masses, including Kepler's laws of planetary motion, can be calculated on the basis of this force law. The left-hand graphic shows some possible trajectories of a "test mass" m, with $m \ll M$, around a stationary mass M. The trajectories, shown as red curves, depend on the central mass M and the energy E of the test mass. When the test mass moves more slowly than the escape velocity, it spirals into the center. At higher energies, a stable orbit becomes possible in a progression of conic sections: circle, ellipse, parabola and hyperbola. (Hyperbolic orbits are not included here.)

Einstein's general theory of relativity gives a completely different picture of gravitation. It is not a force, per se, but rather a consequence of the curvature of spacetime. As John Wheeler said, matter tells spacetime how to curve while spacetime tells matter how to move. The right-hand graphic is a simplified representation of the curvature of space-time caused by the mass M. This has been likened to a cannonball warping a mattress. The test mass then moves along a geodesic path in curved spacetime, which reduces to a straight line in the absence of curvature.

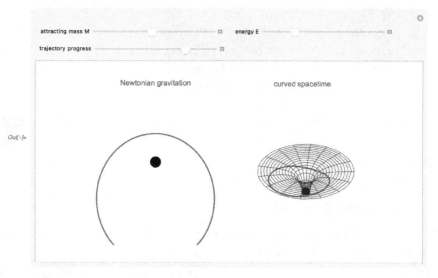

Demonstration 6.4: Gravitation versus Curved Spacetime (https://demonstrations. wolfram.com/GravitationVersusCurvedSpacetime/)

6.1.5. *Relativistic Energy Levels for the Hydrogen Atom*

In non-relativistic quantum mechanics, the energy levels of the hydrogen atom are given by the formula of Bohr and Schrödinger, $E_n = -\frac{1}{2n^2}$, expressed in hartrees (assuming the appropriate correction for the reduced mass of the electron). The energy depends only on the principal quantum number $n = 1, 2, 3, \ldots$ and is $2n^2$-fold degenerate (including electron spin). In Dirac's relativistic theory, this degeneracy is partially resolved and the energy is found to depend as well on the angular momentum quantum number j. To second order in the fine structure constant $\alpha = e^2/\hbar c \approx 1/137$, the hydrogen energy levels are given by $E_{nj} = -\frac{1}{2n^2}\left(1 + \frac{\alpha^2}{n^2}\left(\frac{n}{j+1/2} - \frac{3}{4}\right)\right)$. In Dirac's theory, levels such as $2s_{1/2}$ and $2p_{1/2}$ remain degenerate. The discovery of the Lamb shift showed that these two levels were actually split by 1057.8 MHz. This was a major stimulus for the development of quantum electrodynamics in the 1950s. The Lamb shift, significant only for $l = 0$ (s-states), raises the energy by approximately $\frac{13}{4}\frac{\alpha^3}{n^3}$. The relativistic and radiative correction to hydrogen energy levels can therefore be written $\Delta E_{rel} = -\frac{\alpha^2}{2n^4}\left(\frac{n}{j+1/2} - \frac{3}{4}\right) + \frac{13}{4}\frac{\alpha^3}{n^3}\delta_{l,0}$, to third order in α.

In this Demonstration, you can conceptually vary the fine structure constant from 0 to its actual value, or equivalently the speed of light c from ∞ to 1 (meaning 3×10^8 m/s), to show the transition from non-relativistic to relativistic energies for quantum numbers $n = 1, 2$, and 3. The energies are expressed in MHz (1 hartree $= 6.57966 \times 10^9$ MHz).

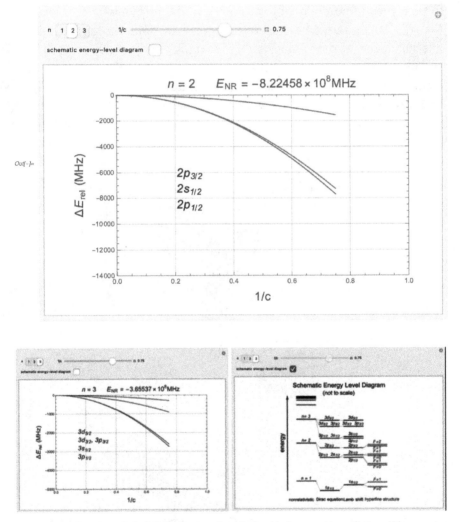

Demonstration 6.5: Relativistic Energy Levels for Hydrogen Atom (https://demonstra tions.wolfram.com/RelativisticEnergyLevelsForHydrogenAtom/)

6.1.6. *Klein-Nishina Formula*

Low-energy (Thomson) scattering of a photon by an electron is approximated by the differential scattering cross-section $\frac{d\sigma}{d\Omega} = \frac{1}{2} \times (1 + \cos^2\theta)r_e^2$, where $r_e = \frac{e^2}{mc^2} = 2.818 \times 10^{-13}$ cm, the classical electron radius. The corresponding total scattering cross-section is given by $\sigma_T = 2\pi \int_0^\pi \frac{d\sigma}{d\Omega} \sin\theta d\theta = \frac{8\pi}{3}r_e^2$. The Thomson formula is, however, inadequate to treat the higher-energy photoelectric and Compton effects. Klein and Nishina (1929) derived the scattering cross-section according to Dirac's relativistic theory of the electron: $\frac{d\sigma}{d\Omega} = \frac{1}{2}r_e^2 f(E_y, \theta)^2[f(E_y, \theta) + f(E_y, \theta)^{-1} - \sin^2\theta]$, where $f(E_y, \theta) = 1/[1 + E_y(1 - \cos\theta)]$ and $E_y = h\nu/mc^2$, the incident photon energy in units of the electron rest energy (511 KeV/c^2). The formulas pertain to the average of the two photon polarizations.

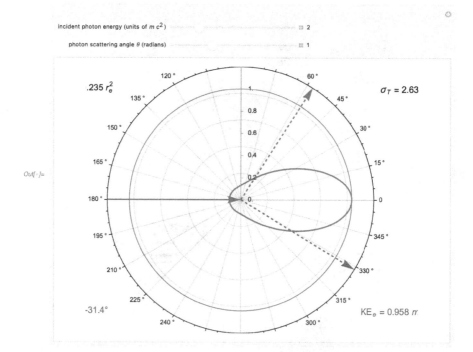

Demonstration 6.6: Klein–Nishina Formula for Compton Effect (https://demonstrati ons.wolfram.com/KleinNishinaFormulaForComptonEffect/)

A polar plot of the differential scattering cross-section is shown in the graphic, with photon energy selectable in the range 0–10 MeV. The cross-section is expressed in units of $r_e^2 \approx 7.94 \times 10^{-26}$ cm$^2 \approx 794$ barns, with a maximum value of $\frac{d\sigma}{d\Omega} = r_e^2 = 1$, as shown by the light red circle. The directions of the scattered photons are shown by a dashed red arrow, while the scattered electron (initially at rest) follows the dashed blue arrow. Numerical values are given for the photon differential and total cross-sections, the electron scattering angle ϕ_e and the electron kinetic energy KE$_e$.

6.1.7. *Penrose Diagrams for Minkowski Space and Black Holes*

On Penrose diagrams, null geodesics, the paths of light rays, are lines at $\pm 45°$ angles, in common with other spacetime pictures. The three figures on the next page show Penrose diagrams for Minkowski space, Schwarzschild black holes and Kruskal-Szekeres maximally extended spacetime, respectively. For Minkowski spacetime, the radial variable r and time t are related to the null geodesics u and v by $r \pm t = \tan(u \pm v)$. The Penrose diagram is a diamond-shaped figure with each corner representing an infinite limit point of space or time. The two upper sides can be associated with future lightlike infinity, the two lower sides to past lightlike infinity. The diagram for a Schwarzschild black hole builds on the Minkowski diagram, adding a wedge-shaped region with boundaries at the event horizon and the antihorizon, both spheres of radius $r = r_S$, and the black hole singularity, represented by a jagged line with $r = 0$. Extended spacetime is seen to consist of four regions, including a duplicate copy of the Schwarzschild geometry, but reversed in time and connected along the antihorizon. The analytic extension contains not only our universe (Region I) and a black hole (Region II), but also a parallel universe (Region III), connected by an Einstein-Rosen bridge, and a white hole (Region IV). This is actually all the product of mathematical construction; any of its predictions may or may not have a basis in reality.

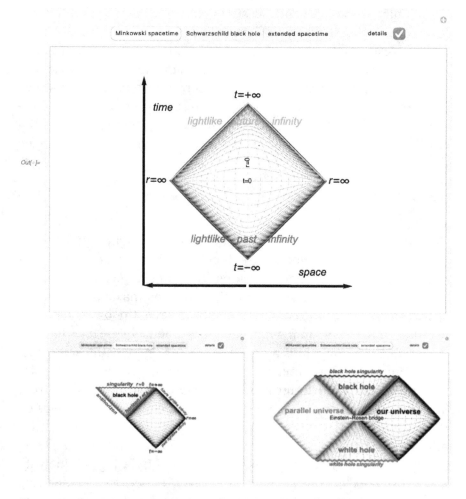

Demonstration 6.7: Penrose Diagrams for Minkowski Space and Black Holes (https://arxiv.org/pdf/1512.02061.pdf)

6.2. Astronomy and Astrophysics

6.2.1. *Celestial Two-Body Problem*

Two celestial bodies interacting gravitationally can establish a stable system in which both trace out elliptical (or possibly circular) orbits about their mutual barycenter (center of mass), marked with a red dot. Each orbit individually follows Kepler's three laws of planetary motion.

Kepler's first law specifies that each orbit is an ellipse with one focus at the barycenter. According to Kepler's second law, each orbit sweeps out equal areas in equal times. Thus for an eccentric orbit, the speed increases closer to the barycenter.

Kepler's third law states that the square of the period of an orbit is proportional to the cube of its semimajor axis. Accordingly, the outer planets of the Solar System have much longer "years" than Earth. When one of the interacting bodies is much more massive than the other, as in the typical case of a planet orbiting a star, the more elementary form of Kepler's laws pertains, with the star itself at the focus of an elliptical orbit. Actually, the barycenter is then located within the body of the star, but not at its exact center. This can cause the star to "wobble" when a Jupiter-sized planet orbits around it. In recent years, the existence of extrasolar planets has been detected in this way.

In this Demonstration, you can vary the mass ratio and the eccentricity ε of the orbit. For a circular orbit, $\varepsilon = 0$, while for an ellipse $0 < \varepsilon < 1$. You can adjust the apoapses, the vectors from the barycenter

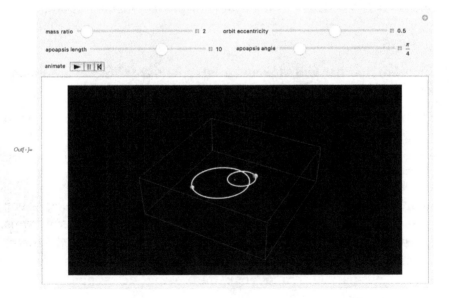

Demonstration 6.8: (*Continued*)

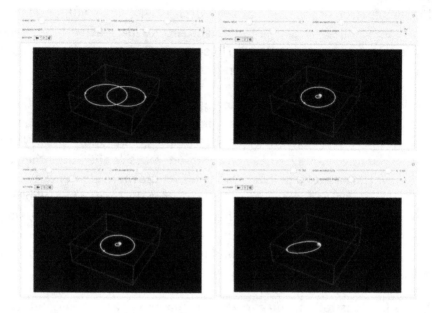

Snapshot 1: the binary or double star 61 Cygni, also known as Bessel's star; the period of rotation is approximately 659 years

Snapshot 2: the dwarf planet Pluto with its companion Charon, with about one-seventh of the mass; the barycenter of the system orbits the Sun with a period of 248.5 years

Snapshot 3: a star with a planet 1/50 of its mass; the star's wobbling motion is apparent

Snapshot 4: approximate representation of a comet in orbit around the Sun; the eccentricity approaches 1

Demonstration 6.8: The Celestial Two-Body Problem (https://demonstrations.wolfram.com/TheCelestialTwoBodyProblem/)

to the farthest point of each orbit, also known as Laplace–Runge–Lenz vectors. (Apogee, aphelion, and apoastron are more familiar synonyms for apoapsis pertaining to specific celestial bodies.) Rotating the three-dimensional figure can show the orbits from different angles. From an edge-on perspective, the motions of the orbiting bodies appear to follow irregular linear trajectories.

6.2.2. *Hodographs for Kepler Orbits*

Kepler orbits are conic sections, most notably ellipses for stable periodic motion of a planet around the Sun. A lesser-known property is the motion of the associated tangential velocity vector, which traces out a circular orbit in velocity space. Hamilton (1864) first introduced the term hodograph to denote this motion.

A Kepler orbit in plane polar coordinates is described by $r = \frac{p}{1-e\cos\theta}$. Here the semi-latus rectum is given by $p = \frac{L^2}{GMm^2}$, where L is the orbital angular momentum, M is the solar mass, m is the planetary mass and G is the gravitational constant. It is assumed that $M \gg m$. The eccentricity of the orbit is given by

$$e = \sqrt{1 + \frac{2EL^2}{G^2M^2m^3}},$$

where E is the energy of the planetary orbit. For an elliptical orbit, $E < 0$, so that $0 \le e < 1$.

For selected values of p and e, the Kepler ellipse and the corresponding hodograph are shown. A set of velocity vectors for evenly spaced values of the true anomaly θ is shown by numbered red arrows, with corresponding values pertaining to the orbit and the hodograph.

The magnitude of the velocity is a minimum at the aphelion, numbered 1, and a maximum at the perihelion, numbered 7.

The spherical components of velocity are converted to Cartesian coordinates using $v = \dot{r}\hat{r} + r\dot{\theta}\hat{\theta}$, $\hat{r} = \cos\theta\hat{x} + \sin\theta\hat{y}$, $\hat{\theta} = -\sin\theta\hat{x} + \cos\theta\hat{y}$.

Taking the time derivative of the orbital formula above and using the angular momentum definition $L = mr^2\dot{\theta}$, we obtain the Cartesian velocity components $v_x = \frac{\sin\theta}{\sqrt{p}}$, $v_y = \frac{e-\sin\theta}{\sqrt{p}}$. The relation

$$v_x^2 + \left(v_y - \frac{e}{\sqrt{p}}\right)^2 = \frac{1}{p}$$

shows that the velocity vector traces out a circle of radius $\frac{1}{\sqrt{p}}$ in velocity space centered at $\left(0, \frac{e}{\sqrt{p}}\right)$.

semi−latus rectum *p* □ 1   eccentricity *e* □ 0.5

Out[ ]=

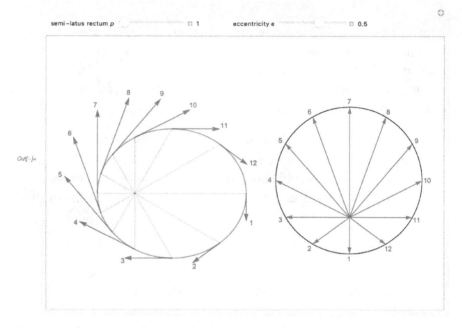

Demonstration 6.9: Hodographs for Kepler Orbits (https://demonstrations.wolfram.com/HodographsForKeplerOrbits/)

6.2.3. *Empty Focus Approximation to Kepler's Second Law*

Ptolemy's model for planetary orbits (ca. 150 AD) entails the idea of an "equant" point, a location from which a imaginary observer would see the planet, along with its epicycles, move with a uniform a angular velocity. The Ptolemaic worldview was superseded by Kepler's laws of planetary motion (ca. 1605). By Kepler's first law, planets move in elliptical orbits around the Sun at one focus. Kepler's second law implies that the planet sweeps out equal areas during equal intervals of time. This is a consequence of the conservation of angular momentum. The angular velocity about the attracting focus is thus variable, except for a perfectly circular orbit. The planet speeds up around its perihelion (nearest distance) and slows down around its aphelion (farthest distance). There is no mention of the "empty" focus of the ellipse in Kepler's laws. However, the realization that angular motion about the empty focus approximates

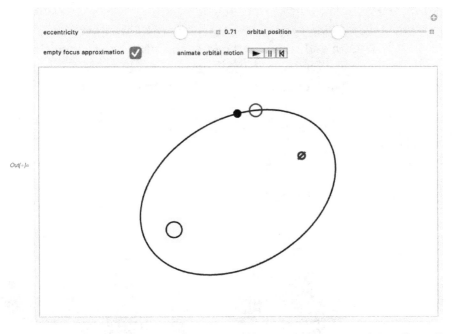

Demonstration 6.10: Empty Focus Approximation to Kepler's Second Law (https://demonstrations.wolfram.com/EmptyFocusApproximationToKeplersSecondLaw/)

the equant property was well known to astronomers in the 17th and 18th centuries.

Determination of an elliptical planetary orbit involves repeated numerical solution of a transcendental equation, carried out in the cited Demonstration on Kepler's second law. In the present Demonstration, you can compare the accurate result to the approximate empty-focus construction, in which the planet's predicted location is shown as a blue circle. The approximation becomes more accurate for smaller values of the eccentricity and, of course, exact for a circle.

6.2.4. *Kepler's Mysterium Cosmographicum*

Johannes Kepler, in his major astronomical work, *Mysterium Cosmographicum* (The Cosmographic Mystery), published in 1595, speculated that the orbits of the six planets known at the time — Mercury, Venus,

Earth, Mars, Jupiter and Saturn — could be arranged in spheres nested around the five Platonic solids: octahedron, icosahedron, dodecahedron, tetrahedron and cube. For the Platonic polyhedra arranged in this order, coinciding circumspheres for a given polyhedron and inspheres for the next polyhedron gave a fair approximation for the relative sizes

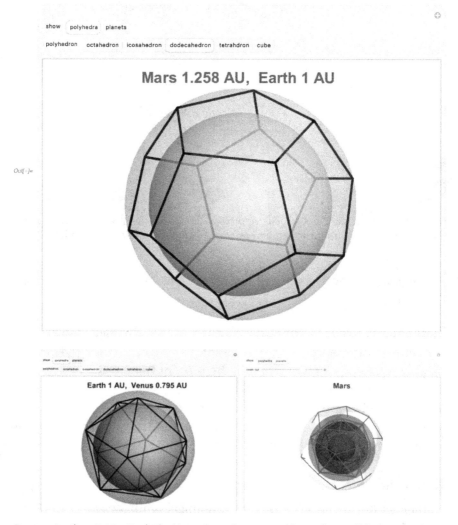

Demonstration 6.11: Kepler's *Mysterium Cosmographicum* (https://demonstrations.wolfram.com/KeplersMysteriumCosmographicum/)

of planetary orbits around the Sun. Kepler later rejected this model as insufficiently accurate, but it remains as an amusing exercise in solid geometry. The predicted orbits are expressed in astronomical units (AU) equal to the average radius of the Earth's orbit. Choose "polyhedra" to display the two planets whose orbits are contained in the circumsphere and insphere of the polyhedron. Choosing "planets" lets you zoom in and out to reveal the Keplerian structure within the orbital sphere of a given planet.

6.2.5. *Gravitational Slingshot Effect*

In astronautical mechanics, the gravitational slingshot maneuver, which NASA calls a "gravity assist", exploits the gravitational attraction of a planet to alter the speed and trajectory of an interplanetary spacecraft. A spacecraft can thereby be accelerated by a near planetary flyby to enable considerable savings of fuel in missions to the outer planets, such as Jupiter and Saturn. At first sight, this might seem like a cosmic something-for-nothing scam. But the physics depends straightforwardly on conservation of momentum and energy and the huge planet-to-spacecraft mass ratio, which leaves the planetary orbit essentially undisturbed.

This Demonstration considers a hypothetical slingshot maneuver around the planet Jupiter (orange sphere with radius $\approx 143,000$ km), which moves at an average speed V of 13.1 km/sec in its orbit around the Sun. A spacecraft, with initial speed v_0, which has a negligible mass and size compared to the planet, follows a hyperbolic path in Jupiter's frame of reference. In the Sun's frame of reference, however, the hyperbolic path is tilted and moves with velocity V, which provides a terrific boost to the spacecraft after it crosses the orbit of the planet. The graphic shown is highly schematic, with both space and time scales significantly distorted.

The encounter of the spacecraft with the planet can be simulated by an elastic collision. In the simplest case of a head-on collision, the initial state can be represented by the diagram: $\bullet \longrightarrow V \ v_0 \longleftarrow \oplus$ and the final state by: $\bullet \longrightarrow V \oplus \longrightarrow v_0 + 2V$. The planet is so massive compared to the spacecraft that its motion is essentially unperturbed. In the actual

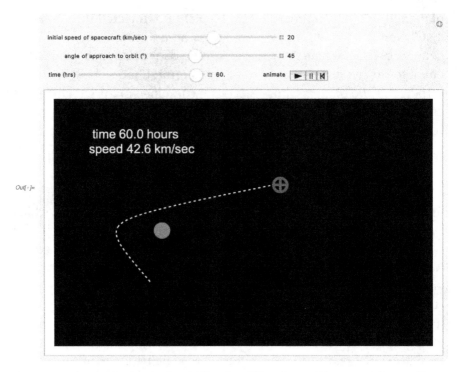

Demonstration 6.12: Gravitational Slingshot Effect (https://demonstrations.wolfram.com/GravitationalSlingshotEffect/)

situation, the final speed of the spacecraft is given by $v_{final}^2 = 4V^2 + v_0^2 + 4Vv_0 \cos \alpha$, where α is the initial angle between v_0 and V.

6.2.6. *Orbital Resonance in the Asteroid Belt*

The asteroid belt, located roughly between the orbits of the planets Mars and Jupiter, about 2.2 to 3.2 astronomical units (310 to 500 million km) from the Sun, is a large collection of several hundred thousand irregularly shaped bodies variously called *asteroids*, *planetesimals* or *minor planets*.

An orbital resonance occurs when two bodies orbiting the Sun exert a regular, periodic gravitational influence on one other, caused by their orbital periods being related by a ratio of small integers, such as 3:1, 5:2, 7:3, 2:1 and so on. In an orbital resonance of an asteroid with the giant planet Jupiter, there is a regular periodic perturbation of the smaller body caused by the gravitational attraction to Jupiter. Over the course of several billion years, the cumulative effect of this perturbation ejects the asteroid into a non-resonant orbit. This gives rise to depleted regions in the asteroid belt, known as *Kirkwood gaps*. In this Demonstration, the formation of the principal Kirkwood gaps is simulated as the time slider is moved over a multi-billion year (Gyr) range.

Also shown on the graphic are the *Trojan asteroids*, which share the orbit of Jupiter, equivalent to a 1:1 resonance. These are clustered around the Lagrange points L4 and L5, at 60° angles ahead of and behind Jupiter in its orbit. The *Hilda asteroids* form an approximate equilateral triangle in a 3:2 resonance with Jupiter, clustered around the Lagrange points L3, L4 and L5.

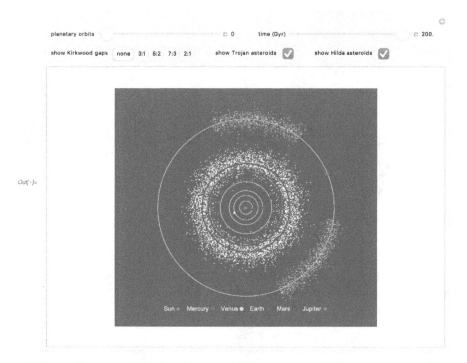

Demonstration 6.13: Orbital Resonance in the Asteroid Belt (https://demonstrations.wolfram.com/OrbitalResonanceInTheAsteroidBelt/)

6.2.7. *Newtonian Reflecting Telescope*

This simple type of reflecting telescope was invented by Sir Isaac Newton. The primary paraboloidal mirror at the closed end of the telescope tube focuses incoming light toward a flat diagonal secondary mirror. The focal length is determined by the curvature of the paraboloid. The secondary mirror directs the focused beam toward the eyepiece. The thin "spider" supporting the secondary mirror is not shown. The telescope happens to be directed toward the planet Saturn and the observed image is shown as an inset.

Demonstration 6.14: Newtonian Reflecting Telescope (https://demonstrations.wolfram.com/NewtonianReflectingTelescope/)

6.2.8. *Blue Sky and Red Sunset*

If the Sun were viewed from beyond the Earth's atmosphere, it would appear to be an intense glowing white sphere. But the Sun's light, as it passes through the atmosphere to an observer on the Earth's surface, undergoes scattering by the molecules in the air.

Nitrogen and oxygen molecules have diameters of the order of $2\,\text{Å}$ or $0.2\,\text{nm}$. Rayleigh scattering of light in the visible spectrum ($\lambda \approx 400$–$700\,\text{nm}$) by objects much smaller than its wavelength is proportional to $1/\lambda^4$. This means that the blue end of the spectrum ($\lambda \approx 400\,\text{nm}$) is scattered by about an order of magnitude more intensely than the red end ($\lambda \approx 700\,\text{nm}$). The observed pale blue color of the sky is determined by sunlight multiply scattered by the atmosphere. More precisely, the blue sky comes from microscopic density fluctuations caused by the random motions of air molecules, which results in fluctuations of the refractive index. Another consequence of Rayleigh scattering is that light coming directly from the Sun is depleted in the blue end of the spectrum, thus giving it the appearance of a yellow sphere.

Clouds consist mainly of tiny water droplets, which are of comparable dimension to the wavelengths of white light. Rayleigh scattering under such conditions approximates Mie scattering, in which all wavelengths are scattered with nearly equal intensity. This accounts for the white or grayish appearance of clouds.

As the Sun nears the horizon, its light must travel a greater distance through the atmosphere. In addition, the more oblique angles of incidence cause the light to be refracted by the atmosphere. This is shown in the inset at the lower-right corner of the graphic. The setting Sun thus enhances the yellow, orange, and red components of the spectrum as it appears to an observer. The great variety of beautiful sunsets is well known to everyone. The detailed appearance of the sunset is dependent on a large number of possible environmental conditions. This Demonstration shows only a highly idealized and simplified representation of the sunset, as it might occur in late summer.

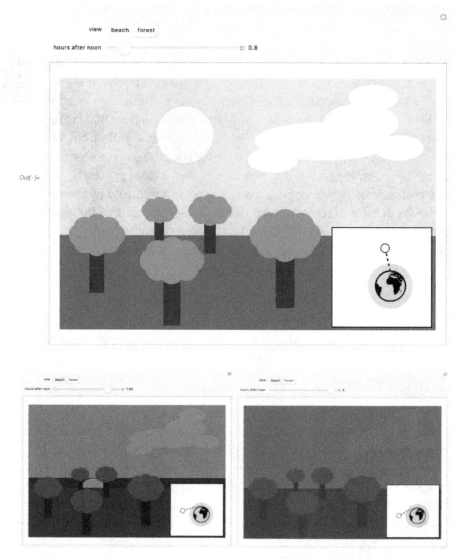

Demonstration 6.15: Blue Sky and Red Sunset (https://demonstrations.wolfram.com/BlueSkyAndRedSunset/)

6.2.9. *White Dwarfs and the Chandrasekhar Limit*

A white dwarf is the remnant of a main-sequence star of mass M (less than about four times the mass $M_\odot$ of the Sun) that has exhausted its hydrogen fuel by fusion into helium. Such a star will first expand to form a red giant as it fuses helium in its core to carbon and oxygen by triple-alpha processes. After the star sheds its outer layers, ejecting a planetary nebula, the remnant will be composed mainly of carbon and oxygen, incapable of further fusion reactions. The surface temperature initially lies in the range 8000 to 40,000 K, which implies a white color, hence the designation *white dwarf*. The gravitational field of the white dwarf causes a collapse to a body about the size of the Earth. Thereby a mass comparable to the Sun's, $M_\odot \approx 2 \times 10^{30}$ kg, is compressed to a radius comparable to that of the Earth, $R_\oplus \approx 6000$ km. Further collapse is resisted by the electrons of the carbon and oxygen atoms, which form a *degenerate electron gas* following a Fermi–Dirac distribution. The outward pressure of the electrons, countering the gravitational compression, is thus a purely quantum-mechanical effect, which can be attributed to the exclusion principle. Among the first identified white dwarfs, in 1915, is Sirius B, the companion to Sirius.

S. Chandrasekhar proposed in 1931 that in a stellar remnant with mass greater than approximately $1.44M_\odot$, known as the *Chandrasekhar limit*, gravitation overcomes the electron degeneracy pressure and the white dwarf collapses into a fraction of its volume to form a *neutron star*. This is associated with the electrons near the Fermi level becoming ultra-relativistic, with energies approaching the electron rest energy mc^2. A neutron star is also a degenerate fermionic quantum system of neutrons, into which the carbon and oxygen nuclei collapse. In a neutron star, a stellar mass is compressed to a radius of the order of 10 km. Some neutron stars can emit beams of electromagnetic radiation, which makes them detectable as pulsars.

It is sometimes said that white dwarfs have densities of the order of tonnes per teaspoon, while neutron stars have densities of billions of tonnes per teaspoon (1 tonne, or metric ton, equals 1000 kg).

If the remnant star has a mass exceeding the Tolman–Oppenheimer–Volkoff limit of around $2M_\odot$, the combination of degeneracy pressure and nuclear forces becomes insufficient to support the neutron star and it continues collapsing to form a black hole.

The inward gravitational pressure must be balanced by the outward pressure of a relativistic Fermi gas of electrons. This results in a differential equation that can only be solved numerically. We have obtained a reasonably accurate analytic approximation to this result in the form

$$\frac{R}{R_\oplus} \approx 1.35 \left(\frac{M}{M_\odot}\right)^{1/3} \left(1 - .615 \left(\frac{M}{M_\odot}\right)^{4/3}\right)^{1/2},$$

where $R_\oplus = 6.371 \times 10^6$ m is the radius of the Earth and $M_\odot = 1.989 \times 10^{30}$ kg is the mass of the Sun. The radius R reduces to zero at the Chandrasekhar mass $M_C = 1.44\,M_\odot$, which is given in our model by $M_C = 0.777 m_p^{-2} \left(\frac{\hbar c}{G}\right)^{3/2}$, where m_p is the proton mass and G is the gravitational constant. Remarkably, $\sqrt{\frac{\hbar c}{G}}$ represents the Planck mass, showing that quantum mechanics, relativity and gravitation are all involved in the theory of white dwarfs.

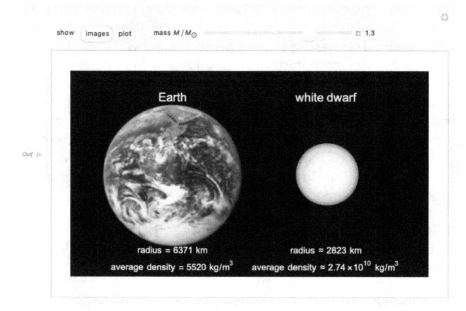

Demonstration 6.16: White Dwarfs and the Chandrasekhar Limit (https://demonstrations.wolfram.com/WhiteDwarfsAndTheChandrasekharLimit/)

6.2.10. *Temperature and Entropy of a Black Hole*

According to the "no-hair theorem" of general relativity, the properties of an electrovac black hole (i.e., a black hole whose exterior is a vacuum and whose interior contains electromagnetic but no other charges) are completely determined by just three parameters: mass M, angular momentum J, and electric (or magnetic monopole) charge Q. While this suggests a possible violation of the second law of thermodynamics, since the entropy of the universe could be reduced by creating single-microstate black holes, the black hole region is classically experimentally inaccessible. Thus, it is possible that a quantum mechanical black hole can possess additional microstates. Moreover, in a series of papers starting in 1973, Jacob Bekenstein showed that the area of a black hole seemed to be a measure of the entropy of a black hole, in precisely the correct magnitude to preserve the second law. In 1974, Stephen Hawking proposed, based on quantum field theory (QFT), that the immense energy density of a black hole's gravitational field could give rise to continual creation and annihilation of virtual particles and antiparticles, with lifetimes consistent with the uncertainty principle, $\Delta E \Delta t \lesssim \hbar$. Should one of the virtual pair be swallowed up by the black hole, its partner would become a real particle which, to an outside observer, would appear to have been radiated by the black hole. Moreover, the effective temperature of the black hole corresponded nicely with Bekenstein's classical derivation, giving a physical justification for the earlier ad-hoc identification.

Thus, Hawking and Bekenstein worked out the principles of black hole thermodynamics. We limit our considerations to the case $Q = 0$, a rotating Kerr black hole. The horizon has a radius $r_h = \frac{GM}{c^2} + \sqrt{\left(\frac{GM}{c^2}\right)^2 - \left(\frac{J}{Mc}\right)^2}$ (for $J = 0$, this reduces to the Schwarzschild radius $r_s = 2GM/c^2$). The spherical horizon is surrounded by an oblate spheroidal ergosphere, which corotates in the same direction, a consequence of frame dragging. The ergosphere, shown in gray, is just a region of spacetime containing no matter. According to the Bekenstein–Hawking theory, the temperature of a black hole is given by $T_{\text{BH}} = \frac{\hbar c^3}{4\pi k_B GM}\left(1 - \frac{r_s}{2r_h}\right)$ and the emitted radiation follows a blackbody distribution. The temperature is inversely proportional to the mass: $T_{BH} \approx \frac{5.64}{M/M_p} \times 10^{30}$ K, where $M_p = (\hbar c/G)^{1/2} \approx$ 2.18×10^{-5} g, the Planck mass. For the Earth's mass, $T_{BH} \approx 0.02$ K, while for a solar mass, $T_{BH} \approx 100$ nK, both less than the temperature of the cosmic microwave background radiation (2.725 K). Evidently, smaller black holes are hotter and, when radiating into empty space, should eventually evaporate.

In the graphic, variations in temperature at the event horizon are simulated by colors of the visible spectrum, but with the scales of space, time, and temperature being grossly exaggerated for display purposes. Black holes of the order of the Planck mass are considered. The Bekenstein–Hawking entropy of a black hole is given by $S_{BH} = \frac{1}{4}A$, where A is the area of the event horizon, equal to $A = 4\pi[r_h^2 + (J/Mc)^2]$, expressed in units of the Planck area, L_p^2 where $L_p = (\hbar G/c^3)^{1/2} \approx 1.62 \times 10^{-33}$ cm, the Planck length. Thus each element of area $\frac{1}{4}L_p^2$ on the horizon represents one Planck unit of entropy. Since a Planck mass contains over 10^{19} proton masses, it can be surmised that 1 Planck unit corresponds to something of the order of 10^{40} bits of information on the atomic level.

While Hawking radiation provides a physical basis for black hole entropy, it also raises new questions. According to the no-hair theorem, the radiation must be perfectly blackbody and therefore devoid of any information. All research into the QFT of black holes supports this conclusion. When the black hole evaporates completely, all of the information from the particles it absorbed disappears, leading to the so-called black hole information paradox. In a more radical direction, since the state of a three-dimensional system can, in concept, be represented on its two-dimensional boundary, Gerard 't Hooft and Leonard Susskind (2001) proposed a general "holographic principle" of nature, which suggests that consistent theories of gravity and quantum mechanics can be represented by lower-dimensional structures. Both the information paradox and the holographic principle remain active areas of investigation.

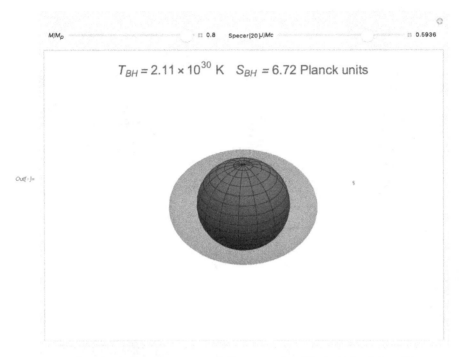

M/M_p 0.8   Specer[20]J/Mc   0.5936

$$T_{BH} = 2.11 \times 10^{30}\ \text{K} \quad S_{BH} = 6.72\ \text{Planck units}$$

Out[ ]=

Demonstration 6.17: Temperature and Entropy of a Black Hole (https://demonstrations.wolfram.com/TemperatureAndEntropyOfABlackHole/)

6.3. Mechanics

6.3.1. *Principle of the Lever*

The lever is balanced when the torque on the two lever arms is equal:

$$x_1 m_1 = x_2 m_2.$$

When it is unbalanced, it tips to the side with the larger torque.

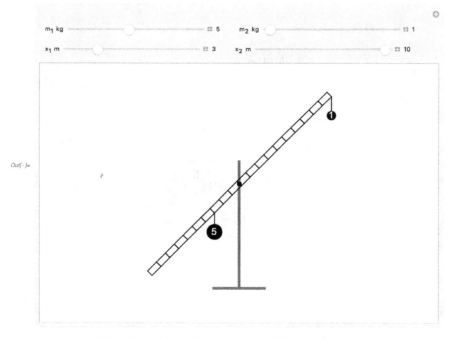

Demonstration 6.18: Principle of the Lever (https://demonstrations.wolfram.com/PrincipleOfTheLever/)

6.3.2. *Rotation of a Rigid Body*

The torque-free rotation of a rigid body can be described by Euler's three equations of motion: $I_1\dot{\omega}_1 - (I_2 - I_3)\omega_2\omega_3 = 0$, and cyclic permutations, where I_1, I_2, I_3 are the principal moments of inertia and ω_1, ω_2, ω_3 are the angular velocities around their respective principal axes in the fixed-body coordinate system. There are two constants of the motion, the angular momentum $L^2 = I_1^2\omega_1^2 + I_2^2\omega_2^2 + I_3^2\omega_3^2$ and the kinetic energy $T = \frac{1}{2}(I_1\omega_1^2 + I_2\omega_2^2 + I_3\omega_3^2)$. Euler's equations can be solved in closed form, giving $\omega_1(t)$, $\omega_2(t)$, $\omega_3(t)$ in terms of Jacobi elliptic integrals.

With no loss of generality, we will limit our considerations to a symmetric rotor with $I_2 = I_1$. The rigid body will be assumed to be a cuboid of dimensions $a \times b \times c$ (with $b = a$) but the same solutions apply to any rigid body with the same ellipsoid of inertia. The angular momentum is a constant vector **L**, oriented vertically. The instantaneous angular velocity ω, along with its component ω_3, is then found to precess around **L** with an angular velocity Ωt. This can be pictured as a red cone rolling around a stationary blue cone, shown in the "Poinsot cones" graphic.

Poinsot also proposed in 1834 a geometric construction that provides an elegant visual representation of rigid body motion. The Poinsot ellipsoid, with principal axes $I_1^{-1/2}$, $I_2^{-1/2}$, $I_3^{-1/2}$, rolls on the invariable angular momentum plane that is perpendicular to the constant angular momentum vector. The path of the angular velocity vector ω within the ellipsoid is called the polhode. Its path on the invariable plane is called the herpolhode. For symmetric rotors, both are circles. In the more general case, they have more complicated shapes. Goldstein summarizes the Poinsot construction in the Jabberwockian-sounding statement: "The polhode rolls without slipping on the herpolhode lying in the invariable plane."

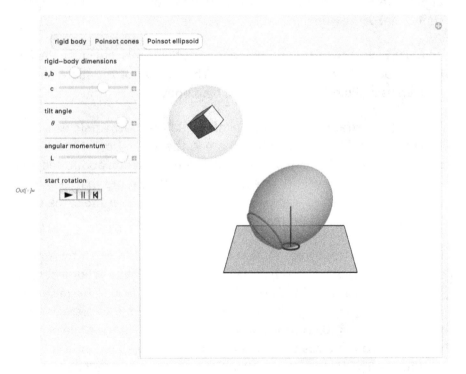

Demonstration 6.19: Free Rotation of a Rigid Body-Poinsot Constructions (https://demonstrations.wolfram.com/FreeRotationOfARigidBodyPoinsotConstructions/)

6.3.3. *Feynman's Wobbling Plate*

In his eccentric collection of autobiographical stories, Richard Feynman recounts: "I was in the cafeteria and some guy, fooling around, throws a plate in the air. As the plate went up in the air I saw it wobble, and I noticed the red medallion of Cornell on the plate going around. It was pretty obvious to me that the medallion went around faster than the wobbling. I had nothing to do, so I start figuring out the motion of the rotating plate. I discovered that when the angle is very slight, the medallion rotates twice as fast as the wobble rate — two to one. It came out of a complicated equation! I went on to work out equations for wobbles. Then I thought about how the electron orbits start to move in relativity. Then there's the Dirac equation in electrodynamics. And then quantum electrodynamics. And before I knew it... the whole business that I got the Nobel prize for came from that piddling around with the wobbling plate." A replica of the Cornell plate is now part of an exhibit marking the centennial of the Nobel Prize.

Actually, Feynman misremembered (or was being mischievous): the factor of 2 actually goes the other way. The motion of the plate can be derived using Euler's equations for a rigid body.

In this Demonstration, the trajectory of the plate is shown in slow motion. The initial conditions to be chosen are θ, the inclination of the plate's symmetry axis to the vertical and $\dot{\psi}$, the rate of rotation about this axis. It is found that the wobble rate is actually slightly more than twice the rotation rate. The ratio approaches 2 as $\theta \to 0$, but, at the same time, the wobble amplitude decreases.

Euler's equations for free rotation of a rigid body are given by $I_1\dot{\omega}_1 = (I_2 - I_3)\omega_2\omega_3$; $I_2\dot{\omega}_2 = (I_3 - I_1)\omega_3\omega_1$; $I_3\dot{\omega}_3 = (I_1 - I_2)\omega_1\omega_2$. For a circular disk of radius R, mass M and negligible thickness, the principal moments of inertia are $I_1 = I_2 = \frac{1}{4}MR^2$, $I_3 = \frac{1}{2}MR^2 = 2I_1$. The third Euler equation reduces to $\dot{\omega}_3 = 0$. Thus $\omega_3 = $ const. This is the angular velocity of the plate about its axis of symmetry, and is taken as one of the initial conditions. The first two Euler equations are then satisfied by $\omega_1(t) = \sqrt{\omega^2 - \omega_3^2}\sin\Omega t$, $\omega_2(t) = \sqrt{\omega^2 - \omega_3^2}\cos\Omega t$, where $\Omega = \frac{I_1 - I_3}{I_1}\omega_3 = -\omega_3$.

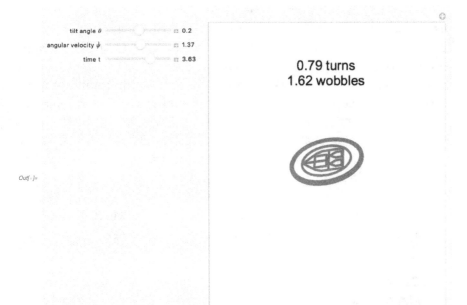

tilt angle θ ⬚ 0.2
angular velocity $\dot{\psi}$ ⬚ 1.37
time t ⬚ 3.63

0.79 turns
1.62 wobbles

Outf=

Demonstration 6.20: Feynman's Wobbling Plate (https://demonstrations.wolfram.com/FeynmansWobblingPlate/)

The motion of the rigid body in the space-fixed frame can be expressed in terms of the Euler angles θ, ϕ, ψ, using the relations $\omega_1 = \dot{\theta}\cos\psi + \dot{\phi}\sin\theta\sin\psi$, $\omega_2 = -\dot{\theta}\sin\psi + \dot{\phi}\sin\theta\cos\psi$, $\omega_3 = \dot{\psi} + \dot{\phi}\cos\theta$. If the axis of the plate is initially inclined by an angle θ from the vertical, with an angular velocity ω_3, then the motion of the plate is given by $\phi(t) = \frac{I_3\omega_3}{I_1\cos\theta}t = \frac{2\omega_3}{\cos\theta}t$, $\psi(t) = \Omega t = -\omega_3 t$, $\theta(t) = \theta = $ const. The rotation of the plate is represented by $\psi(t)$, while its precession or "wobbling" is given by $\phi(t)$. As θ approaches 0, the wobbling frequency approaches twice the rotation frequency, but the wobbling amplitude also decreases.

6.3.4. *Newton's Rotating Bucket Experiment*

In the Scholium to Book 1 of *Principia*, Isaac Newton describes an experiment in which a bucket of water hung by a long cord is twisted and released. Initially, only the bucket rotates while the water remains stationary, as indicated by its flat surface. Gradually, the rotational motion is communicated to the water and centrifugal force distorts its surface into a paraboloid. After the bucket stops turning, the water continues to rotate until frictional forces again bring it to rest, flattening the paraboloid. (Viscosity, which causes this friction, is described by another law proposed by Newton!) Newton cited the rotating bucket experiment to support his notion of absolute space as the reference frame for all motion. His contemporary Leibniz challenged Newton's worldview, arguing that space is actually created by the existence of material bodies. This debate continued into the 20th century, principally associated with the writings of Mach and Einstein, and providing a philosophical underpinning for the general theory of relativity. See the discussion in "The Universe and the Bucket", Chapter 2 in B. Greene, *The Fabric of the Cosmos: Space, Time, and the Texture of Reality*, New York: Knopf, 2004.

This Demonstration is intended to be only qualitatively descriptive. The pictorial representation neglects details such as the torsional behavior

Demonstration 6.21: Newton's Rotating Bucket Experiment (https://demonstrations. wolfram.com/NewtonsRotatingBucketExperiment/)

of the rope and simplifies the time dependence of angular momentum transfer between the bucket and the water.

6.3.5. *Coupled Pendulums*

Consider a system of two identical pendulums swinging in parallel planes and connected at the top by a flexible string. (A recently published Demonstration considered the related version of two pendulums with their bobs connected by a massless spring.) We describe here a more classic form of the problem, going back to the time of Huygens.

Each pendulum consists of a mass m suspended from a fixed support by a massless string of length L, with its coordinate described by the angle θ from the vertical. Under the action of gravity, the equation of motion is given by $mL^2\ddot{\theta} + mgL\sin\theta = 0$. Restricting ourselves to small-amplitude oscillations, we can approximate $\sin\theta \approx \theta$, leading to the elementary solution $\theta(t) = \theta(0)\cos(\omega t)$, where $\omega = \sqrt{g/L}$, the natural frequency of the pendulum, independent of m. For the coupled pendulum system, to the same level of approximation, the Lagrangian can be written $L(\theta_1, \dot{\theta}_1, \theta_2, \dot{\theta}_2) = \frac{1}{2}m(\dot{\theta}_1^2 + \dot{\theta}_2^2) - \frac{1}{2}m\omega^2(\theta_1^2 + \theta_2^2) - mn^2\theta_1\theta_2$, where η is a measure of the coupling between the two pendulums mediated by the connecting string. The equations of motion are readily solved to give $\theta_{1,2}(t) = \frac{1}{2}[\theta_1(0) + \theta_2(0)]\cos(\sqrt{\omega^2 + \eta^2}\,t) \pm \frac{1}{2}[\theta_1(0) - \theta_2(0)]\cos(\sqrt{\omega^2 - \eta^2}\,t)$. The system has two normal modes of vibration. In the in-phase mode, starting with $\theta_1(0) = \theta_2(0)$, the two pendulums swing in unison at a frequency of $\sqrt{\omega^2 + \eta^2}$. In the out-of-phase mode, starting with $\theta_1(0) = -\theta_2(0)$, they swing in opposite directions at a frequency of $\sqrt{\omega^2 - \eta^2}$.

A more dramatic phenomenon is resonance. If one pendulum is started at $\theta(0) \neq 0$ and another at $\theta(0) = 0$, then energy will periodically flow back and forth between the two pendulums.

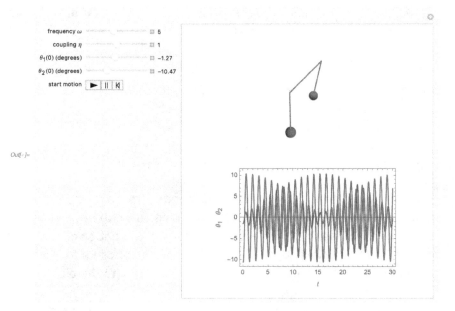

Demonstration 6.22: Dynamics of Coupled Pendulums (https://demonstrations. wolfram.com/DynamicsOfCoupledPendulums/)

6.3.6. *The Wilberforce Pendulum*

In 1896, L. R. Wilberforce, demonstrator in physics at the Cavendish Laboratory, Cambridge, constructed a pendulum that functions simultaneously as a linear oscillator coupled to a torsion pendulum. If the frequencies of the translational and rotational modes of oscillation are nearly equal, energy can be transferred from one mode to the other, while each motion exhibits frequency beats depending on the coupling between the two modes.

The graphic shows the oscillations of the pendulum for selected values of the frequency ω and coupling strength λ. On the right are plots of $z(t)$ (in black) and $\theta(t)$ (in red), the amplitudes of the linear and torsional oscillations, respectively. As shown in the plot, the out-of-phase linear and torsional motions exhibit beat oscillations as energy is exchanged back and forth between the two modes.

The dynamics of an idealized Wilberforce oscillator can be represented by the Lagrangian:

$$L = \frac{1}{2}m\left(\frac{dz}{dt}\right)^2 + \frac{1}{2}I\left(\frac{d\theta}{dt}\right)^2 - \frac{1}{2}Kz^2 - \frac{1}{2}\kappa\theta^2 - \frac{1}{2}\xi z\theta,$$

where m is the mass of the load on the (assumed massless) spring, I is the moment of inertia of the rotating pendulum bob, k is the linear force constant, κ is the torsional force constant and ξ is the linear-torsional coupling strength. We obtain, thereby, two coupled equations of motion:

$$\ddot{z} + \omega_z^2 z + \lambda\theta = 0, \quad \ddot{\theta} + \omega_\theta^2\theta + \lambda z = 0,$$

where $\omega_z = \sqrt{\frac{k}{m}}$, $\omega_\theta = \sqrt{\frac{\kappa}{I}}$ are the linear and torsional oscillation frequencies, respectively, and λ is the scaled coupling constant. Eliminating θ between the coupled equations, we obtain a fourth-order linear differential equation for $z(t)$:

$$\frac{d^4z}{dt^4} + (\omega_z^2 + \omega_\theta^2)\frac{d^2z}{dt^2} + (\omega_z^2\omega_\theta^2 - \lambda^2)z = 0,$$

with an identical equation for $\theta(t)$. These differential equations can be solved exactly to give a linear combination of four complex exponential terms $e^{\pm i\Omega_\pm t}$, where

$$\Omega_\pm^2 = \frac{1}{2}(\omega_z^2 + \omega_\theta^2 \pm \sqrt{(\omega_z^2 - \omega_\theta^2)^2 + 4\lambda^2}).$$

We are interested in solutions for which $\omega_z = \omega_\theta = \omega$, so that $\Omega_\pm = \sqrt{\omega^2\omega \pm \lambda} \approx \omega \pm \frac{\lambda}{2\omega}$, assuming $\omega \gg \lambda$. With an appropriate choice of boundary conditions, we construct the solutions $z(t) = z_0(\cos(\Omega_+ t) + \cos(\Omega_- t))$, $\theta(t) = \theta_0(\sin(\Omega_+ t) - \sin(\Omega_- t))$.

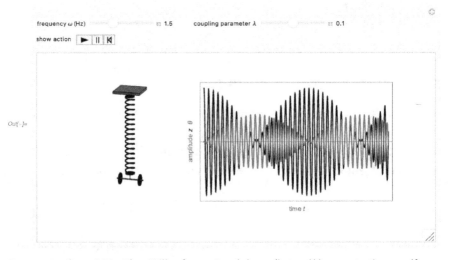

Out[ ]=

Demonstration 6.23: The Wilberforce Pendulum (https://demonstrations.wolfram. com/TheWilberforcePendulum/)

6.3.7. *Newton's Cradle*

"Newton's cradle" (never actually mentioned by Newton himself) is an iconic executive desk toy consisting of five identical polished steel balls aligned with one another, each suspended from a frame by a pair of thin wires. When a ball at one end of the line is pulled back and released, it collides with the middle three balls, which remain stationary, while the ball at the other end of the line swings out to mirror the motion of the first ball. Then the motion reverses itself and repeats through a significant number of cycles. The canonical explanation of this phenomenon, commonly shown in many high school and college physics classes, is simply the conservation of momentum mv and kinetic energy $\frac{1}{2}mv^2$ in elastic collisions, these quantities being exchanged between the first and fifth balls through infinitesimal elastic deformations, similar to sound waves. Sometimes Newton's third law of action and reaction is evoked in the explanation.

So we have a neat experiment with a simple theoretical explanation, which satisfies the majority of physicists. However, several recent references note that, upon closer observation, the middle three balls do, in fact, oscillate very slightly. This can be attributed to the imperfect elasticity of the impacts, together with viscoelastic dissipation and possibly air resistance.

No consensus has yet been achieved for a rigorous solution of this problem. In fact, several videos of Newton's cradle displayed on the internet (YouTube) show small variations in the behavior of the swinging balls, depending evidently on small differences in construction and materials. In all cases, the preponderant tendency appears to be small-amplitude oscillations of the middle three balls, more or less in sync with the motion of the first and fifth balls.

In this Demonstration, we propose an empirical model containing a parameter ξ, to estimate the fraction of kinetic energy transformed into elastic deformation in each collision along with the concomitant dissipation of energy. The canonical behavior is obtained in the limiting case, $\xi \to 0$. The balls are assumed to be of unit diameter with their centers at equilibrium at $x_n = n, n = 0, 1, 2, 3, 4$.

The left-hand ball behaves initially as a simple pendulum, well approximated by the linearized equation $\ddot{x}(t) + \omega^2 x(t) = 0$, with $\omega = \sqrt{g/L}$ and initial condition $\dot{x}(0) = v$, the speed at which the first ball hits the line of four others. The kinetic energy is partially converted into compression energy, which propagates the impulse along the chain. The function $x_0(t)$ approximates a modulated square wave, in which only negative values of x_0 appear. The fifth ball closely follows a complementary positive square-wave sinusoidal motion bounded by $x_4(0) = 4$. The approximate functional forms for the $x_n(t)$ are plotted as functions of time.

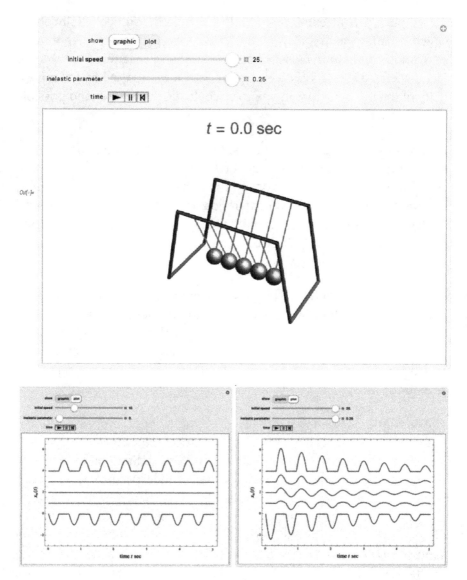

Demonstration 6.24: Phenomenological Approximation to Newton's Cradle (https://demonstrations.wolfram.com/PhenomenologicalApproximationToNewtonsCradle/)

6.3.8. *The Runge-Lenz Vector*

The Runge–Lenz (RL) vector, also commonly known as the Laplace–Runge–Lenz vector, is a "hidden" constant of the motion for both the classical Kepler and quantum Coulomb problems. In classical mechanics, it implies that the energy of planetary motion depends only on the semimajor axis of an elliptical orbit and is independent of the angular momentum. In quantum mechanics, it accounts for the $2s - 2p$, $3s - 3p -$ $3d$, and so on orbital degeneracy in the non-relativistic hydrogen atom. As noted by Goldstein, this vector was actually discovered independently over the years by several other scientists, including possibly Newton himself.

The RL vector can be derived starting with Newton's second law applied to gravitational attraction, written in the form $\frac{d\mathbf{p}}{dt} = -\frac{GMm}{r^2}\hat{\mathbf{r}}$. Now take the cross product of both sides with the orbital angular momentum $\mathbf{L} = \mathbf{r} \times \mathbf{p}$, noting that $\mathbf{L}$ is a constant of the motion. This gives $\frac{d}{dt}\mathbf{p} \times \mathbf{L} = -\frac{GMm}{r^2}\hat{\mathbf{r}} \times \left(\mathbf{r} \times \frac{d\mathbf{r}}{dt}\right)$. Using the vector identities $\hat{\mathbf{r}} \times \left(\mathbf{r} \times \frac{d\mathbf{r}}{dt}\right) = \hat{\mathbf{r}}r\frac{d\mathbf{r}}{dt} - r\frac{d\mathbf{r}}{dt}$ and $\frac{d\mathbf{r}}{dt} = \hat{\mathbf{r}}\frac{dr}{dt} + r\frac{d\hat{\mathbf{r}}}{dt}$, we find $\frac{d}{dt}\mathbf{p} \times \mathbf{L} = GMm\frac{d\hat{\mathbf{r}}}{dt}$ or $\frac{d}{dt}(\mathbf{p} \times \mathbf{L} - GMm\hat{\mathbf{r}}) = 0$, showing that $\mathbf{A} = \mathbf{p} \times \mathbf{L} - GMm\hat{\mathbf{r}}$, defined as the Runge-Lenz vector, is a constant of the motion. Note that $\mathbf{A} \cdot \mathbf{L} = 0$ so that the RL vector is normal to the orbital angular momentum and therefore in the plane of the planetary orbit.

The equation of the orbit is found easily by evaluating the scalar product $\mathbf{A} \cdot \mathbf{r} = Ar\cos\theta = L^2 - GMmr$, which gives the equation of a conic section in plane polar coordinates: $r = \frac{L^2/GMm}{1+e\cos\theta}$, where e is the eccentricity, related to the RL vector magnitude by $e = A/GMm$. The origin of the coordinate system is taken as the location of the heavy particle (M). The perihelion of the orbit (the distance of closest approach) is given by $r_p = \frac{L^2/GMm}{1+e} = \frac{L^2}{GMm+A}$, corresponding to $\theta = 0$. The energy of an orbiting planet is given by $E = \frac{G^2 M^2 m^3}{2L^2}(e^2 - 1)$. The orbit is an ellipse when $E < 0$ with $e < 1$ ($e = 0$ for a circular orbit), a parabola when $E = 0$ and $e = 1$, and a hyperbola when $E > 0$ and $e > 1$.

In this Demonstration, orbits for input values of L and A are shown. For simplicity, we set $GMm = 1$, thus $A = e$. If you trigger the orbital motion, you will see the periodic orbit of an ellipse or circle. For a parabola or hyperbola, there is just a single pass of the planetary body, but this is shown repeatedly.

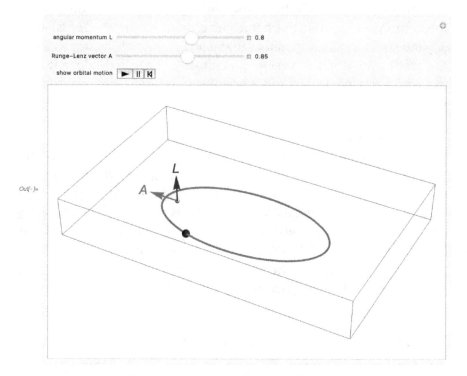

Demonstration 6.25: The Runge–Lenz Vector (https://demonstrations.wolfram.com/ TheRungeLenzVector/)

6.4. Fluid Mechanics

6.4.1. *The Venturi Effect*

A fluid flowing through a constricted section of a tube undergoes a decrease in pressure, which is known as the Venturi effect. This is fundamentally a consequence of Bernoulli's principle, which relates the pressure p_i of a fluid to its velocity $V_i, i = 1, 2$:

$$p_1 + \frac{\rho}{2}V_1^2 = p_2 + \frac{\rho}{2}V_2^2,$$

where ρ is the density, assumed constant for an incompressible fluid. The equation of continuity determines the velocity of a fluid of given density through a section of tube with radius r. You can vary the radius of the constriction between 1 and 5 cm. Quantitative details depend on additional factors, such as the viscosity of the fluid and the roughness of the tube walls. The results given in this Demonstration can be considered as representative. The drop of fluid pressure $p_1 - p_2$ is indicated by the difference in fluid levels in the two vertical capillary tubes. The Venturi tube flowmeter operates on this principle.

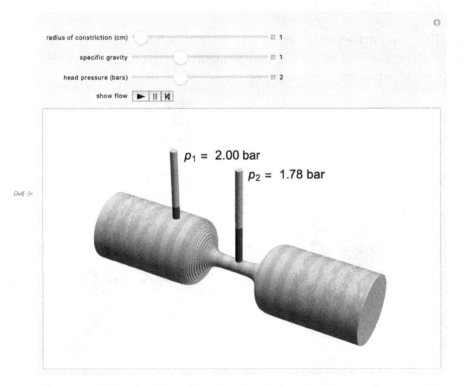

Demonstration 6.26: The Venturi Effect (https://demonstrations.wolfram.com/The VenturiEffect/)

6.4.2. *Von Kármán Vortex Street in Turbulent Flow*

A von Kármán vortex street (named after the fluid dynamicist Theodore von Kármán) is a phenomenon in fluid dynamics occurring with turbulent flow at a high Reynolds number. It consists typically of a pattern of swirling vortices in alternating directions that are caused, for example, by the unsteady separation of a fluid flowing over a rapidly moving cylinder. An empirical relation proposed by Strouhal gives $\frac{fd}{V} \approx 0.198 \times (1 - \frac{19.7}{R_e})$, where f is the vortex shedding frequency, d is the diameter of the cylinder, and V is the flow velocity. For a fluid with kinematic viscosity v, the Reynolds number $R_e = Vd/v$ is generally in the range 100 to 10^7 to exhibit this behavior. The vortex shedding frequency describes the rate at which vortices are formed in the wake of the moving cylinder. This phenomenon can sometimes cause vibrations near the frequency f in wires or antennas subjected to high winds.

This Demonstration is intended to be qualitative and highly schematic. For more realistic photographs and illustrations, see http://en.wikipedia.org/wiki/Karman_vortex_street.

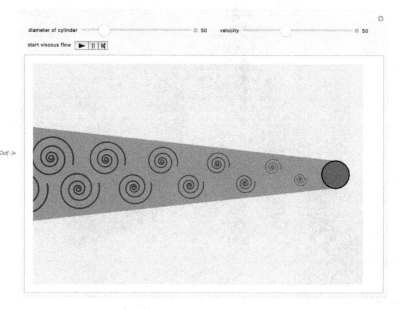

Demonstration 6.27: Von Kármán Vortex Street in Turbulent Flow (https://demonstrations.wolfram.com/VonKarmanVortexStreetInTurbulentFlow/)

6.5. Semiconductors

6.5.1. *Doped Silicon Semiconductors*

In a pure silicon crystal, each Si atom has four valence electrons that can form Lewis octets with four other atoms. A schematic two-dimensional representation of the crystal is shown. When an occasional electron is shaken loose by thermal excitation or a crystalline defect, silicon becomes a weak conductor of electricity (not shown). Much more important to the semiconductor industry are *extrinsic semiconductors*, in which the Si crystal is doped with impurity atoms, usually at concentrations of several parts per million. For example, Si can be doped with P (or As or Sb) atoms, which have five valence electrons. The fifth electron is not needed for bonding and becomes available as a current carrier. This is known as an n-type semiconductor. The mobile electrons are shown in red. If the Si is instead doped with B (or Ga or Al), which have only

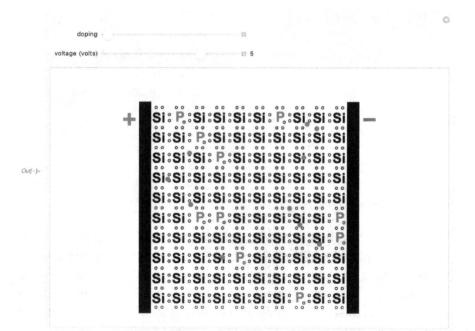

Demonstration 6.28: Doped Silicon Semiconductors (https://demonstrations.wolf ram.com/DopedSiliconSemiconductors/)

three valence electrons, this leaves an electron vacancy or positive hole, shown as a black circle. Positive holes can likewise act as current carriers to produce p-type semiconductors. The mobile holes are shown in blue. The "doping" slider enables you to continuously (in concept) transform the crystal from a p-type to an n-type semiconductor.

6.5.2. *Bipolar Junction Transistors*

This Demonstration shows the operation of an npn bipolar junction transistor as a switch or signal amplifier. Most of the latest transistors, such as MOSFETs, are of the field-effect type, but junction transistors provide a simpler introduction to the basic concepts.

The first graphic shows an npn transistor as a component of an integrated circuit. Three terminals, the collector (C), base (B), and emitter (E), connect to external circuits. The emitter and collector are in contact with layers of n-type silicon — this is Si doped with P (or As or Sb) atoms, so that excess non-bonded electrons can act as negative (n) current carriers. The gate is in contact with a very thin layer ($\sim$.01 mm) of p-type silicon — Si doped with an electron-deficient impurity, such as B, Ga, or Al, so that any current is carried largely by electron vacancies, which act as positive (p) holes. In the absence of any external input, the E-B interface acts as an n-p diode, and when maintained with a small reverse bias (so that there is a depletion zone around the junction) the transistor behaves as an insulator. The free electrons are shown in the graphic as small red dots, while the holes are represented by white dots. Even in the quiescent mode the electrons and holes diffuse within their layers. You can simulate the dynamic behavior using the "time" slider.

When a small current is applied between B and C, a much larger current surges through the transistor, the output signal increasing with the input signal, often at an exponential rate. The ratio of input to output currents is called the *gain*, and is typically in the range of several hundred. The graphic shows the electrons migrating toward the emitter. Recall that the conventional current is in the opposite direction to electron flow (thanks to Benjamin Franklin).

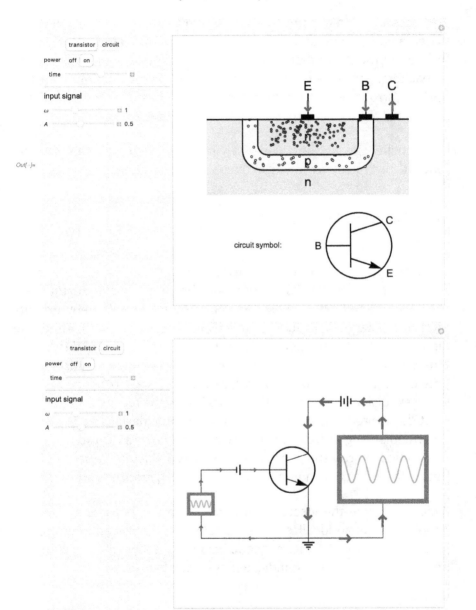

Demonstration 6.29: Primer on Bipolar Junction Transistors (https://demonstrations. wolfram.com/PrimerOnBipolarJunctionTransistors/)

The second graphic shows the transistor in a simplified circuit, in which it can amplify an input signal to a much higher amplitude. To function efficiently, the circuit should also contain several additional resistors and capacitors, which are omitted for simplicity. The current flow is tracked by blue arrows. Note that these are more intense in the output circuit. The signal to be amplified is a simple sine wave $A \sin \omega t$.

An amplifier can also be based on an analogous pnp transistor, with the output currents then running in the opposite directions.

6.6. Superconductivity

6.6.1. *Meissner Effect*

The Meissner effect is the expulsion of magnetic flux from a superconductor when its state is below the threshold curve of the magnetic field-temperature phase diagram. The material thereby exhibits perfect diamagnetism. Superconductivity is destroyed when either the applied field or the temperature is increased to take it out of this region. The threshold curve is shown in black for type-I superconductors. The intercepts are designated B_C and T_C. For type-II superconductors, complete expulsion of magnetic flux occurs below the red curve, with intercept designated B_{C1}. The upper intercept is then designated B_{C2}. In the intermediate region between the two curves, known as a *mixed state*, the magnetic field can still penetrate the superconductor in a series of flux tubes, in which the conducting electrons form quantized vortices.

When you drag the locator to a position on the phase diagram, the graphic shows an idealized representation of the corresponding state of the conductor and the magnetic field lines, shown in blue. Stronger magnetic field intensity is indicated by darker field lines.

Some examples of superconductors:

Type I: lead with $T_C = 7.193$ K, $B_C = 0.0803$ T; mercury with $T_C = 4.153$ K, $B_C = 0.0412$ T; aluminum with $T_C = 1.140$ K, $B_C = 0.0105$ T.

Type II: usually alloys or transition metals, also high-temperature superconductors. Example: niobiumtin with $T_C = 18\,\text{K}$, $B_{C1} = 0.019\,\text{T}$,
$B_{C2} = 24.5\,\text{T}$.

The flux tubes in type-II superconductors exhibit *flux quantization*. The
magnetic flux $\Phi = \int B \cdot d\sigma$ through each vortex is quantized in integral
multiples of $h/2e \approx 2.079 * 10^{-5}\,\text{Tm}^2$.

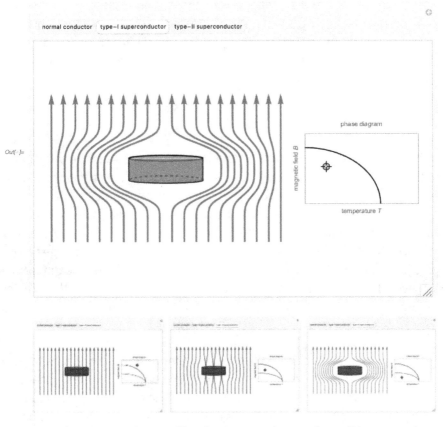

Demonstration 6.30: Meissner Effect in Superconductors (https://demonstrations.
wolfram.com/MeissnerEffectInSuperconductors/)

6.6.2. *DC and AC Josephson Effects*

Brian Josephson discovered in 1962 (and was awarded the Physics Nobel
Prize in 1973) that Cooper pairs of superconducting electrons could

tunnel through an insulating barrier, of the order of $10 \, \text{Å}$ wide, in the absence of any external voltage. This is to be distinguished from the tunneling of single electrons, which does require a finite voltage. This phenomenon is known as the DC Josephson effect.

A superconductor can be described by an order parameter, which is, in effect, the wavefunction describing the collective state of all the Cooper pairs. On the two sides of the barrier the wavefunctions can be represented by $\Psi_1 = \sqrt{\rho_1} e^{i\delta_1}$ and $\Psi_2 = \sqrt{\rho_2} e^{i\delta_2}$, respectively, in which ρ_1 and ρ_2 are Cooper-pair densities and δ_1 and δ_2 are the phases of the wavefunctions. The wavefunctions obey the coupled time-dependent Schrödinger equations

$$i\hbar \frac{\delta \Psi_1}{\delta t} + U_1 \Psi_1 = K \Psi_2 \quad \text{and} \quad i\hbar \frac{\delta \Psi_2}{\delta t} + U_2 \Psi_2 = K \Psi_1,$$

where K is a barrier-opacity constant that depends on the width and composition of the insulating barrier and the temperature. For superconductivity to be operative, the entire system is immersed in a liquid helium cryostat, so $T \leq 4.2K$. For simplicity, the two superconductors are assumed to have the same composition; niobium (Nb) is a popular choice. The energy difference $U_2 - U_1$ is 2 eV, where V is the voltage across the junction and $2e$ is the charge of a Cooper pair. The phase difference is given by $\delta = \delta_2 - \delta_1$. The current I tunneling across the barrier is proportional to the time rate of change of the Cooper-pair densities $\frac{d\rho_1}{dt} = -\frac{d\rho_2}{dt}$.

The preceding can be solved for the two fundamental equations for the Josephson effect: $I = I_c \sin\delta$ and $\frac{d\delta}{dt} = \frac{2e}{\hbar} V(t)$ where I_c is the critical current, above which superconductivity is lost. The critical current depends on K and also on any external magnetic field (which we assume absent here). Suppose first that we apply a DC voltage V_0. The current is then given by $I = I_c \sin(\delta + \frac{2e}{\hbar} V_0 t)$. Since $\hbar$ in the second term is so small, the argument of the sine is immensely large and time-averages to zero. Thus the tunneling supercurrent is zero if $V_0 \neq 0$. Only when $V_0 = 0$ do we observe a current $I = I_c \sin \delta$, with a maximum amplitude of I_c. The lower graphic shows an oscilloscope trace as $V(t)$ is swept over a range of the order of ± 1 or $2V$. This is, in essence, the DC Josephson effect, in which current flows only if $V_0 = 0$, but drops to zero if a DC voltage is applied. The "cross" at $V = 0$ comes from superposed views of the supercurrent flowing in either direction in the course of each oscilloscope cycle.

With a DC voltage V_0 across the junction, the energy difference for a Cooper pair crossing the junction equals $2eV_0$, which would correspond to a photon of frequency $\omega = 2eV_0/\hbar$. Such radiation has been measured with highly sensitive detectors. The AC Josephson effect is observed if the DC voltage is augmented by a small-amplitude, high-frequency AC contribution, such that $V(t) = V_0 + V_1 \cos\omega t$. When RF amplitude is zero, the system reverts to the DC effect. This is most readily accomplished by irradiating the junction with low-intensity microwave radiation in the range of 10–20 GHz. The junction current then given by $I = I_c \sin(\delta + \frac{2e}{\hbar}V_0 t + \frac{2eV_1}{\hbar\omega}\sin\omega t) \approx \frac{V_1}{2V_0}I_c\sin\delta$, for $V_0 = n\frac{\hbar\omega}{2e}, n = 0, \pm 1, \pm 2, \pm 3, \ldots$, again neglecting sinusoidal voltages of unobservably high frequencies. As the voltage V_0 is swept, those points at which the radiation frequency obeys the resonance condition $\omega = 2eV_0/\hbar$ exhibit a series of stepwise increases in current, equal to $\Delta_I \approx \frac{V_1}{2V_0}I_c\sin\delta$. These steps were first observed by S. Shapiro in 1963 and can be considered a definitive validation of the AC Josephson effect. The width of each voltage step is very precisely equal to $\hbar\omega/2e$.

All plots are shown without numerical axes labels, since these magnitudes depend on the specific individual characteristics of instruments and materials. Thus, a qualitative description of these phenomena suffices.

Josephson junctions have important applications in SQUIDs (superconducting quantum interference devices), which can be very sensitive magnetometers, and for RSFQ (rapid single flux quantum) digital electronic devices. They have been suggested in several proposed designs for quantum computers. The Josephson effect provides a highly accurate frequency to voltage conversion, as expressed by the Josephson constant, $2e/\hbar = 483.5979$ MHz/μV. Since frequency can be very precisely defined by the cesium atomic clock, the Josephson effect is now used as the basis of a practical high-precision definition of the volt.

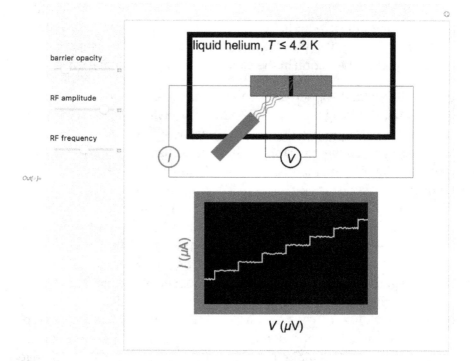

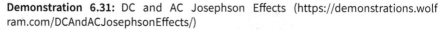

Demonstration 6.31: DC and AC Josephson Effects (https://demonstrations.wolfram.com/DCAndACJosephsonEffects/)

6.7. Solitons

John Scott Russell, a Scottish naval engineer, reported in 1834 on his observation of a remarkable solitary water wave moving a considerable distance down a narrow channel. Korteweg and de Vries (1895) developed a theory to describe weakly non-linear wave propagation in shallow water. The standard form of the Korteweg-de Vries (KdV) equation is usually written $\phi_t + \phi_{xxx} + 6\phi\phi_x = 0$ (in some references with -6). Kruskal and Zabusky (1965) discovered that the KdV equation admits analytic solutions representing what they called "solitons"— propagating pulses or solitary waves that maintain their shape and can pass through one another. These are evidently waves that behave like particles! Several detailed analyses suggest that the coherence of solitons can be attributed to a compensation of non-linear and dispersive effects. A 1-soliton solution to the KdV equation can be written $\phi_1(x,t) = 2k^2\text{sech}^2[k(x-4k^2t)]$. This represents a wavepacket with amplitude $2k^2$ and wave velocity $4k^2$, depending on a parameter k, one of the constants of integration.

In this Demonstration, the function $\phi(x,t)$ is plotted as a function of x for values of t which you can choose and vary. A simulation of the corresponding wave $\phi(x,y,t)$ is also shown as a three-dimensional plot.

Multiple-soliton solutions of the KdV equation have also been discovered. These become increasingly complicated and here only a 2-soliton generalization $\phi_2(x,t)$ is considered. Detailed analysis shows that in

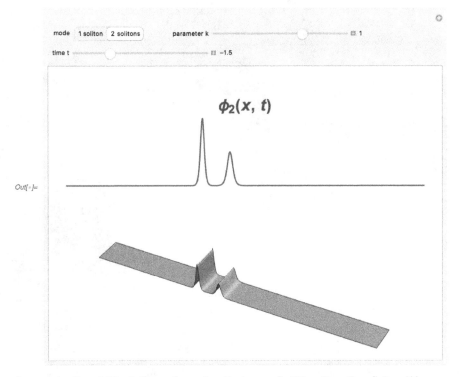

Demonstration 6.32: Solitons from the Korteweg-de Vries Equation (https://demonstrations.wolfram.com/SolitonsFromTheKortewegDeVriesEquation/)

the 2-soliton collision shown, the individual solitons actually exchange amplitudes, rather than passing through one another.

Solitons provide a fertile source of inspiration in several areas of fundamental physics, including elementary particle theory, string theory, quantum optics and Bose-Einstein condensations.

Chapter 7

Theoretical Chemistry

This Chapter is largely on topics in quantum chemistry, dealing with the structure of atoms and molecules and the principles of chemical bonding.

7.1. The Periodic Table

The periodic table is a good starting point for any account of chemistry. To get a picture of the periodic table from Wolfram | Alpha input = periodic table in the Mathematica notebook:

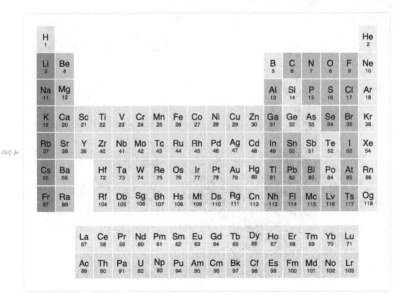

7.1.1. *Mendeleev's Periodic Table*

The graphic shows a fragment of the periodic table of the elements published by Dmitri Ivanovich Mendeleev in 1871. The elements are ordered by increasing atomic weight, such that elements with chemical similarities occur in vertical groups. The headings give the formulas for the most stable oxide for elements in each group. Also shown in blue are the specific gravities of the elements. Mendeleev boldly proposed that there must be missing elements in the three orange boxes, to which he gave the provisional names Ekaboron, Ekaaluminum and Ekasilicon. Try to estimate the atomic weights and specific gravities for these elements. Scandium, Gallium and Germanium were discovered in 1879, 1875 and 1886, respectively, with properties very close to those predicted by Mendeleev. It is now understood, of course, that it is more fundamental to order the elements by atomic number, rather than atomic weight.

element   Ekaboron   Ekaaluminum   Ekasilicon

predicted atomic weight ⌐ 45.   predicted specific gravity ⌐ 3.5

confirm ✅

prediction for Ekaboron:
atomic weight 45.0, specific gravity 3.50

R_2O	RO	R_2O_3	RO_2	R_2O_5
Li = 7	Be = 9.4	B = 11	C = 12	N = 14
0.53	1.85	2.37	1.83	gas
Na = 23	Mg = 24	Al = 27.3	Si = 28	P = 31
0.97	1.74	2.70	2.33	1.82
K = 39	Ca = 40	Sc = 45	Ti = 48	V = 51
0.86	1.55	2.99	4.55	6.11
Cu = 63	Zn = 65	Ekaaluminum	Ekasilicon	As = 75
8.96	7.13			5.73
Rb = 85	Sr = 87	?Yt = 88	Zr = 90	Nb = 94
1.53	2.54	4.46	6.51	6.10

Out[ ]=

Demonstration 7.1: Filling the Gaps in Mendeleev's Periodic Table (https://demonstrations.wolfram.com/FillingTheGapsInMendeleevsPeriodicTable/)

7.2. Atomic Structure

7.2.1. *Build Your Own Atom*

The structure of the atom consists of a cloud of electrons around a nucleus. The nucleus, consisting of Z protons and $A - Z$ neutrons, contains over 99% of the mass of the atom. According to quantum theory, the electrons (shown as red dots) surround the nucleus in shells, with their precise individual positions and momenta being only statistically determined. You can simulate the electron "motions" using the checkbox. The size of the nucleus is greatly magnified in the graphic—it is actually only about 10^{-5} times the radius of the innermost electron shell. In accordance with the Pauli exclusion principle, the innermost shell has a capacity of two electrons, while the second shell can hold a maximum of eight electrons.

This Demonstration considers the first 10 atoms of the periodic table — hydrogen through neon. Only the most stable isotopes are shown. When

Demonstration 7.2: Build Your Own Atoms (https://demonstrations.wolfram.com/BuildYourOwnAtoms/)

the number of electrons equals the nuclear charge Z, the atom is electrically neutral. Otherwise it gives a positive or negative ion, which is labeled on the graphic.

7.2.2. $n + l$ *Rule for Atomic Electron Configurations*

Orbitals in atomic ground-state electron configurations are filled in the order of increasing $n + l$. For equal $n + l$ values, the orbital with the lower n is most often filled first. Here n is the principal quantum

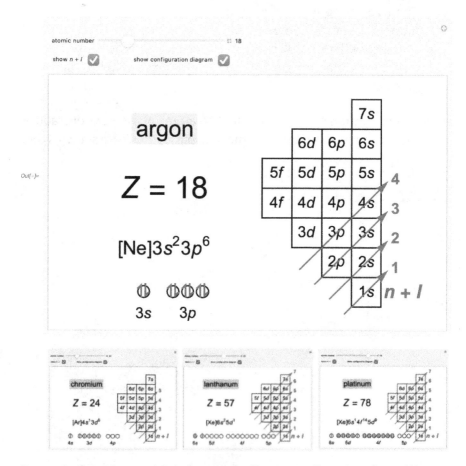

Demonstration 7.3: $n + l$ Rule for Atomic Electron Configurations (https://demonstrations.wolfram.com/NLRuleForAtomicElectronConfigurations/)

number $n = 1, 2, 3, \ldots$ and l is the angular momentum quantum number $l = 0, 1, \ldots, n - 1$, designated by the code s, p, d, f for $l = 0, 1, 2, 3$, respectively. The "$n + l$ rule", also known as the Madelung rule or the diagonal rule, holds with only a small number of irregularities. The designation "diagonal rule" refers to the pattern of atomic orbitals shown in the graphic. The optional configuration diagram also shows the spins of the electrons in occupied orbitals. In accord with the Pauli exclusion principle, each orbital has a maximum capacity of two electrons, with opposite spins. The actual electron configurations are deduced from spectroscopic and chemical characteristics. This Demonstration covers the naturally occurring elements with atomic numbers Z from 1 to 92. The electron configurations of Ni, Pd and Pt show deviations from the simple rule.

7.3. Atomic Orbitals

The electronic structure of an atom is most frequently described by an approximation in which its electrons occupy a set of *atomic orbitals*. Atomic orbitals are solutions of the Schrödinger equation for a hydrogen-like atom, which is the only quantum-mechanical atomic problem which can be solved exactly.

The following diagram represents the general shapes of the atomic orbitals. These pictures are intended as stylized representations of atomic orbitals and should not be interpreted as quantitatively accurate. Blue and yellow indicate, respectively, positive and negative regions of the wavefunctions (the radial nodes of the 2s and 3s orbitals are obscured). The s-orbitals are non-degenerate, while p, d and f-orbitals have degeneracies of 3, 5 and 7, respectively. These degeneracies determine the aufbau of electronic configurations of the atoms in the periodic table.

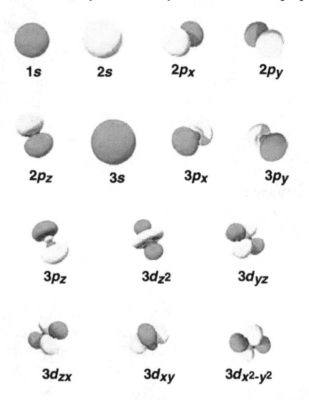

1s   2s   2px   2py

2pz   3s   3px   3py

3pz   3dz²   3dyz

3dzx   3dxy   3dx²-y²

The normalized hydrogen-like wavefunctions in atomic units ($\hbar = m = e = 1$), for arbitrary Z, are given by

$$\psi_{nlm}(r, \theta, \phi) = \sqrt{\left(\frac{2Z}{n}\right)^3 \frac{(n-l-1)!}{2n(n+l)!}}\, e^{-\rho/2} \rho^l L_{n-l-1}^{2l+1}(\rho) Y_l^m(\theta, \phi),$$

$$\rho = 2Zr/n,$$

where L is an associated Laguerre polynomial and Y a spherical harmonic. The orbitals pictures above are all real functions, obtained by taking appropriate linear combinations of spherical harmonics. The real atomic orbitals are used most often in chemical applications.

7.3.1. *Quantum Alchemy*

Schrödinger made use of a factorization method on the hydrogen atom radial equation to show that all solutions can be generated starting with the ground state. Such procedures are now usually categorized as supersymmetric quantum mechanics. In an earlier publication we dubbed this modern form of alchemy "quantum alchemy".

The Schrödinger equation for a non-relativistic hydrogenic atom has the form $(-\frac{1}{2}\nabla^2 - \frac{Z}{r})\Psi = E\Psi$, with use of atomic units and infinite nuclear mass ($\hbar = m_e = e = 1, m_p = \infty$). In our specific examples we take $Z = 1$ for the hydrogen atom itself. The solution is separable in spherical polar coordinates: $\psi_{nlm}(r, \theta, \phi) = R_{nl}(r)Y_{lm}(\theta, \phi)$. The $Y_{lm}(\theta, \phi)$ are spherical harmonics; their transformation properties are well documented and we need not consider them further. We use the value $m = 0$ in our illustrations of atomic orbitals. For bound states with $E_n = -\frac{Z^2}{2n^2}$, the normalized radial function can be expressed $R_{nl}(\rho) = \sqrt{\frac{(n-1-l)!}{2n[(n+l)!]^3}}\left(\frac{2}{n}\right)^{3/2}$ $\rho^l e^{-\rho/2}L_{n-l-1}^{2l+1}(\rho)$, where L is an associated Laguerre polynomial and $\rho = \frac{2Zr}{n}$. It is simpler to work with the reduced radial function $P_{nl}(r) = rR_{nl}(r)$, which obeys the pseudo one-dimensional differential equation $(-\frac{1}{2}\frac{d^2}{dr^2} + \frac{l(l+1)}{2r^2} - \frac{Z}{r})P_{nl}(r) = E_nP_{nl}(r)$. We consider the two "alchemical" transformations $\mathcal{A}_l$ and $\mathcal{N}_{nl}$, which have the following actions: $\mathcal{A}_{l+1}P_{n,l}(r) =$ const$P_{n,l+1}(r)$ and $\mathcal{N}_{nl}P_{n,l}(r) =$ const$P_{n+1,l}(r)$. The first operator, for example, turns a 2s-orbital into a 2p-orbital, while the second turns it into a 3s-orbital.

This Demonstration shows a sequence of steps that can convert the ground state 1s orbital into a chosen orbital with user-specified values of n and l, up to $n = 4$ and $l = 3$. Plots of the radial functions $P_{1\times0}(r)$ and $P_{nl}(r)$ are also shown. The supersymmetric operator is given by $\mathcal{A}_l = \frac{d}{dr} - \frac{l+1}{r} + \frac{Z}{l+1}$. For example, $\mathcal{A}_1r^2e^{-Zr/2} = r(1 - \frac{Zr}{2})e^{-Zr/2}$ (so that $\mathcal{A}_1P_{2S} =$ constP_{2p}). To apply the ladder operator $\mathcal{N}_{nl}$ for principal quantum numbers, we must first express the radial function in the form $P_{nl}(\rho) = \rho F_{nl}(\rho)e^{-\rho/2}$, where $\rho = \frac{2Zr}{n}$. Then the quantum number is increased by 1 in the operation $F_{n+1,l}(\rho) = $ const $[\rho\frac{d}{d\rho} + n + 1 - \rho]F_{nl}(\rho)$, where the square brackets represent the operator $\mathcal{N}_{2\times0}$. For example, operating on a 2s-orbital, for which $n = 2, l = 0, \rho = Zr$, and $F_{20} =$ const $(1 - \frac{\rho}{2})$, we find $[\rho\frac{d}{d\rho} + 2 + 1 - \rho](1 - \frac{\rho}{2}) = (3 - 3\rho + \frac{\rho^2}{2})$. The last expression reduces to const $(27 - 18Zr + 2Z^2r^1) = F_{30}$, after setting $\rho = \frac{2Zr}{3}$.

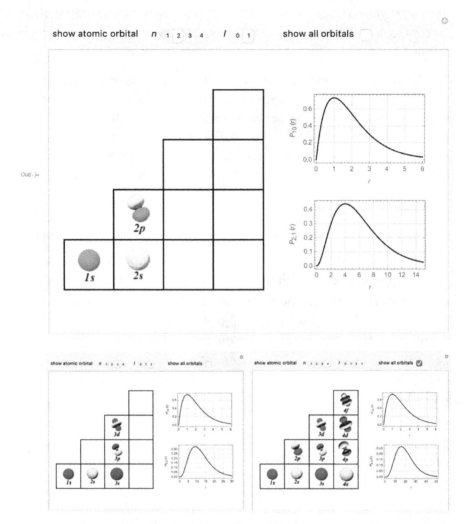

Demonstration 7.4: Quantum, Alchemy (https://demonstrations.wolfram.com/Quan tumAlchemy/)

7.3.2. *Unsöld's Theorem*

A theorem of A. Unsöld states that a filled or half-filled subshell of atomic orbitals with $l > 0$ is spherically symmetrical and thus contributes an orbital angular momentum of zero. This can be illustrated by evaluating the sum of atomic orbital densities $|\psi_{px}|^2 + |\psi_{py}|^2 + |\psi_{pz}|^2$, or equivalently

$|\Psi_{p_{-1}}|^2 + |\Psi_{p_0}|^2 + |\Psi_{p_1}|^2$, giving a spherically symmetrical function (independent of θ and ϕ). The nitrogen atom in its ground state has the configuration ... $2p^3 \,^4S$, with three electrons of parallel spins singly occupying the three degenerate $2p$-orbitals. Neon has a completely filled subshell with configuration ... $2p^6 \,^1S$. Likewise, the half-filled $3d^5$ subshells in Cr and Mn lead to spherically symmetrical ground states. The mathematical proof of Unsöld's theorem follows from the spherical harmonic identity

$$\sum_{m=-l}^{l} |Y_{lm}(\theta, \phi)|^2 = \frac{2l + 1}{4\pi}.$$

In this Demonstration, you can add sums of p, d, or f atomic orbital densities to approach a spherical distribution. A filled or half-filled shell missing one orbital behaves like a positive hole with the same angular momentum as the missing electron. Thus the ground state of C ... $2p^2$

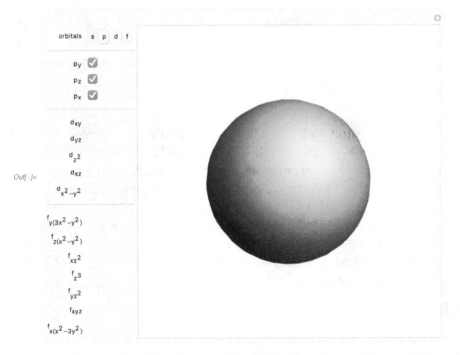

Demonstration 7.5: Unsöld's Theorem (https://demonstrations.wolfram.com/Unso eldsTheorem/)

is a ^{3}P state, constructed, in concept, by removing a $2p$ electron from N ... $2p^3$ ^{4}S.

7.3.3. *Generalized Unsöld Theorem*

According to Unsöld's theorem, the sum over all m states for an l-subshell of hydrogen-like orbitals reduces to a spherically symmetrical function: $\sum_{m=-l}^{l} |\Psi_{nlm}(r, \theta, \phi)|^2 = \rho_{nl}(r)$. For a pure Coulomb potential with any nuclear charge Z, the different l states for a given n are also degenerate. The author has derived a generalization of Unsöld's theorem, an explicit form for the sum over both l and m for hydrogenic orbitals, namely,

$$\sum_{l=0}^{n-1} \rho_{nl}(r) = \rho_n(r) = \frac{Z^3}{\pi n^3} [M'_{n,1/2}(2Zr/n)^2$$

$$- M''_{n,1/2}(2Zr/n) M_{n,1/2}(2Zr/n))],$$

where $M_{m,1/2}(z)$ is a Whittaker function that can alternatively be written as $ze^{-z/2} {}_1F_1(1 - n; 2; z)$. We can define a radial distribution function for a completely filled n-shell by $D_n(r) = 4\pi r^2 \rho_n(r)$. This is normalized according to $\int_0^\infty D_n(r)dr = n^2$, reflecting the orbital degeneracy of the energy level E_n.

In this Demonstration the function $D_n(r)$ is plotted for selected values of Z (1 to 10) and n (1 to 25). The classical analog of $D_n(r)$, in accordance with Bohr's correspondence principle, approaches the quantum result in the limit $n \to \infty$. The checkbox produces a red plot of the classical function.

The generalized Unsöld theorem has found several theoretical applications, including derivation of the canonical Coulomb partition function, density functional computations, supersymmetry, and study of high-n Rydberg states of atoms.

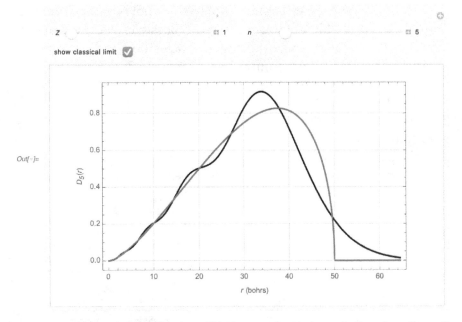

Demonstration 7.6: Generalized Unsöld Theorem for Hydrogenic Functions (https://demonstrations.wolfram.com/GeneralizedUnsoeldTheoremForHydrogenicFunctions/)

7.4. The Helium Atom

7.4.1. *Old Quantum Theory*

Niels Bohr's 1913 model of the hydrogen atom, now known as the old quantum theory (OQT), was a spectacular success in accounting for the spectrum of atomic hydrogen and introducing the concept of energy-level quantization. However, many valiant attempts to extend the Bohr model to the helium atom and beyond met with miserable failure, necessarily awaiting the development of quantum mechanics in 1925–1926. This Demonstration reproduces probably the most creditable OQT model of the helium atom, which was proposed in the doctoral dissertation of J. H. Van Vleck in 1922.

According to this model, the two electrons in helium follow elliptical orbits around the nucleus, in intersecting planes mutually separated by a dihedral angle of Θ, something of the order of 60°. The classical equations of motion, a three-body problem, cannot be solved in closed form, but reasonable approximations are possible. With appropriate choices of the orbital radius and angle of inclination, the experimental ionization energy IP of the atom can be reproduced.

Beyond the original work of Van Vleck, consider the isoelectronic series of two-electron atomic species from $Z = 1$ (H$^-$) to $Z = 10$ (Ne^{+8}). The corresponding singly ionized, one-electron systems can be solved exactly to give energies of $-\frac{1}{2}Z^2$ hartrees. Thus $IP = 27.211|E - \frac{1}{2}Z^2|$ eV, where E is the two-electron energy in hartrees.

For a given atomic number Z, you can vary the angle Θ to fit the experimental ionization energy.

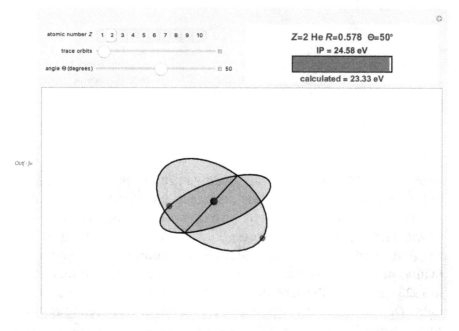

Out[ ]=

Demonstration 7.7: Van Vleck's Model of the Helium Atom in the Old Quantum Theory (https://demonstrations.wolfram.com/VanVlecksModelOfTheHeliumAtomInTheOld QuantumTheory/)

7.4.2. *Variational Calculations*

The Schrödinger equation for a helium-like (two-electron) atom or ion is given by $(-\frac{1}{2}\nabla_1^2-\frac{1}{2}\nabla_2^2-\frac{Z}{r_1}-\frac{Z}{r_2}+\frac{1}{r_{12}}-E)\Psi(\mathbf{r}_1,\mathbf{r}_2)=0$, expressed in atomic units $\hbar=e=m=1$, assuming infinite nuclear mass and neglecting

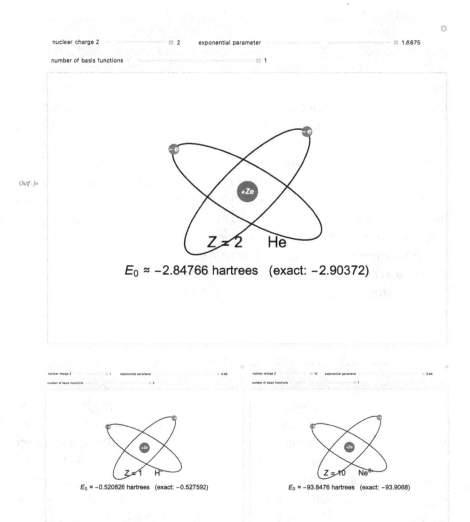

Out[ ]=

Demonstration 7.8: Variational Calculations on the Helium Isoelectronic Series (https://demonstrations.wolfram.com/VariationalCalculationsOnTheHeliumIsoelectronicSeries/)

relativistic corrections. Atomic numbers Z from 1 (H^-) and 2 (He) through 10 (Ne^{8+}) are considered. Unlike the one-electron Schrödinger equation, this problem cannot be solved analytically. E. A. Hylleraas, around 1930, carried out variational calculations giving ground state energies and ionization potentials in essential agreement with experimental results. This, at least to physicists and chemists, could be considered a "proof" of the general validity of the Schrödinger equation. (By contrast, the Bohr theory gave correct energies for the hydrogen atom but failed miserably for helium and heavier atoms.) For spherically symmetrical S states, the helium problem reduces to just three independent variables. Hylleraas introduced the variables $s = r_1 + r_2$, $t = r_1 - r_2$, $u = r_{12}$ and considered linear variational functions of the form $e^{-\zeta s} \sum_{n,m,p} c_{n,m,p} s^n t^m u^p$, with $\zeta = Z - 5/16$ a common choice for the exponential parameter. For N basis functions, the energies are obtained by solution of an $N \times N$ secular equation. This Demonstration can handle a maximum of 10 basis functions, actually going beyond Hylleraas' original capability. You can vary the exponential parameter and number of basis functions for given Z to compute the ground state energy in Hartree atomic units and the first ionization potential (IP) in electron volts. These are compared with the most accurate "exact" non-relativistic results, shown in parentheses. The logo showing two electrons in Bohr orbits is for decorative purposes only.

7.4.3. *Two-Parameter Variational Functions*

We focus in this Demonstration on much simpler variational approxima-tions to the helium wavefunction. The approximate energy is then given by $\mathcal{E} = \langle \psi | H | \psi \rangle / \langle \psi | \psi \rangle$, where the denominator enables us to use non-normalized wavefunctions. The classic first approximation is a product of scaled hydrogen-like 1s functions ($e^{-\alpha r}$): $\psi_l(r_1, r_2) = e^{-\alpha r_1} e^{-\alpha r_2}$. Optimizing the parameter α so that the energy is a minimum, such that $\partial E / \partial \alpha = 0$, it is found that $\alpha = Z - 5/16$ (1.6875 for helium), giving an energy $\mathcal{E} = -(Z - 5/16)^2$ (-2.84766 hartrees for helium). This is compared with the exact non-relativistic value the helium ground-state energy, $E = -2.90372$ hartrees. The first ionization potential is the energy difference with the hydrogen-like He^+ ion, which has an energy of exactly $-Z^2/2$. Thus, expressed in electron volts, IP $= (2.84766 - 2) \times 27.212 = 23.066$ eV, compared to the exact value 24.592 eV.

In addition to $\psi_I(\mathbf{r}_1, \mathbf{r}_2)$, cited above, we consider the two-parameter variational functions:

$$\psi_{II}(\mathbf{r}_1, \mathbf{r}_2) = e^{-\alpha r_1} e^{-\beta r_2} + e^{-\beta r_1} e^{-\alpha r_2},$$

$$\psi_{III}(\mathbf{r}_1, \mathbf{r}_2) = e^{-\alpha(r_1 + r_2)} e^{\gamma r_{12}},$$

$$\psi_{IV}(\mathbf{r}_1, \mathbf{r}_2) = e^{-\alpha(r_1 + r_2)} (1 + \gamma r_{12}).$$

The function $\psi_{II}(\mathbf{r}_1, \mathbf{r}_2)$ first proposed by Eckert (1930) represents an "open shell" modification, in which the "inner" and "outer" 1s orbitals

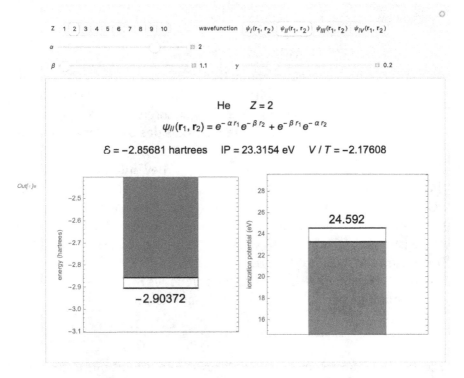

Demonstration 7.9: Two-Parameter Variational Functions for the Helium Isoelectronic Series (https://demonstrations.wolfram.com/TwoParameterVariationalFunctions
ForTheHeliumIsoelectronicSer/)

are allowed to have different shielding constants. The last two functions include explicit dependence on the coordinate r_{12} (Hylleraas, 1929; Baber and Hassé, 1937), which attempts to account for some of the correlation energy—the difference between the instantaneous and averaged interactions between the electrons.

The virial theorem for a Coulombic system requires that the average potential and kinetic energies, given by $V = \langle \psi | - \frac{Z}{r_1} - \frac{Z}{r_2} + \frac{1}{r_{12}} | \psi \rangle$ and $T = \langle \psi | - \frac{1}{2} \nabla_1^2 - \frac{1}{2} \nabla_2^2 | \psi \rangle$, respectively, satisfy the ratio $V/T = -2$. This is true for the exact solution and serves as an additional criterion for a variational function.

You can choose the parameters α and β or α and γ that optimize the computed energy and IP. The results are displayed on two bar graphs, which show how close you come to the exact values.

7.4.4. *Helium with Perimetric Coordinates*

The most accurate computations on the ground state of the helium atom and its isoelectronic series followed from the work of Pekeris. For an S-state, the wavefunction depends on just three coordinates, say r_1, r_2 and r_{12}, which can be represented as the sides of a planar triangle. The *perimetric coordinates* $u = -r_1 + r_2 + r_{12}$, $v = r_1 - r_2 + r_{12}$, $w = r_1 + r_2 - r_{12}$ have the advantage that they automatically satisfy the triangle inequalities and each independently varies from 0 to ∞. Pekeris's original computation made use of an expansion in perimetric coordinates containing 1058 terms, leading to the essentially exact non-relativistic ground-state energy $E_0 = -2.903724375$ hartrees. In this Demonstration, we introduce the use of perimetric coordinates in computations on the two-electron isoelectronic series H^-, He, Li^+, ..., Ne^{8+}, corresponding to $Z = 1, 2, \ldots, 10$ in the Hamiltonian

$$H = -\frac{1}{2}(\nabla_1^2 + \nabla_2^2) - \frac{Z}{r_1} - \frac{Z}{r_2} + \frac{1}{r_{12}}.$$

The wavefunctions considered by Pekeris were expansions in the form $\psi(u, v, w) = e^{-\xi u - \eta v - \zeta w} \sum_{nmk} f_n(u) f_m(u) f_k(u)$.

We consider a much more modest version with $\psi(u, v, w) = e^{-\alpha Z(u+v) - \beta Z w}(1 + \gamma(u + v))$, where α, β, γ can be chosen such as to minimize the variational integral $\mathcal{E} = \int \psi H \psi d\tau / \int \psi^2 d\tau$.

The optimized results can be obtained directly by checking "show optimized values". The corresponding ionization energies of each atom is also shown, given by $IP = -(\mathcal{E} - Z^2/2)$, where $-Z^2/2$ is the ground-state energy of the single-electron ion. The atomic energies and ionization energies are represented on bar graphs, with the exact non-relativistic values written in for reference. The variationally determined energy must, of necessity, be higher (less negative) than the exact value.

Perimetric coordinates for two-electron systems:

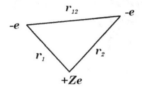

$$u = -r_1 + r_2 + r_{12}, v = r_1 - r_2 + r_{12}, w = r_1 + r_2 - r_{12},$$

$$d^3 r_1 d^3 r_2 = \pi^2 (u + v)(u + w)(v + w) du\, dv\, dw, 0 \le u, v, w \le \infty,$$

$$U = wv(w + v), V = wu(w + u), W = uv(u + v),$$

$$F = 2U + W + 2uvw, G = 2V + W + 2uvw,$$

$$T = -\frac{1}{2}(\nabla_1^2 + \nabla_2^2) = -\frac{8}{(u + v)(u + w)(v + w)}$$

$$\times \left[\frac{\partial}{\partial u} G + \frac{\partial}{\partial u} + \frac{\partial}{\partial v} F + \frac{\partial}{\partial v} + \frac{\partial}{\partial w}(U + V)\frac{\partial}{\partial w} - \frac{\partial}{\partial u} V \frac{\partial}{\partial w} \right.$$

$$\left. - \frac{\partial}{\partial v} U \frac{\partial}{\partial w} - \frac{\partial}{\partial w} V \frac{\partial}{\partial u} - \frac{\partial}{\partial w} U \frac{\partial}{\partial v} \right],$$

$$V = -\frac{Z}{r_1} - \frac{Z}{r_2} + \frac{1}{r_{12}} = -\frac{2Z}{V + W} - \frac{2Z}{u + w} + \frac{2}{u + v}.$$

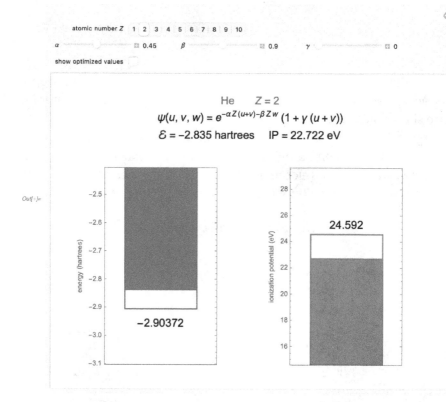

Demonstration 7.10: Energies of Helium Isoelectronic Series Using Perimetric Coordinates (https://demonstrations.wolfram.com/EnergiesOfHeliumIsoelectronicSeriesUsingPerimetricCoordinate/)

7.4.5. *Configuration Interaction*

Configuration interaction (CI) provides a systematic method for improving on single-configuration Hartree–Fock (HF) computations. This Demonstration considers the two-electron atoms in the helium isoelectronic series. The HF wavefunction $\Psi_0(\mathbf{r}_1, \mathbf{r}_2)$ is the optimal product of one-electron orbitals $\phi_{1s}(r_1)\phi_{1s}(r_2)$ approximating the $1s^2$ ground-state configuration. An improved representation of the ground state can be obtained by a superposition containing excited ^1S electronic configurations, including $2s^2, 2p^2, 3d^2, \ldots$, with relative contributions determined by the variational principle.

Shull and Löwdin represented the total wavefunction in the form

$$\Psi(\mathbf{r}_1, \mathbf{r}_2) = \sum_{L=0}^{\infty} f_L(r_1, r_2)\sqrt{\frac{2L + 1}{2}} P_L(\cos\Theta),$$

where Θ is the angle between $\mathbf{r}_1$ and $\mathbf{r}_2$, while $P_L(\cos\Theta)$ is the Legendre polynomial of degree L. Note that the functions $P_L(\cos\Theta)$ contain internal angular dependence but can still represent atomic S states, such as $2p^2\,{}^1S$ and $3d^2\,{}^1S$, with $L = 0$. In the computations presented in this Demonstration, we consider only the $1s^2$, $2s^2$, $2p^2$ and $3d^2$ contributions to CI. The $1s^2$ contribution is taken as the HF function $\Psi_0(\mathbf{r}_1, \mathbf{r}_2)$, which can be very closely approximated using double-zeta orbitals $\phi_{1s}(r) = A(e^{-\alpha r} + ae^{-\beta r})$.

The $2s^2$ contribution is represented by the orthogonalized Slater-type function $\phi_{2s}(r) = B(1 - kr)e^{-\zeta r}$. Together, these two contributions can closely approximate the S-limit to the CI function, as defined by Shull and Löwdin. The P and D contributions are represented using simple Slater-type orbitals:

$$\phi_{2p}(r) = \frac{2}{\sqrt{3}}\zeta^{5/2}re^{-\xi r} \text{ and } \phi_{3d}(r) = \frac{2}{3}\sqrt{\frac{2}{5}}\eta^{7/2}r^2e^{-\eta r},$$

with $\Psi_P = \phi_{2p}(r_1)\phi_{2p}(r_2)\sqrt{\frac{3}{2}}P_1(\cos\Theta)$ for $2p^2$ and $\Psi_D = \phi_{3d}(r_1)\phi_{3d}(r_2)\sqrt{\frac{5}{2}}P_2(\cos\Theta)$ for $3d^2$.

All the relevant matrix elements of the Hamiltonian are then computed; for example,

$$H_{1s, 1s} = 2\left\langle 1s\left|\frac{-1}{2}\nabla^2 - \frac{Z}{r}\right|1s\right\rangle + \left\langle 1s2s\left|\frac{1}{r_{12}}\right|1s1s\right\rangle,$$

$$H_{1s,2s} = \left\langle 1s2s\left|\frac{1}{r_{12}}\right|1s2s\right\rangle,$$

and so forth. All energies are expressed in Hartree atomic units: 1 hartree $= 27.211$ eV. You can select the level of configuration interaction: Ψ_0, S-limit, S+P or S+P+D, and the values of the exponential parameters ζ, ξ and η. The built-in Mathematica function Eigenvalues then finds the lowest eigenvalue for the corresponding Hamiltonian matrix. The results are represented graphically on a barometer display, comparing them to the exact values of the energy.

Plots of the radial distribution function for each component configuration are also shown on the left. The relative magnitudes are not to scale.

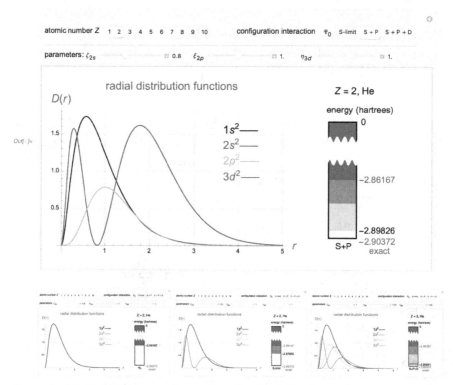

Snapshot 1: the single-configuration Hartree–Fock result

Snapshot 2: approximation to the S-limit; a more accurate computation gives −2.8790 hartrees

Snapshot 3: result using optimized parameters; reaching –2.9 is considered a milestone

Demonstration 7.11: Configuration Interaction for the Helium Isoelectronic Series (https://demonstrations.wolfram.com/ConfigurationInteractionForTheHeliumIsoelectronicSeries/)

7.4.6. *Excited States*

The ground state of the helium atom has the electronic configuration $1s^2 1^1S$. In the lowest excited states, an electron is promoted from the $1s$ to a $2s$ or $2p$ orbital. Although the hydrogenic $2s$ and $2p$ orbitals are degenerate, the $1s2s$ configuration of helium has a lower energy than the $1s2p$. This is attributed to the greater shielding of the nuclear charge experienced by the $2p$ orbital. Each of these lowest excited configurations is further split into a singlet and a triplet state, depending on whether the electron spins are antiparallel or parallel. (They must be antiparallel in the $1s^2$ configuration, by virtue of the Pauli exclusion principle, so that the ground state is a singlet.) The energies of the four lowest excited states can be calculated to fairly reasonable accuracy by self-consistent field (SCF) theory. In this Demonstration, the orbitals are approximated by the simple forms: $\psi_{1s}(r) = N_{1s} e^{-\alpha r}$, $\psi_{2s}(r) = N_{2s}\left(1 - \frac{\alpha+\beta}{3}r\right)e^{-\beta r}$ and $\psi_{2p}(r) = N_{2p}r\cos\theta\, e^{-\lambda r}$. According to the Hartree-Fock method, the energy of a two-electron state is given by $E = H_1 + H_2 + J_{12} \pm K_{12}$. The one-electron integrals $H = \int \psi(r)\left(-\frac{1}{2}\nabla^2 - \frac{2}{r}\right)\psi(r)d^3r$ account for the kinetic energy and nuclear attraction. Atomic units are used, with $\hbar = m = e = 1$. The Coulomb integrals $J_{12} = \iint |\psi_1(r_1)|^2 \frac{1}{r_{12}} |\psi_2(r_2)|^2\, d^3r_1 d^3r_2$ represent the electrostatic repulsion between the two orbital charge distributions. The exchange integrals $K_{12} = \iint \psi_1(r_1)\psi_2(r_1)\frac{1}{r_{12}}\psi_1(r_2)\psi_2(r_2)\, d^3r_1 d^3r_2$ have no classical analog. They are a consequence of the quantum-mechanical exchange symmetry of the atomic wavefunction. Check "turn on K" to include exchange terms in the calculation (they are absent in a simple Hartree SCF computation). The $+$ and $-$ signs in the energy expression pertain to the singlet and triplet states, respectively. The SCF energy can be optimized by variation of the parameters α, β, γ, which you can do in the Demonstration. All energies are expressed in electron volts above the ground state. See how closely you can approximate the exact 2^1S, 2^3S, 2^1P and 2^3P energies, which are represented by black dashes. The 2^3S, 2^1P and 2^3P states are the lowest of their symmetry type, thus the calculated energies are upper bounds to the corresponding exact values, by virtue of the variational principle. This is not true for the 2^1S computation, however, since there exists a lower state of the same symmetry; it is just an approximation which can be higher or lower than the exact value.

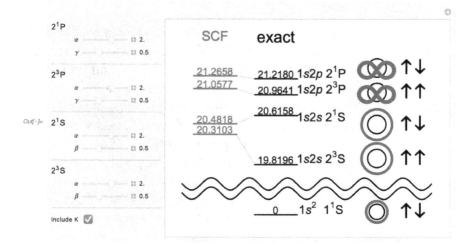

Demonstration 7.12: Lower Excited States of Helium Atom (https://demonstrations. wolfram.com/LowerExcitedStatesOfHeliumAtom/)

7.5. Complex Atoms

7.5.1. *Ions with Noble Gas Configurations*

Atoms and atomic ions with sequences of completely filled electron shells exhibit enhanced stability. The prime examples are the noble gases, He, Ne, Ar, Kr, Xe, and Rn, containing one of the "magic numbers" of electrons: 2, 10, 18, 36, 54, and 86, respectively. These gases are colorless, odorless, and chemically inert (although a few compounds of Kr, Xe, and Rn have been synthesized in recent years). Elements in the extreme right and left portions of the periodic table, whose atoms differ from a closed-shell structure by one or two excess or missing electrons, tend to form stable anions or cations by a gain or loss of one or two electrons. To cite two well-known examples: $Na[1s^2 2s^2 2p^6 3s] \rightarrow Na^+[1s^2 2s^2 2p^6] + e^-$ and $F[1s^2 2s^2 2p^5] + e^- \rightarrow F^-[1s^2 2s^2 2p^6]$, where Na^+ and F^- both have the closed-shell structure of neon.

The graphic shows the relevant fragments of the periodic table as well as a stylized representation of the electron shell structure. You can select the noble gas configuration and the related ion with either positive or negative charges one or two.

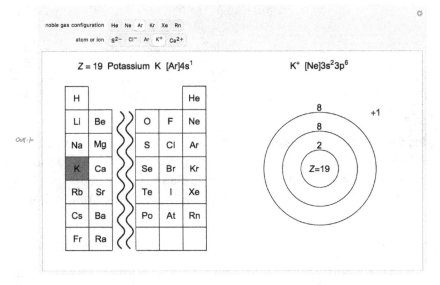

Demonstration 7.13: Ions with Noble Gas Configurations (https://demonstrations.wolfram.com/IonsWithNobleGasConfigurations/)

7.5.2. *Hartree–Fock Computations on Second-Row Atoms*

Modern computational quantum chemistry has developed largely from applications of the Hartree–Fock method to atoms and molecules. A simple representation of a many-electron atom is given by a Slater determinant constructed from N occupied spin-orbitals:

$$\Psi(1 \cdots N) = \frac{1}{\sqrt{N!}} \begin{vmatrix} \Phi_1(1) & \Phi_1(2) & \cdots & \Phi_1(N) \\ \Phi_2(1) & \Phi_2(2) & \cdots & \Phi_1(N) \\ \vdots & \vdots & \ddots & \vdots \\ \Phi_N(1) & \Phi_N(2) & \cdots & \Phi_N(N) \end{vmatrix},$$

where spin-orbitals are products of the form $\Phi(x) = \psi(\mathbf{r})\{^\alpha_\beta$.

A Slater determinant automatically satisfies the Pauli exclusion principle, requiring that spin-orbitals be, at most, singly occupied. The Hamiltonian for an N-electron atom, in hartree atomic units, is given by:

$$H = \sum_{i=1}^{N} \left\{ -\frac{1}{2}\nabla^2 - \frac{Z}{r_i} \right\} + \sum_{i>j=1}^{N} \frac{1}{r_{ij}}.$$

The corresponding approximation to the total energy is then given by

$$E = \sum_{i=1}^{N} H_i + \sum_{i>j=1}^{N} (J_{ij} - K_{ij}),$$

where H, J and K are, respectively, the core, Coulomb and exchange integrals.

This Demonstration carries out a simplified Hartree–Fock computation on the ground states of the atoms He to Ne, $Z = 2$ to 10. Assume a single Slater determinant, thus possibly shortchanging open-shell configurations. The computation involves only $1s$, $2s$ and $2p$ orbitals, approximated by modified Slater-type orbitals:

$$\Psi_{1s} = \frac{\alpha^{3/2}}{\sqrt{\pi}} e^{-\alpha r},$$

$$\Psi_{2s} = \sqrt{\frac{3\beta^5}{\pi(\alpha^2 - \alpha\beta + \beta^2)}} \left(1 - \frac{\alpha + \beta}{3} r\right) e^{-\beta r},$$

$$\Psi_{2p\{x,y,z\}} = \frac{\lambda^{5/2}}{\sqrt{\pi}} r e^{-\gamma r} \{\sin\theta \cos\phi, \sin\theta \sin\phi, \cos\theta\}.$$

These are normalized and mutually orthogonal, which simplifies the computation. The orbital parameters α, β, γ are chosen so as to minimize the total energy, in accordance with the variational principle. You can vary these using the sliders. Actually, since the possible values of α, β, γ vary over inconveniently large ranges, the sliders vary internal parameters that determine them. The values of α, β, γ are shown in the graphic.

The blue bar shows the exact energy of the atomic ground state (actually, the exact non-relativistic value) in hartrees. The red bar shows the calculated energy, given the displayed values of α, β, γ. You should try to adjust the three parameters to get the lowest possible energy. You can never reach the exact energy, however, since a single Hartree–Fock determinant fails to account for *correlation energy*, which involves instantaneous electron-electron interactions.

Following are results for optimized functions Ψ_{1s}, Ψ_{2s} and Ψ_{2p}. For comparison we also include results from the best Hartree-Fock computations and the exact atomic ground-state energies.

Z	atom	configuration	α	β	γ	calculated E	best H-F	exact
2	He	$1s^2\,^1S$	1.6875			−2.84766	−2.86168	−2.903385
3	Li	$1s^2 2s\,^2S$	2.69372	0.766676		−7.41385	−7.43273	−7.477976
4	Be	$1s^2 2s^2\,^1S$	3.70767	1.15954		−14.5300	−14.5730	−14.668449
5	B	$1s^2 2s^2 2p\,^2P$	4.71099	1.57921	1.18716	−24.4506	−24.5291	−24.658211
6	C	$1s^2 2s^2 2p^2\,^3P$	5.71244	1.98775	1.51874	−37.4933	−37.6886	−37.855668
7	N	$1s^2 2s^2 2p^3\,^4S$	6.71293	2.39148	1.84551	−53.9624	−54.4009	−54.611893
8	O	$1s^2 2s^2 2p^4\,^3P$	7.71286	2.79267	2.16972	−74.1624	−74.8094	−75.109991
9	F	$1s^2 2s^2 2p^5\,^2P$	8.71243	3.19236	2.49238	−98.3972	−99.4093	−99.803888
10	Ne	$1s^2 2s^2 2p^6\,^1S$	9.71176	3.59108	2.81404	−126.971	−128.547	−128.830462

Demonstration 7.14: Simplified Hartree-Fock Computations on Second-Row Atoms (https://demonstrations.wolfram.com/SimplifiedHartreeFockComputationsOnSecond RowAtoms/). See also https://arxiv.org/abs/2105.07018.

7.5.3. *Density Functional Computations on Noble Gas Atoms*

Density functional theory (DFT) has now become the predominant technique in computational quantum chemistry, having displaced wavefunction-based computations for atoms, molecules and solids. The key reason is that QFT deals with a single electron density function $\rho(\mathbf{r})$ for an n-electron system, rather than a complicated combination of n orbital functions $\psi(\mathbf{r}_n)$. The fundamental validity of DFT and its practical implementation by a variational principle are expressed in two theorems of Hohenberg and Kohn. For all necessary background on DFT, refer to the definitive monograph of Parr and Yang.

In this Demonstration, a modified version of DFT is applied to compute the energies and electron distributions of the noble gas atoms He, Ne, Ar, Kr and Xe. The energy functional of the spherically symmetric density $\rho(r)$ consists of the following parts: the kinetic energy E_K, the Weizsäcker correction E_W, the electron-nuclear potential energy E_V, the interelectronic Coulomb energy E_J, the Dirac exchange energy E_X and finally, the correlation energy E_C, for which a novel form is suggested. The density functional $\rho(r)$ is designed to take account of the shell structure of the atom, following a computation of Wang and Parr, as well as a curve fitting by the author.

You can select values for one or more exponential parameters σ to optimize the total energy and the radial distribution function. In principle, the exact non-relativistic energies of the noble gas atoms can be reproduced, with the exception of the helium atom, which has too few electrons for a successful statistical model. The default values are chosen to be very close to optimal, to simplify your task.

The total electron density is approximated by a sum of shells (one to five shells for He to Xe):

$$\rho(r) = \sum_k \rho_k(r), \quad \text{where} \quad \rho_k(r) = \text{const}\, r^{2(n^*-1)}\left(e^{-2(Z-\sigma_k)r/n^*}\right),$$

which is suggested by Slater's rules for atomic orbitals. The DFT functional takes the form

$$E[\rho(r)] = E_K + E_W + E_V + E_J + E_X + E_C,$$

with

$$E_K = \frac{3}{10}(3\pi^2)^{2/3}\int \rho(r)^{5/3}dV,$$

$$E_W = \frac{\lambda}{8}\int \frac{\nabla\rho(r)\cdot\nabla\rho(r)}{\rho(r)}dV, \lambda = \frac{1}{5},$$

$$E_V = -Z\int \frac{\rho(r)}{r}dV,$$

$$E_J = \frac{1}{2} \int\int \frac{\rho(r_1)\rho(r_2)}{r_{12}} dV_1 dV_2,$$

$$E_X = -\alpha \frac{3}{4} \left(\frac{3}{\pi}\right)^{1/3} \int \rho(r)^{4/3} dV, \alpha \approx 1.05,$$

$$E_C = (-0.01383Z + 0.1357 - 0.2582/Z) \int \rho(r) dV.$$

The last formula is a conjecture by the author based on computations of atomic correlation energies. It is most convenient to carry out all the integrals numerically. The energy functional $E[\rho(r)]$, based on the selected shielding parameters $\sigma_1, \ldots, \sigma_5$, is computed and compared with the exact (non-relativistic) energy of the atom. By the second Hohenberg–Kohn theorem, the optimized energy for the functional form of $\rho(r)$ is a minimum, although short of the exact energy.

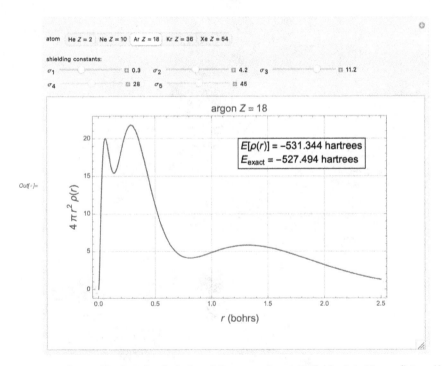

Demonstration 7.15: Density Functional Computations on Noble Gas Atoms (https://demonstrations.wolfram.com/DensityFunctionalComputationsOnNobleGasAtoms/)

7.6. Molecules 1

7.6.1. *Formulas and Structures for Some Simple Molecules*

A chemical formula specifies the number of atoms of each element in a compound. The connection formula shows the topology, how the

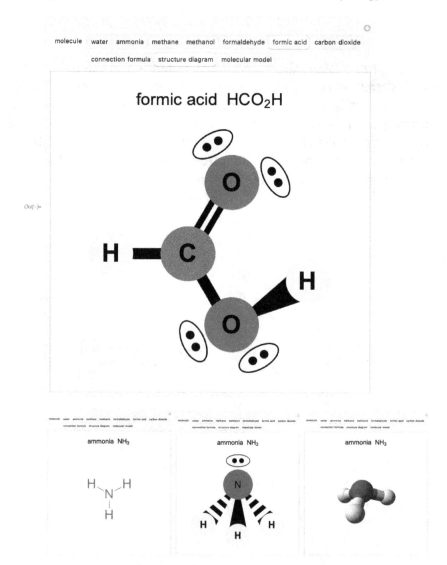

Demonstration 7.16: Formulas and Structures for Some Simple Molecules (https://demonstrations.wolfram.com/FormulasAndStructuresForSomeSimpleMolecules/)

atoms are connected by chemical bonds, usually without regard to their geometry. The actual geometric shape of a molecule can be represented by a structure diagram. This also includes the location of unshared pairs of electrons, which strongly influence the geometry. A Natta projection shows a bond projecting toward the viewer as a solid wedge, while a receding bond is shown as a dashed wedge. In this Demonstration, you can also choose to view a "ball and stick" molecular model. Beginning students in chemistry should become familiar with all these alternative descriptions of molecular structure.

7.6.2. *Making Some Simple Molecules*

The prototype elements with valence 1, 2, 3, and 4 are H, O, N, and C, respectively. Some simple compounds, particularly those of special importance in biology, can be made from combinations of these elements. For each choice of two or more elements, two representative molecules are shown. (The combinations C, N and C, N, O are omitted.)

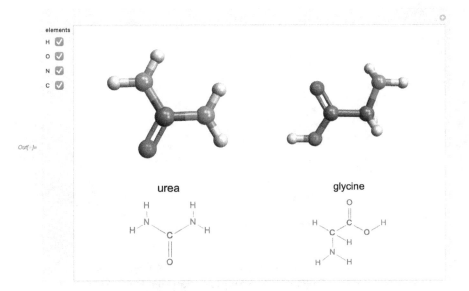

Demonstration 7.17: Making Some Simple Molecules (https://demonstrations.wolfram.com/MakingSomeSimpleMolecules/)

7.6.3. *Bonding and Antibonding Molecular Orbitals*

The lowest-energy bonding and antibonding molecular orbitals (MO) for a homonuclear diatomic molecule are shown, as the internuclear distance R is varied. These MOs are designated $1\sigma_g$ (or $1s\sigma$) and $1\sigma_u$ (or $1s\sigma^*$), respectively. The red contours designate negative values of the wavefunction. In the separated atom limit (large R), the MOs approach a pair of non-interacting $1s$ atomic orbitals. In the united atom limit ($R = 0$), the $1\sigma_g$ and $1\sigma_u$ collapse to $1s$ and $2p_z$ atomic orbitals, respectively. At the equilibrium internuclear distance, when the red dot is at the minimum of the energy curve, the bonding orbital is optimally effective.

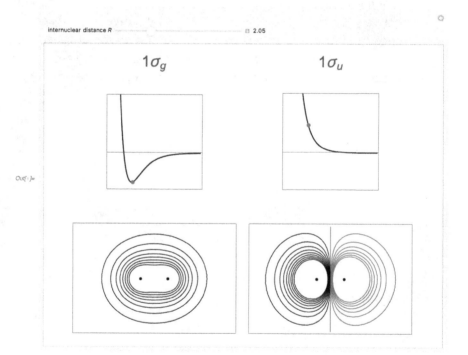

Demonstration 7.18: Bonding and Antibonding Molecular Orbitals (https://demonstrations.wolfram.com/BondingAndAntibondingMolecularOrbitals/)

7.6.4. *Valence-Bond Theory of the Hydrogen Molecule*

The first successful explanation of chemical bonding using quantum mechanics was provided by the simple computation of Heitler and London on the hydrogen molecule H_2 in 1927, only one year after the Schrödinger equation was proposed. This gave the first rational explanation of the chemical concept of the covalent electron-pair bond, proposed by G. N. Lewis in 1916 and Irving Langmuir in 1919. The hydrogen molecule has a binding energy of $D_e = 4.748\,\text{eV}$ (not including the zero-point vibrational energy). This represents the minimum of the Born–Oppenheimer potential curve for H_2 at an internuclear separation of $R_e = 1.401$ bohrs ($0.7414\,\text{Å}$). This is shown as a thick black curve representing the $^1\Sigma_g$ ground electronic state. As $R \to \infty$, the molecule dissociates into two hydrogen atoms in their $1s$ ground states, with antiparallel spins. Also shown, in red, is the antibonding $^3\Sigma_u$ potential curve for two hydrogen atoms with parallel spins.

The Hamiltonian for the H_2 molecule, within the Born–Oppenheimer approximation, consists of the kinetic energies of the two electrons added to six Coulombic potential-energy contributions. In atomic units ($\hbar = m = e = 1$):

$$H = -\frac{1}{2}\nabla_1^2 - \frac{1}{2}\nabla_2^2 - \frac{1}{r_{1a}} - \frac{1}{r_{2a}} - \frac{1}{r_{1b}} - \frac{1}{r_{2a}} + \frac{1}{r_{12}} + \frac{1}{R},$$

where r_{1a} is the distance between electron 1 and proton a, and so forth, r_{12} is the instantaneous distance between the two electrons, and R is the internuclear separation. Since the hydrogen molecule H_2 is formed from a combination of hydrogen atoms a and b, one might consider as a primitive first approximation a product of hydrogen atom $1s$ functions centered on protons a and b, respectively:

$$\Psi(r_1, r_2) \approx \phi_{1s}(r_{1a})\phi_{1s}(r_{2b}).$$

This gives a binding energy $D_e \approx 0.25\,\text{eV}$ at a nuclear separation of $R_e \approx 1.7$ bohrs, indicating that the hydrogen atoms can indeed form a stable molecule. However, the calculated energy is over an order of magnitude too small to account for the strongly bound hydrogen molecule.

Heisenberg had suggested that a wavefunction should be symmetrical (or antisymmetrical) with respect to interchange of its electron labels, to take account of the indistinguishability of identical particles. Heitler and London took this into account by adding a term to the wavefunction in which the electron labels are reversed. The approximate wavefunction with appropriate exchange symmetry can be written

$$\Psi(r_1, r_2) \approx [\phi_{1s}(r_{1a})\phi_{1s}(r_{2b}) \pm \phi_{1s}(r_{1b})\phi_{1s}(r_{2a})]/\sqrt{2 \pm 2S^2}.$$

The function is normalized, with introduction of the overlap integral $S = \langle \phi_{1s}(r_{1a}) | \phi_{1s}(r_{1b}) \rangle$. The plus and minus signs apply to the bonding and repulsive states, respectively. The computed result (augmented by an integral evaluated by Sugiura) gave a much more realistic binding energy value of 3.156 eV, with $R_e \approx 1.64$ bohrs.

A further improvement was implemented by Wang using scaled $1s$ functions of the form $\phi_\alpha(r) = \sqrt{\frac{\alpha^3}{\pi}}e^{-\alpha r}$, with α treated as a variational parameter chosen so as to minimize the molecular energy (rather than keeping $\alpha = 1$, as in the hydrogen atom). The variational energy can be expressed $\varepsilon(R, \alpha) = \frac{H_{11}(R,\alpha)+H_{12}(R,\alpha)}{1+S(R,\alpha)^2}$, with $H_{11}(R, \alpha) = \langle \phi_\alpha(r_{1a})\phi_\alpha(r_{2b})|$ $H\phi_\alpha(r_{1a})\phi_\alpha(r_{2b}) \rangle$ and $H_{12}(R, \alpha) = \langle \phi_\alpha(r_{1a})\phi_\alpha(r_{2b})|H\phi_\alpha(r_{1b})\phi_\alpha(r_{2a}) \rangle$. The minimum is obtained at $R_e = 1.406$ bohr with $\alpha = 1.166$, giving a binding energy of $D_e = \varepsilon - 2E_H = 3.7843$ eV. With selection of the setter "Wang", the graphic shows solid blue curves for varying α in the vicinity of the minimum in the potential curve. The energy values for a given α are not significant for any larger range of R. Also shown, as a dashed blue curve, is the original Heitler–London computation, with $\alpha = 1$ throughout.

The last enhancement we consider explicitly is the inclusion of ionic-covalent resonance. Linus Pauling recognized that the "true" structure of a molecule such as H_2 was actually a "resonance hybrid", an admixture of some ionic character H^+H^- and H^-H^+ into the purely covalent structure $H : H$. Weinbaum suggested a variational function of the form $\sqrt{1-\lambda}\Psi_{cov}(R, \alpha) + \sqrt{\lambda}\Psi_{ion}(R, \alpha)$, to be optimized with respect to the two parameters α and λ. You can generate the curve shown in green by varying these parameters. The optimum values are $\alpha = 1.193$,

$\lambda = 0.0615$, yielding a binding energy of 4.024 eV at $R_e = 1.416$ bohrs. This value λ implies that inclusion of about 6% ionic structure optimizes the computation based on this function.

Further small improvements, which we do not enumerate, were obtained by consideration of "polarization" of each $1s$ atomic function in the direction of the opposite atom by addition of some $2p$ character.

The plots shown can be magnified, to focus in on the region around the minimum.

The definitive computation on the hydrogen molecule, and in a sense an affirming verification of the validity of the many-particle Schrödinger equation, was the work of James and Coolidge. They used a 13-term linear variational method based on prolate spheroidal (also known

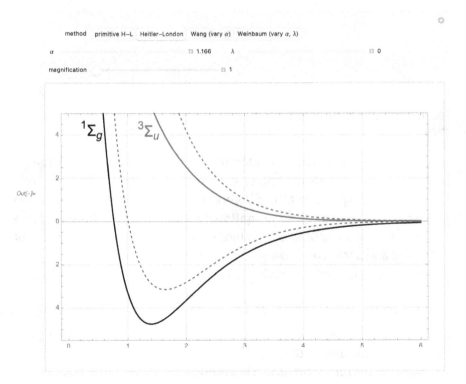

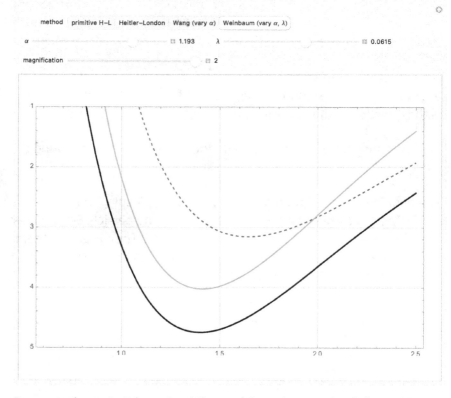

method   primitive H–L   Heitler–London   Wang (vary α)   Weinbaum (vary α, λ)

α ⋯⋯⋯⋯⋯⋯⋯⋯⋯⋯⋯⋯⋯⋯⋯ | 1.193 λ ⋯⋯⋯⋯⋯⋯⋯⋯⋯⋯⋯⋯ | 0.0615

magnification ⋯⋯⋯⋯⋯⋯⋯⋯⋯⋯⋯⋯⋯⋯⋯ | 2

Demonstration 7.19: Valence-Bond Theory of the Hydrogen Molecule (https://demons trations.wolfram.com/ValenceBondTheoryOfTheHydrogenMolecule/)

as confocal elliptical) coordinates to obtain the values $D_e = 4.720\,\text{eV}$, $R_e = 1.40$ bohrs, within the known experimental values at the time. (This is a possible subject of a future Demonstration.) More recently, with the advent of high-powered computational capability, even more accurate results have been obtained, including a 100-parameter extension of Coolidge and James and corrections for the Born-Oppenheimer approximation and relativistic contributions.

7.6.5. *Molecular Orbitals for Diatomic Molecules*

This Demonstration considers the molecular orbitals for the diatomic molecules H_2 through Ne_2. The conceptual relationship to the constituent atomic orbitals is shown in a schematic energy diagram.

Antibonding MOs are shown in red. The bond order of a molecule is defined as the number of electrons occupying bonding MOs minus the number occupying antibonding MOs, all divided by 2, to coincide with the conventional chemical definition of single, double, and triple bonds. The molecules He_2 and weakly Ne_2 have bond orders equal to 0, and exist only as weakly associated van der Waals dimers. Be_2 also has bond order 0, but forms a weak chemical bond attributed to some $2s$-$2p$ hybridization. The "molecular data" checkbox brings up the ground state electron configuration and spectroscopic designation for each diatomic. The dissociation energy D_e is also given, showing an expected increase with bond order.

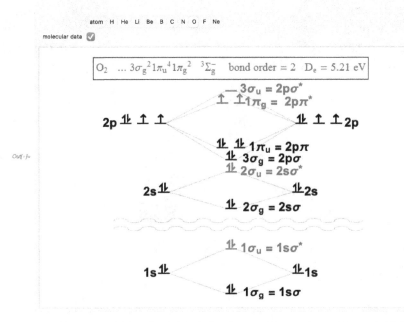

Demonstration 7.20: Molecular Orbitals for First- and Second-Row Diatomic Molecules (https://demonstrations.wolfram.com/MolecularOrbitalsForFirstAndSecondRowDiatomicMolecules/)

7.6.6. *Non-Crossing Rule for Energy Curves*

Let $E_1(R)$ and $E_2(R)$ be energy curves for two different electronic states of a diatomic molecule, both computed within the Born–Oppenheimer approximation. If the two states belong to different symmetry species, say Σ and Π, *u* and *g*, or singlet and triplet, there is no restriction on whether the curves can cross. If, however, the two states have the same symmetry, a non-crossing rule applies. Close approach of the two curves results in mutual repulsion, known as an anticrossing. For near degeneracy of $E_1(R)$ and $E_2(R)$, a perturbation $V_{12}(R)$, representing higher-order contributions in the Born–Oppenheimer approximation, becomes significant, giving mixed states that do not cross.

In this Demonstration, the lower energy state, $E_1(R)$, is drawn in blue. It is assumed to be a bonding state, with dissociation energy D_e and equilibrium internuclear distance R_e, which can both be varied with sliders. The upper energy state, $E_2(R)$, drawn in red, is assumed to be a repulsive state. The mixing parameter V_{12} can also be varied. In certain cases, the upper state can develop a minimum as a result of the V_{12} interaction. The dashed curves in the graphic pertain to the case when $V_{12}(R) = 0$.

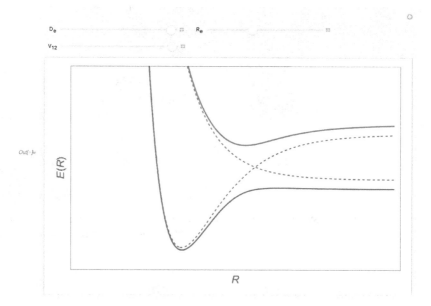

Demonstration 7.21: Non-Crossing Rule for Energy Curves in Diatomic Molecules (https://demonstrations.wolfram.com/NonCrossingRuleForEnergyCurvesInDiatomic Molecules/)

7.7. Molecules 2

7.7.1. *Energy Levels of a Morse Oscillator*

The Morse function $V(R) = D_e(e^{-2a(R-R_e)} - 2e^{-a(R-R_e)})$, where R is the internuclear distance, provides a useful approximation for the potential energy of a diatomic molecule. It is superior to the harmonic oscillator model in that it can account for anharmonicity and bond dissociation. The relevant experimental parameters are the dissociation energy D_e and the fundamental vibrational frequency ω_e, both conventionally expressed in wavenumbers (cm^{-1}), the equilibrium internuclear distance R_e in Angstrom units (Å), and the reduced mass $\mu = m_1 m_2/(m_1 + m_2)$ in atomic mass units (amu). The exponential parameter is given by $a = \omega_e \sqrt{\mu/2D_e}$ in appropriate units. The Schrödinger equation for the Morse oscillator is exactly solvable, giving

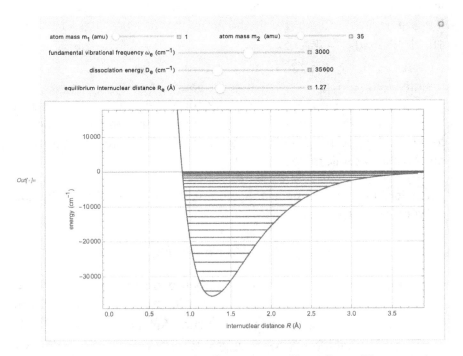

Demonstration 7.22: Energy Levels of a Morse Oscillator (https://demonstrations. wolfram.com/EnergyLevelsOfAMorseOscillator/)

the vibrational eigenvalues $\varepsilon_v = \omega_e\left(v+\frac{1}{2}\right) - \frac{\omega_e^2}{4D_e}\left(v+\frac{1}{2}\right)^2$, for $v = 0, 1, 2, \ldots, v_{max}$. Unlike the harmonic oscillator, the Morse potential has a finite number of bound vibrational levels with $v_{max} \approx 2D_e/\omega_e$.

7.7.2. *WKB Computation on Morse Potential*

The semiclassical Wentzel–Kramers–Brillouin (WKB) method applied to one-dimensional problems with bound states often reduces to the Sommerfeld–Wilson quantization conditions, the cyclic phase-space integrals $\oint \sqrt{2\mu[E - V(x)]}dx = \left(n+\frac{1}{2}\right)h$. It turns out that this formula gives the exact bound-state energies for the Morse oscillator with $V(x) = D(e^{-2a(x-x_0)} - 2e^{-a(x-x_0)})$. The requisite integral can be reduced to $2\int_{x_1}^{x_2}\sqrt{E - V(x)}dx$, in which x_1 and x_2 are the classical turning points $x_{1,2} = x_0 + \frac{1}{a}\log\left[\frac{D}{E}\left(-1\pm\sqrt{1+\frac{E}{D}}\right)\right]$. The integral can be done "by hand", using the transformation $r = e^{a(x-x_0)}$ followed by a contour integration in the complex plane, but *Mathematica* can evaluate the integral explicitly, needing only the additional fact that $\log(-1) = i\pi$. The result reads $\frac{2\pi\sqrt{2\mu}}{a}(\sqrt{D}+\sqrt{-E}) = \left(n+\frac{1}{2}\right)h$, which can be solved for E to give $E_n = -D + a\sqrt{2D}\left(n+\frac{1}{2}\right) - \frac{a^2}{2}\left(n+\frac{1}{2}\right)^2, n = 0, 1, 2, \ldots, n_{max}$, in units with $\hbar = \mu = 1$. The highest bound state is given by $n_{max} = [\sqrt{2D}/a]$, where [ ] represents the integer part of the number. The values of D, a, and x_0 (expressed in atomic units) used in this Demonstration are for illustrative purposes only and are not necessarily representative of any actual diatomic molecule.

A particle in a one-dimensional potential can be described by the Schrödinger equation:

$$-\frac{\hbar^2}{2\mu}\psi''(x) + V(x)\psi(x) = E\psi(x).$$

The semiclassical or WKB method is based on the ansatz $\psi(x) = A(x)e^{iS(x)/\hbar}$. In the limit as $\hbar \to 0$, $S(x)$ in the exponential satisfies the Hamilton-Jacobi equation for the action function $E = \frac{1}{2\mu}\left(\frac{dS}{dx}\right)^2 + V(x)$, with one solution $S(x) = \sqrt{2\mu[E - V(x)]}$. It is then shown in most graduate-level texts on quantum mechanics (e.g. Schiff, Merzbacher,

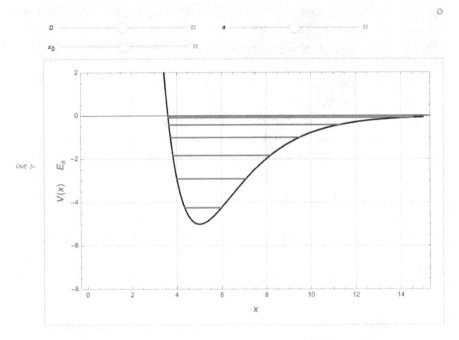

Demonstration 7.23: WKB Computations on Morse Potential (https://demonstrations. wolfram.com/WKBComputationsOnMorsePotential/)

etc.) that this usually leads to the Sommerfeld–Wilson quantum conditions on periodic orbits $\oint \sqrt{2\mu[E - V(x)]}dx = \left(n + \frac{1}{2}\right)h$, $0, 1, 2, \ldots$. For one-dimensional problems, the cyclic integral can be replaced by $2 \int_{x_1}^{x_2}$, where x_1, x_2 are the classical turning points of the motion and $E = V(x)$.

7.7.3. *Franck-Condon Principle*

When a diatomic molecule undergoes a transition to an excited electronic state higher by ΔE_{elec}, it generally changes its vibrational and rotational quantum numbers as well. In the liquid state, the individual rotational levels are not generally resolved and the resulting process is characterized as a *vibronic transition*. Both the ground and excited electronic states are represented by potential energy curves, shown in blue and red, respectively, on the left-hand graphic. The probability densities of the first few ground state and excited-state vibrational levels,

$|\psi_{v'}^{(0)}|^2$, and $|\psi_{v'}^{(1)}|^2$, are shown, superposed on the vibrational energy-level diagrams, with $v = 0, 1, 2, \ldots$. Here the superscripts refer to the electronic state, while the subscripts label the vibrational level.

At normal temperatures, only the $v = 0$ vibrational level of the ground state is occupied. When a molecule absorbs a photon in an electronic transition, the electrons can rearrange themselves much more rapidly than the much heavier nuclei (consistent with the Born–Oppenheimer approximation). Thus, electronic transition can be approximated by the vertical blue arrow to internuclear distances R in the excited state very close to its maximum value in the ground state. This leads to a mixture of several excited-state vibrational levels, predominated by the level that overlaps maximally with the $\psi_0^{(0)}$ wavefunction. According to the Franck–Condon principle, the relative intensities of the individual vibrational peaks are proportional to the factors $|\langle \psi_{v'}^{(1)} | \psi_0^{(0)} \rangle|^2$. This gives rise to an absorption spectrum shown in blue in the right-hand graphic. The

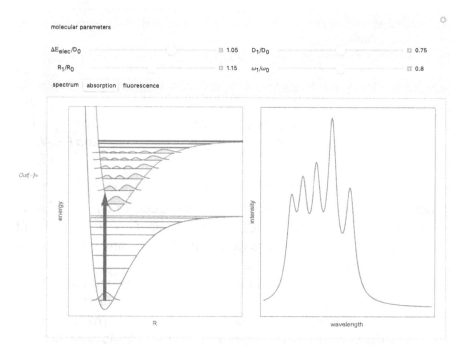

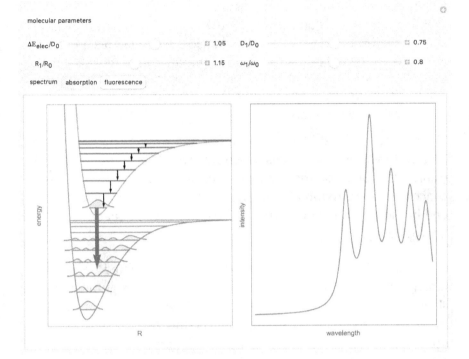

molecular parameters

| $\Delta E_{elec}/D_0$ | 1.05 | D_1/D_0 | 0.75 |
| R_1/R_0 | 1.15 | ω_1/ω_0 | 0.8 |

spectrum   absorption   fluorescence

energy

R

intensity

wavelength

Demonstration 7.24: Franck-Condon Principle in Vibronic Transitions (https://demons trations.wolfram.com/FranckCondonPrincipleInVibronicTransitions/)

relative intensity of the vibrational components depends on the molecular parameters of the two electronic states, but most sensitively on the difference between equilibrium internuclear distances, R_0 and R_1.

A molecule excited in an electronically allowed transition will generally return to its ground electronic state, a process called *fluorescence*, within the order of a few nanoseconds. Before it does so, most of the excited molecules will decay to the lowest vibrational state $\psi_0^{(1)}$ by radiationless transition processes (for example, molecular collisions). These are represented in the upper curve by a series of black arrows. Fluorescence will then produce a series of peaks corresponding to different vibrational levels of the ground state, with intensities proportional to the Franck–Condon factors $|\langle \psi_{v'}^{(0)} | \psi_0^{(1)} \rangle|^2$. Because of the geometry of the energy curves, the fluorescent spectrum is very nearly a mirror image of the absorption spectrum, with the transitions $v' = 0 \leftrightarrow v'' = 0$, meaning that this same transition occurs in both the absorption and fluorescence spectra. In this Demonstration, the Franck–Condon factors and spectral intensities are simulated since explicit computation would take too long.

7.7.4. *Hydrides as Isoelectronic Perturbations of the Neon Atom*

The second-row hydrides hydrogen fluoride HF, water H_2O, ammonia NH_3 and methane CH_4 are isoelectronic with the Ne atom. The electronic structures for these 10-electron systems can be obtained, in concept, by perturbations on the Ne atom, in which protons are embedded in the electron cloud, while the central nuclear charge is reduced appropriately.

The electronic structure of the molecule is represented using density functional theory. You can attempt to minimize the energy by varying the shielding parameters σ_1, σ_2 and the bond distance R. The results will, of necessity, be approximate, owing to the limitation in the density function $\rho(r)$. Computed Hartree–Fock energies and experimental bond distance are shown for comparison. Minimization with respect to R is especially delicate, so do not expect an accurate result for the bond distance.

The 10-electron density function is approximated by

$$\rho(r) = 2\frac{(Z - \sigma_1)^3}{\pi}e^{-2(Z-\sigma_1)r} + 8\frac{(Z - \sigma_2)^5}{96\pi}r^2 e^{-(Z - \sigma_2)r}.$$

The resulting density functional contains the usual forms for kinetic and potential energies, plus the additional contributions from the hydrogen atoms in HF, H_2O, NH_3 and CH_4.

Experimental values of parameters: HF: $R = 1.733$; H_2O: $R = 1.809$, $\Phi = 104.5°$; NH_3: $R = 1.922$, $\Phi = 106.5°$; CH_4: $R = 2.067$, $\Phi = 109.5°$. Approximate Hartree–Fock energies (hartrees): Ne: -128.5, HF: -105.2, H_2O: -76.1, NH_3: -56.2, CH_4: -40.2.

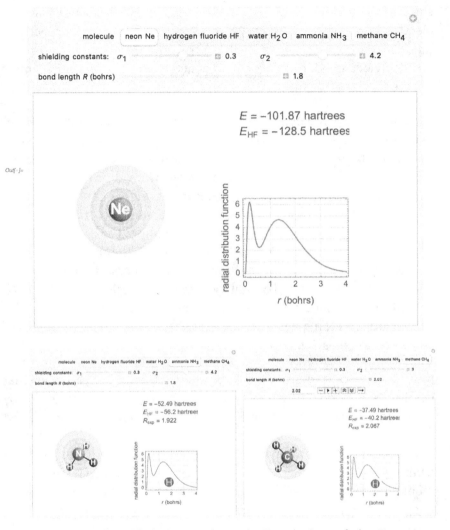

Demonstration 7.25: Hydrides as Isoelectronic Perturbations of the Neon Atom (https://demonstrations.wolfram.com/HydridesAsIsoelectronicPerturbationsOfTheNeon Atom/)

7.7.5. *Second-Row Hydrides*

The simplest hydrides of boron, carbon, nitrogen and oxygen provide a elementary picture of atomic orbitals, hybridization and chemical bonding very instructive for beginning chemistry students. The valence shells of the free atoms of B, C, N and O in their ground states have the electron configurations $2s^2 2p$, $2s^2 2p^2$, $2s^2 2p^3$, and $2s^2 2p^4$, respectively (apart from their $1s^2$ inner shells). The three degenerate $2p$ orbitals are singly occupied, except for O, in which one of the $2p$ orbitals must double up.

Carbon, with its two unpaired electrons, appears to be naturally divalent, and indeed the compound CH_2 can exist in the gas phase. But much more stable compounds can be formed if carbon invests a relatively small amount of energy to excite one of its $2s$ electrons to the remaining $2p$ orbital, and becomes quadrivalent, thus recouping the $2s - 2p$ excitation energy in the formation of two additional chemical bonds. A further transformation, first suggested by Linus Pauling, is the linear combination of the nearly degenerate $2s$ and three $2p$ orbitals into four identically shaped hybrid orbitals, directed toward the corners of a tetrahedron. These are called sp^3 hybrid orbitals, which can be designated t_1, t_2, t_3, t_4. Indeed, the methane molecule CH_4 formed by covalent bonding with four hydrogen atoms has a tetrahedral shape with identical angles of $109.5°$ between each pair of C-H bonds.

Nitrogen and oxygen also tend to produce tetrahedral hybrids in what can be designated as their "valence states", a concept introduced by J. H. Van Vleck and W. E. Moffitt, as the conceptual precursor of bond formation to hydrogens (or other elements). Except when four identical atoms bond to the central atom, the hybrids are slightly distorted from a perfect tetrahedral shape. This picture can be subsumed by the VSEPR model of chemical bonding, in which bonds and lone pairs of electrons adopt a configuration determined by their maximized repulsions.

Nitrogen expresses its natural trivalence to form the ammonia molecule NH_3. It still has an approximately tetrahedral structure with a lone pair of electrons occupying one of the vertices. The N-H bond angles are reduced to $107.8°$ because the lone pair repels the N-H bonds. Adding an additional proton produces the ammonium ion NH_4^+, which is again a perfect tetrahedron.

The best-known compound of oxygen and essential for life is, of course, water H_2O, which forms two bonds to hydrogen atoms in addition to the two lone pairs. The H-O-H angle is reduced to 104.5° by repulsion of the lone pairs. A principal component of acids is the hydronium ion H_3O^+, with a structure analogous to ammonia. When water is involved in hydrogen bonding, the oxygen can momentarily be surrounded by four hydrogen atoms or ions in a tetrahedral configuration. This is approximated in the structure of ice.

Boron is an instance of an "electron-deficient" species. Somewhat boldly we imagine a valence state with one empty tetrahedral orbital. This can also be pictured as a resonance hybrid in which the 3 electrons are distributed among the 4 tetrahedral lobes (with an average of 3/4 of an electron per orbital). This works to account for the tetrahedral structure of the borohydride ion BH_4^-, which requires combination with three hydrogen atoms, as well as a hydride ion H^-. A long controversial problem in chemistry was the structure of diborane B_2H_6. We propose the

hydride formation $C \to CH_4$ $N \to NH_3$ $N \to NH_4^+$ $O \to H_2O$ $O \to H_3O^+$ $B \to BH_4^-$ $B \to B_2H_6$

show   valence state ☑   add hydrogen atoms ☑   molecule plot ☑

Out[ ]=

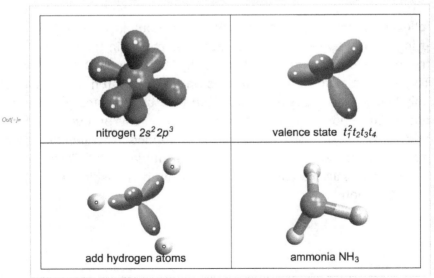

nitrogen $2s^2 2p^3$ valence state $t_1^2 t_2 t_3 t_4$

add hydrogen atoms   ammonia NH_3

hydride formation $C \rightarrow CH_4$ $N \rightarrow NH_3$ $N \rightarrow NH_4^+$ $O \rightarrow H_2O$ $O \rightarrow H_3O^+$ $B \rightarrow BH_4^-$ $B \rightarrow B_2H_6$

show   valence state ☑   add hydrogen atoms ☑   molecule plot ☑

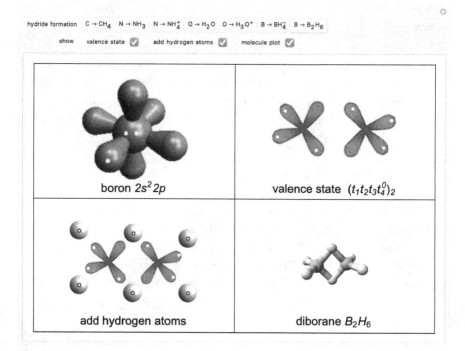

boron $2s^2 2p$	valence state $(t_1 t_2 t_3 t_4^0)_2$
add hydrogen atoms	diborane B_2H_6

Demonstration 7.26: Structure and bonding of second-row hydrides (https://arxiv.org/abs/1409.1190)

following picture, beginning with two boron atoms in juxtaposition occupying their hypothetical valence states, as shown in the graphic. Four hydrogen atoms can be added "normally" to the ends of the molecule. The four remaining valence orbitals on the two boron atoms, having only two electrons between them, can then be imagined to form four one-electron bonds with two hydrogen atoms. This produces a unique bridged structure, which has been amply verified experimentally. One-electron bonds are known to exist, for example in the H_2^+ molecule-ion. Alternatively the two B-H-B bridges can be classified as 3-center, 2-electron bonds.

7.7.6. *Ammonia Inversion*

The ammonia molecule NH_3 has a trigonal pyramidal configuration, with the nitrogen atom connected to three hydrogen atoms. The molecule readily undergoes inversion at room temperature, like an umbrella turning itself inside out in a strong wind. The energy barrier to this inversion is 24.2 kJ/mol. A resonance frequency of 24.87 GHz, in the microwave region, corresponds to the energy splitting of the two lowest vibrational levels. This transition is exploited in the ammonia maser.

In quantum mechanics, ammonia inversion can be described by a simplified Schrödinger equation

$$-\frac{1}{2\mu}\psi_n''(x) + V(x)\psi_n(x) = E_n\psi_n(x),$$

where x is the axial position of the nitrogen atom. The appropriate reduced mass is given by

$$\mu = \frac{3m_N m_H}{m_N + 3m_H}.$$

We consider a model for the potential energy of the form

$$V(x) = \frac{k(x^2 - r^2)^2}{8r^2} = \frac{kr^2}{8} - \frac{kx^2}{4} + \frac{kx^4}{8r^2},$$

where r is the N-H bond distance. The value at $x = 0$ gives the inversion barrier $V_0 = \frac{kr^2}{8}$.

Since the Hamiltonian contains only even powers of p and x, a representation based on the ladder operators a and $a^\dagger$ suggests a generalization of the canonical operator formulation for the harmonic oscillator.

The computation results in a secular equation for the eigenvalues, which are plotted on the graph superposed on the potential energy curve. The blue and red lines correspond to eigenstates that are, respectively, symmetric and antisymmetric with respect to inversion. The eigenvalues tend to occur in closely spaced pairs, with the $E_1 - E_0$ splitting representing the transition in the ammonia maser. The optimal choice of adjustable parameters is shown by clicking "optimize".

The ladder operators can be defined by

$$a = \sqrt{\frac{\mu\omega}{2}}x + i\sqrt{\frac{1}{2\mu\omega}}p,$$

$$a^\dagger = \sqrt{\frac{\mu\omega}{2}}x - i\sqrt{\frac{1}{2\mu\omega}}p,$$

model   classical   quantum

show oscillation   ▶ ‖ ◀

Out[ ]=

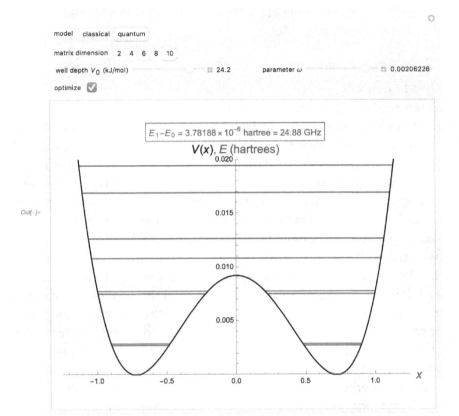

model   classical   quantum

matrix dimension   2 4 6 8 10

well depth V_0 (kJ/mol)   24.2   parameter ω 0.00206226

optimize ✓

$E_1 - E_0 = 3.78188 \times 10^{-6}$ hartree = 24.88 GHz

$V(x)$, E (hartrees)

Demonstration 7.27: Ammonia Inversion — Classical and Quantum Models (https://demonstrations.wolfram.com/AmmoniaInversionClassicalAndQuantumModels/). See also https://arxiv.org/abs/1809.08178

with an adjustable parameter ω introduced. The non-vanishing matrix elements of the Hamiltonian can then be computed, giving

$$H_{n,n} = \frac{1}{32}\left(\frac{(6n^2 + 6n + 3)k}{r^2\mu^2\omega^2} + 4kr^2 - \frac{(8n+4)k}{\mu\omega} + (16n+8)\omega\right),$$

$$H_{n+2,n} = H_{n,n+2} = \sqrt{(n+1)(n+2)}$$
$$\times \frac{(-4r^2\mu^2\omega^3 + (2n+3-2r^2\mu\omega)k)}{16r^2\mu^2\omega^2},$$

$$H_{n+4,n} = H_{n,n+4} = \frac{\sqrt{(n+1)(n+2)(n+3)(n+4)}k}{32r^2\mu^2\omega^2}.$$

The eigenvalues are then determined using the `Eigenvalue` routine for selected dimensions 2 to 10.

7.7.7. *Berry Pseudorotation in Phosphorus Pentafluoride*

The PF_5 molecule has the configuration of a trigonal bipyramid, as predicted by the VSEPR model. Two of the fluorine atoms, designated as *axial*, are aligned with the phosphorus atom, with P-F bond distances of 1.58 Å. The remaining three fluorine atoms, designated as *equatorial*, are arranged in an equilateral triangle with P-F bond distances of 1.53 Å. Even though there exist two geometrically inequivalent types of fluorine atoms, the NMR spectrum of the molecule shows but a single resonance frequency. This indicates that the axial and equatorial ^{19}F nuclei exchange their environments more rapidly than the time it takes to make the NMR measurement. Thus only a single resonance peak is seen. R. S. Berry proposed a mechanism for atomic rearrangement, known as *pseudorotation*, since it simulates a rotation of the axial direction of the molecule. According to the proposed mechanism, one of the equatorial bonds serves as a pivot while the two axial bonds bend into two sides of an equilateral triangle. Simultaneously, the remaining two equatorial bonds line up to become the new axial bonds. Quantum-chemical computations predict a barrier of approximately 16 kJ/mol, which permits rapid tunneling between configurations at room temperature.

Either equilibrium configuration of the PF_5 molecule is a trigonal bipyramid belonging to the symmetry group D_{3h}. The intermediate configuration, or transition state, is a square pyramid belonging to the symmetry group C_{4v}. The check box enables you to see the square pyramid traced out for $t \approx 0.5$. Molecules that can undergo rapid dynamical interchanges between symmetry-equivalent configurations are termed *fluxional molecules*.

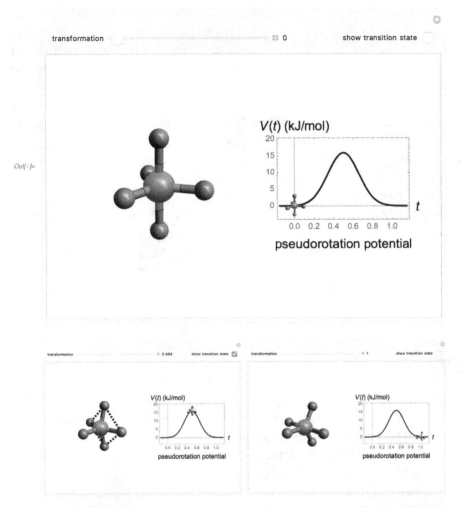

Demonstration 7.28: Berry Pseudorotation in Phosphorus Pentafluoride (https://demonstrations.wolfram.com/BerryPseudorotationInPhosphorusPentafluoride/)

7.8. Molecules 3

7.8.1. *Rotation about Carbon-Carbon Bonds*

Carbon-carbon single bonds enable essentially free rotation about their axes. There is actually a small torsional barrier of about 12 kJ/mol (compared to the C-C bond energy of 350 kJ/mol), which slightly favors the staggered over the eclipsed conformation of the two methyl groups in ethane. To a good approximation, each carbon atom forms four σ bonds from sp^3 hybrid orbitals directed towards the vertices of a regular tetrahedron.

Each carbon atom involved in a C=C double bond forms three σ bonds from sp^2 hybrids, in the same plane, approximately 120° apart. The remaining p-orbitals on the two carbon atoms form a π-bond, which together with the σ constitutes a C=C double bond. In contrast to a single bond, a double bond forms a rigid planar structure, with only a small amplitude of torsional motion allowed. If two of the hydrogen atoms in ethylene (ethene) are replaced by chlorine atoms, cis and trans isomers, molecules with distinct physical properties, become possible. (These isomeric forms can be interconverted at higher temperatures or by UV radiation.)

A C≡C triple bond, which has two orthogonal π-bonds between the two carbon atoms, is, like a single bond, cylindrically symmetrical and allows free rotation. This is most evident in a molecule such as dimethylacetylene. The central C–C bond in the biphenyl molecule represents an instance in which a single bond exhibits restricted rotation. In this case, the cause is steric hindrance between adjacent hydrogen atoms on the two rings. The most stable dihedral angle between the rings is about 39°. Rotation becomes even more restricted when larger groups are substituted for hydrogens.

The ball-and-stick models of the molecules illustrated in the graphics are intended to optimize display of rotational effects. Some distortions of atomic sizes have been introduced.

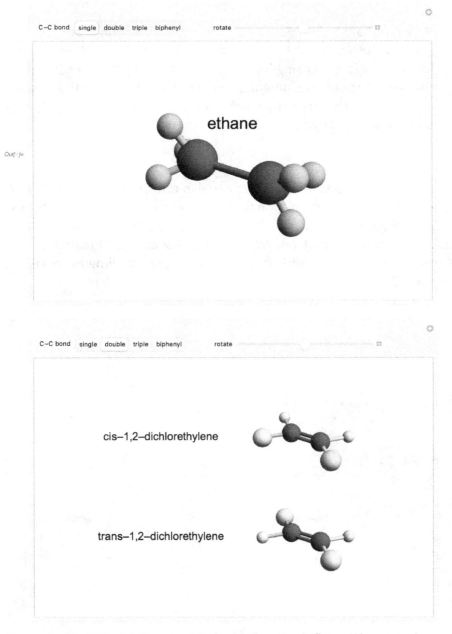

Demonstration 7.29: Rotation about Carbon-Carbon Bonds (https://demonstrations. wolfram.com/RotationAboutCarbonCarbonBonds/)

7.8.2. *Internal Rotation in Ethane*

Rotation about C–C single bonds has been a topic of interest in chemistry since the 1870s. It has been found that the rotation is often hindered by torsional forces arising from interactions among the substituents on the carbon atoms. The potential energy of interaction for the torsional motion of ethane CH_3–CH_3, or substituted ethanes such as CX_3–CY_3, can be approximated by a potential energy of the form

$$V(\theta) = \frac{1}{2}V_0(1 - \cos 3\theta),$$

where the torsional energy is set equal to zero when $\theta = 0, 2\pi/3, 4\pi/3$ or π (or $0°, \pm120°$), corresponding to *staggered* configurations of the two methyl groups. The barrier height V_0 is generally in the range of 10 to 20 kJ/mol. For completely free internal rotation of two methyl groups, we have $V_0 \approx 0$, which is well approximated in dimethyl acetylene CH_3–$C\equiv C$–CH_3.

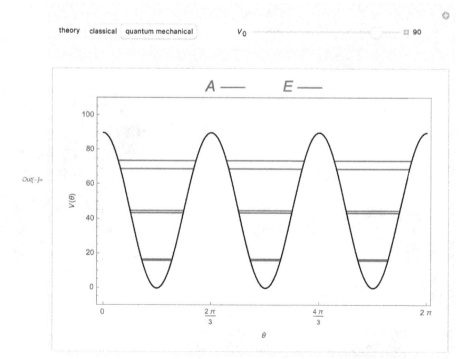

theory classical quantum mechanical V_0 ⚏ 50

energy   ⚏ 40   rotate ▶ ‖ ⏮

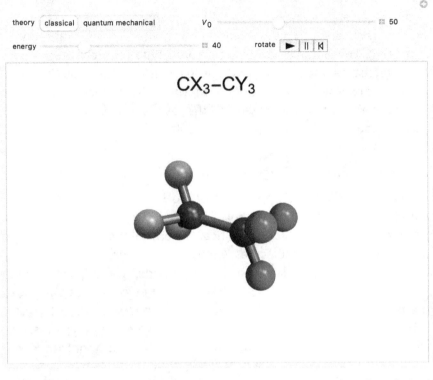

$$CX_3 - CY_3$$

Demonstration 7.30: Internal Rotation in Ethane and Substituted Analogs (https://demonstrations.wolfram.com/InternalRotationInEthaneAndSubstitutedAnalogs/)

The Schrödinger equation for the torsional motion can be written

$$-\frac{\hbar^2}{2\mathcal{I}}\frac{d^2}{d\theta^2}\psi(\theta) + \frac{1}{2}V_0(1 - \cos 3\theta)\psi(\theta) = \varepsilon\psi(\theta),$$

where $\mathcal{I}$ is the reduced moment of inertia of the two counter-rotating methyl groups. This can be put into a standard form of Mathieu's equation,

$$\psi''(\theta) + (a - 2q \cos 3\theta)\psi(\theta) = 0,$$

with the substitutions $q = V_0\mathcal{I}/2\hbar^2$ (≈ 50 to 100), $a = (2\varepsilon - V_0)\mathcal{I}/\hbar^2$. The physically significant solutions are two families of Mathieu functions. One class is periodic in 2π and transforms according to the A representation of the symmetry group C_3; the other is periodic in $2\pi/3$

and belongs to the doubly degenerate E species. If not for tunneling, each energy level would be three-fold degenerate. In reality, a small $A-E$ splitting is observed, which increases with increasing torsional quantum number v. The A and E levels are colored blue and red, respectively. As V_0 decreases, the number of discrete levels decreases, as the higher levels are absorbed into the continuum. The actual results using Mathieu functions are quite complicated and the results have been distilled into approximate formulas for the energy levels.

7.8.3. *Free-Electron Model for Linear Polyenes*

The simplest non-trivial application of the Schrödinger equation is the one-dimensional particle in a box. Remarkably, this simple system can provide a useful model for a significant chemical problem — the structure of linear polyene molecules. A polyene is a hydrocarbon with alternating single and double carbon-carbon bonds, the simplest example being butadiene $CH_2=CH-CH=CH_2$. The series continues with hexatriene, octatetrene, and so on, with the generic structure $CH_2=CH(-CH=CH_2)_{N_c-3}$, a chain of $N_c = 4, 6, 8, \ldots$ conjugated carbon atoms. After all the single bonds are accounted for, each carbon atom contributes one p-electron. Linear combinations of these N_c atomic p-orbitals can form N_c π-molecular orbitals (MOs), delocalized over the entire length of the molecule.

The free-electron model represents these MOs as particle-in-a-box wavefunctions $\psi(x) = \sqrt{\frac{2}{L}} \sin\left(\frac{n\pi x}{L}\right)$, with orbital energies $E_n = \frac{h^2}{8m_e L^2} n^2$, ($n = 1, 2, 3, \ldots$). The length of the box is taken as $L = N_c L_{cc}$, where L_{cc} is the average C$-$C bond length, typically on the order of 1.40 Å. One-half a bond length is added to each end of the molecule to simplify this formula. Taking into account the Pauli principle, two electrons (with α and β spins) are fed into each of the available orbitals of lowest energy. The highest occupied molecular orbital (HOMO) then has $n = 2N_c$. In the lowest-energy electronic transition, one HOMO electron is excited to the lowest unoccupied molecular orbital (LUMO), with $n + 1 = 2N_c + 1$, producing a band with its maximum wavelength in the ultraviolet or visible region. Using $\frac{hc}{\lambda} = E_{n+1} - E_n$, we find $\lambda \approx 4.122 \times \frac{8N_c^2 L_{cc}^2}{N_c+1}$ nm (a useful constant is the Compton wavelength $\frac{h}{m_e c} = 2.426 \times 10^{-12}$ m). The prediction for butadiene is 207 nm, which agrees closely with the observed absorption band at $\lambda_{max} \approx 210$ nm in the ultraviolet. The increase of λ with N_c is correctly predicted; however, quantitative results for the higher polyenes are not very accurate. As the absorption band begins to impinge on the visible region of 400–700 nm a polyene becomes colored. A chain of 10 conjugated carbon atoms, as contained in retinol (vitamin A), shows a pale yellow color.

We propose a modification of the free-electron model to improve results for the longer polyene chains. For the potential energy function within the one-dimensional box, we replace $V(x) = 0$ by $V(x) = V_0 \cos\left(\frac{\pi x}{L_{cc}}\right)$, where V_0 is an additional empirical parameter (in addition to L_{cc}). The rationale for this form is the fact that the C$-$C bonds are not all equivalent (as they are, for example, in benzene). Actually, the bonds exhibit an alternating character, with the C$=$C double bonds in the conventional structural formulas having a slightly greater π-electron density.

N_c 4 6 8 10 12   series of polyenes

L_{cc} (Å)   1.4 V_0 (h/mL_{cc}) 0.018

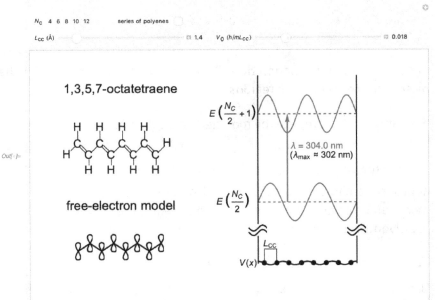

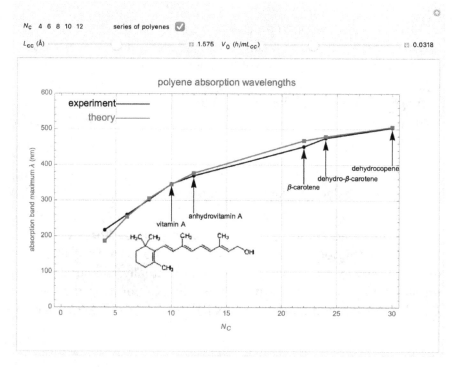

Demonstration 7.31: Free-Electron Model for Linear Polyenes (https://demonstrations.wolfram.com/FreeElectronModelForLinearPolyenes/)

The sinusoidal perturbation describes a lower potential energy for the mobile electrons in these regions.

It is sufficient to compute the modified energies using first-order perturbation theory, such that $E_n^{(1)} = \int_0^{N_c L_{cc}} \psi_n(x) V(x) \psi_n(x)\, dx$. The wavelength formula thereby generalizes to $\lambda(\text{nm}) \approx 4.122 \times \left(\frac{N_c+1}{8N_c^2} + \frac{V_0}{2}\right)^{-1} L_{cc}^2$. With appropriate choices of the empirical parameters, much better agreement can be obtained for the absorption frequencies over a large range of polyenes, as shown in the second snapshot.

7.8.4. *Uranium Enrichment Using Gas Centrifuges*

Natural uranium has an isotopic composition consisting of 99.284% U238 and 0.711% U235 (plus a very small fraction of U234). Only the U235 isotope can undergo nuclear fission for use in nuclear reactors and weapons. For nuclear power reactors, the uranium must be enriched to approximately 3–5% U235. Some research reactors use enrichment to 12–20%, while nuclear weapons require at least 85% enrichment.

The most prevalent method for uranium enrichment makes use of a cascade of gas centrifuges. Uranium hexafluoride UF_6 sublimes into a gas, referred to as "hex", at 56°C (≈ 330 K) under normal atmospheric pressure. Fortunately, fluorine is isotopically pure ^{19}F, so that the mass difference between ^{238}U $^{19}F_6 (M = 352)$ and ^{235}U $^{19}F_6 (M = 349)$ is due entirely to the uranium isotopes. This Demonstration describes a simplified model of the Zippe centrifuge, developed in the years following World War II.

Gas molecules in a rotating cylinder experience a centrifugal force pushing them toward the outer wall of the cylinder. The density distribution has a form analogous to the barometer formula, for the atmospheric density in a gravitational field, specifically, $\rho(r) = \rho(0)e^{Mr^2\omega^2/2RT}$, where ρ is density, r is the distance from the axis of the cylinder, ω is the angular velocity of rotation, T is the absolute temperature and R is the gas constant. The local mole fraction of U235 is given by

$$f(r) = \left(1 + \frac{\rho_{238}(0)}{\rho_{235}(0)}e^{\Delta M r^2 \omega^2/2RT}\right)^{-1},$$

where $\Delta M = M_{238} - M_{235} = .003$ kg/mol.

Typical rotor spin rates are in excess of 60,000 rpm, which corresponds to $\omega = 60\,000 \times 2\pi/60 \approx 6000\,\text{sec}^{-1}$. With cylinder radii of the order of 10 cm, almost all the gas is flattened into a narrow shell clinging to the cylinder walls, known as the Stewartson layer.

The success of the gas centrifuge is made possible by changing the direction of enrichment from radial to axial by inducing vertical circulation of the hex between the top and bottom of the cylinder. Convection in the gas is produced by creating a temperature gradient by heating the bottom of the cylinder. As a result of the vertical circulation, the enriched hex can be withdrawn from the top of the centrifuge, while the depleted hex is drawn out from the bottom.

A single centrifuge can achieve a separation factor in the range of 1.2 to 1.5, meaning that the fraction of U235 is enhanced (from its beginning value of 0.007) by this factor. Clearly, to produce the enrichment required for reactor use, a cascade of connected centrifuges must be used, with the enriched output from one stage fed into a successive stage. The end product might require as many as 20 stages. There are usually multiple banks of centrifuges for each stage, to increase the total output of enriched product.

The graphic is a highly idealized and simplified representation of a gas centrifuge. Hex at some intermediate stage of enrichment is fed into the inlet F, while the outlets P and W withdraw the product (U238 enriched hex) and the waste (U235 depleted hex), respectively.

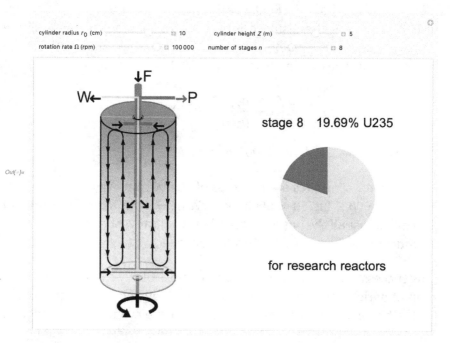

Demonstration 7.32: Uranium Enrichment Using Gas Centrifuges (https://demonstrations.wolfram.com/UraniumEnrichmentUsingGasCentrifuges/)

The pie chart on the right shows the isotopic composition of the uranium after n centrifuge stages.

A simplified model for the operation of the centrifuge gives $x(n)$, the U235 mole fraction at stage n, as a recurrence relation (unpublished work by the author, at Los Alamos):

$$x(n) = \frac{1 + \left(\frac{1}{x(n-1)} - 1\right) e^{\Delta M r_0^2 \omega^2 / 2RT}}{1 + \left(\frac{1}{x(n-1)} - 1\right) e^{\Delta M r_1^2 \omega^2 / 2RT}} x(n-1).$$

Here r_0 is the radius of the centrifuge, Z is its height, and $r_1 = \frac{\lambda}{2} r_0$, with $\lambda \approx 2.77$ m. For larger values of n, say $n > 10$, the recurrence computation becomes time consuming. But a good approximation to $x(n)$ can be constructed as a sigmoid curve with $x(n) \approx (e^{\Delta M (r_0^2 - r_1^2) \omega^2 / 2RT})^n x(0)$ initially, merging into a function such that $x(n) \to 1$ as $n \to \infty$.

7.8.5. *Oxidation States of Carbon*

This Demonstration enumerates the possible oxidation states of carbon in a number of compounds containing one or two carbon atoms (colored

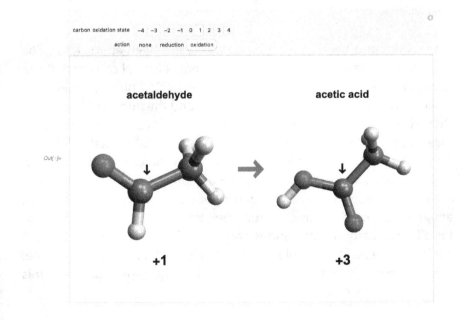

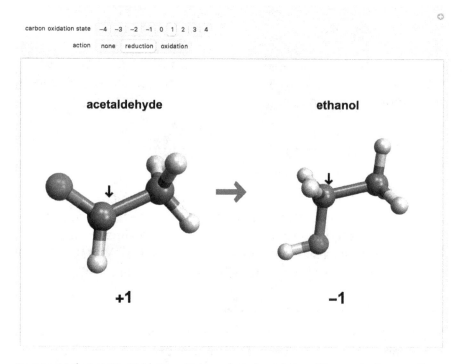

carbon oxidation state   −4   −3   −2   −1   0   1   2   3   4

action   none   reduction   oxidation

acetaldehyde   **ethanol**

+1   **−1**

Demonstration 7.33: Oxidation States of Carbon (https://demonstrations.wolfram.
com/OxidationStatesOfCarbon/)

gray) bonded to hydrogen atoms (white) and oxygen atoms (red). The concept of oxidation state is, to a large extent, a formal construct. It can be defined as the difference between the expected number of valence electrons for a neutral atom of an element and the number of electrons that are actually associated with that atom in a conventional Lewis structure. Carbon atoms can exist in nine different oxidation states, running from −4 to +4. For neutral molecules, the oxidation number of each carbon atom can usually be found by assigning oxidation numbers of +1 and −2, respectively, to bonded hydrogen and oxygen atoms, then assigning the carbon values so that the total sums to zero. It is possible for different carbon atoms in the same molecule to belong in different oxidation states, for example, in ethanol and acetaldehyde. The alkane, alcohol, carbonyl, and carboxylic acid functional groups all appear in this series of compounds.

7.8.6. *The Structure of Diamond*

Diamond has the highest hardness and thermal conductivity of any bulk material while remaining an electrical insulator. The structure of diamond is based on a continuous network of tetrahedrally bonded

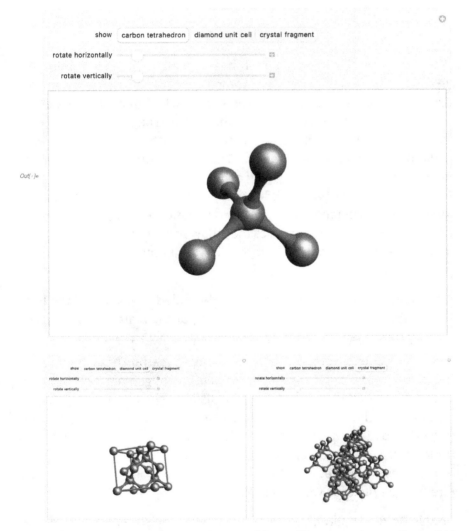

Demonstration 7.34: The Structure of Diamond (https://demonstrations.wolfram.com/TheStructureOfDiamond/)

carbon atoms in which extremely strong covalent bonds are formed between sp^3 hybrid orbitals. The C–C bond length is 154.448 pm. The crystalline structure is of cubic symmetry with unit cell dimension $a = \frac{4}{\sqrt{3}}r_{CC} = 356.682$ pm, containing eight carbon atoms per unit cell. The structure can be characterized as two interpenetrating face-centered cubic lattices, displaced by $a/4$ in each dimension.

7.8.7. *Carbon Nanotubes*

The first synthesis of carbon nanotubes is usually credited to Sumio Ijima in 1991. A single sheet of carbon atoms arranged in a hexagonal lattice is known as graphene. Graphite consists of a stack of graphene sheets held together by van der Waals forces. A single-walled nanotube (SWNT) is, in concept, the result of rolling a graphene sheet into a cylindrical tube with a diameter of several nanometers. The length of the nanotube can be of the order of millimeters, giving a length-to-diameter ratio of up to 20 million. Nanotubes have tensile strengths per unit weight some 10–100 times greater than that of steel. They possess other unique mechanical, electrical, and optical properties that show promise in the development of new nanotechnology and electronics, including, possibly, quantum computers.

Points on the graphene lattice can be described by vectors of the form $na + mb$, where n, m are integers $(n \geq m)$ and a, b are non-orthogonal unit vectors that can be taken as $(1, 0)$ and $\left(\frac{1}{2}, \frac{\sqrt{3}}{2}\right)$, respectively. The chiral indices (n, m) determine the alignment of carbon hexagons around the circumference of the cylinder. Three different geometrical classifications or "flavors" of nanotubes can be distinguished. "Armchair" configurations are characterized by indices (n, n) while "zigzag" configurations are described by $(n, 0)$. Chiral nanotubes have indices (n, m) with $n \neq m$ (and $m \neq 0$) and can occur in two mirror image forms. Armchair nanotubes show metallic electric conductivity, while the other flavors are semiconductors with varying characteristics.

In this Demonstration, you can view a nanotube structure with indices n, m or its conceptual graphene precursor. Pink cylinders are drawn as visual aids.

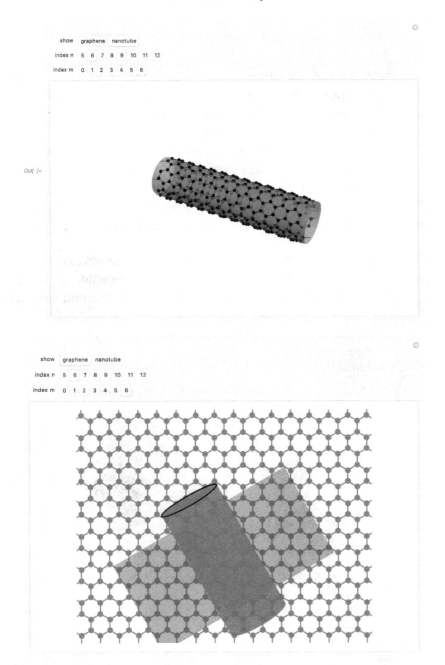

Demonstration 7.35: Carbon Nanotubes (https://demonstrations.wolfram.com/CarbonNanotubes/)

7.9. Molecules 4

7.9.1. *Piezoelectricity in Barium Titanate*

Piezoelectricity is the ability of some materials to generate an electric potential in response to applied mechanical stress. The ceramic mineral barium titanate $BaTiO_3$ is a classic example. The crystal is characterized as a perovskite structure. At temperatures greater than the Curie point (120°C) the unit cell has cubic symmetry. A Ti^{4+} ion, shown as a gray sphere, is located at the center of the cube. It is surrounded by Ca^{2+} ions (green spheres) at the eight corners of the cube and O^{2-} ions (red spheres) at the six centers of the cube faces. The electrical charges of cubic perovskite have a completely symmetrical arrangement.

At temperatures below the Curie point, the crystal distorts to tetragonal symmetry. The titanium ion moves away from the center of the unit cell (chosen as downward in the graphic), thus giving the unit cell a net

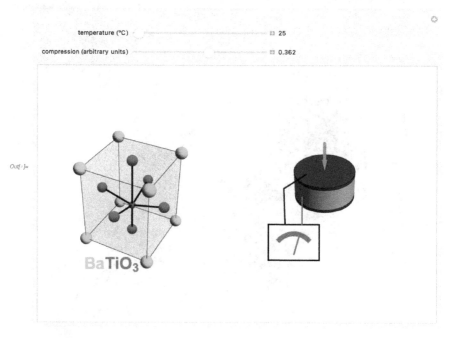

Demonstration 7.36: Piezoelectricity in Barium Titanate (https://demonstrations. wolfram.com/PiezoelectricityInBariumTitanate/)

dipole moment — with the positive end downward. In a single crystal, idealized as a cylindrical slab on the right side of the graphic, this creates a small voltage difference between the top and bottom faces. Even in the absence of external stress, the crystal exhibits a poling voltage, shown as the midpoint reading on the attached voltmeter. The voltage increases from this value if the crystal is compressed, thus increasing the distortion of the unit cell. It decreases as the crystal is stretched. Thus a piezoelectric crystal is a natural oscillator. This is exploited by quartz oscillators, for example, in battery-operated wristwatches.

This Demonstration is intended only as a qualitative description of piezo-electricity. The changes in the dimensions of the slab are greatly exaggerated; they are typically of the order of 0.1%. The piezoelectric constant of $BaTiO_3$ is in the range $100-150 \times 10^{12}$ m/V.

7.9.2. *NMR Spectrum of Ethanol*

Nuclear magnetic resonance (NMR) spectroscopy can measure radio-frequency Zeeman transitions of proton spins in a magnetic field. It is more convenient to sweep the magnetic field through the resonances at a fixed frequency, typically 60 MHz. The resonances are sensitive to the chemical environment of non-equivalent protons, an effect known as the chemical shift. A classic example is the ethanol molecule CH_3CH_2OH, which shows three chemically distinct hydrogen atom sites, thus three NMR peaks with intensity ratios 3:2:1. The relevant parameter is δ, representing the fractional deviation of the chemical shift measured in parts per million (ppm) from that of tetramethylsilane (TMS), a convenient standard assigned the reference value $\delta = 0$. A small amount of TMS is often added to the sample being measured to calibrate the δ-scale.

At higher resolution, it is possible to identify further splitting of the chemically shifted peaks due to spin-spin interactions with neighboring groups of protons. Thus the CH_3 resonance is split into a 1:2:1 triplet by interactions with the two CH_2 protons. Correspondingly, the CH_2 resonance is split into a 1:3:3:1 quartet by interactions with the three CH_3 protons. The OH resonance is not usually split because of the rapid exchange of these protons via hydrogen bonding.

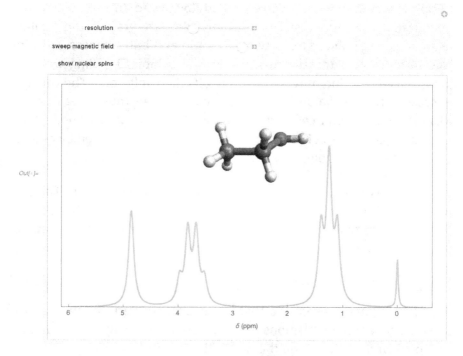

Demonstration 7.37: Nuclear Magnetic Resonance Spectrum of Ethanol (https://demonstrations.wolfram.com/NuclearMagneticResonanceSpectrumOfEthanol/)

The spectroscopic procedures described in this Demonstration are intended as a simplified introduction to the principles of NMR. Modern NMR spectroscopy makes use of Fourier transform techniques, which produce the entire spectrum simultaneously.

7.9.3. *Optical Activity of Tartaric Acid*

Optical activity of compounds in solution can be measured with a polarimeter, shown schematically in the upper part of the graphic. The angle of rotation of plane polarized light, conventionally the sodium D-line at 589 nm, is determined using two polarizers. (In the graphic, an idealized incident polarizer is reduced to a vertical slit coincident with the plane of polarization.) The angle of polarization of the emerging light is given by $\alpha = [\alpha]_D^{20} lc$, where $[\alpha]_D^{20}$ is the specific rotation, referred to the sodium D-line and a temperature of 20°C, l is the path length in decimeters (set equal to 10), and c is the concentration in g/ml. The tartaric acid molecule has three possible stereoisomers:

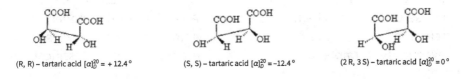

(R, R) – tartaric acid $[\alpha]_D^{20} = +12.4°$ (S, S) – tartaric acid $[\alpha]_D^{20} = -12.4°$ (2 R, 3 S) – tartaric acid $[\alpha]_D^{20} = 0°$

(R,R)-tartaric acid is the naturally occurring form. Its mirror image enantiomer, (S,S)-tartaric acid, as well its diastereoisomer, (2R,3S)-tartaric acid, can also be synthesized. The last is called the meso form and is superposable with its mirror image. Thus the chirality of the two asymmetric carbon atoms cancels and this molecule is not optically active. Thus there is no variation in α with concentration of (R,S). Equal concentrations of (R,R) and (S,S), called a racemic mixture, also exhibits net cancellation of optical rotation.

In this Demonstration, you can choose concentrations for the individual stereoisomers or mixtures of tartaric acid and observe the resultant optical rotation. You can rotate the 3D diagram of (2R,3S)-tartaric acid to show the configurations around the R and S carbon centers.

Louis Pasteur in 1848, using a pair of tweezers and a magnifying glass, was able to separate individual crystals of sodium ammonium tartarate tetrahydrate that were mirror images of one another. (Tartaric acid is found in wine, one of the earliest targets of pasteurization.) Pasteur found that, in water solution, the two varieties were optically active, with equal concentrations of the two different forms rotating the plane of linearly polarized light by exactly the same angle, but in opposite directions. Later, van 't Hoff and Le Bel proposed that the different forms — called stereoisomers — of optically active compounds were right-and left-handed versions of the same molecules, with the chirality (handedness) originating from asymmetric carbon atoms bonded to four non-identical groups.

Tartaric acid $HOOC-C^*H(OH)-C^*H(OH)-COOH$ (2,3-dihydroxybutane-dioic acid) has two asymmetric carbon centers, which are marked with asterisks. Since 1966, the nomenclature for absolute configuration of stereoisomers have been based on the Cahn–Ingold–Prelog system. This replaces the older D (dextro) and L (levo) classification (which is still in use in some biochemical literature). According to the modern system, the four groups attached to the asymmetric carbon are classified by priority, numbered 1 through 4. The details of this classification

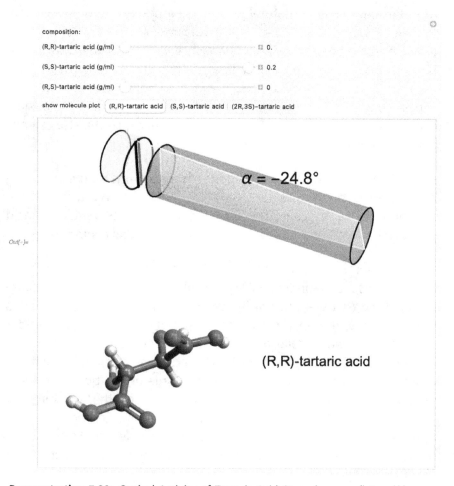

composition:

(R,R)-tartaric acid (g/ml) ⬚ 0.

(S,S)-tartaric acid (g/ml) ⬚ 0.2

(R,S)-tartaric acid (g/ml) ⬚ 0

show molecule plot   (R,R)-tartaric acid   (S,S)-tartaric acid   (2R,3S)–tartaric acid

$\alpha = -24.8°$

(R,R)-tartaric acid

Demonstration 7.38: Optical Activity of Tartaric Acid Stereoisomers (https://demons trations.wolfram.com/OpticalActivityOfTartaricAcidStereoisomers/)

are given in any up-to-date organic chemistry textbook. For present purposes, we need only consider the four groups around the asterisk-marked carbon atoms in tartaric acid, which have the priority ordering OH>COOH>CH(OH)COOH>H. Now imagine the lowest (4th) priority substituent (H) to be the steering column of an automobile and the 1st, 2nd, and 3rd priority groups to be arrayed around the steering wheel. If the ordering 1 → 2 → 3 is clockwise, as if performing a right turn, the configuration is called R (Latin *rectus* = right). If it is counter-clockwise, as in a left turn, the configuration is called S (Latin *sinister* = left).

7.9.4. *d-Orbitals in an Octahedral Field*

A free transition metal atom or ion has five-fold degenerate *d*-orbitals, pictured at the top of the graphic. These can be occupied by a maximum of 10 electrons. The positive and negative regions of the wavefunctions are shown in the blue and yellow spheres, respectively. Transition metals are likely to form compounds in which they are centrally bonded to several molecules or ions, known as ligands. These are shown as white spheres. A common configuration is the highly symmetrical octahedral complex, in which six equivalent ligands are bound to the central ion. The effect of the ligands can be represented by a crystal field parameter Δ, whose magnitude is typically in the range 7,000–30,000 cm^{-1}. The octahedral crystal field partially breaks the five-fold symmetry of the *d*-orbitals. The d_{z^2} and $d_{x^2-y^2}$ orbitals, which have lobes directed at ligands, become a higher-energy doublet which transforms as the e_g representation of the octahedral group. The remaining *d*-orbitals transform as a triply degenerate t_{2g} representation.

When electrons are successively added to the free atom or ion, they follow Hund's rule in occupying different degenerate orbitals, until — with six or more electrons — they are compelled to begin doubling up. In relatively weak crystal fields, roughly for $\Delta < 15,000$ cm^{-1}, the orbitals fill as if they were effectively degenerate. In strong crystal fields, however, the first six electrons fill the lower t_{2g} orbitals before any enter the e_g. High-spin and low-spin alternatives exist for configurations d^4 to d^7, as determined by the magnitude of Δ. These are reflected in the magnetic properties of the corresponding complex ions.

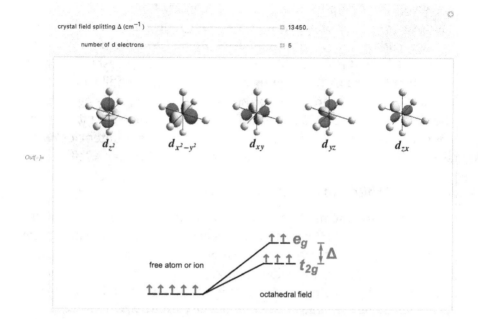

Demonstration 7.39: *d*-Orbitals in an Octahedral Field (https://demonstrations.wol fram.com/DOrbitalsInAnOctahedralField/)

7.9.5. *Orbital Transformations in Diels-Alder Reaction*

The Diels–Alder reaction is a [4+2]-cycloaddition of a conjugated diene (such as butadiene) and a dienophile (such as ethylene):

This is classified as an *electrocyclic reaction*, which involves the four π-electrons of the diene and the two π-electrons of the dieneophile. It is a concerted reaction, with no transition state, in which electrons are transferred usually from the highest occupied molecular orbital (HOMO) of the diene into the lowest unoccupied molecular orbital (LUMO) of the dienophile.

The "orbitals" graphic shows the configurations of *p* atomic orbitals in the π-electron states of the diene and the dienophile. The blue lobes of the *p*-orbitals correspond to positive values of the wavefunction; the yellow lobes correspond to negative values (or vice versa; only the relative

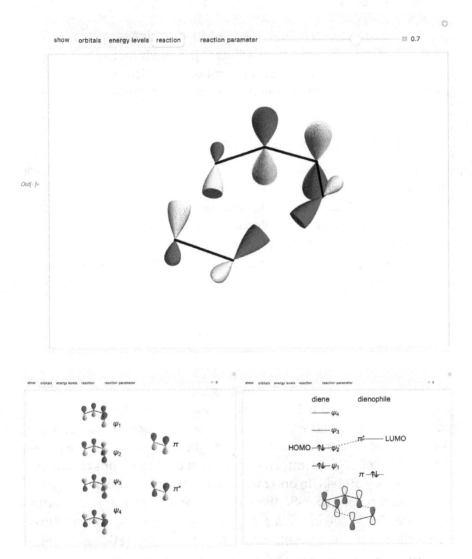

Demonstration 7.40: Orbital Transformations in Diels-Alder Reaction (https://demonstrations.wolfram.com/OrbitalTransformationsInDielsAlderReaction/)

signs are significant). The "energy levels" graphic shows the ground electronic states of the two molecules. In the diene, the two lowest π-orbitals, ψ_1 and ψ_2, are doubly occupied, each with a pair of electrons with opposite spin. The ψ_2 orbital is the HOMO. In the dienophile, the lowest π-orbital is doubly occupied, while the empty π^* is the LUMO.

With "reaction" selected, the slider "reaction parameter" traces out the course of the reaction. The four adjacent *p*-orbitals on the two reactant molecules transform into two new σ-bonds, which are energetically more stable than π-bonds. Thus a cyclic product molecule (cyclohexene) is formed.

7.9.6. *Elementary Processes in Protein Folding*

Biologically active α-amino acids are compounds with the general formula $H_2NCHRCOOH$, where R represents one of about 20 possible side groups (or residues). An amide linkage is formed by the reaction of the carboxyl group of one molecule with the amide group of another. Proteins are built up of chains of amino acids connected by amide (or peptide) linkages, with the general structure . . .HNCH R_1CONHCH R_2 . . .. Chains can vary in length from about 100 to several thousand amino acid units.

The linear sequence of amino acids, identified by the side groups R_1, R_2, . . ., determines the primary structure of the protein. The amide C-N bond is relatively rigid (attributed to its partial double-bond character) and creates a planar unit incorporating six connected atoms. However, the adjacent C-C and N-C bonds can undergo torsional motions, characterized by the angles ψ and ϕ, one set for each amino acid unit. Although possible torsional motions might be restricted by steric and electrostatic effects, an immense number of conformations remain possible for every protein. In order to fulfill its biological function, a protein must attain a very specific three-dimensional secondary and tertiary structure. The "protein folding problem", a very active area of current research, explores the details of how the final configuration is achieved.

This Demonstration presents a simplified schematic representation of the possible motions of a protein chain. Two amino acid units, with side groups R_1 and R_2, are shown. The green cylinders represent the continuation of the protein chain in each direction. Each of the torsional angles ψ and ϕ can be independently varied between 0° and 360°. The immense number of possibilities, for just two of the hundreds or thousands of configuration variables, is soon apparent. Remarkably, a linear sequence of amino acids will biologically self-assemble in a matter of milliseconds!

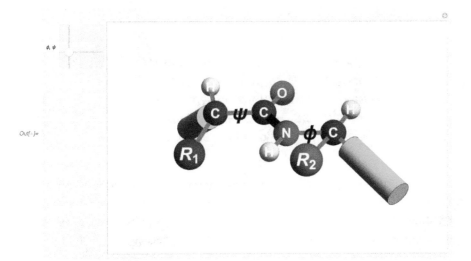

Demonstration 7.41: Elementary Processes in Protein Folding (https://demonstrations. wolfram.com/ElementaryProcessesInProteinFolding/)

Instructions for Accessing Online Supplementary Material

The online supplementary material for this book includes Wolfram Mathematica notebook files containing raw programming codes of more than 180 Wolfram Demonstrations presented in the book. Readers are encouraged to download the files and manipulate the codes/graphics to facilitate their comprehension of the accompanying discussion in the book.

1. Register an account/login at https://www.worldscientific.com
2. Go to: https://www.worldscientific.com/r/12548-SUPP
3. Download the Supplementary Material from https://www.worldscientific.com/worldscibooks/10.1142/12548#t=suppl

For subsequent download, simply log in with the same login details in order to access.

Index